OBSESSED WITH™

STAR WARS®

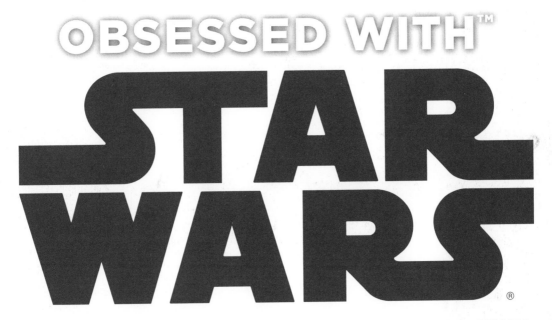

OBSESSED WITH™ STAR WARS®

TEST YOUR KNOWLEDGE OF A GALAXY FAR, FAR AWAY

by Benjamin Harper

CHRONICLE BOOKS

SAN FRANCISCO

Library of Congress Cataloging-in-Publication Data is available.

ISBN: 978-1-4521-3633-2

Manufactured in China

Produced by becker&mayer! LLC, Bellevue, Washington
www.beckermayer.com

Design: Todd Bates and Katie Benezra
Editorial: Kjersti Egerdahl and Sara Addicott
Image Research: Chris Campbell
Production Coordination: Jen Marx

10 9 8 7 6 5 4 3 2 1

Originally published in hardcover with module in 2008 by Chronicle Books LLC.

Chronicle Books LLC
680 Second Street
San Francisco, California 94107

www.chroniclebooks.com

www.starwars.com

CONTENTS

Note: Many questions are drawn from the *Star Wars* Legends continuity.

CHAPTER ONE

STAR WARS

EPISODE I
THE PHANTOM MENACE

1. Who said, "You were right about one thing, Master. The negotiations were short"?
   A. Anakin Skwalker
   B. Qui-Gon Jinn
   C. Obi-Wan Kenobi
   D. Yoda

2. Who was Qui-Gon Jinn's Padawan before he chose Obi-Wan Kenobi?
   A. Kit Fisto
   B. Xanatos
   C. Cerasi
   D. Plo Koon

3. How old was Padmé Amidala when she was elected Queen of Naboo?
   A. Fourteen
   B. Eleven
   C. Nineteen
   D. Sixteen

4. Who did Qui-Gon Jinn run into in the swamps of Naboo?
   A. Captain Tarpals
   B. Boss Nass
   C. Jar Jar Binks
   D. Rep Been

5. Who owned Anakin Skywalker before Watto bought him?
   A. Sebulba
   B. Lana
   C. Gardulla the Hutt
   D. Cliegg Lars

6. What happened to Jar Jar Binks when he brought Obi-Wan Kenobi and Qui-Gon Jinn to Otoh Gunga?
   A. He was welcomed home
   B. Captain Tarpals told him to leave
   C. Captain Tarpals took him to the bosses
   D. He was made General

7. By age seven, Padmé Amidala had enrolled in which of the following?
   A. The Refugee Relocation Service
   B. The Refugee Food Bank
   C. The Refugee Transfer League
   D. The Refugee Relief Movement

8. On which planet did Padawan Obi-Wan Kenobi temporarily decide to leave Qui-Gon Jinn and the Jedi Order?
   A. Coruscant
   B. Melida/Daan
   C. Naboo
   D. Tatooine

9. Who said, "Dis sun doen murder to mesa skin"?

A. Watto   C. Jar Jar Binks

B. Sebulba   D. Anakin Skywalker

10. What did Anakin Skywalker do that made Qui-Gon Jinn think he has Jedi reflexes?

A. He levitated   C. He was a Podracer

B. He trained eopies   D. He had a high midi-chlorian count

11.

12. Who was Anakin Skywalker's father?

A. Mildro Skywalker   C. Orkan Skywalker

B. T'Mell Skywalker   D. He didn't have a father

13. Which Jedi Master at one time tried to convince Qui-Gon Jinn to join the Jedi Council?

A. Ki-Adi-Mundi   C. Yarael Poof

B. Plo Koon   D. Yaddle

14. What was Queen Amidala's birth name?

A. Padmé Nubrie   C. Padmé Naberrie

B. Padmé Taberrie   D. Padmé Oberrie

15. Which aspect of the Force was most important to Qui-Gon Jinn?

A. The unifying Force   C. The Living Force

B. The light side of the Force   D. The dark side of the Force

16. Who was the secret force behind the Trade Federation's blockade of Naboo?

A. Darth Tyranus   C. Darth Plagueis

B. Darth Sidious   D. Darth Bane

17. How old was Padmé when she became an Apprentice Legislator on Naboo?

A. Ten   C. Seven

B. Eleven   D. Thirteen

11.

Queen Amidala barely escaped the Trade Federation's blockade of Naboo when she and her Jedi protectors blasted past the Droid Control Ship and the rest of the Trade Federation fleet. Their ship, however, was damaged during their escape, rendering their hyperdrive engine unusable. They needed to land somewhere to repair their ship, so they chose the planet Tatooine because of its proximity to Naboo in the Outer Rim.

When they landed, Qui-Gon Jinn, Jar Jar Binks, R2-D2, and Queen Amidala's handmaiden Padmé left the ship and went into Mos Espa in search of the parts needed to repair the hyperdrive.

The group searched Mos Espa for a used parts dealer until they finally came to Watto's shop. Padmé met Anakin Skywalker for the first time as Qui-Gon and Watto went off to look for the parts they needed to repair Queen Amidala's ship. What did Anakin think Padmé was when he first saw her?

A. A queen

B. A fairy

C. An angel

D. A princess

OBSESSED WITH *STAR WARS*

18. What did Darth Sidious call Daultay Dofine when Dofine remarked that their plan had failed?

A. "Grimy grub"

B. "Filthy worm"

C. "Stunted slime"

D. "Kowakian monkey-lizard"

19. What did Jar Jar Binks owe Qui-Gon Jinn after Jinn rescued him during the Trade Federation invasion of Naboo?

A. A trip to Otoh Gunga

B. A bongo

C. A life debt

D. 9,000 Republic credits

20. Why did Chancellor Valorum send Qui-Gon Jinn and Obi-Wan Kenobi to Naboo?

A. To acquire a fleet of battle droids

B. To negotiate the release of Queen Amidala

C. To map out alternative trade routes through the system

D. To settle a trade dispute

21. How tall was Jar Jar Binks?

A. 1.74 meters

B. 1.96 meters

C. 0.81 meters

D. 2.20 meters

22. When speaking before the Senate on Coruscant, what action did Queen Amidala move for a vote on?

A. Tariffs on Perlemian Trade Route

B. Disbanding the Trade Federation

C. No confidence in Chancellor Valorum

D. Extending the Chancellor's term limit

23. On which planet did young Obi-Wan Kenobi and Qui-Gon Jinn first form a connection?

A. Tatooine

B. Melida/Daan

C. Bandomeer

D. Telos

24. What did Darth Sidious want Queen Amidala to do?

A. Turn over her reign of Naboo to him

B. Sign a treaty that allowed the Trade Federation to use Naboo's water supply

C. Sign a treaty that legitimized the Trade Federation's blockade of Naboo

D. Run for Senate

The Phantom Menace **Era**

25. According to Obi-Wan, how high was Anakin Skywalker's midi-chlorian count?

A. Off the chart

B. Above average

C. Normal

D. Very weak

26. According to Obi-Wan, how did Anakin's midi-chlorian count compare to master Yoda's?

A. It was the same

B. It was higher

C. It was lower

D. No one knew what Yoda's midi-chlorian count was

27.

28. How old was Anakin Skywalker when Qui-Gon Jinn and Padmé Amidala happened into Watto's junk shop?

A. Seven

B. Eight

C. Nine

D. Ten

29. When working at as a waiter at a party in Boss Nass' mansion, what did Jar Jar Binks do?

A. He broke all of the kaadu eggs

B. He forgot to turn off the stove

C. He flooded Boss Nass' mansion

D. He dropped the cake on the floor

30. What did Queen Amidala do as a security measure whenever she was in public?

A. She emitted an invisible forcefield

B. She wore bulletproof armor

C. She surrounded herself by an elite security force

D. She disguised herself as one of her handmaidens

31. What ruler of Naboo did Queen Amidala replace?

A. King Robena

B. King Flobonka

C. King Veruna

D. Queen Lamtuna

32. What keepsake did Qui-Gon Jinn have from his homeworld?

A. A pebble from the Lake of Dreams

B. A gem from the Cave of Wisdom

C. A rock from the River of Light

D. A bracelet from the Ocean of Time

OBSESSED WITH *STAR WARS*

27.

Anakin Skywalker spent much of his youth collecting spare parts to build his own Podracer. He salvaged Radon-Ulzer racing engines that had been thrown out and rewired them, re-routing the fuel distribution and adding revolutionary technology that created a greater thrust of fuel throughout the engines. He had yet to test his Podracer, though—he had been waiting for the appropriate moment.

When Qui-Gon Jinn, Padmé, R2-D2, and Jar Jar happened upon him in Watto's junkshop and needed assistance, he immediately offered to help—he could enter himself in the Boonta Eve Podrace, which he was sure he would win, and then give the money he earned to the stranded travelers so Qui-Gon could purchase parts to repair the Queen's vessel.

First, however, he needed to make sure the Podracer would work, so he, R2-D2, C-3PO, and Jar Jar set about making the final repairs to ensure perfect performance. Jar Jar, prone to clumsiness, was working very close to a portion of Anakin's Podracer that, if touched, would make his hand go numb for hours. What part was that?

A. Fuel atomizer

B. Thrust ring

C. Fuel injector nozzle

D. Energy binders

33. What did Darth Sidious do to cement the Neimoidians' control of the Trade Federation Directorate?

A. He fabricated scandals that forced all other species to resign

B. He bought out all other species' stock

C. He helped them overpower the other members of the Federation

D. He arranged for all non-Neimoidian members to be assassinated

34. How tall was Queen Amidala?

A. 1.55 meters

B. 1.45 meters

C. 1.65 meters

D. 1.25 meters

35. What did Anakin Skywalker give to Padmé so she would remember him?

A. A collection of his favorite traditional songs

B. A flute he carved out of a branch

C. A carved japor snippet

D. A smooth pebble he found in Mos Espa

36. What evil scientist captured Qui-Gon Jinn, held him prisoner on Simpla-12, and experimented on him in order to learn about the Force?

A. Zenna Fan-fak

B. Zenna Mo'ardor

C. Jenna Zen Arbor

D. Jenna Den Mardor

37. How old was Queen Amidala when she was elected Princess of Theed?

A. Thirteen

B. Ten

C. Fourteen

D. Twelve

38. What was the ceremonial red mark on Queen Amidala's lower lip known as?

A. The tear of Tydria

B. The scar of remembrance

C. The scar of the Great War

D. The tear of Theed

39. What did Qui-Gon Jinn disguise himself as to protect Baroness Omnino five years before the Battle of Naboo?

A. A Tusken Raider

B. A Senate guard

C. A bounty hunter

D. A smuggler

The Phantom Menace Era

40. What tragic event happened when Anakin Skywalker was seven?

A. He was separated from Shmi for a period of time

B. Watto nearly sold him to Jabba the Hutt

C. He crashed his first Podracer, barely escaping

D. Slave traders took his friend Amee's mother

41. From whom did Captain Tarpals rescue Jar Jar Binks almost immediately before arresting Jar Jar and then banishing him from Otoh Gunga?

A. Chef Marshoo

B. Chef Bant

C. Chef Nizzles

D. Grand Chef Parky

42. What compassionate yet dangerous act did young Anakin Skywalker perform on Tatooine?

A. He helped a wounded Sarlacc

B. He helped a wounded Hutt

C. He helped a wounded Dug

D. He helped a wounded Tusken Raider

43. Which Gungan law forbade Jar Jar Binks to return to Otoh Gunga after he had been banished?

A. The Returnendie Law

B. The Noseeum Law

C. The Nocombackie Law

D. The Yousabanished Law

44.

45. What was so special about the fact that Anakin participated in Podraces?

A. He was a self-taught pilot

B. He was the youngest entrant ever in the Boonta Eve Race

C. He was the only human who could do it

D. He came up with the entry fees himself

46. How tall was Qui-Gon Jinn?

A. 1.82 meters

B. 1.93 meters

C. 2.02 meters

D. 2.16 meters

47. What courageous act did Anakin Skywalker perform in the Battle of Naboo?

A. He helped infiltrate Theed Palace

B. He destroyed the main reactor of the Droid Control Ship

C. He aided Jar Jar Binks in the fight against the droid army

D. He assisted Qui-Gon in his fight against the Sith

44.

Amidala, the newly elected Queen of Naboo, had a very difficult situation on her hands. The Trade Federation, displeased with the Senate's vote to approve the taxation of trade routes throughout the galaxy, had decided to show its unhappiness with this decision by setting up a blockade around the small planet of Naboo, allowing no shipments to leave from, or arrive on, the planet.

Queen Amidala contacted Chancellor Valorum about the situation on her planet, and the Chancellor assured her that he was sending two ambassadors from the Republic to negotiate an end to the Trade Federation's blockade.

After she spoke with Trade Federation Viceroy Nute Gunray and heard from him that no ambassadors had arrived to discuss a settlement, she got in touch with Senator Palpatine on Coruscant. While talking to the Senator, however, their communication was disrupted. At that point, Sio Bibble, Governor of Theed, stated that their planet was being invaded. What course of action did Queen Amidala stress that they should take?

A. A course of action that would lead to war

B. They needed to evacuate immediately

C. A course of action that would not lead to war

D. They needed to be patient; it could have been a communications error

OBSESSED WITH *STAR WARS*

48. With which Jedi Knight did Qui-Gon Jinn pledge his love while on a mission to New Apsalon?

A. Rohl

B. Pahl

C. Darh

D. Tahl

49. How did Jar Jar Binks become an orphan?

A. His parents died in a fire

B. His parents were killed by a marauding sea monster

C. His parents were so embarrassed by him that they deserted him

D. His parents were killed by bandits

50. What was Obi-Wan Kenobi's final promise to Qui-Gon Jinn?

A. To carry on the fight against the Sith

B. To train Anakin Skywalker

C. To avenge Qui-Gon's death

D. To find a Padawan worthy of his training

51. Who said, "Feel. Don't think. Trust your instincts"?

A. Obi-Wan Kenobi

B. Shmi Skywalker

C. Qui-Gon Jinn

D. Padmé Naberrie

52. What shocking discovery did Padmé Naberrie make upon landing on Tatooine and visiting Mos Espa?

A. That there was virtually no moisture on the planet

B. That hyperdrives were expensive

C. That slavery still existed in the galaxy

D. That Naboo boots didn't fare well in desert climates

53. Anakin Skywalker had a special ability that made him a very important worker in Watto's shop. What was it?

A. He had been trained as a plumber

B. He spoke 14 different languages

C. He was very mechanically inclined

D. He had Jedi reflexes

54. To whom did Qui-Gon sell Anakin's Podracer after Anakin won the Boonta Eve Classic Podrace?

A. Kitster

B. Watto

C. Sebulba

D. Jira

55. What gift that her parents gave her did Queen Amidala keep with her at all times?

A. A brooch

B. A fan

C. An amulet

D. A ring

The Phantom Menace **Era**

56. Why was Qui-Gon Jinn originally hesitant to take on Obi-Wan Kenobi as a Padawan?

A. He sensed great fear in Obi-Wan

B. Obi-Wan Kenobi was meant to be a farmer

C. His previous Padawan had deserted the Jedi Order in anger

D. Obi-Wan was not in tune with the Living Force

57. How old was Obi-Wan Kenobi at the Battle of Naboo?

A. Twenty-three

B. Twenty-five

C. Seventeen

D. Twenty

58. What one tradition did Queen Amidala retain from her native village on Naboo?

A. She meditated every morning

B. She fasted on Fridays

C. Her thumbnails were painted white

D. She ate no meat

59. How did Jar Jar Binks get his sentence at the Quarry penal colony commuted?

A. He saved Boss Nass' niece, Major Fassa

B. He rescued a rare albino nuna

C. He saved Boss Nass from drowning

D. He taught the other prisoners how to wrangle shaaks

60. Against whom did Amidala run in the election to rule Naboo?

A. Boss Nass

B. Jamilla

C. Sio Bibble

D. Graf Zapalo

61. How did Shmi Skywalker get sold into slavery?

A. She was born a slave

B. Her parents sold her

C. Pirates captured and sold her

D. She was stolen from an orphanage

62. Early in Darth Maul's training, his master taught him to control his fear by trapping him in a room full of what type of venomous creatures?

A. Kouhuns

B. Dinkos

C. Gradlacks

D. Florks

63. How tall was Trade Federation Viceroy Nute Gunray?

A. 2.10 meters

B. 2.03 meters

C. 1.91 meters

D. 1.84 meters

OBSESSED WITH *STAR WARS*

64. What was Rune Haako's primary job during the Battle of Naboo?

A. He was Nute Gunray's Security Officer

B. He was Nute Gunray's legal counsel

C. He was a tactical expert

D. He maintained the droid army

65. What was Lott Dod's position in the Trade Federation?

A. Viceroy Emeritus

B. Senator

C. Secretary of War

D. Secretary of the Treasury

66. What was Daultay Dofine's part in the Trade Federation ship *Revenue*'s battle against pirates at the edge of Dorvalla?

A. He maintained the droid hold

B. He was the ship's commander

C. He was the pilot

D. He monitored the cargo bay

67. Who was elected Governor of Theed during Veruna's reign as King of Naboo?

A. Padmé Amidala

B. Hela Brandes

C. Lufta Shif

D. Sio Bibble

68. Other than racing in the Podraces, how else did Sebulba participate in them?

A. He was in charge of the vendors

B. He personally hired all of the various pilots' pit crews

C. He organized and rehearsed the bands that played whenever he entered the arena

D. He was hired as an after-the-race commentator for the HoloNet

69. How many times had Queen Amidala met Senator Palpatine before her journey to Coruscant to address the Senate?

A. She had never met him

B. Two times

C. Three times

D. One time

70.

After Viceroy Gunray revealed to Darth Sidious that Queen Amidala had managed to escape Naboo and get past the Trade Federation's blockade, an enraged Darth Sidious exclaimed, "I want that treaty signed!" Gunray stated timidly that it would be impossible to locate her ship because it was too far out of the Trade Federation's range. It was at that point that Darth Sidious revealed his secret weapon—his apprentice, Darth Maul. "Not for the Sith," he told Gunray. "This is my apprentice, Darth Maul. He will find your lost ship."

Later, after Darth Maul had tracked and located Queen Amidala's ship, he and Darth Sidious continued their meeting in a secret location on the galaxy's capital planet, Coruscant. "Tatooine is sparsely populated," Maul reported. "If the trace was correct, I will find them quickly, Master."

After this, Darth Sidious gave Darth Maul explicit directions. What was Darth Maul to do first?

A. Find and destroy Queen Amidala

B. Find the boy

C. Move against the Jedi

D. Get Queen Amidala to sign the treaty

71. Who replaced Captain Magneta as head of the Royal Naboo Security Forces?

A. Captain Tarpals

B. Captain Panaka

C. Captain Chronelle

D. Captain Zustuh

The Phantom Menace Era

72. What was Supreme Chancellor Valorum's first name?
- **A.** Tinis
- **B.** Linis
- **C.** Finis
- **D.** Minis

73. How old was Mace Windu during the Battle of Naboo?
- **A.** Thirty-eight
- **B.** Forty
- **C.** Forty-eight
- **D.** Fifty

74. What happened to Yoda twelve years before the Battle of Naboo?
- **A.** He was immortalized as a statue in front of the Jedi Temple
- **B.** He was voted Senior Member of the Jedi Council
- **C.** He was the target of an assassination attempt
- **D.** He temporarily considered running for Senate

75. What was Watto's favorite pastime?
- **A.** Singing
- **B.** Gambling
- **C.** Bargaining
- **D.** Trading

76. How tall was Boss Nass?
- **A.** 2.08 meters
- **B.** 1.99 meters
- **C.** 2.06 meters
- **D.** 2.02 meters

77. Where was Shmi Skywalker's primary workplace?
- **A.** Her home
- **B.** Watto's home
- **C.** Watto's shop
- **D.** A stall in Mos Espa

78. After locating Queen Amidala, what happened to Darth Maul while he was en route to capture her on Tatooine?
- **A.** He needed to replace the crystals in his lightsaber
- **B.** He had to stop to repair his ship
- **C.** He was ambushed by Togorian pirates
- **D.** He had to purchase probe droids

79. Who exclaimed, "At last we will have revenge"?
- **A.** Darth Maul
- **B.** Obi-Wan Kenobi
- **C.** Qui-Gon Jinn
- **D.** Darth Sidious

80. Which Jedi was NOT a member of the Jedi Council?
- **A.** Yaddle
- **B.** Yarael Poof
- **C.** Qui-Gon Jinn
- **D.** Saessee Tiin

83.

After Qui-Gon was unable to get Watto to give him the parts that he needed to repair his ship, Qui-Gon contacted Obi-Wan Kenobi to see if there was anything of value on board that they could trade or sell for parts. After Obi-Wan told him that there was nothing of great value, Qui-Gon started through the streets again. Jar Jar protested, saying, "Wesa be robbed un crunched!"

Qui-Gon replied, "Not likely. We have nothing of value, that's our problem." Jar Jar, however, found a way to get "crunched." As they were walking through the streets of Mos Espa, Jar Jar spotted a tasty snack he couldn't resist.

With his versatile tongue, Jar Jar snagged a gorg from the gorgmonger's cart. When Gragra the gorgmonger insisted that he pay for it, Jar Jar let the gorg go, sending it flying directly into some being's lunch.

After getting splashed, this being leapt across the table and grabbed Jar Jar, ready to turn him into "orange goo," until Anakin Skywalker happened along on his way home. After Anakin spoke to this being in Huttese, the being decided it wasn't such a good idea to fight with Jar Jar and went back to his lunch. Who was it?

A. Jabba the Hutt
B. Sebulba
C. Elan Mak
D. Gasgano

81. What was Lott Dod unable to keep the Senate from taxing?
A. Shipments   **C.** Fuel
B. Free trade zones   **D.** Droid armies

82. Who said to Darth Sidious, "We dare not go against the Jedi"?
A. Rune Haako   **C.** Nute Gunray
B. Daultay Dofine   **D.** Tey How

83.

84. What was Sio Bibble's career prior to entering politics on Naboo?
A. He was a   **C.** He was a philosophy professor
mathematics professor
B. He was an artist   **D.** He was a lawyer

85. How tall was Sebulba?
A. 1.20 meters   **C.** 1.12 meters
B. 1.14 meters   **D.** 1.09 meters

86. Who said, "I *will* be Chancellor"?
A. Queen Amidala   **C.** Senator Palpatine
B. Senator Teem   **D.** Senator Antilles

87. What organization did Captain Panaka belong to as a young man?
A. A Republic Secret   **C.** A Republic Special
Service Force   Service Force
B. A Republic Special Task Force   **D.** A Republic Secret Task Force

88. What was Chancellor Valorum's homeworld?
A. Tatooine   **C.** Veccacopia
B. Coruscant   **D.** Aduba-3

89. How tall was Mace Windu?
A. 2.05 meters   **C.** 1.97 meters
B. 1.88 meters   **D.** 1.78 meters

90. Whose lightsaber skills were second to none on the Jedi Council?
A. Yarael Poof   **C.** Plo Koon
B. Yoda   **D.** Yaddle

The Phantom Menace Era

91. When Watto was younger, in what army did he enlist on his homeworld?

- **A.** The Nossiki Federation
- **B.** The Ossilki Federation
- **C.** The Nossilki Confederacy
- **D.** The Ossiki Confederacy

92. What Gungan competition and test of skill for warriors did Boss Nass win when he was younger?

- **A.** The Heyodalee 500
- **B.** The Big Nasty Free-for-All
- **C.** The Otoh Gunga Big Bomben Challenge
- **D.** The Bigold Racenchase

93. Who came in second place in the Boonta Eve Classic Podrace that Anakin Skywalker won?

- **A.** Sebulba
- **B.** Dud Bolt
- **C.** Gasgano
- **D.** Aldar Beedo

94. Against whom was Darth Maul's final challenge before becoming a Dark Lord of the Sith?

- **A.** Darth Plagueis
- **B.** Darth Bane
- **C.** Darth Sidious
- **D.** Count Dooku

95. What was Nute Gunray's homeworld?

- **A.** Neimoidia
- **B.** Veccacopia
- **C.** Tatooine
- **D.** Malastare

96. Of what Naboo council was Sio Bibble chairman?

- **A.** The Governing Council
- **B.** The Advisory Council
- **C.** The Electorate Council
- **D.** The Arts Council

97. Who was the reigning champion of the Boonta Eve Classic Podrace until Anakin Skywalker won?

- **A.** Mawhonic
- **B.** Ratts Tyerell
- **C.** Ody Mandrell
- **D.** Sebulba

98. How many planets did Senator Palpatine represent in the Senate?

- **A.** Thirty-two
- **B.** Thirty-six
- **C.** Forty-one
- **D.** Twenty-nine

99. What did Chancellor Valorum propose that led to the deadly summit on Eriadu?

- **A.** The purchase of droid armies
- **B.** The incorporation of an army of the Republic
- **C.** The taxation of trade routes
- **D.** The taxation of shipments from outlying mining colonies

100. Who rescued the orphaned Depa Billaba and brought her to the Jedi Temple?

A. Yaddle   C. Ki-Adi-Mundi
B. Mace Windu   D. Yoda

101. Who was the oldest member of the Jedi Council at the time of the Battle of Naboo?

A. Saesee Tiin   C. Oppo Rancisis
B. Adi Gallia   D. Yoda

102. Over how many years had Yoda been alive at the time of the Battle of Naboo?

A. Six hundred   C. Nine hundred
B. Seven hundred   D. Eight hundred

103. To whom was the following graffiti, discovered in Mos Espa, referring? "His flippers stink like bantha curd / His breath smells even worse."

A. Sebulba   C. Titi Chronelle
B. Kitster   D. Watto

104. What act did a foolish, young Boss Nass perform?

A. He swam through Naboo's core and broke a record   C. He stole faamba eggs
B. He went in search of and found a sando aqua monster   D. He tried to tame a colo claw fish

105. What work did Shmi Skywalker do at home to earn extra income?

A. She repaired communication devices   C. She wove belts
B. She wove tunics   D. She cleaned computer memory devices

106.

By the time of the Battle of Naboo, this Jedi Master had traveled to hundreds of worlds of his own accord in his quest to understand the many aspects of the Force. He had helped to re-establish the Jedi Order as peacekeepers in the galaxy and was revered by all for his knowledge, wisdom and insight. He became a Jedi Master at the age of one hundred and trained many Jedi Knights. His final Padawan was Ki-Adi-Mundi. After Ki-Adi-Mundi passed the trials to become a Jedi Knight, his former Master retired from having a single Padawan—instead he turned his talents to training the youngest of the Jedi in groups, helping them learn to control their abilities.

When Qui-Gon Jinn came before the Jedi Council and told them that he believed young Skywalker to be the Chosen One who would bring balance to the Force, this Master was reluctant to proceed; however, he relented and Anakin Skywalker went before the Council to be tested. As the Jedi were asking Anakin questions, this Master let the boy know that they could see through him. Which member of the Jedi Council was it?

A. Mace Windu
B. Saesee Tiin
C. Yoda
D. Yarael Poof

107. How old was Darth Maul when Darth Sidious discovered the Force-sensitive child and spirited him away?

A. Two   C. An infant
B. Three   D. Four

108. Whose deciding vote expelled the Pulsar Supertanker corporation from the Trade Federation?

A. Rune Haako   C. Nute Gunray
B. Lott Dod   D. Daultay Dofine

The Phantom Menace Era

109. In what Malastarian city was Sebulba born?
- **A.** Pixelito
- **B.** Pixaleddo
- **C.** Pixoludo
- **D.** Pixeleeko

110. How tall was Captain Panaka?
- **A.** 1.75 meters
- **B.** 1.83 meters
- **C.** 1.95 meters
- **D.** 2.09 meters

111. Why did Darth Sidious send Darth Maul to kill Neimoidian Hath Monchar prior to the Battle of Naboo?
- **A.** He stole the designs to build battle droids
- **B.** He had discovered Darth Sidious's true identity
- **C.** He was threatening to assassinate Nute Gunray
- **D.** He fled the Trade Federation with information on Darth Sidious's invasion plans

112. What job did a young Valorum have on the planet Vecaccopia?
- **A.** Bailiff
- **B.** Attorney
- **C.** Judge
- **D.** Security officer

113. What was one of Darth Maul's earliest memories?
- **A.** Building his lightsaber
- **B.** Going to the Jedi Temple with Darth Sidious to watch the Jedi enter and exit the building
- **C.** Relentless martial arts training
- **D.** Traveling from his homeworld to Coruscant

114. On which planet did young Padawan Mace Windu fight pirates aboard the ship Temblor?
- **A.** Malastare
- **B.** Wroona
- **C.** Worvat-6
- **D.** Kiki

115.

116. Who was in charge of the Space Fighter Corps on Naboo?
- **A.** Captain Panaka
- **B.** Ric Olié
- **C.** Major Fassa
- **D.** Officer Ellberger

117. What was Captain Tarpals' first name?
- **A.** Gunt
- **B.** Lurdo
- **C.** Roos
- **D.** Dooth

115.

After Queen Amidala explained her plan to retake Naboo from the droid armies of the Trade Federation, Boss Nass agreed that the Gungans would go to the plains to distract the droid army so the Queen and her party could infiltrate Theed Palace. Boss Nass had forgiven Jar Jar Binks for all of his idiosyncrasies and allowed him to take part in the battle—an occurrence Jar Jar wasn't very happy about.

Out on the battlefield, the Gungans had started up their shield generators and were all well protected under the blankets of blast-deterring plasma that surrounded their entire army. The AATs were completely ineffective against the Gungans' brilliant organic technology.

The tables turned, however, when the Trade Federation's MTTs opened their doors and revealed the racks of battle droids contained within. The droids were able to break through and ultimately shut down the Gungans' shields. After a strong and well-fought battle, the Gungans were surrounded by the droids. Jar Jar was racking his brains to come up with a strategy when his companion said, "No given up, General Jar Jar. Wesa tinka sumpting!" Which Gungan hero said this?

- **A.** Rep Been
- **B.** Captain Tarpals
- **C.** Boss Nass
- **D.** General Ceel

118. What did Captain Tarpals do before he enlisted in the Gungan Grand Army?

A. He played in a street band

B. He was Boss Nass's personal chef

C. He was a potter

D. He was leader of a gang of swindlers

119. Who was often referred to as "the quickest eyes on Naboo"?

A. Captain Tarpals

B. Captain Typho

C. Captain Panaka

D. General Binks

120. What was Sebulba's most prized possession?

A. His collection of trophy coins

B. His famed Podracer

C. His Twi'lek twin masseuses

D. His reputation

121. Who trained Aurra Sing as a Jedi hopeful?

A. Ki-Adi-Mundi

B. Kit Fisto

C. The Dark Woman

D. Don'naah Tehlah

122. Which of Queen Amidala's handmaidens was chosen to act as her decoy?

A. Eirtaé

B. Yané

C. Rabé

D. Sabé

123. How did Kitster, along with Anakin Skwalker, infiltrate Gardulla the Hutt's fortress to release the Ghostling slaves?

A. He disguised himself as a Tusken Raider

B. He disguised himself as a chef's aide

C. He disguised himself as a wealthy Offworlder's son

D. He disguised himself as a Jawa

124. What was Clegg Holdfast's actual job when not Podracing?

A. He wrote for *Podracers Quarterly*

B. He was an illustrator

C. He was a poacher on his homeworld

D. He was a bounty hunter

125. What Senate committee had Orn Free Taa recently been appointed to prior to the Battle of Naboo?

A. The Free Trade Committee

B. The Financial Appropriations Committee

C. The Tariff Balance Committee

D. The Trade Route Exploration Committee

The Phantom Menace Era

126. What was Jedi Council member Even Piell's homeworld?

A. Lannik

B. Melida/Daan

C. Nemoidia

D. Malastare

127. What did Queen Amidala's handmaiden Saché do when Queen Amidala and her entourage were escaping Naboo?

A. She went with them

B. She went to a prison camp

C. She stayed behind

D. She stowed away on an AAT to investigate the droid army

128. How old was Anakin's Rodian friend Wald at the time of the Boonta Eve Classic Podrace?

A. Seven

B. Six

C. Eight

D. Nine

129. What was Aldar Beedo's Podracing nickname?

A. "Lightning Bolt"

B. "Stumpy"

C. "Hit Man"

D. "Blaster"

130. What sector of the galaxy did Senator Horox Ryyder represent?

A. The Ballorai sector

B. The Raioballo sector

C. The Rebollo sector

D. The Bellarayo sector

131. What special skill did Yarael Poof possess?

A. He could make himself invisible

B. He could pass through walls

C. He could force objects to implode

D. He could cast flawless illusions

132. What was handmaiden Eirtaé's special skill?

A. She was a strong negotiator

B. She was well-versed in etiquette

C. She was a martial arts expert

D. She served as a translator

133. What was Lufta Shif's position on Queen Amidala's Advisory Council?

A. Master of the Arts

B. Education Regent

C. Master of Sciences

D. Music Advisor

134. What was Anakin's friend Amee's mother's name?

A. Holla

B. Hala

C. Halle

D. Hola

OBSESSED WITH *STAR WARS*

141.

This Podracer piloted an oversized, garishly painted, awkward craft that contained twin-turbined Vokoff-Strood Plug-8G 927 Cluster Array engines. An open-air channel in the center of the engine cluster allowed these enormous engines the cooling they needed to sustain the high speeds involved with Podracing. While they looked ungainly, these engines offered the pilot the speed he needed—he hated letting anyone pass him.

Diva Funquita, acting on orders of Gardulla the Hutt, hired him to sabotage Anakin Skywalker's Podracer so the boy would have no chance of winning the race. This podracer, who Skywalker had nearly overtaken in a previous race, jumped at the chance to ensure that the boy would have no way to beat him.

He was not a fast thinker—in fact, he was known for being a bit of a dolt. It should have come as no surprise to anyone that he mistakenly sabotaged Ben Quadinaros' Podracer.

Even if he had been bright enough to tamper with the right Podracer, it wouldn't have mattered—he collided with Dud Bolt during the third lap of the Boonta Eve Classic in a treacherous stretch of the track known as "the Coil." Which Podracer was this?

A. Mawhonic
B. Gasgano
C. Ark "Bumpy" Roose
D. Wan Sandage

135. How did Ebe Endocott begin his racing career?
- **A.** As a pit assistant on Malastare
- **B.** As a pit assistant on Boonta
- **C.** As a landspeeder driver on Malastare
- **D.** As a landspeeder driver on Boonta

136. What planet did Senator Passel Argente represent?
- **A.** Tatooine
- **B.** Naboo
- **C.** Boonta
- **D.** Kooriva

137. What Jedi trained Jedi Council member Saesee Tiin?
- **A.** Master Umo Buri
- **B.** Master Emo Bore
- **C.** Master Omo Bouri
- **D.** Master Oma Boure

138. What position did Hugo Eckener hold on Queen Amidala's Advisory Council?
- **A.** Master of the Arts
- **B.** Chief Architect
- **C.** Galactic Etiquette Master
- **D.** Master of Sciences

139. How old was Anakin Skywalker's friend Seek at the time of the Boonta Eve Classic Podrace on Tatooine?
- **A.** Ten
- **B.** Eight
- **C.** Nine
- **D.** Eleven

140. How many brothers and sisters did Podracer Wan Sandage have?
- **A.** Ninety-seven
- **B.** Eighty-one
- **C.** One hundred twenty-seven
- **D.** One hundred fifty-one

141.

142. What was Dud Bolt's homeworld?
- **A.** Vultur
- **B.** Vulptaar
- **C.** Vulpter
- **D.** Veltor

143. From which planet did Senator Aks Moe hail?
- **A.** Kashyyyk
- **B.** Malastare
- **C.** Ryloth
- **D.** Mon Calamari

144. What Jedi-in-hiding did Aurra Sing hunt down and murder on Tatooine?
- **A.** A'Sharad Hutt
- **B.** Sharad Hett
- **C.** Shorodd Hutt
- **D.** Shredda Hott

The Phantom Menace Era

145. How many wives did Ki-Adi-Mundi have?
- **A.** One
- **B.** Five
- **C.** Four
- **D.** Three

146. What special function did Gungan Rep Been serve on the Gungan High Council?
- **A.** He was Diplomat to Naboo
- **B.** He was keeper of all ancient records
- **C.** He was Boss Nass's bodyguard
- **D.** He was head military strategist

147. What position did Graf Zapalo hold on Queen Amidala's Advisory Council?
- **A.** Master of Hydroponics
- **B.** Master of Sciences
- **C.** Chief Horticulturist
- **D.** Master of the Arts

148. What were the names of Sebulba's twin Twi'lek masseuses?
- **A.** Gan and Tann Gella
- **B.** Ann and Tann Gella
- **C.** Ann and Tann Della
- **D.** Ann and Fan Jella

149. On what planet was Podracer Ody Mandrell born?
- **A.** Naboo
- **B.** Tatooine
- **C.** Lannik
- **D.** Dantooine

150. Who presided over the Boonta Eve Classic Podrace?
- **A.** Fode and Beed
- **B.** Jabba the Hutt
- **C.** Gardulla the Hutt
- **D.** Bib Fortuna

151. What species was Senator Mot-Not Rab?
- **A.** Tarnab
- **B.** Tornob
- **C.** Taanab
- **D.** Tornab

152. How old was Eeth Koth when he was taken as a student at the Jedi Temple?
- **A.** Four
- **B.** Newborn
- **C.** Five
- **D.** Six

153. How old was Jedi Master Oppo Rancisis at the Battle of Naboo?
- **A.** One hundred seventy-four
- **B.** One hundred eighty
- **C.** One hundred eighty-nine
- **D.** One hundred ninety-four

OBSESSED WITH *STAR WARS*

156.

When he was younger, this Senator from Kashyyyk wanted little out of life other than to take over his family's business and live a full life on his homeworld. In an unfortunate turn of events that changed his life forever, his father died in an accident and left him the family patriarch at the tender age of one hundred twenty.

As leader of a family group, this Wookiee taught himself to deal with situations calmly and diplomatically. Although he, like all Wookiees, possessed a fierce, unpredictable temper, he trained himself to deal with situations calmly and diplomatically instead of lashing out. Because of his calm demeanor in the face of adversity, he quickly earned the respect of the Kashyyyk elders, who urged him to run for Senator when his predecessor retired.

He detested the current state of corruption in the Galactic Senate and worked diligently to return true democracy to the Republic, supporting the Jedi through the Battle of Kashyyyk. What was this Senator's name?

A. Tarfful
B. Chewbacca
C. Yarua
D. Lumpawarrump

154. How tall was Podracer Teemto Pagalies?
A. 1.19 meters **C.** 1.48 meters
B. 1.37 meters **D.** 1.24 meters

155. What was Ratts Tyerell's species?
A. Allem **C.** Aleena
B. Alluna **D.** Alooma

156.

157. After the Boonta Eve Classic Podrace, why did Gardulla the Hutt offer Watto a large sum of money?
A. As payment for an old debt **C.** As payment for Anakin's win
B. To purchase Anakin's Podracer **D.** To regain custody of Anakin Skywalker

158. What color was Diva Funquita's hair?
A. Blue **C.** Red
B. Brown **D.** Black

159. What was Sei Taria's relationship with Chancellor Valorum?
A. She was his administrative aide **C.** She was his translator
B. She was his servant **D.** She was his publicist

160. From which planet did Senator Bail Antilles hail?
A. Coruscant **C.** Malastare
B. Tatooine **D.** Alderaan

161. How old was Jedi Master Yaddle at the Battle of Naboo?
A. Two hundred seventy-six **C.** Four hundred seventy-seven
B. Three hundred ninety-nine **D.** Five hundred thirteen

162. What was Mas Amedda's role in the Senate?
A. Assistant Chancellor **C.** Vice Chair
B. Vice Chancellor **D.** Assistant Chair

163. What is Fode and Beed's Troig name?
A. Fodenbeed **C.** Fodesbeed
B. FodeBeed **D.** FodesinBeed

The Phantom Menace Era

164. What Jedi Council member was Oppo Rancisis' Master?

A. Mace Windu

B. Yoda

C. Ki-Adi-Mundi

D. Yaddle

165. What was Queen Amidala's handmaiden Rabé's special skill?

A. She was the Queen's spiritual advisor

B. She was skilled at preparing the Queen's elaborate hairstyles

C. She served as negotiator in difficult situations

D. She acted as the Queen's double if Sabé wasn't available

166. What was Hela Brandes' position on the Royal Advisory Council of Naboo?

A. Master of Arts

B. Music Advisor

C. Education Regent

D. Political Advisor

167. How tall was Podracer Gasgano?

A. 1.77 meters

B. 1.22 meters

C. 0.99 meters

D. 1.44 meters

168. Who was Jabba the Hutt's major-domo?

A. Bib Futrona

B. Bib Fortuna

C. Bid Fanturna

D. Dib Futura

169. For how long had Senator Yarua of Kashyyyk served at the time of the Battle of Naboo?

A. More than two hundred years

B. More than three hundred years

C. More than one hundred years

D. More than fifty years

170. What was Dud Bolt's secret job during the Boonta Eve Podrace?

A. He was a spy

B. He was hired to make sure racers didn't cheat

C. He was Sebulba's mid-air bodyguard

D. He was Gasgano's mid-air bodyguard

171. From which planet did Senator Ainlee Teem hail?

A. Xagobah

B. Malastare

C. Tatooine

D. Naboo

172. Who was one of two aides to the Senator from Alderaan?

A. Liana Merian

B. Lann Maran

C. Lenai Mirand

D. Lian Mierana

OBSESSED WITH *STAR WARS*

179.

This member of the Jedi Council was born in squalor on the smuggler's moon Nar Shaddaa, a slimy criminal hotbed orbiting Nal Hutta. This planet is a dark reflection of Coruscant, completely covered in interlocking spaceports that harbor criminals, smugglers, thieves, bounty hunters, and any other underworld characters hoping to evade justice.

It was no surprise, then, that this Jedi's abilities were not discovered until he was older. It was a widely accepted rule that in order to be fully and completely trained as a Jedi Knight, one had to start near infancy, so this Jedi almost missed his chance to train. He proved himself worthy of bending the rules by demonstrating extreme mental discipline.

An Iridonian Zabrak, he had vestigial horns and facial tattoos received during his rite of passage. He had very strong self-control and the ability to withstand intense pain.

This Jedi Master trained the fabled Jedi Sharad Hett, who disappeared to live among the Tusken Raiders on the desert planet of Tatooine. Which member of the Jedi Council was he?

A. Yarael Poof
B. Plo Koon
C. Eeth Koth
D. Saesee Tiin

173. Who was the other aide to the Senator from Alderaan?
  A. Agrippo Adonte
  B. Agrinda Aldodo
  C. Agrippa Aldrete
  D. Agridda Algrente

174. Who was Kitster's father?
  A. Miner Rookir Bonni
  B. Miner Rekir Benii
  C. Smuggler Rakir Banai
  D. Smuggler Rokir Bonak

175. What species was Jedi Master Plo Koon's Padawan during the Battle of Naboo?
  A. Gungan
  B. Wookiee
  C. Trandoshan
  D. Twi'lek

176. How did Jedi Master Even Piell lose his eye?
  A. It was shot out during target practice in the Jedi Temple
  B. It was shot out in the Stark Hyperspace War
  C. He lost it in a battle against Red Iaro terrorists
  D. He was trying to break up a brawl in a cantina

177. Why did Podracer Ben Quadinaros and his family have to flee their homeworld?
  A. The cost of living had gotten too high
  B. He was wanted for a crime he did not commit
  C. The planet suffered from environmental poisoning
  D. Their planet was being invaded by an alien species

178. What was Jedi Master Adi Gallia's homeworld?
  A. Naboo
  B. Coruscant
  C. Yavin 4
  D. Corellia

179.

180. In what Mos Espa bar did Podracer Boles Roor perform his glimmik singing?
  A. The Happy Hutt
  B. The Bloody Bantha
  C. The Poodoo Lounge
  D. The Jawa Barn

181. Who was Anakin Skywalker's friend Melee's owner in Mos Espa?
  A. Watto
  B. Gardulla the Hutt
  C. Jabba the Hutt
  D. Sebulba

The Phantom Menace Era

182. With whom was Podracer Mars Guo enamored?
- **A.** Diva Shaliqua
- **B.** Tann Gella
- **C.** Ann Gella
- **D.** Diva Funquita

183. What was Podracer Ark "Bumpy" Roose's homeworld?
- **A.** Stump
- **B.** Sump
- **C.** Slump
- **D.** Skump

184. What color was Diva Shaliqua's hair?
- **A.** Red
- **B.** Green
- **C.** Blue
- **D.** Orange

185. What differentiated Ki-Adi-Mundi from other members of the Jedi Council?
- **A.** He was married
- **B.** He was not Force-sensitive
- **C.** He embraced the dark side
- **D.** He took no Padawans

186. What was Gran Podracer Mawhonic's homeworld?
- **A.** Malastare
- **B.** Hok
- **C.** Kinyen
- **D.** Tatooine

187.

188. Why did Elan Mak enter the Boonta Eve Classic Podrace?
- **A.** To win glory for his homeworld
- **B.** To get revenge on Sebulba
- **C.** To get the prize money and pay off gambling debts
- **D.** To kill Aldar Beedo, his father's assassin

189. What was Neva Kee's homeworld?
- **A.** Dagobah
- **B.** Dantooine
- **C.** Xagobah
- **D.** Tatooine

190. What distinctive article of clothing did Jedi Council member Adi Gallia wear?
- **A.** A Nabooian cape
- **B.** A Tholoth headdress
- **C.** Green leather gloves
- **D.** A large gold bracelet

187.

Qui-Gon Jinn had won Anakin Skywalker's freedom from Watto by betting that Anakin would win the Boonta Eve Podrace. He returned to Mos Espa, while his companions were repairing Queen Amidala's Royal Starship, to find Anakin and bring him along. On his way through the slave quarters of Mos Espa, Qui-Gon found Anakin surrounded by children, fighting with another child. When the two noticed Qui-Gon's shadow looming over them, they lost their will to fight and rolled over to see who was towering over them. "What's this?" Qui-Gon asked Anakin.

"He said I cheated!" Anakin responded. Qui-Gon then asked Anakin if he had cheated, to which he responded no, and then turned to the other boy and asked him if he still thought Anakin had cheated.

"Yes," the boy said.

"Well, Ani. You know the truth. You will have to tolerate his opinion. Fighting won't change it," Qui-Gon lectured. Who was Anakin's adversary?

- **A.** Greedo
- **B.** Greedo the Elder
- **C.** Kitster
- **D.** Wald

191. What was Nute Gunray's species?
A. Devaronian   **C.** Chagrian
B. Neimoidian   **D.** Human

192. What was Jabba's species?
A. Charon   **C.** Hutt
B. Xexto   **D.** Squib

193. What was Mas Amedda's species?
A. Twi'lek   **C.** Iridonian Zabrak
B. Chagrian   **D.** Rodian

194. What was Sebulba's species?
A. Wookiee   **C.** Malastarian
B. Dug   **D.** Gran

195. What was Jar Jar Binks' species?
A. Nabooian   **C.** Gungan
B. Hutt   **D.** Rodian

196. What was Orn Free Taa's race?
A. Lethan Twi'lek   **C.** Rutian Twi'lek
B. Twi'lek   **D.** Human

197. What was Watto's species?
A. Gungan   **C.** Jawa
B. Toydarian   **D.** Dug

198. What was Adi Gallia's species?
A. Chalactan   **C.** Human
B. Twi'lek   **D.** Cerean

199. What was Darth Maul's species?
A. Human   **C.** Nemoidian
B. Iridonian Zabrak **D.** Rodian

The Phantom Menace **Era**

200. What was Aldar Beedo's species?
- **A.** Fluggrian
- **B.** Glymphid
- **C.** Dug
- **D.** Hutt

201. What was Boss Nass' race?
- **A.** Otolla Gungan
- **B.** Ankura Gungan
- **C.** Lethan Twi'lek
- **D.** Rutian Twi'lek

202. What was Toonbuck Toora's species?
- **A.** Ssi-ruuk
- **B.** Sy Myrthian
- **C.** Slivilith
- **D.** Shistavanen Wolfman

203. What was Captain Tarpals' race?
- **A.** Ankura Gungan
- **B.** Rutian Twi'lek
- **C.** Otolla Gungan
- **D.** Lethan Twi'lek

204.

205. What distinguishes a Lethan Twi'lek from other Twi'leks?
- **A.** Four lekku
- **B.** Red skin
- **C.** Three lekku
- **D.** Blue skin

206. What was Neva Kee's species?
- **A.** Xamster
- **B.** Er'kit
- **C.** Lannik
- **D.** Devlikk

207. What was Mars Guo's species?
- **A.** Phuii
- **B.** Xamster
- **C.** Nuknog
- **D.** Talz

208. What was Yarael Poof's species?
- **A.** Y'bith
- **B.** Xexto
- **C.** Cerean
- **D.** Quermian

209. What was Mawhonic's species?
- **A.** Dug
- **B.** Gran
- **C.** Jawa
- **D.** Toydarian

204.

This species is descended from colonial Duros travelers who settled away from their homeworld. They have the exact same genetic structure as Duros, but have adapted to an entirely different way of life. While Duros are preoccupied with space travel and exploration, their genetic cousins are much greedier and fiscally motivated. Money and power drive them to their goals, and they are raised to believe that those two things are all that matter in life.

Brought up from eggs, these aliens are thrown into a colony situation at birth and have limited access to food. Their keepers believe that the lesson to be learned is that he who hoards the most will be the one who ends up on top. Many of their young die due to starvation; the adults feel that those were the weak ones, who did not deserve to live. Those who survive leave their colony at age seven, instilled with an intense fear of death and a severe sense of greed.

Due to these two learned traits, these aliens are keen businessmen, amassing great fortune, sometimes by nefarious means. They shy away from battle, fleeing the scene or sending other, more gullible, toadies to do their dirty work. What is this species?

- **A.** Dug
- **B.** Hutt
- **C.** Neimoidian
- **D.** Rodian

210. In what form are Neimoidians at birth?

A. Grubs
B. Maggots
C. Tadpoles
D. Worms

211. What is unique about Dugs' physiology?

A. They developed a second set of teeth to help chew bark
B. They walk on their upper limbs
C. They developed a second stomach to better digest bark
D. They developed very thick nails to assist in tree climbing

212. What was Plo Koon's species?

A. Kaleesh
B. Gossam
C. Kel Dor
D. Givin

213. Which term best describes the Er'Kit, of which Ody Mandrell was a prominent example?

A. Insectoid
B. Amphibious
C. Mammalian
D. Reptilian

214. What was Coruscant taxi driver Rayno Vaca's species?

A. Besalisk
B. Tarnab
C. Anzati
D. Clawdite

215. What was Clegg Holdfast's species?

A. Dug
B. Nosaurian
C. Gran
D. Xexto

216. How many arms do Xexto have?

A. Three
B. Four
C. Six
D. Two

217. How many eyes do Gran have?

A. Four
B. Three
C. Two
D. One

The Phantom Menace Era

218. How many fingers do Gungans have on each hand?

A. Four

B. Three

C. Six

D. Five

219. How do Iridonian Zabrak identify their various races?

A. By their vestigial horn patterns

B. By their eye colors

C. By their tribal haircuts

D. By their tribal tattoos

220.

221. How do Neimoidians raise their young?

A. In communal hives

B. As only children

C. At boarding schools

D. In military training camps

222. Which species refers to their ears as haillu?

A. Gran

B. Gungans

C. Dugs

D. Twi'leks

223. What was Saesee Tiin's species?

A. Ithorian

B. Ishi Tib

C. Iktotchi

D. Imzig

224. How fast do Toydarians' wings beat?

A. As fast as thirty times a second

B. As fast as fifteen times a second

C. As fast as ten times a second

D. As fast as five times a second

225. Which Podracer belonged to the Fluggrian species?

A. Dud Bolt

B. Ark "Bumpy" Roose

C. Elan Mak

D. Sebulba

226. What was Jedi Master Even Piell's species?

A. Cerean

B. Shawda Ubb

C. Nautolan

D. Lannik

227. Which humanoid species has tall craniums that contain binary brains?

A. Iridonian Zabraks

B. Cereans

C. Twi'leks

D. Gungans

220.

This orange-skinned species is native to a planet in the Expansion Region. Their society and economy are based on technology and their lives are family-based. Many generations of a family may live together, and couples begin having children almost immediately after marriage.

The atmosphere on their planet consists of helium and a mysterious gaseous substance unique to their system. These hairless beings have adapted so thoroughly to the gases in their atmosphere that they cannot breathe or see in other atmospheres without using equipment designed to provide them a constant supply of these gases.

They must be fitted with an antiox breathing mask and goggles in order to travel offworld. The masks are equipped with tubes that extend downward from their faces and supply a constant flow of atmospheric isotopes equal to those of their homeworld's. This species also fits its offworld dwellings with airlocks so they can create artificial atmospheres similar to that found on their planet. The goggles they wear when offworld keep their eyes from burning and actually improve their eyesight.

What species is this?

A. Dug

B. Kel Dor

C. Kubaz

D. Gand

228. What distinguishes male Rodians from females?
- **A.** Females can grow hair
- **B.** Males are shorter
- **C.** Males have a dewlap
- **D.** Females have prehensile tails

229. How many hands do Thisspiasians like Jedi Master Oppo Rancisis have?
- **A.** Six
- **B.** Four
- **C.** None
- **D.** Two

230. Which apparently chubby species actually has spongy tissue full of gas allowing them to fly with ease?
- **A.** Jawas
- **B.** Dugs
- **C.** Toydarians
- **D.** Lepi

231. How did dewbacks get their name?
- **A.** Their backs glisten
- **B.** They lick dew off each other's backs
- **C.** They exude lipids that look like dew
- **D.** They are constantly damp

232. How large can male sando aqua monsters grow?
- **A.** 200 meters long
- **B.** 350 meters long
- **C.** 50 meters long
- **D.** 10 meters long

233. Falumpasets roam the Naboo swamps in family groups of what size?
- **A.** Two males, one female and their young
- **B.** One male, four to seven females and their young
- **C.** One male, three females and their young
- **D.** Two males, ten females and their young

234. Which creature is the largest terrestrial herbivore of the Naboo swamp?
- **A.** Kaadu
- **B.** Reek
- **C.** Spore newt
- **D.** Fambaa

The Phantom Menace Era

235. Which Naboo animal is farmed for its succulent meat?

A. Colo claw fish C. Falumpasets

B. Shaaks D. Spore newts

236. How does the colo claw fish push prey down its gullet?

A. Butting its head against outcroppings C. Temporomandibular claws

B. Dual tongues D. Multiple layers of mobile teeth

237. What annoying trait do eopies display when startled?

A. They emit gas C. They charge

B. They spit undigested stomach contents D. They scream

238. How many sets of ears do Rontos have?

A. One C. Three

B. Two D. Four

239.

240. How does the colo claw fish accommodate large prey?

A. It breaks its prey into pieces before consuming it C. It shares its kill with other colo claw fish

B. Its stomach stretches to fit its prey's size D. It injects its prey with an acidic substance that breaks it down before it consumes it

241. What are sando aqua monsters?

A. Insects C. Mammals

B. Amphibians D. Reptiles

242. The sando aqua monster was thought to be a myth until one beached itself on the shore near which Naboo port?

A. Port Landien C. Port Nandien

B. Port Landier D. Port Londien

243. How does the opee sea killer attract prey?

A. It has phosphorescent tips on the ends of its antennae C. It hides among algae clusters

B. It releases pheromones D. It buries itself in the sand

239.

Although they're technically amphibians and get along perfectly above or under water, this species, native to the swamplands of Naboo, is covered in thick, leathery scales. These scales are soft at birth but harden as these creatures mature. They are also born with gills that are absorbed into their bodies as they age. These creatures sometimes knock down trees to reach their fruits and berries, but they are also happy to consume underwater plants.

In the wild, these slow, lumbering creatures travel in herds of up to twelve, but in captivity they are kept in groups of

244. How long does it take for young eopies to be able to walk on their own?

- **A.** Several months
- **B.** Several days
- **C.** Several weeks
- **D.** Several minutes after their birth

245. Though generally slow, how fast can dewbacks run in short bursts?

- **A.** Up to 60 kph
- **B.** Up to 40 kph
- **C.** Up to 50 kph
- **D.** Up to 30 kph

246. How many eggs do female dewbacks produce per year?

- **A.** Twenty to forty eggs
- **B.** Fifty to eighty-five eggs
- **C.** One hundred to two hundred eggs
- **D.** Ten to twenty-five eggs

247. What are tee fish known for?

- **A.** Their ability to swallow single Gungans whole
- **B.** Their ability to glow in the dark
- **C.** The eerie hum they produce when mating
- **D.** Their elongated fins, which are a delicacy

248. How do male nunas display aggression?

- **A.** They hiss and inflate their wattles
- **B.** They extend dewlaps
- **C.** They inflate their throats
- **D.** They howl

249. What makes the peko-peko an integral part of the Naboo swamp ecosystem?

- **A.** Many nuts and seeds won't germinate unless they pass through its gastrointestinal system
- **B.** It is the sole food source of many swamp species
- **C.** Its guano fertilizes a large portion of the swamp floor
- **D.** Its egg shells provide calcium to the falumpasets

250. What is the average amount of young per mott birth?

- **A.** Ten
- **B.** Fifteen
- **C.** Five
- **D.** Twenty

251. Where in the Naboo swamp do motts dwell?

- **A.** Underwater
- **B.** In low-hanging nests
- **C.** Inside tree trunks
- **D.** In underground burrows

three. Gungans have domesticated these dimwitted, docile creatures and use them as beasts of burden and transport. They also use this creature's skin to make saddles. Gungan breeding herds of these creatures are often so large that they keep them in their sacred places or in the swamps.

During wartime, these enormous beasts transport the Gungans' shield generators and massive projectile weapons. Which Naboo swamp creature is this?

- **A.** Kaadu
- **B.** Falumpaset
- **C.** Fambaa
- **D.** Terazod

The Phantom Menace Era

252. How do ikopi consume their food?
- **A.** They scrape bark with their teeth
- **B.** They suck it through an elongated, hollow tongue
- **C.** They swallow nuna eggs whole
- **D.** They ingest moisture through padding in their hooves

253. What creature did Jabba flick off the balcony of his private box at the Boonta Eve Classic Podrace?
- **A.** A dwarf eopie
- **B.** A dwarf dewback
- **C.** A dwarf bantha
- **D.** A dwarf nuna

254. Into which category do gorgs fall?
- **A.** Amphibian
- **B.** Reptilian
- **C.** Mammalian
- **D.** Insectoid

255. What do gorgmongers sell?
- **A.** Nunas
- **B.** Dewback eggs
- **C.** Gorgs
- **D.** Eopie steaks

256. How do opee sea killers catch their prey?
- **A.** With their claws
- **B.** With hinged, finger-like fins
- **C.** With double dentition
- **D.** With a long, sticky tongue

257. What body part do young fambaas have that disappears as they mature?
- **A.** Wings
- **B.** Fins
- **C.** Gills
- **D.** Tails

258. How do eopies get most of their moisture?
- **A.** They receive it from moisture farms
- **B.** They collect it from desert lichens and tubers
- **C.** They have glands that produce moisture for them
- **D.** They have evolved to no longer need moisture

259. What is unique about opee sea killer egg-laying practices?
- **A.** They lay their eggs into a protective, weblike substance
- **B.** Their eggs hatch immediately
- **C.** The male holds the eggs in his mouth for three months
- **D.** They bury their eggs on land

260. What do banthas do with their dead?
- **A.** They eat them
- **B.** They bury them
- **C.** They abandon them
- **D.** They take them to "bantha graveyards"

269.

The Boonta Eve Classic is one of the most popular and profitable Podrace circuits in the Outer Rim, attracting fans from all over the galaxy eager to watch Podracers battle it out to see who is the bravest, the fastest, and in some cases, the most devious.

The circuit's starting point is the immense Mos Espa Arena. Podracers zoom past the starting line through Starlite Flats and on into Waldo Flats and the treacherous curves of Waldo Cradle to reach Mushroom Mesa, a dangerous field of outcroppings where Podracers must careen through alternating harsh sunlight and shadow in order to move on

261. What was the name of the Gungan underwater city?
- **A.** Otoh Gunga
- **B.** Mos Espa
- **C.** Theed
- **D.** Bestine

262. What is the name of the wide, flat mountain around which the Mos Espa Podrace course winds?
- **A.** Jawa Mesa
- **B.** Ben's Mesa
- **C.** Toond Mesa
- **D.** Olari's Mesa

263. What is Otoh Gunga made up of?
- **A.** Transparisteel bubbles
- **B.** Glass bubbles
- **C.** Hydrostatic bubbles
- **D.** Plastisteel bubbles

264. In which canyon on the Northern edge of the Dune Sea is the Tatooine spaceport Mos Espa located?
- **A.** The Zeltric Gap
- **B.** The Xeltric Draw
- **C.** The Xeltric Gap
- **D.** The Zeltric Draw

265. What did Watto place in the upper dome of his junkshop?
- **A.** A cooling unit
- **B.** A secret safe
- **C.** A nest where he rests
- **D.** A solar panel

266. How do Mos Espa slave hovels receive their power?
- **A.** From massive solar panels
- **B.** From wind power
- **C.** From plasma conduits
- **D.** From bio-converter power generators

267. What was the name of Senator Palpatine's apartment building on Coruscant?
- **A.** 40 Republica
- **B.** 500 Republica
- **C.** 1138 Republica
- **D.** 3000 Republica

268. How many spectators can fit into the grandstands of the Mos Espa Arena to watch the Podraces?
- **A.** 300,000
- **B.** 100,000
- **C.** 60,000
- **D.** 10,000

269.

to Ebe Crater Valley. The next section of the course contains such dangerous turns that some have been named Diablo Cut, Dead Man's Turn, and Stone Needle.

On non-race days, daring would-be pilots race their own skyhoppers and landspeeders to test their skill. The winding curves of one dry riverbed have been host to many dreams gone awry as less-talented pilots crash their vehicles into one of its many sharp turns. What is the name of this famous stretch of the Tatooine desert?

- **A.** The Whip
- **B.** Beggar's Canyon
- **C.** The Corkscrew
- **D.** Canyon Dune Turn

The Phantom Menace Era

270. What lies behind each of the detachable Senate platforms in the Galactic Senate building on Coruscant?

A. Repulsorlifts to landing platforms

B. Power generators

C. Hallways leading to the outer greeting areas of the Senate

D. The Senators' private offices

271. How many towers does the Jedi Temple have?

A. Four

B. Six

C. Five

D. Three

272. Where in the Mos Espa Podrace course do the Tusken Raiders lie in wait to shoot at unsuspecting contestants?

A. The Whip

B. Jett's Chute

C. Canyon Dune Turn

D. Mushroom Mesa

273. Where did the confrontation between the Gungans and the Trade Federation droid army take place?

A. The Theedian Grass Knoll

B. The Great Green Plains

C. The Theedian Grass Plains

D. The Great Grass Plains

274. What type of energy does the Theed Generator produce?

A. Wind

B. Solar

C. Biowaste

D. Plasma

275. In which area of Mos Espa was Anakin and Shmi Skywalker's hovel located?

A. City Center

B. Slave Quarters Row

C. The Outskirts

D. Slaver's Corner

276. What makes Naboo a unique planet?

A. Its core is a honeycomb of caves and tunnels

B. Its core was artificially produced and is regularly maintained

C. It has more than one active core

D. Its core contains an air-like atmosphere

277. Where is the Gungan City of Otoh Gunga located?

A. Deep within the River Solleu

B. Suspended in the depths of Lake Cuuro

C. On the rim of the planet's core

D. Anchored to a cliff in Lake Paonga

OBSESSED WITH *STAR WARS*

285.

When Anakin Skywalker found the structural framework of a protocol droid, he carried it home in hopes of creating a functioning droid to relieve some of his mother's workload. Many parts had been stripped from the droid's frame, most of which was well over eighty years old, but Anakin scrounged what he needed from Watto's shop or wherever he could. He even built some of the parts himself.

This fortunate droid contains a very important piece of hardware: a TranLang III communications module, which Anakin smuggled out of Watto's shop from a droid that Gardulla the Hutt had destroyed. This piece of hardware allows C-3PO to speak in more than six million forms of communication, including Tusken Raider and Jawa.

Although he was largely finished, C-3PO still had some kinks that needed to be worked out. When Anakin turned C-3PO on and introduced him to Padmé for the first time, the hapless droid couldn't see anything. "Where is everybody?" C-3PO asked. At that point, Anakin remembered that he had left out one very important part. What part was that?

A. Oculotron
B. Photoreceptor
C. Orbital CamLens
D. Visio-Lite Masquer

278. Where is the Gungan Sacred Place located?
A. In the swampy foothills of the Gallo Mountains
C. On top of Mount Gunga
B. In the Ankura Swamp
D. In the Theed Swamp

279. At which location in the Mos Espa Podrace course did Ratts Tyerell run his Podracer into a stalactite?
A. Jawa Forge
C. Jawa Mesa
B. Laguna Caves
D. The Xeltric Draw

280. What are Coruscant's coordinates on standard navigation charts?
A. Zero-zero-zero
C. One-one-one
B. One-zero-zero
D. Zero-zero-one

281. What was the designation of the protocol droid who attended the Jedi Ambassadors on the Droid Control Ship?
A. TC-14
C. AB-C13
B. BB-KM
D. SAGGS.5

282. What droid repaired the shield generator on Queen Amidala's Royal Starship?
A. R4-B9
C. R2-D2
B. R5-D4
D. R4-D2

283. How do droidekas, or destroyer droids, travel at top speed?
A. They fly
C. They run
B. They hover just above the ground
D. They fold into a wheel and roll

284. What type of droid was Anakin Skywalker building to help his mother?
A. Astromech
C. Protocol
B. Destroyer
D. Probe

285.

286. What dangerous species did the Trade Federation commission to create their droideka forces?
A. Iridonian Zabraks
C. Hutts
B. Colicoids
D. Tusken Raiders

The Phantom Menace Era

287. What did Darth Maul use to locate Qui-Gon Jinn on Tatooine?
- **A.** Astromech droids
- **B.** Probe droids
- **C.** Mouse droids
- **D.** Battle droids

288. What unfortunate trait did R2-D2 point out to his new friend C-3PO when they met?
- **A.** That C-3PO was naked
- **B.** That C-3PO was unfinished
- **C.** That C-3PO was fat
- **D.** That C-3PO was lopsided

289. How did the Trade Federation control its battle droid armies?
- **A.** The droids were pre-programmed to destroy living beings
- **B.** The droids were trained to follow orders
- **C.** The droids acted on their own free will
- **D.** Orders were sent to officer droids from Central Control Computer processors

290. What makes droidekas particularly deadly enemies?
- **A.** They have reasoning capabilities
- **B.** They have individual shield generators
- **C.** They can become invisible
- **D.** They can see in the dark

291. What job function do battle droids with red detailing perform?
- **A.** Security droid
- **B.** Command Officer
- **C.** Pilot droid
- **D.** Infantry droid

292. How many battle droids can be carried in the deployment rack of an MTT?
- **A.** 250
- **B.** 144
- **C.** 112
- **D.** 120

293. What job function do battle droids with blue detailing perform?
- **A.** Pilot droid
- **B.** Security droid
- **C.** Infantry droid
- **D.** Command Officer

294. What species designed the Trade Federation's droid starfighters?
- **A.** Neimoidians
- **B.** Xi Charrians
- **C.** Colicoids
- **D.** Geonosians

295.

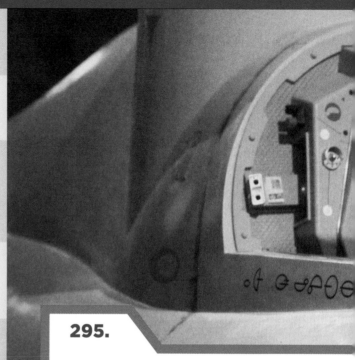

295.

The astromech droid R2-D2 was assigned to the Queen's Royal Starship. After he distinguished himself by repairing the ship's shields during Queen Amidala's escape from Naboo, she treated the droid as a member of the team. It was no surprise that Queen Amidala brought R2-D2 with her when she returned to Naboo to infiltrate Theed. Her team also included Qui-Gon Jinn, Obi-Wan Kenobi, Anakin Skywalker, and Captain Panaka.

In the Theed Hangar, Anakin Skywalker was told to stay out of harm's way, so he hid in the cockpit of an N-1 Naboo Starfighter. R2-D2, positioned under the starfighter when

296. What makes pit droids effective mechanics in the Podracing circuit?

A. They are pre-programmed with a permanent sense of urgency

B. They are their own tool kits

C. They are pre-programmed to fix anything

D. They can stand in for pilots

297. What service do GNK droids provide?

A. They host parties

B. They are mobile power generators

C. They collect and process garbage

D. They act as translators

298. How many crystals powered Darth Maul's lightsaber?

A. Three

B. Six

C. Two

D. Four

299. What color was Qui-Gon Jinn's lightsaber blade?

A. Green

B. Red

C. Purple

D. Blue

300. What do Gungan boomas consist of?

A. Poisonous gel sapped from aquatic plant roots

B. Sharp wooden spikes encased in a charged organic membrane

C. Unstable plasmic energy encased in a charged organic membrane

D. Shrapnel particles extracted from colo claw fish

301. On what planet did Obi-Wan retrieve the crystals to build his lightsaber?

A. Naboo

B. Ilum

C. Coruscant

D. Dantooine

302. What color was Obi-Wan's lightsaber blade?

A. Blue

B. Red

C. Green

D. Purple

303. What is the traditional Tusken Raider weapon of choice?

A. Blaster

B. Bow and arrow

C. Club

D. Gaffi stick

304. What special feature does the Security S-5 blaster have that aids Queen Amidala and her party when fighting the Trade Federation?

A. Infrared sensors

B. Liquid cable shooter with a grappling hook tip

C. Rapid fire trigger function

D. Net shooter

Anakin inadvertently activated it, was pulled up into the droid socket behind the cockpit, which was placed there so the droid could assist with the ship's computers and systems during battle. How did R2-D2 fit into this socket?

A. The socket was designed to fit astro-mech units perfectly

B. He was pulled underneath the cockpit and clamped in place

C. His head telescoped up from his body

D. His body folded away from his head at a ninety-degree angle

The Phantom Menace Era

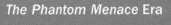

305. What do Gungans use atlatls for?

A. To shield themselves

B. To disrupt enemy communication signals

C. To throw single small energy balls

D. To track enemies

306. How many fambaas carrying shield generator components does it take to create a functioning plasma shield for the Gungan Grand Army?

A. Two

B. Three

C. Six

D. Nine

307. What color were Darth Maul's lightsaber blades?

A. Green

B. Blue

C. Red

D. Purple

308. How many twin high energy blasters does a destroyer droid come equipped with?

A. Four

B. Six

C. Two

D. Eight

309. What makes a battle droid's blaster particularly dangerous?

A. It has a limitless power supply

B. It has a continuous-fire trigger

C. It fires more than one laser bolt at a time

D. It has sensors that lock in on targets

310. Other than acting as a starfighter, what else can a droid starfighter do?

A. Submerge in water

B. Walk

C. Fold flat for storage

D. Cloak themselves

311.

312. How many legs do destroyer droids have?

A. Eight

B. Two

C. Four

D. Three

313. What happens when a pit droid gets hit on the nose?

A. It attacks

B. It stands still

C. It deactivates and collapses

D. It falls apart

311.

In order to create a particularly deadly weapon, this being had to build a specialized furnace from plans housed in an ancient Sith Holocron. Producing this device was one of his fondest memories—the care he took in building it proved how deep and intense his devotion to this underground sect was.

He chose to build a weapon that was primarily used as a training device. Due to its dangerous nature, this weapon had to be wielded by someone who was a master; otherwise it could be just as dangerous to its owner as to its opponent. In order to utilize this weapon to its

314. What makes battle droids easy to transport in great numbers?
- **A.** They disassemble
- **B.** They each fold up tightly
- **C.** They shrink
- **D.** They link together like puzzle pieces

315. What makes Darth Maul's Sith Infiltrator unique among small spacecraft?
- **A.** It is powered with a solar sail
- **B.** It contains a cloaking device
- **C.** It contains a hyperdrive engine
- **D.** It has a chromium exterior

316. How do Gungans construct their bongos?
- **A.** They grow them
- **B.** They carve them out of stone
- **C.** They fit them together using bone
- **D.** They construct them from wood

317. What was the name of the Republic Cruiser that brought ambassadors Qui-Gon Jinn and Obi-Wan Kenobi to Naboo?
- **A.** The *Millennium Falcon*
- **B.** The Naboo Royal Starship
- **C.** The *Invisible Hand*
- **D.** The *Radiant VII*

318. What company designed the Trade Federation's MTT (Mult-Troop Transport)?
- **A.** Bactoid Armory Inc.
- **B.** Baktoid Armory and DroidWorks
- **C.** Baktoid Armor Workshop
- **D.** Bactoid Armor Envoy

319. What type of hyperdrive core does the Queen's Royal Starship contain?
- **A.** Nubian 327
- **B.** Theed Palace Space Vessel Engineering Corps 327
- **C.** FreiTek Inc. 327
- **D.** Incom Corporation 327

320. What was Sebulba's Podracer's maximum recorded speed?
- **A.** 1047 kph
- **B.** 829 kph
- **C.** 657 kph
- **D.** 420 kph

321. What company designed the Trade Federation's Droid Control Ship?
- **A.** Baktoid Armor Workshop
- **B.** Kuat Drive Yards
- **C.** Hoersch-Kessel Drive, Inc.
- **D.** Sienar Fleet Systems

322. What type of engines did Anakin Skywalker's Podracer have?
- **A.** Radon-Ulzer 620c racing engines
- **B.** Elsinore-Cordova Turbodyne 99-U racing engines
- **C.** JAK Racing J930 Dash-8 racing engines
- **D.** Bin Gassi Quadrijet 4Barrel 904E racing engines

fullest capacity, its creator had to perfect an esoteric form of fighting.

During the ritual of building this weapon, he went for days without food, sleep, or water. Creating this weapon was his rite of passage.

It incorporated two activators, four control locks, two blade-modulation controls, and two blade-projection plates, and it proved deadly when used in the Battle of Naboo. Who built this weapon?

- **A.** Obi-Wan Kenobi
- **B.** Darth Sidious
- **C.** Darth Maul
- **D.** Qui-Gon Jinn

The Phantom Menace Era

323. What type of engines did Sebulba's Podracer have?

A. Exelbrok XL 5115 racing engines

B. Irdani Performance Group IPG-X1131 LongTail racing engines

C. Collor Pondrat Plug-F Mammoth racing engines

D. Radon-Ulzer 620c racing engines

324. What does the rear "rat tail" finial on the Naboo N-1 Starfighter do?

A. It serves as an antenna

B. It stores weapons

C. It plugs into a power source in the Theed Hangar

D. It houses a plasma engine

325. What company manufactured the Republic Cruiser?

A. Corellian Engineering Corporation

B. Kuat Drive Yards

C. Hoersch-Kessel Drive, Inc.

D. Kuat Systems Engineering

326. How do Podracers' twin engines keep from flying apart while in use?

A. A thin cable attaches them

B. They have repulsorlifts that keep them in position

C. They are connected by an energy binder arc

D. The control cables connecting them to the cockpit lock in place when in use

327. How many droids fit into an AAT (Armored Assault Tank)?

A. Five

B. Three

C. Four

D. Two

328. What craft do the Royal Naboo Security Forces use for standard patrol?

A. Gian speeders

B. N-1 Starfighters

C. STAPs

D. Flash Speeders

329. What does STAP stand for?

A. Single Trapdoor Air Platform

B. Solo Tailwind Airlift Positioning

C. Single Trooper Aerial Platform

D. Solo Traveler Air Port

330. Who designed the exterior portion of Queen Amidala's Royal Starship?

A. Commerce Guild

B. Cygnus Spaceworks

C. Theed Palace Space Vessel Engineering Corps

D. Corellian Engineering Corporation

335.

This Podracer was a Triffian who had three consecutive semi-pro victories on Malastare. He used his winnings to purchase a freighter that transported both him and his Podracer to Tatooine for the most famous of all Podracing events, the Boonta Eve Classic.

He was towed into a third-row starting position on the speedway of the Mos Espa Arena by a dewback. Although he didn't finish as glamorously as he had hoped, this Podracer came in fourth with a time of 16.04:994 and an average speed of 827 kph. He fared better than most—at least he crossed the finish line!

He had an enormous ego and therefore had the cockpit of his Podracer modified so that he was seated high on his

acceleration chair, giving his fans maximum opportunity to gaze at him. His Podracer was blue, with split-X engines boasting fin-like steering vanes. His split-X engines were far less overpowering in size than Sebulba's; he favored sleekness over intimidation. In an effort to exert control over his powerful JAK Racing J930 Dash-8 engines, he tethered them to his cockpit. The attempt at control was misguided—the tethers made it almost impossible to right an oversteering mishap. Who was the owner of this powerful, unfortunately modified Podracer?

A. Gasgano
B. Dud Bolt
C. Ebe Endocott
D. Wan Sandage

331. What company manufactures Gungan Bongos?
- **A.** Ankura Bongo Growengroup
- **B.** Otoh Gunga Bongamaken Cooperative
- **C.** Otolla Bongo Yards
- **D.** Bongo Bubble Growen Council

332. How are Podracers' engines connected to the cockpit?
- **A.** Steelton control cables
- **B.** Steel beams
- **C.** A web of Plastisteel cables
- **D.** Durasteel chains

333. How many quad laser emplacements did the Trade Federation's Droid Control Ship contain?
- **A.** 400
- **B.** 102
- **C.** 42
- **D.** 14

334. What is an AAT's maximum speed?
- **A.** 55 kph
- **B.** 50 kph
- **C.** 45 kph
- **D.** 40 kph

335.

336. What did Anakin's air scoops act as on his Podracer?
- **A.** Stabilizers
- **B.** Steering brakes
- **C.** Power converters
- **D.** Thrusters

337. What type of weapon did Darth Maul's Sith speeder contain?
- **A.** Twin blasters
- **B.** Ion cannons
- **C.** None
- **D.** Harpoons

338. Why do Neimoidians use mechno-chairs?
- **A.** They are lazy
- **B.** They can only walk on land for short periods of time
- **C.** They remind them of home
- **D.** They are status symbols

339. What does the Republic Cruiser's red color signify?
- **A.** Its political neutrality
- **B.** Its use as a hospital ship
- **C.** Its allegiance with the Jedi
- **D.** Its allegiance with the Trade Federation

The Phantom Menace Era

340. How do Bongo cockpits remain airtight in water?
A. They are protected by transparisteel bubbles
B. They are protected by a watertight forcefield
C. They are protected by glass
D. They are protected by hydrostatic bubbles

341. What racing engines did Teemto Pagalies' Podracer use?
A. Elsinore-Cordova Turbodyne 99-U
B. Irdani Performance Group IPG-X1131 LongTail
C. Exelbrok XL 5115
D. Radon-Ulzer 620c

342. What armament did the Queen's Royal Starship have?
A. Four turret-mounted cannons
B. None
C. Two laser cannons
D. Eight torpedo launchers

343. What Podracer did Ratts Tyerell race in the Boonta Eve Classic?
A. Galactic Power Engineering GPE-3130
B. Vorkoff-Strood Titan 2150
C. Farwan & Glott FG 8T8-Twin Block2 Special
D. Kurtob KRT 401-C

344. How many control cables did Ben Quadinaros' Podracer utilize?
A. Four
B. Six
C. Three
D. Two

345. To which prison camp were Queen Amidala and her party sentenced when the droid army invaded Naboo?
A. Camp Seven
B. Camp Three
C. Camp Four
D. Camp Two

346. Whose transmission to Queen Amidala was interrupted when the Trade Federation blocked all communications to Naboo?
A. Chancellor Valorum
B. Senator Antilles
C. Senator Palpatine
D. Mas Amedda

347. Whom did Daultay Dofine suggest should entertain the Jedi ambassadors?
A. Nute Gunray
B. TC-14
C. Rune Haako
D. Tey How

353.

This evil mastermind lived and worked on Coruscant, center of the galaxy, plotting the downfall of the Republic and the Jedi Order right under their noses. He maneuvered events in the galaxy that would throw the Force out of balance and topple the revered Jedi from their pedestal for decades to come. Then, the Dark Lords of the Sith would return to glory.

He manipulated the Neimoidian Trade Federation into invading the planet Naboo. When Queen Amidala escaped his clutches, he unleashed his henchman to track her across the galaxy, and, in a bold move, revealed himself indirectly to the Jedi. They had cause for worry now that their worst and longest-standing adversaries, considered extinct for a millennium, were back in the galaxy.

His schemes with the Trade Federation seemed to have failed, thanks in part to Queen Amidala's devotion to her people and her recent allegiance with the Gungans. In addition, Senator Palpatine had been elected Supreme Chancellor of the Republic and had promised an end to corruption. His game, however, was just beginning. Who was he?

A. Darth Plagueis
B. Darth Maul
C. Darth Sidious
D. Darth Bane

348. Why did the Queen send Padmé along with Qui-Gon and Jar Jar when they landed on the outskirts of Mos Espa?
- **A.** Padmé wanted a walk
- **B.** The Queen was curious about the planet
- **C.** The Queen wanted to make sure Qui-Gon didn't do anything foolish
- **D.** The Queen wanted to make sure Jar Jar didn't do anything foolish

349. According to Anakin Skywalker, where did angels live?
- **A.** The moons of Dantooine
- **B.** The moons of Ilum
- **C.** The moons of Iego
- **D.** The moons of Tatooine

350. How did Qui-Gon propose to raise the money to purchase the replacement hyperdrive they needed to leave Tatooine?
- **A.** Selling the Queen's wardrobe
- **B.** Betting on Anakin in the Podrace
- **C.** Entering the Podrace
- **D.** Using Jedi mind tricks on Watto

351. What did Master Yoda tell Obi-Wan that he should be mindful of?
- **A.** The dark side
- **B.** The Living Force
- **C.** The Trade Federation
- **D.** The future

352. According to Ki-Adi-Mundi, how long had the Sith been extinct?
- **A.** For five thousand years
- **B.** For centuries
- **C.** For a millennium
- **D.** For two millennium

353.

354. Why did the Trade Federation stop all shipping to the planet Naboo?
- **A.** To show their support of the taxation of trade routes
- **B.** To boycott the taxation of trade routes
- **C.** To attempt to get exclusive shipping rights through Naboo's system
- **D.** To entice the Galactic Senate into creating new trade routes

355. What did Obi-Wan Kenobi tell Boss Nass the Naboo and the Gungans formed?
- **A.** A deadly army
- **B.** A well-rounded population
- **C.** A symbiont circle
- **D.** A false alliance

The Phantom Menace Era

356. What, according to Watto, wasn't worth trading two slaves?
- **A.** A T-14 hyperdrive
- **B.** An astromech droid
- **C.** A starship
- **D.** A Podracer

357. How had Anakin Skywalker destroyed Watto's old Podracer?
- **A.** He smashed it while racing it
- **B.** He didn't—Sebulba flashed him with his vents
- **C.** He was joyriding around Ben's Mesa
- **D.** He made bad repairs

358. Why did the Jedi and Queen Amidala have to land on Tatooine?
- **A.** Their hyperdrive engine had been damaged
- **B.** They needed navigational assistance
- **C.** They wanted to see the Boonta Eve Classic
- **D.** To find Anakin Skywalker

359. What unusual circumstance arose on Tatooine that made it urgent for the Jedi to get to Coruscant?
- **A.** They had found the Chosen One
- **B.** The Sith had revealed themselves to Qui-Gon Jinn
- **C.** Queen Amidala was due to speak at the Senate
- **D.** Obi-Wan was scheduled to take the trials

360. Who sent a communication to Queen Amidala stating that the death toll on Naboo was catastrophic?
- **A.** Sio Bibble
- **B.** Captain Typho
- **C.** Senator Palpatine
- **D.** Boss Nass

361. What did Yoda have to say to Qui-Gon Jinn about Anakin Skywalker's future?
- **A.** The dark side surrounded everything
- **B.** It was clouded
- **C.** He was the Chosen One
- **D.** He would bring balance to the Force

362. Who said, "And you, young Skywalker, we shall watch your career with great interest"?
- **A.** Master Yoda
- **B.** Obi-Wan Kenobi
- **C.** Chancellor Palpatine
- **D.** Queen Amidala

OBSESSED WITH *STAR WARS*

363. Why did Mace Windu say that Anakin Skywalker would not be trained as a Jedi?

- **A.** He was too young
- **B.** His future was clouded
- **C.** He was too old
- **D.** He couldn't stop thinking about his mother

364. What did Qui-Gon Jinn tell the Jedi Council he was going to do?

- **A.** Find someone to train Anakin Skywalker
- **B.** Take Anakin as his Padawan
- **C.** Take Anakin back to Tatooine
- **D.** Leave Anakin at the Temple

365.

Queen Amidala escaped the Trade Federation's blockade of Naboo in an attempt to plead her planet's case in front of the galactic Senate on Coruscant. Along with Senator Palpatine, Queen Amidala appeared before the Senate. Palpatine told the Senate that Naboo had been engulfed in the oppression of the Trade Federation due to the taxation of trade routes, and then introduced Queen Amidala. The Queen stated that she had come to speak to them under the gravest of circumstances: Naboo had been invaded by the droid armies of the Trade Federation. As she spoke, however, the Senator representing the Trade Federation interrupted, asserting that her claims were outrageous. The Senator from Malastare concurred with this accusation.

At that point, Senator Palpatine leaned over and said, "This is where Chancellor Valorum's strength will disappear." What did Chancellor Valorum do next?

- **A.** He told the Trade Federation Senator to retreat from Naboo
- **B.** He told Queen Amidala that her issues would be addressed
- **C.** He asked Queen Amidala to wait until a commission could explore the validity of her accusations
- **D.** He asked the Senate to vote on how to act

366. Why, according to Senator Palpatine, was Chancellor Valorum an ineffectual leader?

- **A.** He was mired in baseless allegations of corruption
- **B.** He had confessed to taking bribes
- **C.** He had been proven to be corrupt
- **D.** He favored big business over real problems

367. What, according to Mace Windu, did the Jedi need to do in order to unravel the mystery of the Sith?

- **A.** Accompany the Queen on her journey back to Naboo
- **B.** Discover the identity of the Dark Lord
- **C.** Assist in the resolution of the Trade Federation conflict on Naboo
- **D.** Await the Senate's vote on a new Supreme Chancellor

368. When Obi-Wan ran a test on Anakin's blood sample, how high was the midi-chlorian count?

- **A.** Over 10,000
- **B.** Over 20,000
- **C.** Over 1,000
- **D.** Over 5,000

369. What dream did Anakin Skywalker have?

- **A.** That he had won the Boonta Eve Classic Podrace
- **B.** That he had escaped from Watto's shop
- **C.** That he had been taken away from Tatooine to become a Jedi
- **D.** That he was a Jedi and came back to Tatooine to free the slaves

The Phantom Menace Era

370. Why did Captain Panaka disagree with Qui-Gon Jinn about stopping on Tatooine?

A. He knew the Hutts were gangsters

B. He knew that Tusken Raiders were dangerous

C. The desert climate would damage the Queen's hair

D. He wanted to stay on schedule

371. What did Boss Nass give Queen Amidala as a token of continuing allegiance after the Battle of Naboo?

A. A ceremonial shield

B. A Medal of Friendship

C. A Globe of Peace

D. A signed peace treaty

372. What were Captain Panaka's parting words to Nute Gunray?

A. "I think you can kiss your trade franchise goodbye."

B. "Kiss the Trade Federation goodbye."

C. "Say goodbye to your little franchise."

D. "I think you can kiss your business goodbye."

373. How many Sith did Jedi Master Yoda say were always present?

A. Four

B. Three

C. One

D. Two

374. How many Republic credits did Qui-Gon offer Watto for his used T-14 hyperdrive?

A. 20,000

B. 5,000

C. 40,000

D. 60,000

375. Who seconds the Trade Federation's senatorial motion to send a commission to Naboo to ascertain whether or not a blockade of the planet was in effect?

A. The Congress of Rodia

B. The Senator from Kashyyyk

C. The Congress of Malastare

D. The Senator from Ando

376. What did C-3PO say he wasn't sure was entirely stable?

A. R2D2's programming

B. His legs

C. The building

D. The floor

377.

Qui-Gon Jinn was sure he had found the Chosen One, the one to bring balance to the Force, in young Anakin Skywalker. He presented his findings to an incredulous Jedi Council, saying that he had discovered a vergence in the Force centered on a person. The Jedi Council finally agreed to test the boy to see whether he had Jedi powers, and so Anakin came before them.

After the tests were over, Qui-Gon went before the Jedi Council to discuss the boy's future; they let him know that he was not to train the boy, although he would remain in Qui-Gon's charge. "Clouded this boy's future is," Master Yoda warned.

As the two were preparing to go back to Naboo, Anakin stopped Qui-Gon to ask him about something he had heard Master Yoda talking about. Qui-Gon told Anakin that the things Yoda had mentioned were symbiotes that existed in all living cells. Without them, the Jedi would have no knowledge of the Force, and no special abilities. What were these symbiotes?

A. Midi-chlorians

B. Mitochondria

C. Force-energies

D. Microcrystals

OBSESSED WITH *STAR WARS*

378. Who did Watto bet all of his money on to win the Boonta Eve Classic Podrace?
A. Sebulba
B. Teemto Pagalies
C. Anakin Skywalker
D. Ratts Tyerell

379. What did Ki-Adi-Mundi think Anakin Skywalker's thoughts dwelled on?
A. His Jedi training
B. Being in a strange place
C. His mother
D. Padmé

380. What did Darth Sidious think was an unexpected, aggressive move on the part of Queen Amidala?
A. Returning to Naboo from Coruscant
B. Joining forces with the Gungans
C. Leaving Naboo and presenting her case to the Senate
D. Capturing Viceroy Gunray

381. How did Queen Amidala convince Boss Nass to join forces to fight the Trade Federation?
A. She offered a great deal of money
B. She fell on her knees and begged
C. She invited the Gungans to move to Theed
D. She promised him land

382. What creature first attacked Obi-Wan, Qui-Gon, and Jar Jar as they traveled through Naboo's core?
A. Opee sea killer
B. Sando aqua monster
C. Fambaa
D. Colo claw fish

383. What, according to Queen Amidala, was the Gungan Army's role in the Battle of Naboo?
A. The most important part of the battle
B. The first wave of battle
C. A diversion to get the droid army out of the city
D. A backup if her plan failed

384. What did Captain Panaka feel would happen as soon as Queen Amidala returned to Naboo?
A. She would be killed
B. She would be forced to sign the treaty
C. There would be a revolt
D. The Gungans would come to her aid

The Phantom Menace Era

385. Although Qui-Gon felt that Obi-Wan was ready to face the trials to become a Jedi Knight, what flaws did he find in his apprentice?

A. He was headstrong and had much to learn of the Living Force

B. He was headstrong and not skilled with a lightsaber

C. He had much to learn of the dark side of the Force

D. He was far too stubborn and arrogant

386. After Queen Amidala's ship blasted through the Trade Federation blockade and disappeared, who did Darth Sidious say would be able to locate it?

A. Darth Bane

B. Darth Maul

C. Darth Plagueis

D. A tracking Droid

387. What did Boss Nass accuse Queen Amidala of doing?

A. Bringen da bombad bomben

B. Bringen da Droideneeks

C. Bringen da Mackineeks

D. Bringen da maxibig starshippen

388. What did Darth Sidious tell Darth Maul when Queen Amidala's ship was found in the swamp?

A. To be mindful and let them make the first move

B. To seek her out and capture her

C. To organize a war party

D. To attack the Jedi immediately

389. What did Obi-Wan Kenobi say would happen if Queen Amidala's plan to capture Viceroy Gunray failed?

A. The Viceroy would take his case to the Senate

B. The battle would be over and the Viceroy would retreat into hiding

C. The Viceroy would return with another droid army

D. Naboo would be in the hands of the Trade Federation forever

390.

391. According to Sio Bibble, what was the only thing a communications disruption could mean?

A. Negotiations were taking place

B. The Ambassadors were not coming

C. Invasion

D. Retreat

OBSESSED WITH *STAR WARS*

390.

Long before Darth Sidious became the shadowy master of its ancient power and used it to attack the Galactic Republic, many fell prey to the dark side's allure. A rogue Jedi who believed that power emanated from the dark side founded the group after the Jedi Council rejected his concepts. As time went on, many other fallen Jedi joined him. In the beginning, the Sith worked as a group to battle the Jedi. Over a thousand years, however, internal power struggles divided the Sith until the order finally fell into a violent conflict. The few who survived the battle were finished off by the Jedi Order.

One Sith Lord, however, survived to restructure the order. To make sure that power struggles would never again destroy the Sith order, he dictated that a Sith Lord could only take one apprentice and that they would work together for the downfall of the Jedi. His teachings were later expanded so that there would only be two Sith in existence at a time— a master and an apprentice. Who was the Sith Lord who ensured that generations of secret knowledge could be passed down to Darth Sidious?

A. Darth Bane

B. Freedon Nadd

C. Darth Zannah

D. Lord Kaan

392. How did Queen Amidala and her troops enter the city to retake the palace from the Trade Federation?

A. They used a secret passage on the waterfall side of the city
B. They used a secret passage directly into the palace
C. They used a secret passage through the swamp
D. They used a secret passage through the sewer

393. How attentive was Jabba the Hutt during the Boonta Eve Classic Podrace?

A. He was on pins and needles
B. He fell asleep
C. He had to leave
D. He was talking to friends

394. What, according to Yoda, was the path to the dark side?

A. Fear
B. Pain
C. Suffering
D. Hate

395. How much did the gorg that Jar Jar was trying to eat in Mos Espa cost?

A. Seven wupiupi
B. Nine wupiupi
C. Ten wupiupi
D. Six wupiupi

396. How did Obi-Wan kill Darth Maul?

A. He used his lightsaber
B. He threw him down the generator core shaft
C. He used Qui-Gon's lightsaber
D. He used half of Darth Maul's lightsaber

397. To what rank did Boss Nass promote Jar Jar for bringing the Naboo and the Gungans together?

A. Captain
B. General
C. Admiral
D. Yoeman

398. How did Queen Amidala finally overtake the Viceroy and regain control of Theed?

A. She got him to get his troops to run after her, leaving him unprotected so her decoy could arrest him
B. She cornered him
C. Her decoy tricked him into getting his troops to chase after her, leaving him unprotected
D. Her decoy cornered him

399. How did Yoda feel about Obi-Wan taking Anakin Skywalker as his Padawan?

A. He did not agree with it
B. He had reservations
C. He approved
D. He had no opinion

The Phantom Menace Era

400. Which Senator was chosen to replace Valorum as Chancellor of the Republic?
A. Senator Moe
C. Senator Palpatine
B. Senator Teem
D. Senator Antilles

401. Who portrayed Boss Nass in *The Phantom Menace*?
A. Steven Speirs
C. Frank Oz
B. Brian Blessed
D. Ahmed Best

402. What actress played Sabé?
A. Natalie Portman
C. Keira Knightley
B. Sofia Coppola
D. Candice Orwell

403. Who was production designer for *The Phantom Menace*?
A. Gavin Bocquet
C. Tina Mills
B. Robin Gurland
D. Phil Harvey

404. Who portrayed the voice of Darth Maul?
A. Ray Park
C. Ian McDiarmid
B. James Earl Jones
D. Peter Serafinowicz

405. Who was the costume designer for *The Phantom Menace*?
A. Grant Tarbox
C. Trisha Biggar
B. Terryl Whitlatch
D. Sharon Long

406. Who was stunt coordinator/swordmaster for *The Phantom Menace*?
A. Joss Gower
C. Rob Inch
B. Nick Gillard
D. Dani Biernat

407. Who was animation director for *The Phantom Menace*?
A. Rob Coleman
C. Kun Chang
B. Ben Burtt
D. Barry Angus

408.

409. Where was the Naboo Palace courtyard set built?
A. Reggia Palace
C. Tunisia
B. Leavesden Studios
D. San Francisco, California

408.

In *The Phantom Menace*, this actress provided the voice of the Trade Federation Droid Control Ship's ingratiating protocol droid TC-14. This silver droid greeted the Jedi ambassadors Qui-Gon Jinn and Obi-Wan Kenobi after they boarded the Trade Federation craft and then told the Trade Federation Viceroy that she believed the ambassadors were Jedi Knights.

Born in Edinburgh, Scotland, she has had a long, award-winning career. She has starred in numerous television productions, including HBO's *Rome*, in which she portrayed Servilia of the Junii. She has also appeared in many films, including *Under the Tuscan Sun*, *Mansfield Park*, *Prick Up Your Ears*, and *Starter for Ten*.

Over the course of her career in theater, she has won a Tony Award, a Drama Desk Award, a Laurence Olivier Theatre Award, a London Evening Standard Award, and a London Critics Circle Theatre Award, and has been nominated for many other awards. Most recently, she was awarded Broadway's 2002 Tony Award as Best Actress for her role in the revival of Noel Coward's *Private Lives*. Who is this actress?

A. Sandy Duncan
B. Sandra Duncan
C. Lisa Duncan
D. Lindsay Duncan

410. Who portrayed Fighter Pilot Bravo 5 in *The Phantom Menace*?
- **A.** Ralph Brown
- **B.** Benedict Taylor
- **C.** Clarence Smith
- **D.** Celia Imrie

411. Where were the Tatooine exteriors filmed?
- **A.** Death Valley
- **B.** Tunisia
- **C.** Leavesden Studios
- **D.** Arizona

412. Who portrayed Kitster?
- **A.** Hassani Shapi
- **B.** Silas Carson
- **C.** Dhruv Chanchani
- **D.** Clarence Smith

413. Who portrayed Chancellor Valorum in *The Phantom Menace*?
- **A.** Ian McDiarmid
- **B.** Silas Carson
- **C.** Terence Stamp
- **D.** Jerome Blake

414. Where were the interiors of the Royal Palace filmed?
- **A.** Reggia Palace
- **B.** Leavesden Studios
- **C.** Ealing Studios
- **D.** Studio City, California

415. Who portrayed Shmi Skywalker?
- **A.** Natalie Portman
- **B.** Sofia Coppola
- **C.** Keira Knightley
- **D.** Pernilla August

416. Who portrayed Yaddle in *The Phantom Menace*?
- **A.** Frank Oz
- **B.** Phil Eason
- **C.** Silas Carson
- **D.** Michelle Taylor

417. Who played Jabba the Hutt in *The Phantom Menace*?
- **A.** He played himself
- **B.** Silas Carson
- **C.** Frank Oz
- **D.** Jerome Blake

418. Who played Yoda?
- **A.** Phil Eason
- **B.** Jerome Blake
- **C.** Michelle Taylor
- **D.** Frank Oz

The Phantom Menace Era

CHAPTER TWO

STAR WARS
ATTACK OF THE CLONES
WARS

419. According to Anakin Skywalker, from what nightmare did he rescue Obi-Wan Kenobi?
- **A.** A nest of gundarks
- **B.** A nest of Krayt dragons
- **C.** A nest of dewbacks
- **D.** A nest of Tusken Raiders

420. How old was Anakin Skywalker during the battle on Geonosis?
- **A.** Twenty-one
- **B.** Nineteen
- **C.** Twenty
- **D.** Twenty-two

421. What dark presence did Anakin Skywalker meet in the frozen caverns of Ilum while collecting crystals for his lightsaber?
- **A.** Darth Maul
- **B.** Darth Sidious
- **C.** Darth Plagueis
- **D.** Darth Bane

422. Obi-Wan Kenobi specialized in which type of lightsaber combat?
- **A.** Form II
- **B.** Form V
- **C.** Form III
- **D.** Form I

423. How did Jedi elders feel about Anakin Skywalker's choice of a dark uniform?
- **A.** They were indifferent
- **B.** They thought it fit his personality
- **C.** They assigned it to him
- **D.** They were concerned

424. How did Obi-Wan Kenobi feel about flying?
- **A.** He loved it
- **B.** He hated it
- **C.** He was indifferent
- **D.** It depended on the situation

425. What did Obi-Wan give to Anakin Skywalker on Anakin's thirteenth birthday?

A. A new lightsaber
C. A crystal
B. A river stone
D. A seashell

426.

427. What illicit activity did Anakin Skywalker secretly participate in, down in the bowels of Coruscant's Wicko district?

A. Sewer tunnel racing
C. Air ventilation racing
B. Garbage pit racing
D. Water duct racing

428. What was Anakin's first personal experience with the dark side of the Force?

A. Killing a Blood Carver on Melida/Daan
C. Killing a Corellian pilot on Coruscant
B. Killing the Geonosian drones on Geonosis
D. Killing a Blood Carver on Zonoma Sekot

429. Where did space pirate Krayn take Anakin Skywalker and throw him into slavery working in the spice mines?

A. Naboo
C. Ylesia
B. Nar Shaddaa
D. Bespin

430. What act was Senator Amidala fighting when she returned to Coruscant to speak to the Senate?

A. The Military Insurgence Act
C. The Military Creation Act
B. The Republic Armed Forces Act
D. The Republican Military Act

431. How long had Senator Amidala been fighting the passage of this act?

A. One month
C. Two years
B. Two months
D. One year

432. How did Anakin Skywalker feel about seeing Senator Amidala again after so many years?

A. He found it disagreeable
C. He was polite but impartial
B. He found it intoxicating
D. He felt like a child

OBSESSED WITH *STAR WARS*

426.

After the attempt on Senator Amidala's life as she returned to Coruscant, Jedi Knight Obi-Wan Kenobi and his Padawan Anakin Skywalker had been sent to her apartment to protect her during her stay. After getting reacquainted, Senator Amidala stated that she did not need additional protection—what she wanted were answers. She had an idea who was trying to assassinate her and why, but she wanted proof. "We're here to protect you, Senator, not to start an investigation," Obi-Wan told the Senator.

"We will find out who's trying to kill you, Padmé, I promise you." Anakin countered. Obi-Wan and Anakin then began a heated debate in front of the Senator over the extent of their assignment. "Protection is a job for local security, not Jedi. It's overkill, Master. Investigation is implied in our mandate," Anakin said. How did Obi-Wan respond to this?

A. "We will do exactly as the Council has instructed. And you will learn your place, young one."
B. "I shall bring your case to the Council and let them decide."
C. "You are wise, young one, and correct."
D. "I shall meditate on the situation and decide how to proceed."

433. What galactic sector did Senator Amidala represent in the Senate?

A. The Alderaan sector
C. The Illodia sector
B. The Chommell sector
D. The Coruscant sector

434. What did Anakin Skywalker often have nightmares about?

A. His mother
C. Darth Maul
B. Qui-Gon Jinn
D. Tusken Raiders

435. Why were Anakin Skywalker and Obi-Wan Kenobi sent to Ansion?

A. To observe trade negotiations
C. To further Anakin's training
B. To resolve a border dispute
D. To help resolve a civil war

436. How many terms did Amidala serve as Queen of Naboo before becoming Senator?

A. Two
C. One
B. Three
D. Four

437. Of which political group was Senator Amidala a member?

A. The Separatist Committee
C. The Loyalist Committee
B. The Military Creation Committee
D. The Anti-Separatist Committee

438. Why were Anakin Skywalker and Obi-Wan Kenobi sent on a mission to the planet Euceron?

A. To serve as peacekeepers during the Galactic Games
C. To compete in the Galactic Games
B. To serve as mediators at a trade dispute
D. To serve as mediators during a border dispute

439. Which form of lightsaber combat did Anakin Skywalker study?

A. Form I
C. Form III
B. Form IV
D. Form II

440. According to Obi-Wan Kenobi, what is a Jedi's lightsaber?

A. His best friend
C. His security
B. His life
D. His protection

Attack of the Clones Era

441. Where did Senator Amidala plan to go while she and Anakin Skywalker were in hiding on Naboo?

A. The canyon
B. The plains
C. The lake country
D. The ocean shore

442. When Anakin Skywalker was assigned to protect Senator Amidala, how long had it been since he'd last seen her?

A. Nine years
B. Ten years
C. Seven years
D. Eleven years

443. How did Obi-Wan Kenobi feel about politicians?

A. They are morally responsible
B. A few are trustworthy
C. They're not to be trusted
D. They should be obeyed

444.

445. How tall was Anakin Skywalker?

A. 1.74 meters
B. 2.07 meters
C. 1.97 meters
D. 1.85 meters

446. When on Kamino, how did Obi-Wan ask R4 to contact the Jedi Council?

A. "Scramble code 5 to Coruscant care of the Old Folks' Home"
B. "Scramble code 4 to Coruscant immediately"
C. "Scramble code 9 to Coruscant through C-3PO"
D. "Scramble code 6 to Coruscant care of the Senior Center"

447. What did Anakin Skywalker do on Nar Shaddaa during the slave revolt that he and fellow Jedi Padawan Siri initiated?

A. He captured Krayn and turned him over to the authorities
B. He used his newly created lightsaber to kill Krayn
C. He captured Krayn and handed him over to the slaves
D. He felt sympathy for Krayn and allowed him to escape

448. What planet was Anakin Skywalker on when Obi-Wan Kenobi tried to contact him from Geonosis?

A. Naboo
B. Tatooine
C. Coruscant
D. Geonosis

444.

There was an important meeting going on in the Chancellor's office. Several systems had made clear their intentions to secede from the Republic, and one Senator had just escaped an assassination attempt. As Chancellor Palpatine was discussing the Separatist situation with Mace Windu, Yoda, and other Jedi Masters, Senator Amidala entered his offices with the Loyalist Committee, including Senators Orn Free Taa and Bail Organa. "Senator Amidala. Your tragedy on the landing platform—terrible. Seeing you alive brings warm feelings to my heart," Master Yoda told her.

"Do you have any idea who was behind this attack?" Senator Amidala asked. The Jedi told her who their intelligence reports had pointed out as possible suspects. She disagreed with their information, but they dismissed her suspicions. Master Yoda added, "But for certain, Senator, in grave danger you are." At that point, Chancellor Palpatine suggested that she be placed under Jedi protection. How did Senator Amidala react to this suggestion?

A. She wholeheartedly refused any additional protection
B. She welcomed the idea
C. She didn't think the situation was serious
D. She relented, but only after personally selecting the Jedi who would protect her

449. When Obi-Wan was discussing Anakin with Masters Yoda and Mace Windu, how did he feel Anakin's abilities had affected him?

A. Anakin had become violent

B. Anakin had become arrogant

C. Anakin had become untrustworthy

D. Anakin had become jealous

450. What, according to Anakin Skywalker, were "aggressive negotiations"?

A. Negotiations with a blaster

B. Negotiations with a lightsaber

C. Negotiations with Force lightning

D. Negotiations with Jedi backup

451. Who, according to Mas Amedda, would have the courage to push for an amendment granting the Chancellor emergency powers in order to approve the creation of an army of the Republic?

A. Senator Organa

B. Senator Amidala

C. Representative Binks

D. Senator Moe

452. How tall was Obi-Wan Kenobi?

A. 1.58 meters

B. 1.79 meters

C. 1.87 meters

D. 1.64 meters

453. Who would never join Count Dooku, according to Obi-Wan Kenobi?

A. Qui-Gon Jinn

B. Yoda

C. Anakin Skywalker

D. Padmé Amidala

454. Who accompanied Anakin Skywalker to Tatooine to look for his mother?

A. Obi-Wan Kenobi

B. C-3PO

C. Senator Amidala

D. Kitster

455. Why did the people of Naboo try to amend their constitution?

A. To extend Amidala's term as Queen

B. To extend Amidala's term as Senator

C. To extend Jamillia's term as Queen

D. To unseat Amidala as Senator

456. If Anakin had spent as much time practicing his lightsaber techniques as he did his wit, who, according to Obi-Wan Kenobi, would he rival as a swordsman?

A. Qui-Gon Jinn

B. Ki-Adi-Mundi

C. Yoda

D. Yaddle

Attack of the Clones Era

457. What did Anakin and Padmé disguise themselves as when they left Coruscant to go into hiding on Naboo?
- **A.** Miners
- **B.** Refugees
- **C.** Hobos
- **D.** Bounty hunters

458.

459. Who replaced Captain Panaka as Senator Amidala's head of security?
- **A.** Captain Typho
- **B.** He was not replaced
- **C.** Captain Chronelle
- **D.** Captain Mukkuh

460. Who told Senator Amidala that they believed the attempt on her life was carried out by disgruntled spice miners on the moons of Naboo?
- **A.** Captain Typho
- **B.** Yoda
- **C.** Mace Windu
- **D.** Ki-Adi-Mundi

461. Who suggested that Obi-Wan Kenobi and Anakin Skywalker protect Senator Amidala while she was on Coruscant?
- **A.** Senator Organa
- **B.** Chancellor Palpatine
- **C.** Mas Amedda
- **D.** Yoda

462. Who exclaimed, "Around the survivors, a perimeter create!" on Geonosis?
- **A.** Yoda
- **B.** Kit Fisto
- **C.** Mace Windu
- **D.** Obi-Wan Kenobi

463. What was Zam Wesell?
- **A.** A Clawdite
- **B.** A Luddite
- **C.** A Leitbrite
- **D.** A Changeling

464. What type of armor did Jango Fett wear?
- **A.** Mandalay
- **B.** Mandaloovian
- **C.** Mondolary
- **D.** Mandalorian

465. Which member of the Jedi Council took A'Sharad Hett as a Padawan after discovering him on Tatooine?
- **A.** Oppo Rancisis
- **B.** Ki-Adi-Mundi
- **C.** Yaddle
- **D.** Yarael Poof

458.

The Jedi Council had given Anakin Skywalker a solo assignment: He and Senator Amidala were to disguise themselves as refugees and take unregistered transport to Naboo, where he would protect her from potential assassination attempts. Anakin told the council that the Senator would resist leaving Coruscant before she could address the Senate regarding the act she had come to strike down, but Mace Windu told him to speak to Chancellor Palpatine about the situation. Chancellor Palpatine in turn ordered Amidala to leave the planet for her own safety.

At Amidala's apartment, Anakin and Amidala talked as she packed for their journey. As Amidala complained about her orders to return to Naboo, Anakin countered, "Sometimes we must let go of our pride and do what is requested of us."

"Anakin, you've grown up," Amidala observed. Anakin then told her that he didn't feel that Obi-Wan could see his progress. He believed that he was ahead of Obi-Wan in many ways and ready for the trials, but that Obi-Wan thought he was too unpredictable. What advice did Padmé give him?

- **A.** "You should speak to him about the way you feel."
- **B.** "Anakin, don't try to grow up too fast."
- **C.** "You should take your complaints to the Council."
- **D.** "He is your mentor and you must obey his orders."

OBSESSED WITH *STAR WARS*

466. Who, according to Ki-Adi-Mundi, was "a political idealist, not a murderer"?

A. Darth Sidious   C. Nute Gunray

B. Count Dooku   D. Darth Tyranus

467. Who was the Senator from Alderaan?

A. Senator Bail Organa   C. Senator Ask Aak

B. Senator Orn Free Taa   D. Senator Padmé Amidala

468. Before becoming a Representative to the Galactic Senate, what diplomatic role did Jar Jar Binks hold on Naboo?

A. He was Gungan Mayor of Theed   C. He was Gungan Rep on the Advisory Council

B. He was Gungan Associate to Queen Jamillia   D. He was Gungan ambassador to Theed

469. Which of Senator Amidala's handmaidens remained on Coruscant with Captain Typho when Senator Amidala went into hiding on Naboo?

A. Dormé   C. Saché

B. Cordé   D. Yané

470. Who was Prime Minister of Kamino?

A. Taun We   C. Ko Sai

B. Lama Su   D. Pho Pa

471. Who said, "There hasn't been a full-scale war since the formation of the Republic"?

A. Sio Bibble   C. Chancellor Palpatine

B. Senator Amidala   D. Senator Bail Organa

472. Who did Anakin Skywalker discover in the Tusken Raider camp?

A. Cliegg Lars   C. Beru Whitesun

B. Owen Lars   D. Shmi Skywalker

473. Who hadn't seen a Kamino saberdart since prospecting on Subterrel beyond the Outer Rim?

A. Dexter Jettster   C. Hermione Bagwa

B. Captain Typho   D. Obi-Wan Kenobi

Attack of the Clones Era

474. Who was elected Queen of Naboo after Padmé Amidala's term ended?
- **A.** Queen Darphalea
- **B.** Queen Apailana
- **C.** Queen Jamillia
- **D.** Queen Noruda

475. Who exclaimed, "Truly wonderful, the mind of a child is!"?
- **A.** Yoda
- **B.** Madame Jocasta Nu
- **C.** Obi-Wan Kenobi
- **D.** Mace Windu

476. Who lost a leg in a skirmish with Tusken Raiders?
- **A.** Anakin Skywalker
- **B.** Owen Lars
- **C.** Cliegg Lars
- **D.** Shmi Skywalker

477.

478. How tall was Poggle the Lesser?
- **A.** 1.42 meters
- **B.** 1.64 meters
- **C.** 1.83 meters
- **D.** 2.05 meters

479. Who said, "Dellow Felegates" while addressing the Senate?
- **A.** Representative Binks
- **B.** Chancellor Palpatine
- **C.** Senator Amidala
- **D.** Senator Organa

480. Where did Jango Fett live?
- **A.** Tatooine
- **B.** Sullust
- **C.** Galidraan
- **D.** Kamino

481. Who was Captain Panaka's nephew?
- **A.** Captain Chronelle
- **B.** Captain Toydo
- **C.** Captain Typho
- **D.** Captain Tarnak

482. Who said, "I was recruited by a man called Tyranus on one of the moons of Bogden"?
- **A.** Zam Wesell
- **B.** Jango Fett
- **C.** Boba Fett
- **D.** Elan Sleazebaggano

OBSESSED WITH *STAR WARS*

477.

This bounty hunter worked alongside the legendary Jango Fett to break into a maximum-security asteroid prison to free fellow bounty hunter Bendix Fust. After this, Fett trusted this bounty hunter to work with him in tracking down the leader of the Bando Gora criminal empire. Fitted with a malleable armorweave suit, this killer created a reputation across the galaxy as one of the deadliest bounty hunters. Some believed the hunter to be a Stennes Shifter working incognito, while others whispered that the skilled killer was actually a Shi'ido. No one knew for certain, though. It was certain, however, that the being was a shape-shifter, although with only limited ability to mimic the specific features of particular individuals, a weakness seldom shared.

After many jobs with the talented Jango Fett, this bounty hunter finally met young Boba Fett. Boba Fett enjoyed hearing the jokes that this hunter had collected in trips across the galaxy, and even picked up a love of reading from this being.

Jango Fett tasked this hunter with an important job on Coruscant, one that would ultimately end the killer's career. Who was this bounty hunter?

- **A.** Aurra Sing
- **B.** Zam Wesell
- **C.** Florian
- **D.** Dane

483. What ancient order of warrior-knights did Zam Wessell emulate in her discipline as a bounty hunter?
A. The Mawala
B. The Manarin
C. The Marrain
D. The Mabari

484. Who was Project Coordinator for the clone army on Kamino?
A. Lama Su
B. Taun We
C. Pho Ka
D. Ka Lai

485. Which Jedi Knight planned to visit the cloners on Kamino and inspect the army they had created for the Republic?
A. Ki-Adi-Mundi
B. Mace Windu
C. Yoda
D. Oppo Rancisis

486. Who claimed that Geonosians didn't trust bounty hunters?
A. Count Dooku
B. Poggle the Lesser
C. Jango Fett
D. Boba Fett

487. How did Jango and Boba Fett spend quiet time together on Kamino?
A. Fishing for rollerfish
B. Riding aiwhas
C. Fishing for jobonfish
D. Working on their ship

488. Who asked Anakin, "Maybe you could help with some deadbeats who owe me a lot of money"?
A. Cliegg Lars
B. Sebulba
C. Watto
D. Mawhonic

489. Why was Jango Fett adopted and raised by the Mandalorians?
A. His parents were murdered
B. He was kidnapped
C. His parents lost him betting on Podraces
D. His parents deserted him

490. Who thought that Jedi should be able to know the difference between knowledge and wisdom?
A. Zam Wesell
B. Kit Fisto
C. Hermione Bagwa
D. Dexter Jettster

Attack of the Clones Era

491. On what planet did Zam Wesell learn to be a bounty hunter?
- **A.** Coruscant
- **B.** Denon
- **C.** Tatooine
- **D.** Geonosis

492. What was Shmi Skywalker doing when she disappeared from the Lars homestead?
- **A.** Picking mushrooms
- **B.** Monitoring the moisture vaporators
- **C.** Herding dwarf nunas
- **D.** Collecting moisture

493. When did Captain Typho lose his left eye?
- **A.** During his training for the Royal Security Force
- **B.** During the Battle of Naboo
- **C.** Battling disgruntled miners on the moons of Naboo
- **D.** When he was a small boy

494. Who said to Count Dooku, "I am not signing your treaty until I have her head on my desk," referring to Senator Amidala?
- **A.** Rune Haako
- **B.** Nute Gunray
- **C.** Po Nudu
- **D.** Passel Argente

495. Whose voice did Yoda hear when Anakin Skywalker attacked the Tusken Raiders on Tatooine?
- **A.** Anakin Skywalker's
- **B.** Darth Sidious'
- **C.** Qui-Gon Jinn's
- **D.** Mace Windu's

496.

497. Where did Obi-Wan Kenobi first meet Dexter Jettster?
- **A.** Ord Mantell
- **B.** Ord Beale
- **C.** Ord Sigatt
- **D.** Ord Nizzles

498. Who was Count Dooku's former Padawan?
- **A.** Shaak Ti
- **B.** Coleman Trebor
- **C.** Obi-Wan Kenobi
- **D.** Qui-Gon Jinn

499. Who said, "For a mechanic, you do an excessive amount of thinking"?
- **A.** R2-D2
- **B.** C-3PO
- **C.** Anakin Skywalker
- **D.** Dexter Jettster

OBSESSED WITH *STAR WARS*

496.

So admired was Count Dooku that he had been memorialized by a bronzium bust placed in the Archives of the Jedi Temple. Although he had never sat on the Jedi Council, he was well respected throughout the Jedi Order. His expertise as a lightsaber instructor had been invaluable—he was a master of a classical, elegant form of combat.

Having studied the ways of the Force for almost eight decades, he became one of its most powerful practitioners. Truer to his own sense of right and wrong than to the protocols of the Jedi Order, he began to be a voice of dissent in the Order—a voice that had trickled down to his former Padawan, Qui-Gon Jinn. Finally, Count Dooku announced his resignation from the Jedi Order, stating that he could no longer serve a Republic he saw as mired in corruption. Although several Council members agreed that the government needed reform, they argued that to leave the Order would be to turn their backs on those they had sworn to protect.

After what galactic event did Count Dooku wash his hands of the Republic, leave the Jedi Order, and disappear?

- **A.** The Battle of Eriadu
- **B.** The Battle of Zonoma Sekot
- **C.** The Battle of Naboo
- **D.** The Battle of Geonosis

500. Who introduced Obi-Wan Kenobi to Jango Fett?
- **A.** Lama Su
- **B.** Boba Fett
- **C.** Taun We
- **D.** Ko Sai

501. What was Mas Amedda's homeworld?
- **A.** Chagria
- **B.** Kamino
- **C.** Champala
- **D.** Coruscant

502. How long did Cliegg Lars say Shmi Skywalker had been missing?
- **A.** Two weeks
- **B.** A month
- **C.** Two months
- **D.** A week

503. What was Count Dooku's homeworld?
- **A.** Kamino
- **B.** Bogden
- **C.** Serenno
- **D.** Coruscant

504. What was Zam Wesell's special ability?
- **A.** She could shape-shift
- **B.** She could become invisible
- **C.** She could fly
- **D.** She could pass through solid objects

505. Who chose Count Dooku to be his Padawan when Dooku was thirteen?
- **A.** Thame Cerulian
- **B.** Yoda
- **C.** Shaak Ti
- **D.** Yaddle

506. What "delicacy" was Dexter Jettster's diner famous for serving?
- **A.** Shaak patties
- **B.** Sliders
- **C.** Reek hoagies
- **D.** Grinders

507. Who did Poggle the Lesser topple from power in order to become Archduke of Geonosis?
- **A.** Haggis the Vaunted
- **B.** Haddis the Greater
- **C.** Hadiss the Vaulted
- **D.** Haddis the Grand

508. According to Lama Su, who commissioned the creation of a clone army for the Republic?
- **A.** Jedi Master Sidio-Dious
- **B.** Jedi Master Sifo-Dyas
- **C.** Jedi Master Sifer
- **D.** Jedi Master Tyranus

Attack of the Clones Era

509. Who, disguised as Senator Amidala, died in the attack on Amidala's ship as she arrived to vote on the Military Creation Act?
- **A.** Dormé
- **B.** Saché
- **C.** Yané
- **D.** Cordé

510. Who told Anakin Skywalker that he was the most gifted Jedi he had ever met?
- **A.** Obi-Wan Kenobi
- **B.** Yoda
- **C.** Chancellor Palpatine
- **D.** Mace Windu

511. Who watched Boba Fett when Jango Fett was away on business?
- **A.** Taun We and MU-12
- **B.** Lama Su and MU-12
- **C.** Ko Sai and MU-12
- **C.** MU-12

512. According to Sio Bibble, how many trials had Nute Gunray had before the Supreme Court for his involvement the Battle of Naboo?
- **A.** Four
- **B.** Two
- **C.** Five
- **D.** Three

513. According to Lama Su, how many units were ready when Obi-Wan Kenobi arrived on Kamino?
- **A.** 50,000
- **B.** 200,000
- **C.** 400,000
- **D.** 1,000,000

514. In what Coruscant neighborhood was Dexter Jettster's diner located?
- **A.** Popo Town
- **B.** Nono Town
- **C.** Coco Town
- **D.** Dodo Town

515. Who made the following statement: "No friends, no enemies. Only allies and adversaries."?
- **A.** Aurra Sing
- **B.** Boba Fett
- **C.** Jango Fett
- **D.** Zam Wesell

516. Who told Obi-Wan Kenobi that, if the prophecy was true, Anakin Skywalker was the only one who could bring the Force into balance?
- **A.** Yoda
- **B.** Mace Windu
- **C.** Padmé Amidala
- **D.** Luminara Unduli

517. What was Ki-Adi-Mundi's homeworld?
- **A.** Cerea
- **B.** Tatooine
- **C.** Champala
- **D.** Malastare

520.

The Death Watch, a mercenary group led by Vizsla, were tracking a sworn enemy on Concord Dawn and happened across the Fett farm. They murdered all of the child Jango Fett's family, leaving him an orphan. Jango then helped the Death Watch's quarry escape. The thankful man took Jango in and raised him, and for seven years Jango fought at his side along with the Mandalorians, a group of warriors. Soon after this man was finally captured by the Death Watch, Jango Fett was chosen to be the leader of the Mandalorian Warriors.

Many years later, Jango Fett was betrayed by someone who had secretly been working for Vizsla and the Death Watch.

518. Count Dooku was one of how many Jedi to have left the Jedi Order?

A. Forty
B. Fifty
C. Thirty
D. Twenty

519. Who was the Techno Union Foreman?

A. Wat Tambor
B. San Hill
C. Poggle the Lesser
D. Nute Gunray

520.

521. What was Jedi Council member Coleman Trebor's homeworld?

A. Naboo
B. Coruscant
C. Cerea
D. Sembla

522. Who replaced Jedi Master Yaddle on the Jedi Council?

A. Shaak Ti
B. Aayla Secura
C. Coleman Trebor
D. Pablo-Jill

523. Who was Magistrate of the Corporate Alliance?

A. Toonbuck Toora
B. Wat Tambor
C. Passel Argente
D. San Hill

524. Who pompously exclaimed, "If an item does not appear in our records, it does not exist"?

A. Mace Windu
B. Madame Jocasta Nu
C. SP-4
D. JN-66

525. Who was the human waitress in Dexter's Diner?

A. Homioni Bagwa
B. Donnanne Bagwa
C. Hermione Bagwa
D. Myphanwy Bagwa

526. Who was Poggle the Lesser's aide on Geonosis?

A. Sun Fac
B. Sun Faa
C. Soon Fah
D. Soon Fac

Jango was eventually sold to slavers, who locked him away on a spice transport for many years. When space pirates attacked this ship, Jango was able to make his escape. He acquired a suit of Mandalorian armor and set out to track Vizsla, the being responsible for the deaths of everyone who had ever cared for him. Jango finally found and killed Vizsla, and embarked on a career that would eventually make him one of the most sought-after bounty hunters in the galaxy, as well as the genetic material for an entire army.

Who was the man Jango Fett helped escape, starting him down his path in life?

A. Joster Moreen
B. Jesten Merael
C. Juster Meroe
D. Jaster Mareel

Attack of the Clones Era

527. What was Shaak Ti's homeworld?

A. Ryloth   C. Ansion

B. Shili   D. Rodia

528. Which youngling drew the shades for Master Yoda when Obi-Wan asked for his assistance with the map reader?

A. Leit   C. Liam

B. Lium   D. Liah

529. Who replaced Jedi Master Yarael Poof on the Jedi Council?

A. Bultar Swan   C. Pablo-Jill

B. Shaak Ti   D. Coleman Trebor

530. What was Madame Jocasta Nu's position in the Jedi Temple?

A. Administrator   C. Information Technician

B. Archivist   D. Analyst

531. What was Wat Tambor's homeworld?

A. Mon Calamari   C. Skako

B. Geonosis   D. Hypori

532. What did Elan Sleazebaggano try to sell Obi-Wan Kenobi in the Outlander nightclub?

A. Rancor nail blades   C. Slyth

B. Death sticks   D. Sleep sticks

533. How did Coruscant underworld con man Dannl Faytonni disguise himself to make himself appear dignified?

A. As a Colonel of Coruscant's Republic Guard   C. As a Lieutenant of Coruscant's Republic Guard

B. As a Captain of Naboo's Royal Security Forces   D. As a Lieutenant of Naboo's Royal Security Forces

534. Who was Chairman of the InterGalactic Banking Clan?

A. San Hill   C. Lexi Dio

B. Wat Tambor   D. Passel Argente

OBSESSED WITH *STAR WARS*

539.

Anakin, Padmé, and Obi-Wan had all been brought out into the middle of the execution arena and had been sentenced to be killed by three ferocious beasts. The three had managed to escape their shackles and were holding their own against the creatures—two were dead and the third had been subdued. Anakin, Obi-Wan, and Padmé were all on the creature's back, apparently victorious, when droidekas rolled into the arena and surrounded them. Surrounded, they had little hope of escaping. Then, looking up into the arena, they saw lightsabers igniting. The Jedi had arrived.

Just when they thought they were safe, hundreds of battle droids, super battle droids, and droidekas marched into the arena, making their plight much worse. "There's been some mistake! I'm programmed for etiquette, not destruction!" the confused C-3PO said as he marched with the battle droid troops onto the field. He grew even more confused as he began saying things like "Die, Jedi dogs!" while firing a blaster at his compatriots. As he was about to fire at a Jedi, he shouted, "Oh dear, I'm terribly sorry about all this!" but the Jedi used a Force push to knock him over, trapping him under a fallen super battle droid. Which Jedi saved C-3PO from firing any more shots on the Republic troops?

A. Kit Fisto
B. Pablo-Jill
C. Coleman Trebor
D. Bultar Swan

535. How did Senator Ister Paddie wear his hair?
    A. In the orthodox Bespin style   **C.** In the orthodox Corellian style
    B. In the orthodox Nabooian style   **D.** In the orthodox Halbara style

536. Who was Kaminoan Chief Scientist?
    A. Ko Sai   **C.** Lama Su
    B. Taun We   **D.** La Shu

537. What was Senator Po Nudo's homeworld?
    A. Alderaan   **C.** Anzat
    B. Ando   **D.** Antar

538. Who was Commerce Guild President?
    A. Wat Tambor   **C.** San Hill
    B. Shu Mai   **D.** Senator Tikkes

539.

540. What was Madame Jocasta Nu's homeworld?
    A. Naboo   **C.** Coruscant
    B. Tatooine   **D.** Corellia

541. Who was Senator Orn Free Taa's blue-skinned Rutian Twi'lek aide?
    A. Pampy   **C.** Pampin
    B. Supin   **D.** Supy

542. Who was Jedi Luminara Unduli's Padawan?
    A. Barrix Uffuh   **C.** Coley Twilley
    B. Barriss Offee   **D.** Bultar Swan

543. Where did criminal Achk Med-Beq spend a brief stint before escaping in a laundry speeder?
    A. Coco Town Prison   **C.** Coco Penitentiary
    B. Coco Gaol   **D.** Coco Men's Camp

544. What group did Jedi Knight Stass Allie and Padawan Barriss Offee belong to?
    A. The Jedi Medics   **C.** The Company of Jedi Mediators
    B. The Circle of Jedi Healers   **D.** The Jedi Medical Combination

Attack of the Clones **Era**

545. Who was Anakin Skywalker's step-brother?
A. Owen Lars
B. Ofa Lars
C. Oman Lars
D. Oken Lars

546. What was Jedi Master Kit Fisto's homeworld?
A. Chagria
B. Glee Anselm
C. Tatooine
D. Melida/Daan

547. Who was Chancellor Palpatine's Rodian aide?
A. Dah Wah
B. Greeata
C. Dar Wac
D. Greeiago

548.

549. What was San Hill's homeworld?
A. Yaga Minor
B. Dubrillion
C. Muunilinst
D. Agamar

550. Who was Owen Lars' mother?
A. Aika
B. Aila
C. Aida
D. Anika

551. What was Senator Lexi Dio's homeworld?
A. Ator
B. Uyter
C. Coruscant
D. Rodia

552. Who was Chancellor Palpatine's Umbaran aide?
A. Sy Snootles
B. Cly Snoopes
C. Sye Moor
D. Sly Moore

553. How did San Hill support the Confederacy of Independent Systems?
A. In secret
B. With a non-exclusive agreement
C. With financial restrictions
D. Fully and devotedly

548.

This being rose to be one of the most prominent business-people in the galaxy, heading a massive galactic organization involved in the acquisition, refinement, and reselling of raw materials. This organization was so powerful that it had its own private army.

When a worldwide economic depression decimated her homeworld, her species brutally butchered each other for the things they used to take for granted, like food, jobs, and offworld travel. A mixed blessing occurred when an off-world concern came to the ravaged planet's rescue, buying up devalued real estate and boosting the planet's economy. What did this massive organization want in return? The servitude of the planet's native people, of course.

This being found a job with the offworld concern and worked her way up the corporate ladder to the position of Chief of Property Resources. At that stage, she had the opportunity to become a hero by repurchasing her home-world from the offworld concern. She did indeed buy her planet back, but instead of freeing her people, she raised their rents, deepening their servitude. The offworld concern was so impressed with her greed that they promoted her again. She was without morals, but always stayed within the law. She was present at the infamous Separatist meeting on Geonosis. Who was she?

A. Zam Wesell
B. Shu Mai
C. Toonbuck Toora
D. Lexi Dio

554. What was the name of the merchandising conglomerate for which Passel Argente acted as Chairman?

A. Clathe
B. Cleit
C. Lethe
D. Leafeth

555. Who was the Ongree Jedi Knight fighting alongside Kit Fisto during the Battle of Geonosis?

A. Pablo-Jill
B. Ki-Adi-Mundi
C. Mace Windu
D. Stass Allie

556. Who went to the Bounty Hunters' Guild a year before the Battle of Geonosis to hire Bossk and Cradossk to kill conspirators trying to destroy the Fondor shipyards?

A. San Hill
B. Wat Tambor
C. Count Dooku
D. Nute Gunray

557. What was Shu Mai's homeworld?

A. Gossam
B. Coruscant
C. Geonosis
D. Castell

558. What was Madame Jocasta Nu's position in the Jedi Temple prior to becoming Jedi Archivist?

A. She served on the Jedi Council for ten years
B. She served in the Jedi Farming League
C. She trained Jedi pilots
D. She trained Jedi in Style IV lightsaber combat

559. What was Elan Sleazebaggano studying before he got in with the wrong crowd and became a slythmonger?

A. Philosophy
B. Law
C. Medicine
D. Music

560. Why was Hermione Bagwa grateful to be working at Dexter's Diner?

A. She grew up in the Coruscant underlevels and was happy to be close to the surface
B. She needed to pay off loans
C. She was hoping to steal his business from him
D. She hoped to meet a space pilot who would take her away

Attack of the Clones Era

561. Where did Beru Whitesun grow up?
- **A.** Near Mos Entha
- **B.** Near Mos Eisley
- **C.** Near Mos Olaf
- **D.** Near Mos Espa

562. Who was the young Togruta member of the twenty Jedi hopefuls Yoda was training in the lightsaber arts?
- **A.** Sasha
- **B.** Ashla
- **C.** D'Needria
- **D.** Liam

563. Who was Dannl Faytonni's Swokes Swokes companion in the Outlander Nightclub?
- **A.** Oakie Dokes
- **B.** Orlie Dotes
- **C.** Omie Dokes
- **D.** Opse Dopse

564.

565. Who was Senator Orn Free Taa's green-skinned Twi'lek aide?
- **A.** Pampi
- **B.** Supi
- **C.** Pamsy
- **D.** Supsy

566. Who was Senator Padmé's sister?
- **A.** Sola
- **B.** Sona
- **C.** Sota
- **D.** Sopa

567. Who held sole authority over the mysterious Red Guard?
- **A.** Mas Amedda
- **B.** Dar Wac
- **C.** Chancellor Palpatine
- **D.** Sly Moore

568. What did slythmonger Elan Sleazebaggano try to sell Jango Fett and Zam Wesell?
- **A.** Death sticks
- **B.** Rancor nail blades
- **C.** Wifmaks
- **D.** Snoders

569. What was Jobal Naberrie's relationship to Padmé?
- **A.** Cousin
- **B.** Sister
- **C.** Mother
- **D.** Niece

564.

Before Jedi hopefuls were chosen as Padawans, they lived in communal groups called "clans." There were generally ten different clans in existence at one time, under the blanket care of Jedi Master Yoda. In addition to Master Yoda's overall interest, each clan was assigned a Master of its own.

These younglings varied in age from four to eight and belonged to many different species. The Force-sensitive children were too young to be sent offworld on missions, but from time to time they were transferred to training centers on different planets, such as the Jedi training center on Kamparas.

Younglings were trained in the lightsaber arts at a very young age. With special training lightsabers that operated at lower frequencies and with protective helmets, they followed Master Yoda's patient instructions in a special training room in the Jedi Temple. Members of this particular clan included Mari Amithest, J.K. Burtola, Jempa, and Chian. They were hard at work with their lightsaber training when Master Obi-Wan walked in and interrupted, stating that he had a very important question for Master Yoda. Yoda, together with the children, solved Master Obi-Wan's puzzle, but found that the solution left several sinister questions unanswered. What was the name of this particular clan?

- **A.** The Gnashing Acklay Clan
- **B.** The Mighty Reek Clan
- **C.** The Mighty Bear Clan
- **D.** The Gnashing Nexu Clan

OBSESSED WITH *STAR WARS*

570. On what planet was Owen Lars born?

A. Ator

B. Dantooine

C. Naboo

D. Tatooine

571. Who was Kit Fisto's Padawan?

A. Garen Muln

B. Reeft

C. Bant Eerin

D. Bruck Chun

572. Who was Passel Argente's aide?

A. Neva Kee

B. Denaria Kee

C. Lenudia Kee

D. Seairia Kee

573. What was Ruwee Naberrie's occupation in Theed?

A. He tended the Royal Gardens

B. He was Palace sculptor

C. He was on Queen Jamillia's Advisory Council

D. He taught at the university

574. To which planet did the Techno Union Foreman relocate from his homeworld Skako?

A. Mustafar

B. Metalorn

C. Metrigorn

D. Malastare

575. How did Shu Mai pledge her, and the Commerce Guild's, support for the Confederacy of Independent Systems?

A. With financial restrictions

B. Fully and openly

C. In secret

D. With many clauses designed to bring the Guild more business

576. Who were Padmé's nieces?

A. Ryoo and Pooja

B. Rioo and Pooka

C. Ryoo and Pooma

D. Sola and Darred

577. How long was Jocasta Nu employed in the Jedi Archives?

A. Over twenty years

B. Over thirty years

C. Over forty years

D. Over ten years

578. Where did Beru Whitesun meet Owen Lars?

A. Mos Olaf

B. Anchorhead

C. Mos Espa

D. Mos Eisley

Attack of the Clones Era

579. What was Senator Zo Howler's species?

A. Mandalorian   C. Geonosian

B. Toydarian   D. Anx

580. What special ability do Clawdites have?

A. They are shape-shifters   C. They can fly

B. They can change their   D. They are telekinetic
body mass

581. What language do Skakoans speak?

A. Cheunh   C. Skakoverbal

B. Skakoform   D. Frumund

582. What was Elan Sleazebaggano's species?

A. Koorivar   C. Twi'lek

B. Balosar   D. Nautolan

583. What was Senator Tikkes' species?

A. Aqualish   C. Gungan

B. Quarren   D. Trandoshan

584.

585. What prominent feature do male Kaminoans have that female Kaminoans lack?

A. A dewlap   C. Gills

B. A head fin   D. A tail

586. What was Passel Argente's species?

A. Kaminoan   C. Mandalorian

B. Rodian   D. Koorivar

587. What is unusual about Umbarans like Sly Moore?

A. They are blind   C. They see only infrared

B. They see only in ultraviolet   D. They have compound eyes
light ranges

OBSESSED WITH *STAR WARS*

584.

These beings live in giant underground hive colonies in order to escape the notice of the large predators that roam the surface of their planet. Their hives are built upon pre-existing natural structures that have been modified with a paste created from excretions and rock powder.

This species is born into a strict caste system with three main groups: aristocrats, warriors, and drones. The aristocrats and warriors are fortunate enough to have been born with wings, while the drones are flightless. The warriors grow to adulthood very quickly and are ready for battle by age six. They are trained to act en masse and to be fearless in battle, making them an excellent defense force. They carry sonic blasters.

The wingless drones have been genetically altered into several subgroups, each with a particular occupational focus. Overseer drones manage service, labor, soldier, farmer, and maker drones. The latest drone type is the pilot drone, which is in itself a caste. From their pupa stage, they pair with a flight computer and develop specific skills to make their actual adult flights more coordinated. This species plays an integral role in the Clone Wars. What species is it?

A. Neimoidian

B. Toydarian

C. Gossam

D. Geonosian

588. What is the most distinguishing feature of the Koorivar species?

A. The spiraling horn on top of their heads

B. Their long tail

C. Their six-fingered hands

D. Their insectoid exoskeleton

589. What type of creature are the Nautolans, of which Kit Fisto was a prominent example?

A. Insects

B. Mammals

C. Amphibians

D. Reptiles

590. What do Balosars like Elan Sleazebaggano have on their heads?

A. Flexible antenepalps

B. Flexible eyestalks

C. Flexible tendrils

D. Flexible sensor organs that pick up odors

591. How many levels are involved in the very intricate Umbaran caste system?

A. Nearly one hundred

B. Nearly two hundred

C. Nearly thirty

D. Nearly fifty

592. What was Jedi Knight Pablo-Jill's species?

A. Human

B. Ongree

C. Twi'lek

D. Umbaran

593. What was San Hill's species?

A. Hutt

B. Skakoan

C. Anx

D. Muun

594. What happens if a Skakoan's pressure suit is punctured?

A. The suit has a repair mechanism that fixes any breach

B. There is a massive explosion

C. The Skakoan disintegrates

D. The Skakoan instantly replaces the suit

595. What do Nautolans' head tentacles act as?

A. Secondary hands

B. Fierce weapons

C. Sensory organs that pick up scents

D. Sensory organs that pick up on the emotions of others

Attack of the Clones Era

596. How many facial tentacles do Quarren have?
A. Three
B. Six
C. Nine
D. Four

597. What was Dexter Jettster's species?
A. Besalisk
B. Quarren
C. Hutt
D. Rodian

598. What secret species is Senator Po Nudo's aide?
A. Clawdite
B. Aqualish
C. Shi'ido
D. Ghostling

599. What was Jedi Master Coleman Trebor's species?
A. Human
B. Vurk
C. Twi'lek
D. Semblarian

600. What was Shaak Ti's species?
A. Togruta
B. Muun
C. Clawdite
D. Shili

601. What is unusual about the Kaminoans' vision?
A. They only see in the ultraviolet spectrum
B. They only see infrared
C. They are colorblind
D. They only see black and white

602. What do Gossams do with their eggs?
A. Place them in communal incubators
B. Bury them in warm sand
C. Construct elaborate, colorful nests and throw "egg parties"
D. Place them in a bacta solution to ensure healthy births

603. What, unlike the Shi'ido, troubles Clawdites when shape-shifting?
A. They can only maintain their altered state for very small periods of time
B. It is very painful
C. Their lifespan is reduced every time they shape-shift
D. It is illegal in Clawdite society to shape-shift

604. In what form are Chagrians like Mas Amedda when born?
A. Babies
B. Tadpoles
C. Invertebrate
D. Grubs

OBSESSED WITH *STAR WARS*

605. What type of creature are the Gossams, of which Shu Mai was a prominent example?

A. Amphibians

B. Reptiles

C. Mammals

D. Insects

606.

These mysterious beings travel the barren wastelands of Tatooine in nomadic tribes. They live in temporary utrya, tents made from skins, tendons, and organic matter they scavenge from the desert floor, and set up semipermanent camps during the planet's hottest months. Scattered across Tatooine's vast desert, they tend to roam the most barren wastes of the planet, areas where human settlers would surely perish.

They are vicious enemies of Tatooine's moisture farmers, with whom they fight for the planet's most precious and rare of elements—water. They have been known to slaughter anyone foolish enough to venture near their wells, which they consider sacred. They have even been rumored to spit streams of blood at their enemies.

Their all-enveloping clothing allows them to blend into the desert's expanse with ease. Any member of the tribe foolish enough to expose his or her skin is immediately banished, and in some extreme cases, killed. The male and female adults have distinguishing wardrobes, while the children, who are called Uli-ah, wear unisex garments that protect them from the brutal weather of Tatooine while conserving body moisture.

Travelers and Tatooine natives both know to steer clear of these deadly beings if they want to keep their lives and limbs. Who are they?

A. Tusken Raiders

B. Jawas

C. Klatooinians

D. Twi'leks

606.

607. Why do Skakoans wear special environmental control suits?

A. They are aquatic

B. They are not used to regular sunlight because they live underground

C. They breathe only methane and live in a high-pressure environment

D. They have no immune systems

608. What type of creature are Besalisks?

A. Mammalian

B. Avian

C. Reptilian

D. Amphibious

609. How many fingers do Ongree like Pablo-Jill have on each hand?

A. Three fingers and an opposable thumb

B. Two fingers and an opposable thumb

C. Four fingers and an opposable thumb

D. Three fingers

610. How many nostrils do Ongree like Jedi Master Pablo-Jill have?

A. Two

B. Six

C. Nine

D. Four

611. How many head-tails do Togrutas have?

A. Three

B. Four

C. Five

D. Two

612. What are the display bulbs on Nuknogs' heads actually used for?

A. They store separate brainlets

B. They sense emotions

C. They store fat

D. They sense air quality

613. How many hearts do Muuns like San Hill have?

A. One

B. Three

C. Four

D. Two

Attack of the Clones Era

614. What purpose does the disruptive coloration on Togrutas' lekku serve?
- **A.** It confuses predators
- **B.** It marks their tribe
- **C.** It distinguishes their sex
- **D.** It is decorative

615. What race of Aqualish was Senator Po Nudo?
- **A.** Aquala
- **B.** Ualac
- **C.** Quara
- **D.** Nola

616. How many arms do male besalisks have?
- **A.** Four
- **B.** Six
- **C.** Eight
- **D.** Two

617. How many arms do female besalisks have?
- **A.** Up to eight
- **B.** Up to four
- **C.** Two
- **D.** Up to six

618.

619. Which of the arena beasts on Geonosis focused on Obi-Wan as its prey?
- **A.** The tan'ya
- **B.** The reek
- **C.** The acklay
- **D.** The nexu

620. What animal is an easy means of transportation on Kamino?
- **A.** Colo claw fish
- **B.** Bantha
- **C.** Giant sea worm
- **D.** Aiwha

621. In bantha herds, which individual is the leader?
- **A.** The oldest male
- **B.** There is no leader; they live in a communal herd
- **C.** The oldest female
- **D.** The youngest adult male

622. What planet do reeks come from?
- **A.** Muunilinst
- **B.** Ylesia
- **C.** Yavin 4
- **D.** Dathomir

623. What planet do acklays come from?
- **A.** Vendaxa
- **B.** Kamino
- **C.** Geonosis
- **D.** Dantooine

618.

This testy species hails from the Mid Rim planet Ando and is legendary throughout the galaxy for a bad temper that seems to be pervasive. This species is well suited to its homeworld, being able to breathe both in the murky waters that cover the majority of the planet and on the few rocky outcroppings and swampy islands. The species is known for having thick tusks that protrude downward from the mouth. They have large, black eyes designed for sharp underwater vision and they tend to avoid bright lights at all costs.

There are three races within this species. The Aquala have fin-like hands reminiscent of their watery ancestors; they

OBSESSED WITH *STAR WARS*

are able to operate on land but prefer to stay close to a water source. The Quara, the least prominent race, have fingered hands and more-developed motor skills. The Ualaq have fingered hands and a secondary set of eyes. The Quara and Ualaq tend to have a grey or black skin tone, while the Aquala's skin tone is dark green to blue.

The Quara and Ualaq, due to their improved dexterity, tend to travel offworld more frequently than their finned relatives, and can be seen throughout the galaxy frequenting seedier places. What species is this?

A. Aqualish
B. Quarren
C. Gungan
D. Mon Calamari

624. How many stone mite individuals merge to form a symbiotic triont?
A. Four
B. Three
C. Thirteen
D. Two

625. What planet do nexus come from?
A. Kowak
B. Coruscant
C. Kegan
D. Cholganna

626. How were duracrete slugs introduced to Coruscant?
A. They were originally sold as pets at the Coruscant Livestock Exchange
B. They were attached to a meteor that landed on the planet
C. They were inadvertently introduced to the ecosystem from off-world freighters
D. A traveler accidentally brought one back in his luggage

627. What are the nexu's secondary eyes used for?
A. Peripheral vision
B. Ultraviolet sight
C. Infrared sight
D. They are decorative

628. What moon maintains reek ranches?
A. Codian Moon
B. Coleyan Moon
C. Sadgiean Moon
D. Twilleyan Moon

629. What creature infests millions of miles of electric wiring channels on Coruscant?
A. Wire worm
B. Electropin worm
C. Cordworm
D. Conduit worm

630. What type of creature are acklays?
A. Insects
B. Crustaceans
C. Mammals
D. Reptiles

631. What do duracrete slugs consume?
A. Lipids
B. Grease trap sludge
C. Plastisteel
D. Duracrete

632. On its homeworld of Vendaxa, what is the acklay's primary source of food?
A. Lemnai
B. Lowaca newts
C. Drell
D. Orbalisks

Attack of the Clones Era

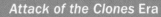

633. What purpose does the nexu's semi-prehensile tail serve?
  A. It works as a brutal whip
  B. It fans away snitchflies
  C. It wraps around branches for stability
  D. It is decorative

634. How does the aiwha corral fish underwater?
  A. It exudes pheromones
  B. It uses high-pitched sounds
  C. It emits a lipid that attracts fish
  D. It corners them in caverns

635. What do stone mites emit from their mouths to help predigest food?
  A. Acid
  B. Electric pulses
  C. Grit
  D. Bile

636. What is the nexu's primary food source on its home planet?
  A. Nooseworts
  B. Kliphids
  C. Arboreal octopi
  D. Arboreal banthas

637. According to xenobiologists, on which planet did the aiwha species originate?
  A. Kamino
  B. Bespin
  C. Vorzyd-5
  D. Naboo

638.

639. What do conduit worms feed on?
  A. Wiring
  B. Copper
  C. Electrical fields
  D. Plastisteel

640. What creatures were fighting with each other in the Tusken Raider camp in which Shmi Skywalker was being held on Tatooine?
  A. Massiffs
  B. Banthas
  C. Toenays
  D. Fangruhnays

641. In the wild, what category would the reek fall into?
  A. Carnivore
  B. Scavenger
  C. Herbivore
  D. Omnivore

638.

These pack animals have thick, leathery skin and can carry very heavy loads. In the wild, these beasts have defensive tail stingers, but the domesticated animals have all had their tail stingers amputated, making them more docile.

Before these beasts of burden were domesticated on rocky, dangerous Geonosis, they used their long snouts to root down into the delicate egg chambers of new Geonosian hives, consuming thousands of larvae in one sitting. Recognizing the damage these beasts could cause, the Geonosians took it upon themselves to train these creatures to do their bidding.

Geonosian picadors, those responsible for corralling the dangerous execution arena beasts and monitoring prisoners, ride these creatures throughout the deadly ordeal atop beaded saddles.

These beasts pulled the cart that brought Anakin Skywalker and Padmé Amidala into the execution arena and into the beginning of the Clone Wars. What are they?

  A. Acklays
  B. Orrays
  C. Dewbacks
  D. Reeks

642. Why do Coruscant Underworld dwellers fear power outages?

A. Duracrete slugs come out in the dark

B. Conduit worms can sense electrical activity in humanoid brains

C. Stone mites are attracted to heat sources

D. Duracrete slugs are attracted to heat sources

643. What creature has had a new mutant subspecies, larger and deadlier than its relative, appear on Geonosis due to pollution?

A. Acklay

B. Orray

C. Reek

D. Nexu

644. How does the aiwha collect its food?

A. A filter-like baleen

B. Its jaws

C. Its jaws and a filter-like baleen

D. Its claws

645. What carnivorous, star freighter-sized insect is the acklay's only known predator on Geonosis?

A. The merdeth

B. The meredith

C. The mardock

D. The mordet

646. Of the three beasts utilized in the arena on Geonosis, which has a thriving wild population on the planet?

A. Nexu and reek

B. Nexu

C. Reek

D. Acklay

647. What is the reek's primary source of nourishment in the wild?

A. Wood-moss

B. Whid-moss

C. Whorl-moss

D. Wool-moss

648. Where do aiwhas make their homes on Kamino?

A. On the undersides of stilt cities

B. Underwater caverns

C. In pens the Kaminoans created

D. Nest-like pods on the ocean surface

649. What was the name of the Kaminoan city that housed the cloning facility?

A. Tapoca City

B. Tupoca City

C. Tipoca City

D. Tepoca City

Attack of the Clones Era

650. In what section of Galactic City did Darth Sidious and Darth Tyranus meet to discuss the war?

A. The Graveyard

B. The Works

C. The Metalworks District

D. The Entertainment District

651. When Anakin and Padmé travel to the the Nabooian Lake Country, in which villa do they stay?

A. Varykino

B. Lake Tower

C. Varikyno

D. Lake Villa

652.

653. Where, according to Dexter Jettster, is Kamino located?

A. Twelve parsecs outside the Ricki Maze

B. Thirteen parsecs outside the Rishi Maze

C. Twelve parsecs outside the Rishi Maze

D. Twelve parsecs outside the Rishi Conundrum

654. Where did Boba Fett's friend Whrr work on Kamino?

A. The Ha Zurh Military Training Complex

B. The Ha Zurh Library and Records Office

C. The City Library and Records Office

D. The Kamino Central Military Training Complex

655. What Tatooine landmark, which translated into Basic means "bantha horn turned to stone," did Anakin pass on his path to find Shmi Skywalker?

A. B'Thazoshe Bridge

B. B'thasoszhe Rim

C. B'Tlasisch Ridge

D. B'tatomine Coil

656. What dominates the land below the great cliffs of Theed?

A. Theed Spaceport

B. Theed Palace

C. Theed Palace Courtyard

D. Theed Generator

657. On what street in the Entertainment District of Galactic City did Obi-Wan land his speeder after chasing Zam Wesell?

A. Von Glare Street

B. Vos Gesal Street

C. Van Galilee Street

D. Vas Geisel Street

652.

Obi-Wan Kenobi had been assigned to track down the bounty hunter responsible for the attempt on Senator Amidala's life—an assignment that had taken him to the mysterious water world Kamino. Adding to the mystery surrounding the entire ordeal was the fact that the Kaminoans had been expecting his arrival. Lama Su, Prime Minister of Kamino, assured Obi-Wan Kenobi that his order was going to be finished on schedule. Obi-Wan played along as Lama Su outlined for him the clone army that awaited shipment to the Republic, supposedly ordered by the now-deceased Jedi Master Sifo-Dyas.

Touring the cloning facility, Obi-Wan Kenobi saw clones in all stages of development, from a group created five years ago to thousands of clone troopers ready for deployment.

During the tour, Lama Su told Obi-Wan, "They are totally obedient, taking any order without question." How did the Kaminoans make this possible?

A. The clones were brain-washed from birth

B. The genetic structure of the clones makes them less independent

C. The clones have implants that make it impossible for them to misbehave

D. The clones' brains were not fully developed

658. To which planet did Obi-Wan Kenobi track Jango and Boba Fett after they fled Kamino?

A. Tatooine

B. Utapau

C. Geonosis

D. Naboo

659. In what spaceport did Anakin and Padmé land on Tatooine?

A. Mos Espa

B. Mos Olaf

C. Mos Eisley

D. Mos Entha

660. In which portion of the Jedi Temple was Yoda training the younglings when Obi-Wan asked for assistance?

A. The Training Room

B. The Training Pod

C. The Training Annex

D. The Training Veranda

661. From what box did Count Dooku, Poggle the Lesser, Nute Gunray, and the Separatists watch the executions of their prisoners?

A. The royal box

B. The archducal box

C. The Hive Leader box

D. The Hive Honor box

662. In which area of Coruscant is the Jedi Temple located?

A. The Jedi Precinct

B. The Temple Ward

C. The Jedi Ward

D. The Temple Precinct

663. What famous act had occurred centuries earlier on the balcony where Anakin Skwalker and Padmé Amidala were married?

A. The beloved Naboo essayist Verenko was kidnapped

B. The controversial Naboo poet Berenko was kidnapped

C. The controversial Naboo sculptor Berenko was assassinated

D. The exiled Coruscant painter Verenko was kidnapped

664. Where did Taun We take Obi-Wan Kenobi to introduce him to Jango Fett?

A. The library

B. A conference room

C. Jango's apartment

D. The troop barracks

665. What did Anakin Skywalker encounter on the edge of the Western Dune Sea?

A. A Jawa Sandcrawler caravan

B. A Tusken Raider camp

C. A Sarlacc pit

D. Three dead farmers

Attack of the Clones Era

666. What Tatooine landmark was near the Tusken Raider camp where Shmi Skywalker was held?

A. Ben's Mesa
B. Fort Tusken
C. Anchorhead
D. Bestine

667. Where on Kamino is Tipoca City located?

A. The eastern equator
B. The western equator
C. The north pole
D. The south pole

668. What Naboo festival is held every spring in the Lake Country?

A. The Festival of Glad Arrival
B. The Festival of Spring
C. The Festival of Good Tidings
D. The Festival of the Waterfalls

669. What dominates Tipoca City?

A. The Clone Military Training Complex
B. The Clone Education and Training Compound
C. The Clone Military Education Compound
D. The Clone Military Education Complex

670. In what Coruscant district is the Outlander Nightclub located?

A. The Uhuruh entertainment district
B. The Uscru entertainment district
C. The Utuluth entertainment district
D. The Uscram entertainment district

671. Where did Geonosian drone workers rest in between shifts in the droid factory?

A. Drone Relaxation Kiosks
B. Drone apartments
C. Restoration kiosks
D. Storage alcoves

672. Where did Obi-Wan Kenobi go to get information about the dart that had killed Zam Wesell?

A. Dex's Dugout
B. Dex's Diner
C. Dex's Café
D. Dex's Slider Stop

673. How do Kaminoan cities stay above water?

A. They are built with repulsorlifts
B. The cities descend all the way to the ocean floor
C. They are built on stilts
D. They are actually giant boats

676.

Obi-Wan Kenobi had spotted an assassin droid outside of Padmé's window after Anakin had thwarted an attack on her life by deadly kouhuns. To find out who had dispatched the droid, Obi-Wan jumped through the window and caught it, but the droid persisted and dragged Obi-Wan kicking through the skylanes of Coruscant. Anakin maneuvered his borrowed speeder below the dangling Jedi to catch him after Zam Wesell shot and destroyed the droid.

Zam attempted to lose her pursuers by nose-diving from the upper city down into the lower levels. The Jedi followed her down into the canyons of Corusca Circus, narrowly missing an enormous transport. Seeing that they were still pursuing

674. What is located at the deepest level of a Geonosian hive?

A. The Archduke's residence   C. The drone quarters

B. The food caverns   D. The queen's quarters

675. Where did Senator Amidala speak to Master Yoda about the attempt on her life?

A. The Jedi Temple   C. Chancellor Palpatine's office

B. The main Senate chamber   D. The landing platform

676.

677. Where did Anakin Skywalker receive instructions to protect Senator Amidala on her journey to Naboo?

A. The Jedi Council Chamber   C. Chancellor Palpatine's office

B. The Jedi Temple training veranda   D. Senator Amidala's apartment

678. What was being assembled on the conveyor belt where C-3PO landed in the droid factory?

A. Welding machines   C. Droid weapons

B. Astromech droids   D. Droideka thorax shells

679. Where did the Clone Wars start?

A. Tatooine   C. Naboo

B. Geonosis   D. Coruscant

680. Where did Count Dooku meet with the Separatists?

A. The tower rotunda   C. The factory boardroom

B. The factory rotunda   D. The archducal offices

681. What occurred when a moonlet orbiting Geonosis was destroyed by a two-kilometer wide comet?

A. The moonlet struck the surface and created the natural core of the execution arena   C. The Geonosians were forced offworld for several centuries

B. An asteroid belt was created   D. The planet shifted its orbit

her, Zam flew into the flaming exhaust vents of the Kerdos Company recycling plant. She had noted that the Jedi had a speeder with an open cockpit, and she hoped the flames would hinder their pursuit. She was mistaken. She zoomed past the recycling plant and on toward Goreth Lan-Dwu Corp. Seeing another opportunity to thwart their progress, Zam took out her blaster and fired, causing a reaction. With time to alter his course, Anakin plowed through the ensuing electrical bolts, and the two Jedi received an electric shock.

What had Zam Wesell fired at, causing massive electrical bolts to form a barrier in front of the Jedi's airspeeder?

A. Power nodes

B. Electrical towers

C. Power couplings

D. Electromagnetic towers

Attack of the Clones Era

682. What spacious Theed location was built over a portion of the city that had been bombed in the Battle of Naboo?

A. The Palace Courtyard
B. The Palace Gardens
C. The Theed Market
D. The Theed Courtyard

683. Where did Jango Fett land the *Slave I* on Geonosis?

A. In the ventilation shaft of the droid factory
B. In a secret hangar inside the droid-loading bays
C. On an outcropping of the arena
D. On a landing platform above the droid factory

684. Where on Coruscant did Representative Binks greet Jedi Master Obi-Wan Kenobi and Anakin Skywalker?

A. Chancellor Palpatine's office
B. The Jedi Temple
C. The Senate
D. Senator Amidala's apartment

685. Where did Padmé and Anakin land their ship on Geonosis?

A. Next to Obi-Wan's ship
B. In a secret hangar
C. On the outskirts of the droid factory
D. In the ventilation shaft of the droid factory

686. What group maintains the communally owned meadows of Naboo's Lake Country?

A. The Meadow Collective
B. The Arbor Collective
C. The Pastoral Collective
D. The Naboo Gardens Collective

687. In which room in their villa did Anakin and Padmé share their meals?

A. The Room of Morning Mists
B. The Room of Dewy Meadows
C. The Room of a Thousand Fountains
D. The Room of Vista Lake

688.

689. What type of droid served Jawa Juice in Dex's Diner?

A. I-5YQ
B. BLX
C. Otoga-222
D. WA-7

690. Who referred to Anakin Skywalker as "The Maker"?

A. R2-D2
B. C-3PX
C. C-3PO
D. Watto

688.

Anakin Skywalker and Padmé Amidala hid themselves away from possible threats of violence, enjoying the seclusion of the Lake Country of Naboo. They stayed at Varykino, an island retreat on the shores of a beautiful lake that had been in the Naberrie family for years. Anakin and Padmé roamed the the countryside together, and grew to have deep feelings for each other, though Padmé tried her hardest to fight them off. "I will not give in to this," she stated firmly when Anakin finally made his feelings for her known. Ultimately, however, she would allow her emotions to guide her actions.

When she heard Anakin having a terrible nightmare, she confronted him about it. "Jedi don't have nightmares," Anakin lied.

"I heard you," she replied.

Anakin told her that he had been dreaming about his mother, and that she was in pain. "I know I'm disobeying my mandate to protect you, Senator, but I have to go," he told Padmé. "I have to help her." Padmé, wanting to help, said she would go with him. The two left Naboo in Padmé's yacht and soon arrived on Tatooine to search for Shmi. Where did they stop first?

A. Watto's junkshop
B. Shmi's hovel
C. Jira's stand
D. The Lars homestead

691. Who screamed, "Hey, no droids!" at R2-D2 as R2 was collecting food for Anakin and Padmé aboard the Coruscant freighter en route to Naboo?

A. C-3PO

B. COO-2180

C. COO-BBKM

D. C-3PX

692. What droid's infrared photoreceptors and echolocation emitter allow it to function in total darkness?

A. Astromech

B. Dwarf spider droid

C. Battle droid

D. Protocol droid

693. What manufacturer produced the homing spider droids?

A. Colicoid Creation Nest

B. Industrial Automaton

C. Baktoid Armor Workshop

D. Commerce Guild

694. What droid pulls a rickshaw in Mos Espa?

A. Mouse droid

B. Roller droid

C. Wheel droid

D. Unipod droid

695. What newer, more powerful droid soldier did the Separatists reveal to the Jedi during the Battle of Geonosis?

A. Battle droids

B. Super battle droids

C. Droidekas

D. Super droidekas

696. What type of droid could be seen attacking Obi-Wan Kenobi at the end of his transmission from Geonosis to the Jedi Council?

A. Droideka

B. Super battle droid

C. Battle droid

D. Dwarf spider droid

697. What was Count Dooku's lightsaber designed specifically to enhance?

A. Form IV lightsaber combat

B. Form III lightsaber combat

C. Form II lightsaber combat

D. Form I lightsaber combat

698. What is another name for the Tusken Raiders' gaffi stick?

A. Gaderffi

B. Blood wand

C. Gradeffi

D. Blood pike

699. What droid delivered the deadly kouhuns to Padmé's apartment?

A. ANN-428

B. ASN-121

C. SAN-122

D. NAS-346

Attack of the Clones **Era**

700. What droid was actually a Baktoid Combat Automata B2?
A. Super battle droid
B. Droideka
C. Battle droid
D. Dwarf spider droid

701. What color was Luminara Unduli's lightsaber blade?
A. Blue
B. Green
C. Purple
D. Red

702. What did the InterGalactic Banking Clan originally use hailfire droids for?
A. Security
B. Border patrol
C. Debt collection
D. Hostile takeovers

703. What deadly bomb did Jango Fett think would deter Obi-Wan's pursuit through the asteroid belt surrounding Geonosis?
A. Seismic charge
B. Seismic bomb
C. Stealth charge
D. Stealth bomb

704. What nightmare did the Corporate Alliance unleash on populations unwilling to go along with its business deals?
A. The NR-44 dwarf spider droid
B. The TK-23 battle droid
C. The NR-99 tank droid
D. The TI-99 battle droid

705. Where did the Cybot Galactica SP-4 and JN-66 droids work?
A. Dex's Diner
B. The Senate
C. Geonosis
D. The Jedi Temple

706. Which droid replaced the window of Senator Amidala's apartment on Coruscant after an attack on her life?
A. INT-218
B. INS-444
C. INF-023
D. INQ-444

707. What manufacturer produced the dwarf spider droids?
A. Techno Union
B. Serv-O-Droid
C. Commerce Guild
D. Kalibac Industries

708.

709. How tall are super battle droids?
A. 1.84 meters
B. 2.07 meters
C. 1.91 meters
D. 2.20 meters

708.

When Anakin and Padmé landed on Geonosis to search for Obi-Wan, they left R2-D2 and C-3PO behind to watch Padmé's ship. Although C-3PO was reluctant as always, R2-D2 insisted on following the two humans into the droid foundry. As the Geonosians attacked Padmé and Anakin, R2-D2 and C-3PO ventured on to see how they could be of assistance. As the two droids happened upon an abrupt dropoff, C-3PO peered cautiously over the edge. R2-D2, however, wanted to get in on the action—and pushed C-3PO over.

R2-D2 used his rocket boosters to follow Padmé, who had fallen into an empty vat, while Anakin fought off Geonosians

710. Who acquired the plating that made C-3PO complete?
- **A.** Shmi Skywalker
- **B.** Cliegg Lars
- **C.** Owen Lars
- **D.** Beru Whitesun

711. What did CLE-004 do?
- **A.** It cleaned the Outlander gambling club
- **B.** It cleaned Senator Amidala's windows
- **C.** It did maintenance work on Senator Amidala's apartment
- **D.** It performed security scans in Chancellor Palpatine's office

712. What blaster did Zam Wesell use?
- **A.** KYD-42
- **B.** KYD-21
- **C.** KYD-23
- **D.** KDY-21

713. What weapon do Geonosian picadors use?
- **A.** Static pike
- **B.** Electropike
- **C.** Lightning pike
- **D.** Firepike

714. What color was Anakin Skywalker's lightsaber blade?
- **A.** Red
- **B.** Blue
- **C.** Green
- **D.** Purple

715. What color was Kit Fisto's lightsaber blade?
- **A.** Blue
- **B.** Purple
- **C.** Red
- **D.** Green

716. What manufacturer produced the ASN-121 assassin droid?
- **A.** Malkite Poisoners
- **B.** Malco Poisoners
- **C.** Mudguh Poisoners
- **D.** Cerebra Poisoners

717. What did Dexter Jettster nickname his WA-7 droid?
- **A.** Flo
- **B.** Rose
- **C.** Dorothy
- **D.** Blanche

718. What devastating weapon do Geonosian soldier drones carry?
- **A.** Ion blaster
- **B.** Seismic blaster
- **C.** Laser blaster
- **D.** Sonic blaster

719. What color was Count Dooku's lightsaber blade?
- **A.** Blue
- **B.** Green
- **C.** Red
- **D.** Purple

on a conveyor belt. C-3PO, however, was picked up by a Short Range Transport droid and dropped onto an empty conveyor belt. "What did I do to deserve this?" the prissy droid lamented. As C-3PO stumbled forward, he questioned, "I wonder what happened to poor little R2. He's always getting himself into trouble . . ."

Standing up and looking around, it turned out that C-3PO had spoken too soon. What happened to him?

- **A.** He was disintegrated
- **B.** His head was chopped off
- **C.** He was surrounded by droidekas
- **D.** He fell into an empty vat himself

Attack of the Clones Era

720. Which clone trooper rifle utilizes Tibanna gas?
- **A.** CD-1334
- **B.** GPO-23
- **C.** DC-16L
- **D.** DC-15S

721. What type of blaster did Jango Fett use?
- **A.** Godstar-23
- **B.** Westar-34
- **C.** Yonstar-29
- **D.** Whitestar-34

722. Which droid exclaimed, "I'm quite beside myself"?
- **A.** R2-D2
- **B.** WA-7
- **C.** COO-2180
- **D.** C-3PO

723. What unusual weapon very quickly put an end to Zam Wesell's career as a bounty hunter?
- **A.** Kamino kyberdart
- **B.** Kamino hyperdart
- **C.** Kamino saberdart
- **D.** Kamino slayerdart

724.

725. What color was Coleman Trebor's lightsaber blade?
- **A.** Blue
- **B.** Red
- **C.** Green
- **D.** Purple

726. Who retrieved C-3PO's head in the Battle of Geonosis?
- **A.** Padmé
- **B.** R2-D2
- **C.** Anakin
- **D.** Obi-Wan

727. What color was Barriss Offee's lightsaber blade?
- **A.** Blue
- **B.** Red
- **C.** Purple
- **D.** Green

728. What blaster was issued to the clone troopers?
- **A.** CD-1334
- **B.** DC-270
- **C.** DC-15
- **D.** CD-1408

729. What does AT-TE stand for?
- **A.** All Terrain Training Enhancer
- **B.** All Terrain Troop Enforcer
- **C.** All Terrain Tactical Enforcer
- **D.** All Terrain Tactical Enhancer

724.

After its disgrace during the Battle of Naboo, the Trade Federation realized that its battle droids were too easy to overcome, even when supplemented by droidekas. In lieu of training an actual army, Nute Gunray opted to go back to the drawing board and create a stronger, more durable battle droid.

Baktoid Combat Automata, the manufacturers of the original battle droids, were once again commissioned to design the new powerhouse droid. Trying to improve upon the basic design, Baktoid retained the cranial shape and many of the internal components. These droids violated the Republic's regulations on private security forces, due to their military-grade construction. Each droid is encased in a heat-, flame-, and blaster fire–retardant shell. They operate without the assistance of a central computer, but lack intelligence, stampeding through everything in their way.

These droids were introduced in the arena battle on Geonosis, plowing onto the floor amid the standard battle droids and droidekas. They battered the Jedi relentlessly, unleashing a steady flow of laser blasts. Where did these blasts generate?

- **A.** Firing impulse generators on the right shoulder
- **B.** Firing impulse generators on the right hand
- **C.** Firing impulse generators on the left shoulder
- **D.** Firing impulse generators on the left hand

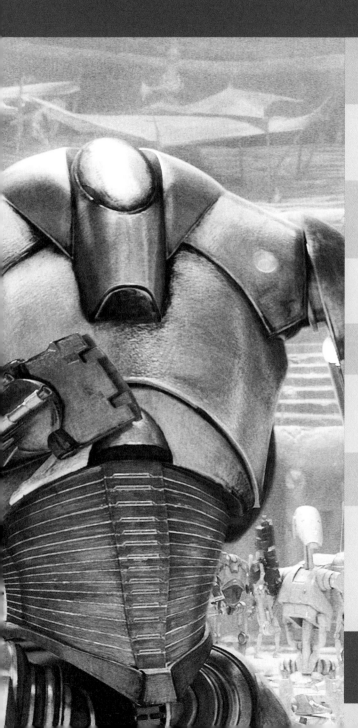

730. What class are the Republic assault ships?

A. *Eradicator*-class
B. *Destroyer*-class
C. *Acclamator*-class
D. *Vindicator*-class

731. What make was Zam Wesell's airspeeder?

A. *Cor*-2 interplanetary exodrive airspeeder
B. *Koro*-2 all-environment exodrive airspeeder
C. *Kora*-2 all-environment endodrive airspeeder
D. *Kor*-2 interplanetary endodrive airspeeder

732. What manufacturer produced Senator Amidala's Naboo cruiser?

A. Theed Palace Space Vessel Engineering Corps
B. Theed Palace Royal Engineering Company
C. Theed Palace Royal Space Vessel Corporation
D. Theed Palace Royal Vessel Design Guild

733. Who owned the airspeeder that Anakin Skywalker borrowed to chase Zam Wesell?

A. Senator Amidala
B. Senator Greyshade
C. Senator Moe
D. Senator Taa

734. What manufacturer produced the Delta-7 Jedi starfighter?

A. Incom
B. Republic Sienar Systems
C. Kuat Systems Engineering
D. Rothana Heavy Engineering

735. What does LAAT/i stand for?

A. Level Altitude Assault Tank/infantry
B. Low Altitude Attack Tank/infantry
C. Level Altitude Assault Transport/infantry
D. Low Altitude Attack Transport/infantry

736. What is the Geonosian fighter's frame constructed of?

A. Duracrete
B. Laministeel
C. Transparisteel
D. Plastisteel

737. How fast could Count Dooku's speeder bike go at top speed?

A. 692 kph
B. 643 kph
C. 634 kph
D. 690 kph

Attack of the Clones Era

738. How many quad turbolaser turrets does the Acclamator-class transgalactic military transport ship (republic assault ship) boast?
A. Fourteen
B. Ten
C. Twelve
D. Sixteen

739. What make is the Naboo Yacht that Senator Amidala takes from Naboo to Tatooine?
A. J-type Nabooian
B. H-type Nubian
C. K-type Nabooian
D. M-type Nubian

740. What make is Owen Lars' swoop bike?
A. Zephyr-G
B. Zephyr-D
C. Zephyr-12
D. Zephyr-94

741. How did Jango Fett acquire the *Slave I*?
A. He won it in a game of Dejarik
B. He stole it on the gambling planet Vorzyd-5
C. He stole it on the asteroid prison Oovo IV
D. He won it in a game of sabacc

742.

743. What is the LAAT/c's primary function?
A. To deploy troops to the surface
B. To deploy AT-TEs
C. To recover damaged craft
D. To act as roving repair ship

744. How many Techno Union starships escaped the ground battle on Geonosis?
A. One hundred sixty-nine
B. Two hundred nine
C. Forty-five
D. One hundred fourteen

745. How many passengers can an AT-TE carry?
A. Forty
B. Twenty
C. Fifty
D. Sixty

746. How many landing legs do the Trade Federation's core ships have?
A. Six
B. Eight
C. Ten
D. Four

742.

As a token of gratitude, the Geonosians gave Count Dooku an elegant craft, his solar sailer. The ship's interior, painstakingly crafted to fit Count Dooku's sense of refinement, was ornately decorated and included a vast library. The sail attached to Count Dooku's ship had been found in an antiques dealership near the Gree Enclave; it was composed of an exotic matter that reflected energies from space and allowed Dooku to travel great distances, piloted by an FA-4 droid, without much fuel. The enigmatic power with which the ship sailed made Count Dooku more mysterious and powerful in the Geonosians' eyes.

OBSESSED WITH *STAR WARS*

This craft harkened back to the ancient Geonosians' sailing traditions: in years past, they fashioned cargo kites to fly through their low-gravity world. Their first craft capable of space travel was made of huge, solar-powered robotic sheets. As the Geonosians' technological abilities grew, they depended less and less on sailers and eventually abandoned them. They were startled, then, when they were instructed to attach this sail to the ship. Who made a point of adding the sail to the ship?

A. Poggle the Lesser
B. Darth Sidious
C. Count Dooku
D. Sun Fac

747. What make is the *Slave I*?
A. *Firefly*-class patrol ship
B. *Firespray*-class patrol and attack ship
C. *Firespray*-class scout ship
D. *Firefly*-class prison transport

748. What does SPHA-T stand for?
A. Self Propelled Heavy Artillery—Tank
B. Self Propelled Heavy Artillery—Trooper
C. Self Propelled Heavy Artillery—Turbolaser
D. Self Propelled Heavy Artillery—Turbocharger

749. What was the name of the Coruscant freighter that Anakin Skywalker and Padmé Amidala took to Naboo?
A. The *Denedrian Valley*
B. The *Jendirian Valley*
C. The *Toydarian Valley*
D. The *Jedian Valley*

750. What manufacturer produced the Geonosian fighter?
A. Hoopla Denton Tisc Shipwrights Collective
B. Huppla Pasa Tisc Shipwrights Collective
C. Huppla Poseur Shipwrights Collective
D. Hoopla Danton Tisc Shipwrights Collective

751. How many laser or blaster cannons does the *Slave I* have?
A. Four
B. Three
C. Six
D. Two

752. How many antipersonnel turrets does the LAAT/i have?
A. Four
B. Six
C. Two
D. Three

753. What make is Count Dooku's solar sailer?
A. *Pudundruh 116*-class intergalactic sloop
B. *Punworrca 116*-class interstellar sloop
C. *Punworrca 115*-class interstellar cruiser
D. *Pudundruh 115*-class interstellar transport

Attack of the Clones Era

754. How did Obi-Wan Kenobi's Delta starfighter jump into hyperspace?

A. It had a built-in class 1.0 hyperdrive generator

B. It docked with a Syliure-31 long-range hyperdrive module

C. It docked with a Syliure-45 mid-range hyperdrive module

D. It had a built-in class 0.6 hyperdrive generator

755. What manufacturer constructed the Republic assault ships?

A. Rothana Heavy Engineering

B. Kuat Systems Engineering

C. Desler Gizh Outworld Mobility Corporation

D. Baktoid Armor Workshop

756. What advantage does the Geonosian fighter's laministeel frame give it?

A. It is flexible on impact

B. It is porous

C. It is lightweight

D. It is laser-resistant

757. How many Trade Federation Core Ships escaped the ground battle on Geonosis?

A. Forty-six

B. Sixty

C. Twenty-nine

D. Forty-two

758. Who was Obi-Wan Kenobi's Delta-7 co-pilot?

A. R4-P4

B. R5-P9

C. R4-P17

D. R5-P22

759.

760. To whom did Obi-Wan Kenobi say, "You don't want to sell me death sticks. You want to go home and rethink your life"?

A. Elan Sleazebaggano

B. Achk Med-Beq

C. Zam Wesell

D. Dannl Faytonni

761. According to Chancellor Palpatine, how long had the Republic been in existence?

A. Two thousand years

B. Four thousand years

C. One thousand years

D. Three thousand years

762. How did Obi-Wan Kenobi track the assassin droid who placed the kouhuns in Senator Amidala's room?

A. He grabbed it with his hands

B. He threw a homing beacon on it

C. He captured it with a net

D. He used the Force

OBSESSED WITH *STAR WARS*

759.

Zam Wesell thought she had outsmarted the Jedi. After she lost sight of them, Zam soared into a skytunnel, racing through the traffic at speeds of up to 400 kph in a strict 200-kph zone in an attempt to lose her Jedi pursuers once and for all.

"Where are you going? He went that way!" Obi-Wan shouted as Anakin Skywalker circumvented the tunnel, taking what he told Obi-Wan was a shortcut. Anakin came to a standstill as Obi-Wan lectured, "That was some shortcut, Anakin. He went completely the other way. Once again you've proved . . ." Obi-Wan was cut off as his Padawan leapt from the cockpit of their speeder and dropped toward the Coruscant floor.

As he careened downward, Anakin grabbed onto the variable air intake of Zam's speeder before sliding out onto the front of the ship. Zam fired her blaster at him, but Anakin managed to maneuver himself to the top of her ship and cut a hole in the roof before wrestling her blaster hand into shooting the controls. The ship spun down and crash-landed on the Coruscant streets. Zam managed to free herself from the wreckage. Where did she run?

A. The Vos Gesal Hotel

B. The Outlander gambling club

C. The Vos Gesal Jawa Juice Joint

D. The Revwien Comedy Playhouse

763. What, according to Dexter Jettster, gave away the fact that he was holding a Kamino saberdart?

- **A.** Funny little cuts on the side
- **B.** Kaminoan symbols
- **C.** Lines along the fins
- **D.** Grooves in the tip

764. What, according to Lama Su, made clones preferable to droids?

- **A.** They were more flexible
- **B.** They cost less to create
- **C.** They could think creatively
- **D.** They were easier to train

765. Who said, "The day we stop believing democracy can work is the day we lose it"?

- **A.** Sio Bibble
- **B.** Chancellor Palpatine
- **C.** Queen Jamillia
- **D.** Senator Amidala

766. What creature was Anakin Skywalker riding in the meadow?

- **A.** A falumpaset
- **B.** A shaak
- **C.** A kaadu
- **D.** A Fambaa

767. Who was Jango Fett's son?

- **A.** Doda Fett
- **B.** Toba Fett
- **C.** Doba Fett
- **D.** Boba Fett

768. What surprised Obi-Wan Kenobi when he was greeted by Taun We on Kamino?

- **A.** He was expected
- **B.** She was belligerent
- **C.** The planet was entirely covered in water
- **D.** She spoke Basic

769. Who said, "I think it is time we inform the Senate that our ability to use the Force is diminished"?

- **A.** Mace Windu
- **B.** Yoda
- **C.** Obi-Wan Kenobi
- **D.** Ki-Adi-Mundi

770. What did Obi-Wan notice about the surface of Geonosis as he was landing?

- **A.** There was an unusual concentration of Commerce Guild ships
- **B.** There was an unusual concentration of Techno Union ships
- **C.** There was an unusual concentration of Trade Federation ships
- **D.** The planet appeared to be barren

Attack of the Clones **Era**

771. How could Obi-Wan tell from his map reader that the planet Kamino was supposed to be there, even though it wasn't showing up?

A. Gravity was pulling all the stars in the area toward where Kamino should have been

C. The map reader was showing a silhouette where the planet should have been

B. It was south of the Rishi Maze

D. It was clearly marked

772. Who was R2-D2 carrying a message from when he showed up at the Lars homestead?

A. Mace Windu

C. Yoda

B. Obi-Wan Kenobi

D. Chancellor Palpatine

773. Who said, "The Commerce Guilds are preparing for war, there can be no doubt of that"?

A. Senator Antilles

C. Senator Aak

B. Senator Organa

D. Senator Amidala

774. Who said, "Why do I have the feeling you're going to be the death of me?" to Anakin Skywalker?

A. Padmé Amidala

C. Chancellor Palpatine

B. Count Dooku

D. Obi-Wan Kenobi

775. What happened to Anakin Skywalker during his battle with Count Dooku?

A. He lost his left arm

C. He lost his left leg

B. He lost his right arm

D. He lost his right leg

776. How far away from Tatooine was Geonosis?

A. Two parsecs away

C. Three parsecs away

B. Less than a parsec away

D. Four parsecs away

777. Who said, "I'm haunted by the kiss you should never have given me"?

A. Obi-Wan Kenobi

C. Padmé Amidala

B. Anakin Skywalker

D. Queen Jamillia

778.

778.

Obi-Wan's primary mission on Kamino was to find the bounty hunter who had been responsible for the attempt on Senator Amidala's life. He had happened upon much more—a discovery that would change the course of history in the Republic. As the mystery of the clones unfolded before him, Kamino's Prime Minister told him that the clones' genetic host was a bounty hunter named Jango Fett. Obi-Wan asked to be introduced to the hunter, and the Kaminoans obliged.

After an unsettling meeting with Fett, Obi-Wan contacted Jedi Masters Yoda and Mace Windu, who instructed him to capture Fett and bring him to Coruscant for questioning. Obi-Wan discovered that Jango and his son Boba were planning to flee Kamino and got to their landing platform just as they were about to board. In the driving rain, Obi-Wan battled very intensely, lightsaber versus blaster, jetpack, grappling hook, and the *Slave I*'s blaster cannons. The Jedi fought gallantly, but ultimately, after Jango tied his hands with a grappling hook, found himself dangling off the side of the landing platform above the churning depths of the Kamino ocean. During the battle, how many times did Obi-Wan lose his lightsaber?

A. Three

B. One

C. Four

D. Two

779. After Padmé told Anakin she wouldn't allow him to give up his future for her, what did he suggest?

- **A.** That they get married
- **B.** That he leave the Jedi Order
- **C.** That she leave the Senate
- **D.** They they keep their love a secret

780. What was Anakin Skywalker having a nightmare about on Naboo?

- **A.** Padmé
- **B.** His mother
- **C.** Obi-Wan Kenobi
- **D.** His future

781. What, according to the Jedi youngling on the training veranda, was the reason that Kamino didn't show up in the archive memory?

- **A.** The archive database was incomplete
- **B.** Someone had erased it from the archive memory
- **C.** There was no such planet
- **D.** Obi-Wan had given the wrong coordinates

782. Why did Yoda say the Jedi were blind?

- **A.** Their ability to use the Force had been diminished
- **B.** They couldn't tell that Count Dooku had turned to the dark side
- **C.** They couldn't predict the creation of the clone army
- **D.** They couldn't predict the attack on Senator Amidala's life

783. What message did Taun We ask Obi-Wan to tell the Jedi Council?

- **A.** That the first battalions would be ready soon
- **B.** That the first battalions were ready
- **C.** That they would receive no troops until the Kaminoans had received payment
- **D.** That the first battalions were en route to Coruscant

784. What did Count Dooku say his Master's reaction would be to the formation of the Republic army?

- **A.** That he would order more droids made at once
- **B.** Everything was proceeding according to his design
- **C.** He would never allow them to get away with such treachery
- **D.** That the dark side would prevail

Attack of the Clones Era

785. What plans did Count Dooku take with him before he fled to his secret hangar?

A. The Confederacy of Independent Systems' battle plans

B. The plans for super battle droids

C. Plans for the "ultimate weapon"

D. The blueprints for Star Destroyers

786. Who said, "I'm just a simple man trying to make my way in the universe"?

A. Boba Fett

B. Obi-Wan Kenobi

C. Anakin Skywalker

D. Jango Fett

787. What was Anakin Skywalker's first assignment on his own?

A. To track down Jango Fett

B. To rescue Obi-Wan on Geonosis

C. To escort Senator Amidala to Naboo

D. To inspect the clone army

788. What surrounded Anakin and Padmé when they were riding the reek?

A. Geonosian soldier drones

B. Droidekas

C. Battle droids

D. Super battle droids

789. How did Anakin mount the reek?

A. He jumped it from behind

B. He jumped on it from the top of an execution pillar

C. He lassoed it

D. He calmed it with the Force and then jumped on it

790. Who attacked Senator Amidala's ship on the landing platform?

A. Zam Wesell

B. Aurra Sing

C. Boba Fett

D. Jango Fett

791. Who killed Jedi Master Coleman Trebor in the arena on Geonosis?

A. Count Dooku

B. Jango Fett

C. A droideka

D. The acklay

792. Who said, "This party's over"?

A. Count Dooku

B. Obi-Wan Kenobi

C. Mace Windu

D. Yoda

OBSESSED WITH *STAR WARS*

793. What did Senator Amidala tell Queen Jamillia she was sure would happen if the Senate voted to create an army?

A. A stronger government
B. Mass destruction
C. Increased security
D. Civil war

794. Who captured Anakin Skywalker after his long struggle to get through the droid factory on Geonosis?

A. Jango Fett
B. Poggle the Lesser
C. Wat Tambor
D. Count Dooku

795.

796. Who ambushed Anakin Skywalker and Padmé Amidala in the entrance to the droid factory on Geonosis?

A. Geonosian drones
B. Battle droids
C. Droidekas
D. Super battle droids

797. What did Anakin Skywalker do after Shmi Skywalker died?

A. He left quietly
B. He slaughtered the entire camp of Tusken Raiders
C. He killed the Tusken Raiders who were guarding her
D. He meditated on the Force

798. Who represented Naboo in the Senate when Senator Amidala went into hiding?

A. Chancellor Palpatine
B. Representative Binks
C. Dormé
D. Captain Typho

799. Who said, "As a member of the Senate, maybe I can find a diplomatic solution to this mess"?

A. Senator Organa
B. Senator Amidala
C. Representative Binks
D. Chancellor Palpatine

800. Who did Senator Amidala think was behind the attempt on her life?

A. The Sith
B. Disgruntled spice miners on the moons of Naboo
C. The Trade Federation
D. Count Dooku

795.

As the Army of the Republic sent the Confederacy of Independent Systems' troops into retreat on Geonosis, Anakin and Obi-Wan spotted Count Dooku fleeing the scene on a speeder bike. The two Jedi followed Dooku to a hangar and challenged him. "You're going to pay for all the Jedi that you killed today, Dooku," Anakin seethed. He flew into battle, only to be knocked unconscious when Dooku attacked him with Force lightning. Obi-Wan Kenobi then took up the fight, but Dooku overpowered him. As Dooku was about to finish Obi-Wan off, Anakin regained consciousness and flew to his side, blocking the attack. Anakin fought with both his own and Obi-Wan's lightsabers, until Dooku severed his arm. At that point, Master Yoda entered the hangar.

Dooku used the Force to hurl objects at Yoda, but the Jedi Master pushed them aside with ease. "Powerful you have become, Dooku. The dark side I sense in you," Yoda said to his former student.

"I've become more powerful than any Jedi," Dooku boasted. "Even you." At this point, what did Dooku do?

A. He projected Force lightning at Yoda
B. He projected ceiling chunks at Yoda
C. He used his lightsaber
D. He fled the scene

Attack of the Clones Era

801. Who said, "We are encouraged to love"?
- **A.** Padmé Amidala
- **B.** Anakin Skywalker
- **C.** Obi-Wan Kenobi
- **D.** Yoda

802. Apart from his pay, which was considerable, what was the only thing that Jango Fett asked for from the Kaminoans?
- **A.** An apartment
- **B.** A personal landing pad
- **C.** A ship
- **D.** An unaltered clone

803. Who killed the kouhuns that were attacking Padmé?
- **A.** R2-D2
- **B.** Captain Typho
- **C.** Anakin Skywalker
- **D.** Obi-Wan Kenobi

804. Who told Count Dooku, "With these new battle droids we've built for you, you'll have the finest army in the galaxy"?
- **A.** Nute Gunray
- **B.** Shu Mai
- **C.** Wat Tambor
- **D.** San Hill

805. How did Obi-Wan Kenobi follow Jango Fett to Geonosis after their fight on the landing platform on Kamino?
- **A.** He stowed aboard their ship before they took off
- **B.** He used the Force
- **C.** He immediately took off after them
- **D.** He threw a tracer beacon onto *Slave I*'s hull

806.

807. What, according to Mace Windu in Chancellor Palpatine's office, were the Jedi?
- **A.** Keepers of the peace
- **B.** Warriors
- **C.** Soldiers
- **D.** Leaders

808. Who proposed granting the Supreme Chancellor emergency powers in the Senate?
- **A.** Senator Taa
- **B.** Representative Binks
- **C.** Senator Tikkes
- **D.** Senator Amidala

809. Who did Lama Su think was a leading member of the Jedi Council?
- **A.** Master Yoda
- **B.** Master Tiin
- **C.** Master Sifo-Dyas
- **D.** Master Windu

806.

Anakin had been having recurring nightmares about his mother, and they were getting worse. While staying with Padmé on Naboo, he had a vision of his mother that was so horrific that he told Padmé he had to leave at once and save her. Padmé told him that she would travel to Tatooine with him.

When Anakin and Padmé arrived on Tatooine, they immediately set about finding information that would lead him to his mother. They stopped and talked to Anakin's former master, who gave them the name of the person who bought Shmi from him, as well as information regarding their

810. How did Amidala get free of her shackles in the execution arena on Geonosis?

A. She picked the lock

B. The acklay cut them

C. A Jedi cut them

D. A laser blast cut through them

811. What was Chancellor Palpatine's first act after being granted emergency power by the Senate?

A. To veto the creation of the grand army of the Republic

B. To place sanctions on Geonosis

C. To create a grand army of the Republic

D. To blockade Geonosis

812. What did Count Dooku tell Obi-Wan he must do?

A. Join with him—together they would rule the galaxy

B. Destroy Darth Sidious

C. Join with him—together they would destroy the Sith

D. Turn to the dark side

813. Who told Obi-Wan to track down the bounty hunter who had killed Zam Wesell?

A. Saesee Tiin

B. Mace Windu

C. Oppo Rancisis

D. Yoda

814. Who killed Jango Fett?

A. Mace Windu

B. Anakin Skywalker

C. Obi-Wan Kenobi

D. Yoda

815. How did Obi-Wan evade the concussion missile Jango Fett launched on his Delta-7 starfighter in the asteroid belt surrounding Geonosis?

A. He led the missile into an asteroid

B. He told R4 to jettison the spare parts canisters and the missile detonated against the debris

C. He hid in a cavernous asteroid

D. He detonated it with a blast from his laser cannon

816. Why did Count Dooku escape his battle with Yoda?

A. Yoda had to use the Force to keep himself from being crushed by falling pipes

B. Yoda was temporarily knocked unconscious in the battle

C. Yoda allowed him to escape

D. Yoda had to use the Force to keep Obi-Wan and Anakin from being crushed by gas-release trunking

location. They rushed off to the site, only to find that Shmi was missing. A search party had looked for her but returned with no success. Anakin, determined to find her, went off in search of her himself. He found her, but in a tragic state. She died in his arms, and Anakin returned with her body.

What did Anakin vow to Padmé after Shmi died?

A. That he would devote himself to the Force

B. That he would learn to control his anger

C. That he would learn to stop people from dying

D. That he would leave the Jedi Order

Attack of the Clones Era

817. After the Battle of Geonosis, what did Anakin Skywalker and Padmé Amidala do?
- **A.** They prepared for further battles
- **B.** They secretly married
- **C.** Anakin returned to the Jedi Temple and Padmé returned to Naboo
- **D.** They returned to Coruscant

818. Who said the Battle of Geonosis was a defeat?
- **A.** Chancellor Palpatine
- **B.** Yoda
- **C.** Mace Windu
- **D.** Senator Organa

819.

In *Attack of the Clones*, this actor portrayed Jango Fett, infamous bounty hunter and genetic source for the Kaminoans' clone army. The Maori actor was born on December 26, 1960, in Rotorua, North Island, New Zealand. He portrayed Dr. Hone Ropata from 1992–95 on the soap opera *Shortland Street*. The film role that brought him international attention, though, was that of an abusive husband in *Once Were Warriors*, a film adaptation of Alan Duff's novel of the same name. He received the 1994 award for best male performance in a dramatic role from the Guild of Film and TV Arts. He has also appeared in *The Island of Dr. Moreau*, *Speed 2: Cruise Control*, *Vertical Limit*, and *The Beautiful Country*, among many others. In addition to regular film and television work, he has starred as the host of a talk show on New Zealand television.

His role in *Once Were Warriors* caught the attention of casting director Robin Gurland, who spoke to George Lucas about meeting with him for the role of Jango Fett. He was cast in the role, and has voiced many other roles for Lucasfilm. Who is he?

- **A.** Daniel Logan
- **B.** Jay Laga'aia
- **C.** Temuera Morrison
- **D.** Matt Sloan

820. Who played Dormé in *Attack of the Clones*?
- **A.** Ayesha Dharker
- **B.** Phoebe Yiamkiati
- **C.** Rose Byrne
- **D.** Pernilla August

821. Who was the droid unit supervisor and R2-D2 operator for *Attack of the Clones*?
- **A.** Justin Dix
- **B.** Don Bies
- **C.** Trevor Tighe
- **D.** Zeynep Selcuk

822. Where in Italy was the wedding of Padmé and Anakin shot?
- **A.** Lake Toblino
- **B.** Lake Como
- **C.** Lake Lavarone
- **D.** Lake Molveno

823. Who played Captain Typho in *Attack of the Clones*?
- **A.** Hugh Quarshie
- **B.** Bodie "Tihoi" Taylor
- **C.** Temuera Morrison
- **D.** Jay Laga'aia

824. Who played Boba Fett in *Attack of the Clones*?
- **A.** Temuera Morrison
- **B.** Jeremy Bulloch
- **C.** Daniel Logan
- **D.** Matt Doran

825. Who played Elan Sleazebaggano in *Attack of the Clones*?
- **A.** Alan Ruscoe
- **B.** Matt Doran
- **C.** Matt Sloan
- **D.** Ahmed Best

826. Who provided the voice of Taun We in *Attack of the Clones*?
- **A.** Rose Byrne
- **B.** Ayesha Dharker
- **C.** Veronica Segura
- **D.** Rena Owen

827. Who played Ki-Adi-Mundi and Nute Gunray in *Attack of the Clones*?
- **A.** Jerome Blake
- **B.** Silas Carson
- **C.** Joel Edgerton
- **D.** Matt Rowan

828. Who was first assistant director for *Attack of the Clones*?
- **A.** Paul Sullivan
- **B.** Claire Richardson
- **C.** Fred Meyers
- **D.** James McTeigue

829. Who played Queen Jamillia in *Attack of the Clones*?
- **A.** Ayesha Dharker
- **B.** Natalie Portman
- **C.** Susie Porter
- **D.** Leanna Walsman

830. Who played Madame Jocasta Nu in *Attack of the Clones*?
- **A.** Susie Porter
- **B.** Alethea McGrath
- **C.** Leeanna Walsman
- **D.** Veronica Segura

831. Who was the creatures supervisor for *Attack of the Clones*?
- **A.** Stuart Roswell
- **B.** Jason Baird
- **C.** Gab Facchinei
- **D.** Steven Boyle

832. Who was Count Dooku's stunt double for *Attack of the Clones*?
- **A.** Kyle Rowling
- **B.** Nash Edgerton
- **C.** Scott McClean
- **D.** Daniel Stevens

833. What *Attack of the Clones* scene was shot at the Plaza d'Espana in Seville, Spain?
- **A.** Theed Palace
- **B.** Varykino
- **C.** Jedi Archives
- **D.** Theed Palace Courtyard

834. Who played Count Dooku in *Attack of the Clones*?
- **A.** Christopher Lee
- **B.** Samuel L. Jackson
- **C.** Temuera Morrison
- **D.** Ian McDiarmid

Attack of the Clones Era

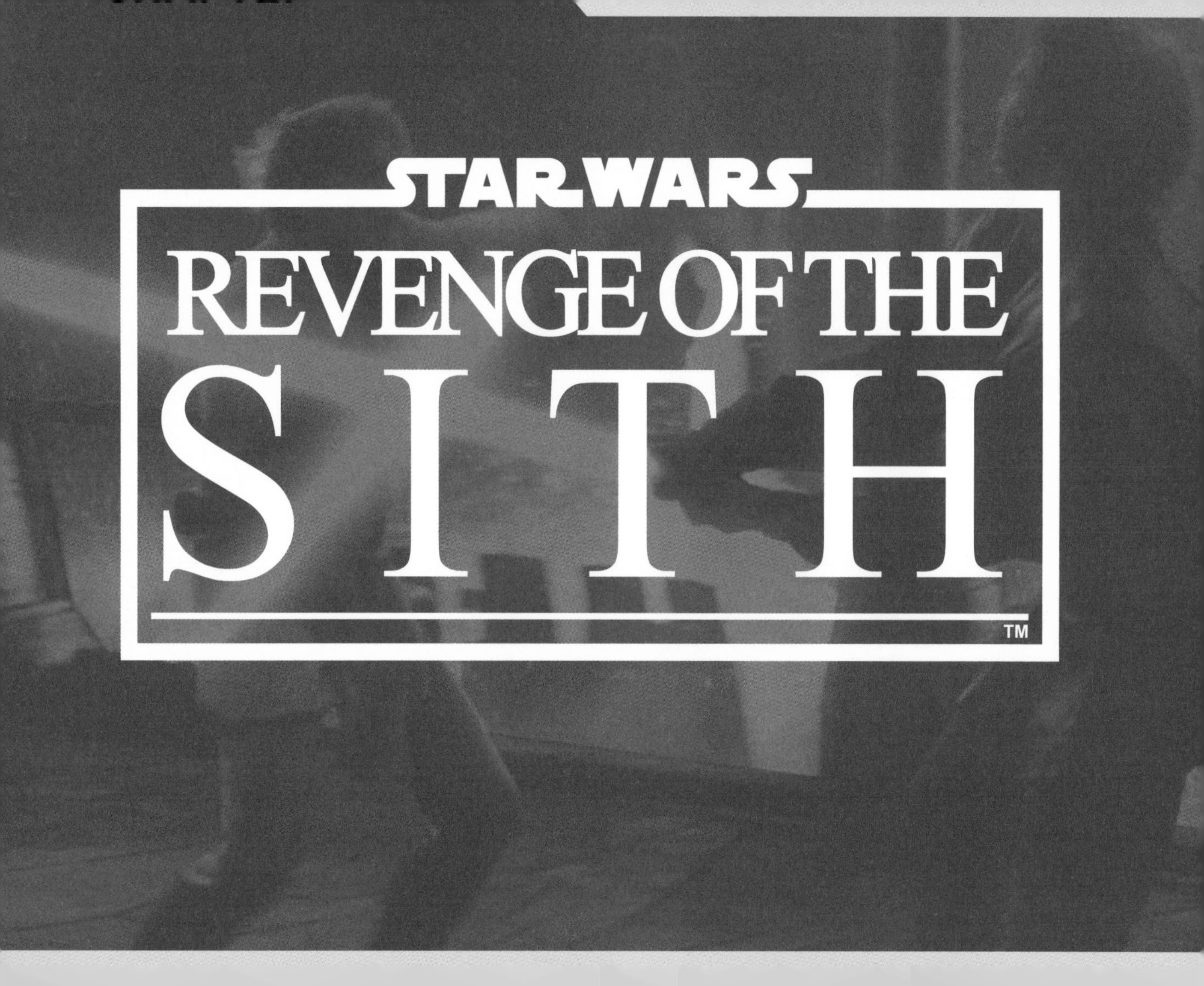
STAR WARS
REVENGE OF THE
SITH
TM

835. On which planet was Commander Bacara when Order 66 was executed?
- **A.** Felucia
- **B.** Mygeeto
- **C.** Kashyyyk
- **D.** Coruscant

836. Who discovered a secret Techno Union laboratory on Nelvaan?
- **A.** Obi-Wan Kenobi
- **B.** Mace Windu
- **C.** Anakin Skywalker
- **D.** Shaak Ti

837. What news did Padmé have for Anakin when he returned from rescuing Chancellor Palpatine from General Grievous?
- **A.** She was pregnant
- **B.** She had joined the Separatists
- **C.** She was no longer a member of the Senate
- **D.** She was moving back to Naboo

838. Who said, "What an incredible smell you've discovered!" to Anakin?
- **A.** Padmé Amidala
- **B.** Obi-Wan Kenobi
- **C.** Asajj Ventress
- **D.** Ki-Adi-Mundi

839. Who helped Yoda defeat the Separatists and rescue Luminara Unduli and Barriss Offee on Ilum?
- **A.** Anakin Skywalker
- **B.** Obi-Wan Kenobi
- **C.** Padmé Amidala
- **D.** Mace Windu

840. What eerie vision did Anakin have on Nelvaan?
- **A.** He saw Obi-Wan die
- **B.** He saw Padmé die
- **C.** He saw Yoda die
- **D.** He saw Darth Vader

841. What did Padmé place in a box along with the japor snippet Anakin carved for her?
- **A.** A picture of Anakin
- **B.** A ring
- **C.** Anakin's Padawan braid
- **D.** Anakin's journal

842. What did Chancellor Palpatine say when Mace Windu placed him under arrest?

A. "I control the courts."

B. "I will not give in to this!"

C. "You can't arrest me—I am Chancellor."

D. "I *am* the Senate."

843. Who was captured by Asajj Ventress and placed in a Sith torture mask that hindered his ability to use the Force?

A. Mace Windu

B. Obi-Wan Kenobi

C. Yoda

D. Kit Fisto

844.

845. Who, according to Obi-Wan Kenobi, had to be the poster boy?

A. Anakin Skywalker

B. Mace Windu

C. Yoda

D. Saesee Tiin

846. Who led the Battle of Kashyyyk?

A. Luminara Unduli

B. Yoda

C. Plo Koon

D. Mace Windu

847. How did Anakin lose his right arm a second time?

A. Destroying the Techno Union laboratory on Geonosis

B. Destroying the Banking Clan laboratory on Muunilinst

C. Destroying the Techno Union laboratory on Felucia

D. Destroying the Techno Union laboratory on Nelvaan

848. What was Obi-Wan Kenobi's rank in the Grand Army of the Republic?

A. General

B. Captain

C. Major

D. Lieutenant

849. Where did Padmé want to have her baby?

A. Coruscant

B. Geonosis

C. Tatooine

D. Naboo

844.

The Jedi Order had fallen prey to a hideous plot hatched by none other than Chancellor Palpatine. Jedi across the galaxy were wiped out by their troops after a sinister order was given. Palpatine sat smugly in his office below the main Senate chamber with Mas Amedda behind him when a surprise visitor entered the room.

Master Yoda had escaped an attack on Kashyyyk and returned to Coruscant to get to the bottom of the plot against the Jedi, only to discover through security recordings in the Jedi Temple that Palpatine was the Sith Lord for whom the Jedi had been searching since Qui-Gon Jinn was murdered. Entering Palpatine's office, Yoda easily dispatched the two Royal Guards standing at attention on either side of the door.

"I hear a new apprentice you have, Emperor," Yoda said as the Emperor turned to face him. Yoda then called the Emperor something else. What was it?

A. Darth Bane

B. Sith Lord

C. Darth Sidious

D. Chancellor

850. How long had Chancellor Palpatine been in office when he was kidnapped?

A. Twelve years   **C.** Fifteen years

B. Thirteen years   **D.** Eleven years

851. What was Obi-Wan Kenobi's favored style of lightsaber combat?

A. Ataru   **C.** Soresu

B. Djem So   **D.** Jung Ma

852. After his actions on which planet was Anakin awarded the title of Jedi Knight, forgoing the Trials?

A. Utapau   **C.** Coruscant

B. Geonosis   **D.** Nelvaan

853. Who was with Anakin in his vision of the cave on Dagobah?

A. Qui-Gon Jinn   **C.** Darth Vader

B. Obi-Wan Kenobi   **D.** Yoda

854. What did Obi-Wan tell Padmé about Anakin before he departed for Utapau?

A. That he had turned to the dark side   **C.** That he had been under a lot of stress

B. That he had killed younglings   **D.** That he was being promoted to Jedi Master

855. Who did Anakin follow to Yavin 4?

A. Asajj Ventress   **C.** Darth Tyranus

B. Darth Sidious   **D.** Durge

856. When Obi-Wan was complaining, who said, "No loose wire jokes" to him?

A. C-3PO   **C.** Padmé Amidala

B. Anakin Skywalker   **D.** Yoda

857. Who said "Well, did you notice the shields are still up?" during the battle over Coruscant?

A. Obi-Wan Kenobi   **C.** Odd Ball

B. Anakin Skywalker   **D.** General Grievous

Revenge of the Sith **Era**

858. What did Yoda tell Obi-Wan he had for him on Tatooine?

A. A house

B. Training

C. An eopie farm

D. A secret mission

859. Who said, "Chancellor Palpatine, Sith Lords are our specialty"?

A. Anakin Skywalker

B. Mace Windu

C. Yoda

D. Obi-Wan Kenobi

860. What were Padmé's last words?

A. "Find him and destroy him."

B. "Make sure he never finds out."

C. "I know there is still good in him."

D. "You were right, Obi-Wan."

861. How did Anakin receive the scar on his face?

A. He was injured during the space battle above Coruscant

B. He received it during a duel with Asajj Ventress

C. He received it during a duel with Count Dooku

D. He was injured during a ground battle in the Outer Rim

862. What did Padmé beg Anakin to ask Chancellor Palpatine?

A. To bless their wedding

B. To fight to the finish

C. To give in to the Separatists

D. To allow diplomacy to resume

863. What were Anakin's last words to Mace Windu?

A. "I need him!"

B. "He must stand trial."

C. "It's not the Jedi way."

D. "Kill him!"

864. What did Padmé give to Anakin in honor of his being given the rank of Jedi Knight?

A. A new speeder

B. R2-D2

C. A shaak leather tunic

D. A crystal pendant

865.

Anakin was very confused. He was having horrible nightmares about Padmé, dreams that echoed the prophetic dreams he had endured about his mother, Shmi Skywalker. When Anakin met with Chancellor Palpatine at the Galaxies Opera House, Palpatine told him things about the Sith that raised questions in his mind regarding his recurring nightmares about Padmé.

Anakin had another horrible nightmare in which he saw Padmé dying as Obi-Wan looked on, telling her not to give up. Later, in Padmé's apartment, he sensed that Obi-Wan had been there without him and he questioned Padmé about it. "He's worried about you," Padmé told Anakin. "He says you've been under a lot of stress."

Anakin paused and then confided in Padmé that he felt lost. "Obi-Wan and the Council don't trust me," he told Padmé. What did she say in response?

A. "I think you are right."

B. "They trust you with their lives."

C. "You should confront them about it."

D. "Obi-Wan trusts you. He told me so himself."

866. Who lamented, "So this is how liberty dies—with thunderous applause"?

A. Padmé Amidala

B. Jar Jar Binks

C. Terr Taneel

D. Bail Organa

867. What appointment did Chancellor Palpatine give Anakin Skywalker, much to the Jedi's surprise?

A. He made him a Senator

B. He made him Chief of Security

C. He made him a General in the Grand Army of the Republic

D. He made him his personal representative on the Jedi Council

868. What were Anakin's last words to Obi-Wan Kenobi before he turned to the dark side?

A. "I hate you!"

B. "Good luck, Obi-Wan."

C. "Obi-Wan, may the Force be with you."

D. "I've been selfish and I'm sorry."

869. Which of the following did Chancellor Palpatine say after his battle with Mace Windu?

A. "Use my knowledge, I beg of you!"

B. "You're fulfilling your destiny, Anakin."

C. "Unlimited power!"

D. "I have the power to save the ones you love."

870. Which pilot exclaimed, "Flying is for droids!"?

A. Anakin Skywalker

B. Odd Ball

C. Obi-Wan Kenobi

D. Mace Windu

871. What did Yoda have to say about the prophecy of the Chosen One before he left for Kashyyyk?

A. That a recently discovered Holocron had disproved it

B. That it was a fable

C. That he believed that Anakin was the Chosen One

D. That it may have been misread

Revenge of the Sith Era

872. What did Anakin tell Chancellor Palpatine about the Jedi Council?

A. That he trusted them with his life

B. That they knew Chancellor Palpatine was a Sith Lord

C. That he knew there were things about the Force they weren't telling him

D. That they were planning to take over the Senate

873. Who had good relations with the Wookiees?

A. Mace Windu

B. Yoda

C. Bariss Offee

D. Aayla Secura

874. What name did Darth Sidious give his new apprentice?

A. Darth Maul

B. Darth Vader

C. Darth Offal

D. Darth Plagueis

875. What did General Grievous collect?

A. Bones

B. Blasters

C. Lightsabers

D. Padawan braids

876. Who demanded, "Your swords, please. We don't want to make a mess of things in front of the Chancellor" to Anakin Skywalker and Obi-Wan Kenobi?

A. Darth Sidious

B. General Grievous

C. Count Dooku

D. Nute Gunray

877.

878. How many arms did General Grievous have?

A. Four

B. Three

C. Two

D. Six

879. How old was Mace Windu when he joined the Jedi Council?

A. Twenty-eight

B. Thirty-two

C. Thirty-four

D. Twenty-seven

OBSESSED WITH *STAR WARS*

877.

Seeing the Jedi Temple in flames, Senator Bail Organa sped toward it and landed on a platform. As he attempted to enter the Temple, he saw a battalion of clone troopers standing guard. "What's going on here?" he demanded of a clone trooper.

"There's been a rebellion, sir," the trooper responded. "Don't worry. The situation is under control."

Senator Organa then attempted to push past the guards and enter the Temple so he could see what was going on, only to be met by raised weapons. "I'm sorry, sir, but it's time for you to leave," the clone trooper ordered him.

"And so it is," Organa responded. As he headed toward his speeder, a Padawan leapt out onto the platform and began fighting the clone troopers. After defeating several of them, the young Jedi was finally struck down, and a panicked Organa leapt into his craft and sped away from the scene.

What was his next course of action?

A. He went directly to the Chancellor to report the matter

B. He boarded the *Tantive IV* and left in search of surviving Jedi

C. He gathered troops to battle the clones and enter the Temple

D. He went about his business

880. Who did Ki-Adi-Mundi battle on the planet Hypori?
- **A.** Count Dooku
- **B.** Darth Sidious
- **C.** General Grievous
- **D.** Asajj Ventress

881. How tall was Bail Organa?
- **A.** 1.91 meters
- **B.** 1.82 meters
- **C.** 1.69 meters
- **D.** 2.04 meters

882. What Sith artifact did Darth Tyranus unleash on the Republic during the Clone Wars?
- **A.** The Grim Reaper
- **B.** The Dark Harvester
- **C.** The Grim Harvester
- **D.** The Dark Reaper

883. Where was Ki-Adi-Mundi when Order 66 was executed?
- **A.** Felucia
- **B.** Mygeeto
- **C.** Geonosis
- **D.** Cato Neimoidia

884. What bounty hunter did Count Dooku pair with Asajj Ventress in his fight against the Republic?
- **A.** Durge
- **B.** Boba Fett
- **C.** Aurra Sing
- **D.** Jango Fett

885. What was General Grievous' official title after the Battle of Geonosis?
- **A.** Supreme Commander of the Droid Armies
- **B.** Supreme Commander of Separatist Combat
- **C.** Supreme Commander of the Droid Legions
- **D.** Supreme Commander of Separatist Troops

886. What was Ki-Adi-Mundi's rank during the Clone Wars?
- **A.** Captain
- **B.** General
- **C.** Admiral
- **D.** Governor

887. What was Bail Organa's wife Breha's position on Alderaan?
- **A.** Minister of Music
- **B.** Minister of the Arts
- **C.** Minister of Education
- **D.** Minister of Peace

Revenge of the Sith **Era**

888. To whom did Count Dooku say, "Don't let your pursuit of trinkets cloud your reality"?
- **A.** Darth Sidious
- **B.** Asajj Ventress
- **C.** General Grievous
- **D.** Darth Tyranus

889. Against what species were General Grievous and the Kaleesh in a battle before he joined the Separatists?
- **A.** Rodians
- **B.** Huks
- **C.** Muuns
- **D.** Nautolans

890. How many daughters did Ki-Adi-Mundi have?
- **A.** Six
- **B.** Seven
- **C.** Ten
- **D.** Four

891. With which Jedi Master did Bultar Swan lead forces on the planet Aargonar?
- **A.** Yoda
- **B.** Mace Windu
- **C.** Stass Allie
- **D.** Ki-Adi-Mundi

892. Who said to Anakin, "There is much fear that clouds your judgment"?
- **A.** Mace Windu
- **B.** Obi-Wan Kenobi
- **C.** Yoda
- **D.** Chancellor Palpatine

893. Who trained General Grievous in the lightsaber arts?
- **A.** Count Dooku
- **B.** Darth Maul
- **C.** Darth Bane
- **D.** Darth Sidious

894. How tall was General Grievous?
- **A.** 1.72 meters
- **B.** 2.16 meters
- **C.** 2.38 meters
- **D.** 2.23 meters

895. What did Mace Windu say surrounded the Chancellor?
- **A.** Separatist sympathies
- **B.** Whispers of corruption
- **C.** Sycophants
- **D.** The dark side of the Force

899.

After General Kenobi reported that his mission had been successful, effectively ending the war, Mace Windu and three other Jedi were preparing to go to Chancellor Palpatine's office to ensure that he would restore control to the Senate when Anakin confided to Windu that Palpatine was the Sith Lord they had been searching for since the Battle of Naboo.

"In the name of the Galactic Senate of the Republic, you are under arrest, Chancellor," Mace Windu said upon entering Palpatine's office.

"Are you threatening me, Master Jedi?" the Chancellor responded, before igniting his hidden lightsaber.

896. According to legend, on what planet did Mace Windu retrieve the crystals to create his purple lightsaber?
A. Ilum
B. Korriban
C. Hurikane
D. Haruun Kal

897. In which form of lightsaber combat was Mace Windu a master?
A. Vaapad
B. Shien
C. Shii-Cho
D. Ataru

898. Which cause that Bail Organa championed allowed refugees to immigrate to Alderaan during the Clone Wars?
A. Refugee Placement Movement
B. Refugee Relief Movement
C. Refugee Resettlement Organization
D. Refugee Relief Organization

899.

900. What did General Grievous call Anakin Skywalker aboard the *Invisible Hand*?
A. "Jedi slime"
B. "Jedi fool"
C. "Jedi scum"
D. "Foul Jedi"

901. To whom was Anakin Skywalker entrusted as a Padawan when Obi-Wan Kenobi was presumed killed in battle?
A. Mace Windu
B. Ki-Adi-Mundi
C. Oppo Rancisis
D. Plo Koon

902. Where was Count Dooku's hidden base in which he trained General Grievous?
A. The *Malevolent* cruiser
B. The *Trenchant* cruiser
C. Muunilinst
D. Geonosis

903. What Separatist leader was initially interested in General Grievous due to his particularly gruesome war record?
A. San Hill
B. Shu Mai
C. Wat Tambor
D. Po Nudo

It was clear that Palpatine was a Sith Lord when he dispatched three of the Jedi with ease, leaving only Windu to combat him. The two fought a hard battle in the Chancellor's office. As the battle progressed, they moved up the stairs toward the window, which Palpatine smashed with his lightsaber blade. Windu finally ended the battle by kicking Palpatine and sending the Chancellor's blade flying out the broken window. What did Mace Windu first say to Palpatine, who he had pinned against the ledge with his lightsaber?

A. "The oppression of the Sith will never return."
B. "You have lost."
C. "You are under arrest, my Lord."
D. "The Sith are weak."

Revenge of the Sith Era

904. What was Mace Windu's homeworld?

A. Muunilinst
B. Alderaan
C. Haruun Kal
D. Vorzyd-5

905. Who retrieved Yoda after his battle with Emperor Palpatine?

A. Obi-Wan Kenobi
B. Padmé Amidala
C. Bail Organa
D. Anakin Skywalker

906. On Polis Massa, who told Yoda that Obi-Wan Kenobi had made contact?

A. C-3PO
B. Bail Organa
C. Padmé Amidala
D. Anakin Skywalker

907.

908. Who suggested that Master Kenobi should lead the mission to Utapau?

A. Yoda
B. Ki-Adi-Mundi
C. Stass Allie
D. Mace Windu

909. Who killed Count Dooku?

A. Obi-Wan Kenobi
B. Darth Sidious
C. Anakin Skywalker
D. Chancellor Palpatine

910. What did General Grievous call Obi-Wan Kenobi on Utapau?

A. "Jedi slime"
B. "Jedi scum"
C. "Foolish Jedi"
D. "Republic toadie"

911. Who made contact with General Kenobi after Kenobi escaped Utapau?

A. Mas Amedda
B. Bail Organa
C. Yoda
D. Anakin Skywalker

907.

Under orders from Darth Sidious, General Grievous staged a daring attack on the city planet of Coruscant. As thousands of battle droids stormed the streets of the city planet, General Grievous himself had a more important mission: to kidnap the Chancellor. Shaak Ti and two other Jedi spirited the Chancellor away from his private apartment and sped toward his bunker, but little did they know that Grievous would be there waiting for them.

In another section of Coruscant, Yoda and Mace Windu were leading the battle against legions of droids until they realized that the battle was a diversion. The two sensed that the Chancellor was at risk, and Mace Windu sped toward the Chancellor's location in hopes of beating Grievous to his quarry.

Windu arrived too late: Grievous was already boarding a shuttle with the Chancellor. He did, however, manage to do something to General Grievous that left him with the nagging cough that plagued him until his untimely demise. What did Mace Windu do?

A. He crushed Grievous' chest with a Force push
B. He hurled a canister at Grievous, smashing his plating
C. He kicked Grievous in the chest
D. He stabbed Grievous in the chest with his lightsaber

912. From what animal's skull was General Grievous' facemask carved?
- **A.** Nuna
- **B.** Mumuu
- **C.** Huk
- **D.** Karabacc

913. How tall was Ki-Adi-Mundi?
- **A.** 2.08 meters
- **B.** 1.80 meters
- **C.** 2.18 meters
- **D.** 1.98 meters

914. Who adopted Padmé's daughter Leia?
- **A.** Bail Organa
- **B.** Captain Antilles
- **C.** Owen and Beru Lars
- **D.** Giddean Danu

915. What was Senator Mon Mothma's home planet?
- **A.** Bespin
- **B.** Alderaan
- **C.** Chandrila
- **D.** Yavin

916. What stranded Jedi trained Asajj Ventress when she was a child?
- **A.** Ki-Adi-Mundi
- **B.** Ky Narec
- **C.** A'Sharad Hett
- **D.** Plo Koon

917. What Jedi Master was taken prisoner on Brentaal IV?
- **A.** Agen Kolar
- **B.** Shaak Ti
- **C.** Eeth Koth
- **D.** Kit Fisto

918. What Jedi fell prey to Order 66 on Felucia?
- **A.** Stass Allie
- **B.** Aayla Secura
- **C.** Ki-Adi-Mundi
- **D.** Yaddle

919. Who was the Utapaun Master of Port Administration?
- **A.** Koogi Sia
- **B.** Blipson Blu
- **C.** Tion Medon
- **D.** Nizz Zel

Revenge of the Sith Era

920. Into whose care did Bail Organa place R2-D2 and C-3PO?

A. Colton Antilles　　C. Bail Antilles

B. Raymus Antilles　　D. Ignatius Antilles

921. What Senator wore a molf-tasseled overcloak?

A. Chi Eekway　　C. Fang Zar

B. Terr Taneel　　D. Mon Mothma

922. Who was the consort of Duke Teta?

A. Mussuh Crussuh　　C. Koyi Mateil

B. Aayla Secura　　D. Koya Bama

923. What was Captain Davijaan's nickname?

A. Bad Egg　　C. Sad Sack

B. Happy Camper　　D. Odd Ball

924.

925. Which was one of Padmé's handmaidens?

A. Ruweé　　C. Yaueé

B. Moteé　　D. Eneé

926. Who was the administress to the Commerce Guild Presidente?

A. Cat Mandu　　C. Cat Miin

B. Cat Wanda　　D. Cat Corlath

927. Who was the Ithorian Jedi assigned to protect Chancellor Palpatine on Coruscant?

A. Roron Corobb　　C. Drake Lo'gaan

B. Foul Moudama　　D. Drake Rogherrs

924.

A small, red planet in the far reaches of the Outer Rim housed a being who was to become one of the great villains of the Clone Wars. This being was born into a barbaric world ruled by cruel overlords who were constantly warring for global domination. Orphaned as a child, this being was taken in and trained by a stranded Jedi who sensed that she was strong in the Force. His ruthless murder soon left her alone and vengeful.

Through her knowledge of the Force, this being bested most of the warlords on the small planet. She was also continuously victorious in her planet's vicious gladiatorial games. A chance to exact revenge on those she felt had turned their backs, the Jedi and the Republic, came when Count Dooku arrived on the planet. He was searching the gladiatorial games to find a relentless warrior to fight under his command; he found her.

This being had already played an active role in the Separatist movement under Count Dooku when Anakin Skywalker, who was leading the space battle above the planet Muunilinst, noticed the being's incredible piloting, disobeyed orders from Obi-Wan Kenobi, and pursued the adversary. The unknown pilot landed on Yavin 4, where a trap had been set for Anakin. After his ship was destroyed by this powerful being, Anakin was left to fight the warrior alone among the rainforests and ancient temples of the mysterious planet. Who was this being?

A. Asajj Ventress

B. Aurra Sing

C. Zam Wesell

D. Tanya Madera

928. Who was Darth Sidious' Sith Master?
A. Darth Bane
B. Darth Mordris
C. Darth Tyranus
D. Darth Plagueis

929. What clone trooper shot down Jedi Master Plo Koon when Order 66 was given?
A. Captain Jak
B. Captain Jag
C. Captain Cordy
D. Captain Zak

930. Who urged Padmé to allow him to accompany her to Mustafar?
A. Captain Panaka
B. Captain Typho
C. Obi-Wan Kenobi
D. Jar Jar Binks

931. Who was Tion Medon's aide?
A. Bok Bok Chuckuh
B. Dorla Skal
C. Lampay Fay
D. Orgae Ford

932. Which Wookiee was the leader of the city Kachirho on Kashyyyk?
A. Chewbacca
B. Tarfful
C. Guanta
D. Lachichuk

933. Where is Rystáll Sant from?
A. New Bornelax
B. Vorzyd V
C. Dantooine
D. Muunilinst

934. Who was the Senatorial representative from Mon Calamari?
A. Haelee Mills
B. Taylee Sills
C. Meena Tills
D. Quella Norvanto

935. In the battle above Coruscant, who was Squad Seven leader?
A. Captain Breemu
B. Captain Antilles
C. Captain Faytonni
D. Captain Davijaan

Revenge of the Sith **Era**

936. What Jedi Master was riding a BARC speeder on Saleucami when Order 66 was given?
- **A.** Adi Gallia
- **B.** Kit Fisto
- **C.** Stass Allie
- **D.** Oppo Rancisis

937. Sheltay Retrac worked for which senator?
- **A.** Bail Organa
- **B.** Giddean Danu
- **C.** Fang Zar
- **D.** Sweitt Concorkill

938. Who was the Talz Jedi assigned to protect Chancellor Palpatine from General Grievous on Coruscant?
- **A.** Mord Larkiss
- **B.** Enstrelle Pwistrax
- **C.** Foul Moudama
- **D.** Ro-to Mislits

939. What was Delva Racine's occupation?
- **A.** Reporter
- **B.** Waitress
- **C.** Spy
- **D.** Fashion designer

940. What Jedi Padawan did Senator Organa see gunned down on the Jedi Temple hangar platform?
- **A.** Mixy Pixo
- **B.** Zett Jukassa
- **C.** Papis Dain
- **D.** Be Preatchin

941. How old was Queen Apailana at the time of Padmé's funeral procession on Naboo?
- **A.** Twelve
- **B.** Nine
- **C.** Thirteen
- **D.** Fifteen

942. Who was speaking with Chi Eekway at the Galaxies Opera House on Coruscant?
- **A.** Baron Papanoida
- **B.** Barriss Offee
- **C.** Sebulba
- **D.** Duke Gilfor

943. Which Wookiee was considered a master of the ryyk blade?
- **A.** Mallatobuck
- **B.** Tarfful
- **C.** Chewbacca
- **D.** Salporin

947.

During a meeting of the Jedi Council, Ki-Adi-Mundi brought up the plight of Kashyyyk, which had recently been overrun by the droid armies of the Confederacy of Independent Systems. The lush, forested world of Kashyyyk served as a pivotal planet in the Clone Wars. It was close to a major trade route for the southwestern quadrant of the galaxy and housed an important navigation and communications relay station. The Jedi, spread out as they were throughout the galaxy, realized that Kashyyyk was too important a planet to allow it to fall to the enemy.

Master Yoda volunteered to oversee the battle on Kashyyyk, stressing that he had good relations with the native

944. Following his duel with Master Yoda, what clone Captain did Emperor Palpatine ask to prepare his shuttle?

A. Captain Kogge
B. Captain Kagi
C. Captain Cargo
D. Captain Clog

945. What Vurk was seated in Chancellor Palpatine's box at the Galaxies Opera House?

A. Sweitt Concorkill
B. Coleman Trebor
C. Shoo Gaxe
D. Twan Nunnuh

946. Who represented Kuat in the Senate?

A. Veedaaz Awmetth
B. Giddean Danu
C. Brookish Boon
D. Gume Saam

947.

948. Which Jedi was not killed by Chancellor Palpatine?

A. Agen Kolar
B. Kit Fisto
C. Eeth Koth
D. Mace Windu

949. What politician split his time between estates on Coruscant, Ghorman, and Sern Prime?

A. Chancellor Palpatine
B. Fang Zar
C. Meena Tills
D. Bail Organa

950. Who retrieved Obi-Wan Kenobi's lightsaber on Utapau?

A. Commander Cody
B. Captain Kagi
C. Lieutenant Galle
D. Commander Neyo

951. Who established a new droid factory on Metalorn at the request of Count Dooku?

A. Wat Tambor
B. San Hill
C. Shu Mai
D. Poggle the Lesser

Wookiees. A Wookiee greeted him as he headed offworld toward Kashyyyk and the impending battle.

Jedi Masters Quinlan Vos and Luminara Unduli were heavily involved in the initial defenses of the Wookiee planet Kashyyyk. The Wookiee who had escorted Yoda from Coruscant to Kashyyyk worked very closely with Masters Vos and Unduli to set up initial defenses and allocate the Wookiees to different areas of defense. He served as direct liaison for Master Yoda and considered Yoda to be a member of his honor family.

Who was this Wookiee?

A. Chewbacca
B. Tarfful
C. Guanta
D. Yarua

Revenge of the Sith Era

952. Who, along with Tarfful, escorted Yoda to an escape pod after the battle on Kashyyyk?

A. Chewbacca **C.** Merumeru
B. Salporin **D.** Lachichuk

953. Who shouted, "Then he's not dead!" when clone troopers said they couldn't find Yoda in the Senate chamber?

A. Mas Amedda **C.** Emperor Palpatine
B. Sly Moore **D.** Darth Vader

954. Who represented the Humbarine sector in the Senate?

A. Bana Breemu **C.** Ask Aak
B. Giddean Danu **D.** Veedaaz Awmetth

955. Who financed the rehabilitation of General Grievous?

A. Wat Tambor **C.** Po Nudo
B. San Hill **D.** Rune Haako

956. To whom did Obi-Wan entrust the care of young Luke Skywalker?

A. Owen and Beru Lars **C.** Cliegg Lars
B. Shmi Skwalker **D.** Bail Organa

957. Which Jedi helped fight the Quarren Isolationist League on Mon Calamari?

A. Agen Kolar **C.** Shaak Ti
B. Kit Fisto **D.** Bant Eerin

958. According to legend, who could use the dark side of the Force to create life?

A. Darth Sidious **C.** Darth Plagueis
B. Darth Bane **D.** Darth Maul

959. Who replaced Senator Lexi Dio after she was assassinated?

A. Malé-Dee **C.** Passel Argente
B. Fang Zar **D.** Terr Taneel

OBSESSED WITH *STAR WARS*

960. Why was Aayla Secura assigned to Felucia?

A. To find the Trade Federation's secret base

B. To keep the Techno Union from opening a new droid factory

C. To keep the Geonosians from opening a new droid factory

D. To stop the Commerce Guild from poisoning the planet's water table

961. Which General in the Grand Army of the Republic was assigned to protect Tipoca City when the Separatists attacked Kamino?

A. Shaak Ti

B. Plo Koon

C. Stass Allie

D. Kit Fisto

962. Who narrowly escaped an assassination attempt by Boba Fett on Xagobah?

A. San Hill

B. Shu Mai

C. Count Dooku

D. Wat Tambor

963. Who led the beachfront defense during the Battle of Kachirho?

A. Chewbacca

B. Tarfful

C. Merumeru

D. Guanta

964. Who said, "There's no war here, unless you brought it with you"?

A. Lampay Fay

B. Gume Saam

C. Tion Medon

D. Baron Papanoida

965.

Padmé rushed to Mustafar after meeting with Obi-Wan, who had told her of Anakin Skywalker's fall to the dark side. Padmé knew that if she were to confront Anakin, she would be able to talk him into turning away from the dark side and helping her raise their child. But when Obi-Wan revealed that he had stowed aboard Padmé's vessel, Anakin thought that Padmé had brought Obi-Wan there to fight him. In a fit of rage, Anakin used the Force to choke Padmé until she passed out. He released her, but not in time to save her spirit.

Though physically healthy, for some unknown reason Padmé lay dying as she gave birth to her children. With a few final words to Obi-Wan, Padmé closed her eyes, leaving behind the future of the galaxy.

On Naboo, Padmé's funeral procession was enormous. The streets of Theed were flooded with thousands of mourners who had gone to pay their final respects to the Queen who had led them out of the Trade Federation's occupation. Leading the procession was Queen Apailana, successor to Queen Jamillia. Directly behind her was an Ankura Gungan. Who was it?

A. Jar Jar Binks

B. Captain Tarpals

C. Rep Been

D. Boss Nass

---

966. Who was seated to Chancellor Palpatine's left in his Galaxies Opera House box?

A. Mas Amedda

B. Sly Moore

C. Sweitt Concorkill

D. Sei Taria

967. Which Wookiee was left-handed?

A. Chewbacca

B. Tarfful

C. Lachichuk

D. Guanta

Revenge of the Sith **Era**

968. Who was Captain Antilles' mentor?
- **A.** Captain Yeltin
- **B.** Captain Tralo
- **C.** Captain Colton
- **D.** Captain Ahl

969. Who was the Senatorial representative from the Senex sector?
- **A.** Terr Taneel
- **B.** Ask Aak
- **C.** Fang Zar
- **D.** Male-Dee

970. At the time of the Clone Wars, who was the youngest Senator ever to hold office?
- **A.** Mon Mothma
- **B.** Chi Eekway
- **C.** Padmé Amidala
- **D.** Fang Zar

971. Who was the first to receive Order 66?
- **A.** Commander Yar
- **B.** Captain Kagi
- **C.** Captain Fezz
- **D.** Commander Cody

972.

973. With whom did Bail Organa meet, pretending he was interested in joining the Confederacy of Independent Systems?
- **A.** Count Dooku
- **B.** Nute Gunray
- **C.** Passel Argente
- **D.** Wat Tambor

974. Who represented Sern Prime in the Senate?
- **A.** Gume Saam
- **B.** Giddean Danu
- **C.** Mon Mothma
- **D.** Fang Zar

975. What species performed *Squid Lake* in the Galaxies Opera House on Coruscant?
- **A.** Nautolans
- **B.** Aqualish
- **C.** Quarren
- **D.** Mon Calamari

972.

Chancellor Palpatine told Anakin Skywalker that General Grievous' location had been discovered, and Anakin at once delivered the news, which was key to the Republic's victory, to the Jedi Council. As the Council discussed the matter, Anakin told them that the Chancellor wanted him to lead the attack against the dreaded Grievous. "The Council will make up its own mind who is to go, not the Chancellor," Mace Windu declared.

"A Master is needed with more experience," Yoda added. The group then voted that Obi-Wan Kenobi would lead the mission to the decisive planet and bring an end to the fighting.

"You're going to need me on this one, Master," Anakin told his mentor afterward. Obi-Wan agreed, but then stressed that the mission could turn out to be a false lead. The two old friends then parted ways and Obi-Wan boarded a Star Destroyer bound for the Outer Rim.

Obi-Wan met with the leader of the planet and discovered the truth of the situation. He gave the administrator some advice before leaving. "Is he bringing additional warriors?" one of the administrator's aides asked after Obi-Wan had departed. What was the administrator's response?

- **A.** "He didn't say."
- **B.** "We can expect an invasion."
- **C.** "Reinforcements are not far behind."
- **D.** "They are already here."

976. What color is Nelvaanian fur?
- **A.** Yellow
- **B.** Blue
- **C.** Red
- **D.** Orange

977. How many fingers do Polis Massans have on each hand?
- **A.** Three
- **B.** Two
- **C.** Four
- **D.** Five

978. What was Jedi Master Agen Kolar's species?
- **A.** Ithorian
- **B.** Iktotchi
- **C.** Iridonian Zabrak
- **D.** Nautolan

979. Who trained the varactyls on Utapau?
- **A.** Pau'ans
- **B.** Utai
- **C.** Human settlers
- **D.** Skakoans

980. Which subspecies of Mustafarian is tall and thin?
- **A.** Southern
- **B.** Eastern
- **C.** Northern
- **D.** Western

981. What language do Wookiees speak?
- **A.** Wookiee
- **B.** Shyriiwook
- **C.** Wookieese
- **D.** Kashwook

982. Who had set up a secret laboratory on Nelvaan?
- **A.** Skakoans
- **B.** Gossams
- **C.** Geonosians
- **D.** Neimoidians

983. Before his transformation into a cyborg general, what species was General Grievous?
- **A.** Vurk
- **B.** Kaleesh
- **C.** Trandoshan
- **D.** Barabel

Revenge of the Sith Era

984. What do Pau'ans eat?
- **A.** Raw meat
- **B.** Grains
- **C.** Vegetables
- **D.** Fruit

985. Which of the following species has a chitinous exoskeleton?
- **A.** Utai
- **B.** Polis Massans
- **C.** Mustafarians
- **D.** Wookiees

986. How do Polis Massans communicate?
- **A.** Sign language
- **B.** Spoken language
- **C.** High-pitched clicks
- **D.** With written code

987. What arthropods with insectoid eyes evolved in the underground tunnels of their homeworld?
- **A.** Mustafarians
- **B.** Neimoidians
- **C.** Kaminoans
- **D.** Koorivar

988. What species has retractable claws on its hands and feet, used primarily for climbing?
- **A.** Geonosians
- **B.** Mustafarians
- **C.** Wookiees
- **D.** Utai

989. How many throats do Ithorians have?
- **A.** Three
- **B.** Four
- **C.** Two
- **D.** One

990. What did Ishi Tib evolve from?
- **A.** Birds
- **B.** Fish
- **C.** Reptiles
- **D.** Rodents

991. What is unusual about Pau'ans' teeth?
- **A.** They have triple rows
- **B.** They have double rows
- **C.** They are hollow
- **D.** They are black

997.

Polis Massans are strange, featureless beings native to the Subterrel Sector who obsessively mine the asteroid field they have colonized, known as Polis Massa, for clues as to its history. The planet Polis Massa was reduced to rubble by some unknown catastrophe in the distant past, and very few clues remain as to its original inhabitants. In addition to being compulsive archaeologists, the Polis Massans are also skilled xenobiologists, studying alien species and their cultures. Although interested in alien beings, Polis Massans tend to study from afar instead of confronting or capturing their subjects.

In a rare departure from their standoffish behavior, the Polis Massans did make contact and exchange information with one alien species, who gave them the knowledge to create clones, among other things.

When researching a planet in the Subterrel sector, the Polis Massans used a weapon given to them by the natives in order to fend off the planet's wild beasts. While there, they ran into a being who, in turn, used what he learned from the Polis Massans to help Obi-Wan Kenobi solve a mystery that would have a huge impact on the history of the Galactic Republic. This being had taken a particular interest in the weapons the Polis Massans were using: saberdarts. Who was this being?

A. Jar Jar Binks
B. Chewbacca
C. Agen Kolar
D. Dexter Jettster

992. What is special about Mustafarians' skin?
A. It does not absorb water
C. It is scaled
B. It can withstand the heat radiated from laser blasts
D. It changes color with their emotional state

993. What was Jedi Neb Bees' species?
A. Devaronian
C. Talz
B. Ithorian
D. Ortolan

994. What subspecies of Mustafarian is short, squat, and able to withstand hotter temperatures?
A. Northern
C. Southern
B. Western
D. Eastern

995. What was Koyi Mateil's species?
A. Twi'lek
C. Rodian
B. Nemoidian
D. Mon Calamari

996. How many pairs of eyes do Talz have?
A. Four
C. One
B. Three
D. Two

997.

998. What was Cat Miin's species?
A. Lannik
C. Skakoan
B. Gossam
D. Wroonian

999. What was Baron Papanoida's species?
A. Ortolan
C. Human
B. Muun
D. Wroonian

Revenge of the Sith Era

1000. Which of the following species pledges its existence to a being who saves them?
  A. Mustafarians
  B. Wookiees
  C. Weequays
  D. Pau'ans

1001. What is the prominent feature on the Utai's faces?
  A. Elephantine noses
  B. Huge fangs
  C. Sharp beaks
  D. Large, distended eyes

1002. What species was Meena Tills?
  A. Quarren
  B. Mon Calamari
  C. Human
  D. Quermian

1003. What is special about Kaleesh eyesight?
  A. They see only in the ultraviolet spectrum
  B. They have X-ray vision
  C. They have thermoreceptor glands next to their eyes, allowing them to see the infrared spectrum
  D. They have insectoid vision

1004. What species believed that Anakin Skywalker was the holt kazet, or "ghost hand"?
  A. Nelvaanians
  B. Gungans
  C. Muuns
  D. Mustafarians

1005. What was Lampay Fay's species?
  A. Utai
  B. Pau'an
  C. Neimoidian
  D. Polis Massan

1006. How many toes do Utai have on each foot?
  A. Three
  B. Six
  C. Four
  D. Two

1007. What was Lachichuk's species?
  A. Mustafarian
  B. Pau'an
  C. Wookiee
  D. Nautolan

1011.

The ancestors of this tranquil species were predators who hunted in packs, leaving their descendants the tendency to live in large communal groups in the dense forests and valleys of their homeworld. This species still hunts in large packs, and as a communal tribe, every being is expected to participate in the hunt in some way, including all children old enough to grasp weapons. As a result of their upbringing, this species believes that anyone not willing or able to participate in the communal hunts should be left to die.

This species is proud of its hunts and wears trophies of its kills in the forms of skins, teeth, and bones, some fashioned

1008. What color is Talz fur?
- **A.** Black
- **B.** White
- **C.** Grey
- **D.** Brown

1009. What was Senator Gume Saam's species?
- **A.** Swokes Swokes
- **B.** Gotal
- **C.** Gungan
- **D.** Ishi Tib

1010. What are Wookiees famous for?
- **A.** Their poetry
- **B.** Their humor
- **C.** Their tempers
- **D.** Their pottery

1011.

1012. What species worships the Great Mother?
- **A.** Nelvaanians
- **B.** Gungans
- **C.** Wookiees
- **D.** Quarren

1013. What was Waks Trode's species?
- **A.** Iridonian Zabrak
- **B.** Ithorian
- **C.** Ishi Tib
- **D.** Iktotchi

1014. What is special about the Utai's eyes?
- **A.** They are colorblind
- **B.** They are sightless
- **C.** They see only in the ultraviolet spectrum
- **D.** They have night vision

1015. How many legs do dactillions have?
- **A.** Six
- **B.** Four
- **C.** Two
- **D.** Eight

into elaborate jewelry pieces that form an important part of their rites of passage. Particularly important are the teeth of the akul, a deadly carnivore that stalks the planet. Only a member of this species who has killed an akul by himself or herself has the privilege to wear the teeth as a sign of bravery.

This species has evolved to blend in with the natural environment on their planet. Their skin acts as a natural camouflage in their homeworld's thigh-high turu-grass, which is generally black, red, and white in color. What species is it?

- **A.** Togruta
- **B.** Wookiee
- **C.** Twi'lek
- **D.** Nautolan

Revenge of the Sith **Era**

1016. What do Mustafarians use as a mount?
- **A.** Mustafar lava dog
- **B.** Mustafar lava flea
- **C.** Mustafar lava gru
- **D.** Mustafar lava beast

1017. What huge creature did Anakin slay on Nelvaan, not realizing he was interfering with a Nelvanian ritual?
- **A.** Bantha
- **B.** Yanfa
- **C.** Horax
- **D.** Tauntaun

1018. What is a ginntho?
- **A.** A spider
- **B.** An insect
- **C.** A reptile
- **D.** A bird

1019. What species has semitranslucent skin in its larval stage that metabolizes UV-filtering chemicals from its planet's native plant life?
- **A.** Varactyl
- **B.** Dactillion
- **C.** Yanfa
- **D.** Gelagrub

1020. What do dactillions use as a rudder during flight?
- **A.** Their beaks
- **B.** Their tails
- **C.** A dewlap
- **D.** Fins on their underbellies

1021. What did Obi-Wan ride to the Lars homestead on Tatooine?
- **A.** A bantha
- **B.** A landspeeder
- **C.** An eopie
- **D.** A swoop bike

1022. How many spinnerets do ginnthos have?
- **A.** Six
- **B.** Two
- **C.** Four
- **D.** Twenty

1023. What did Obi-Wan ride on Utapau?
- **A.** A yanfa
- **B.** A dactillion
- **C.** A speeder bike
- **D.** A varactyl

1024. What did prehistoric dactillions prey on?
- **A.** Varactyls
- **B.** Utapauns
- **C.** Ginnthos
- **D.** Grotto fish

OBSESSED WITH *STAR WARS*

1025. What service did the ginnthos provide during the war on Utapau?
- **A.** They spun webs to capture droids
- **B.** They chewed through droids' wiring
- **C.** They attempted to poison the Separatist invaders
- **D.** They acted as messengers

1026. Why did the Felucia Star Corps employ gelagrubs as a means of ground transport?
- **A.** They were over budget and needed alternative transportation
- **B.** The Felucian tradition insisted that troops use the native species as transportation
- **C.** Gelagrubs formed telepathic bonds with the troopers
- **D.** The gelagrubs were undetectable by enemy sensors

1027. How many horns do dactillions have on their beaks?
- **A.** One
- **B.** Three
- **C.** Two
- **D.** None

1028.

1028.

These cold-blooded quadrupeds are most active during the day, searching for food in the rocky terrain of their home-world. As vegetarians, they prefer eating the green algae that grows on the rocks in the wetter portions of their world, or snacking on arterial roots dug from porous rocks in arid climates.

They are well equipped for life on their unusual planet. Their five-digit feet have large claws that enable them to climb easily and rapidly. Their heads have armor-plated skulls as well as giant beaks, and their necks are extremely flexible. They have ridges of defensive spines down their backs. While generally docile creatures, they can be extremely dangerous if provoked. Females in particular are very protective of their eggs, which other species native to the planet prey upon.

Both males and females, while reptilian, show many qual-ities similar to birds, particularly the crown of feathers on their heads and feathers on their spines and tails. When domesticated, these highly intelligent, loyal creatures are used as steeds.

What species is this?

- **A.** Dactillions
- **B.** Rancors
- **C.** Varactyls
- **D.** Tauntauns

1029. How long was Boga?
- **A.** Fifteen meters
- **B.** Ten meters
- **C.** Twenty-five meters
- **D.** Twenty meters

1030. How did Anakin get his tribal markings on Nelvaan?
- **A.** Scorpions
- **B.** Leeches
- **C.** Slugs
- **D.** Mites

1031. What creature were the Wookiees hunting on Kashyyyk when they discovered a hidden MTT?
- **A.** Knu
- **B.** Gazekke
- **C.** Gne
- **D.** Grantaloupe

1032. How do Utapauns use varactyls to monitor the weather?
- **A.** They send them to the planet's surface carrying weather sensors
- **B.** They know that when dactillions leave the sinkholes, surface winds are heavy
- **C.** They know that when dactillions leave the sinkholes, surface winds are weak
- **D.** They send them to the surface carrying weather balloons

Revenge of the Sith Era

1033. What do Utapauns keep as domestic pets?
- **A.** Movaks
- **B.** Ginnthos
- **C.** Ylenniks
- **D.** Tralliks

1034. What is the purpose of the varactyl's mid-body spine ridge?
- **A.** It is used during courting rituals
- **B.** It is a defense mechanism
- **C.** It is used as wind resistance
- **D.** It is decorative

1035. What do gelagrubs transform into after their larval stage?
- **A.** Mantids
- **B.** Butterflies
- **C.** Beetles
- **D.** Arachnids

1036. What creature found on Tatooine has a subspecies, adapted to climbing, that lives on Kashyyyk?
- **A.** Eopie
- **B.** Ronto
- **C.** Dewback
- **D.** Bantha

1037.

1038. Over which planet was Chancellor Palpatine being held captive?
- **A.** Kashyyyk
- **B.** Coruscant
- **C.** Felucia
- **D.** Boz Pity

1039. How many residents live in Pau City?
- **A.** Almost a million
- **B.** Almost two hundred thousand
- **C.** Almost two million
- **D.** Almost five hundred thousand

1040. In what sector of the Mid Rim is Kashyyyk located?
- **A.** Baykuh
- **B.** Kashyyyk
- **C.** Meridian
- **D.** Mytaranor

1041. On which planet did Obi-Wan Kenobi learn that Asajj Ventress was still alive?
- **A.** Onderon
- **B.** Korriban
- **C.** Boz Pity
- **D.** Sump

1037.

Anakin Skywalker had fallen to the dark side, and his new Master had sent him on a very important mission involving the Separatists. After taking care of this mission, Anakin remained on the planet he'd been sent to, only to discover that Padmé had followed him. As Padmé was begging Anakin to leave this new life behind and run away with her to raise their child, Obi-Wan Kenobi revealed that he had stowed onboard Padmé's ship in order to find and defeat Anakin.

"Liar!" Anakin screamed at Padmé. "You're with him!" Anakin then attacked Padmé, rendering her unconscious, and the former Master and apprentice began a long, epic lightsaber battle.

Battling through a mining facility, the two toppled into a molten river and were saved only by landing on repulsorlift technology that was protected by heat-retardant shielding. Obi-Wan was on a harvester when Anakin jumped from a collector droid onto the platform with Obi-Wan. The two began to battle again, until Obi-Wan leapt onto a ridge on the edge of the river. At that point he claimed that the battle was over. What gave him that impression?

A. The light side always wins

B. He had the high ground

C. Anakin was not as proficient at lightsaber battle as Obi-Wan

D. Obi-Wan had a vision of the future and knew he was going to win

1042. What sacred Sith artifact was located in the Emperor Palpatine Surgical Reconstruction Center?
A. Naga Sadow's Sith Holocron **C.** Freedon Nadd's coffin
B. The Great Crystal of Aantonaii **D.** The Bane Manifesto

1043. Where did Emperor Palpatine take Darth Vader after his failure on Mustafar?
A. Naboo **C.** Coruscant MedLab
B. EmPal SuRecon **D.** His own home

1044. On what level of Pau City were General Grievous and the battle droids located?
A. Ninth level **C.** First level
B. Eighth level **D.** Tenth level

1045. Who lived on Polis Massa before the Polis Massans?
A. The Eellayin **C.** The Pernidik Gaks
B. The Yarglatch **D.** The Orcon Felarcics

1046. What is Mustafar's twin planet?
A. Pzob **C.** Jestefad
B. Toola **D.** Helska

1047. How does one gain access to the Sith medical facility?
A. Eye scan **C.** Sith code
B. Bio-key **D.** Access card

1048. What is Kashyyyk sometimes erroneously referred to as?
A. Endor **C.** Wookiee Planet 4
B. Wookiee World **D.** Wookiee Planet C

1049. How long ago was Utapau settled by humanoid colonists?
A. 58,000 years **C.** 28,000 years
B. 57,000 years **D.** 27,000 years

1050. To what organization does the Wawaatt Archipelago offer shelter on Kashyyyk?
A. The Claatuvac Guild **C.** The Cholotovat Guild
B. The Mythriis Guild **D.** The Kirhitchi Guild

Revenge of the Sith Era

1051. Where did Chancellor Palpatine tell Anakin about Darth Plagueis the Wise?

A. In the Senate Rotunda C. In the Galaxies Opera House
B. In his office D. In his apartment

1052. What planet was also referred to as the "Graveyard World"?

A. Boz Pity C. Sullust
B. Korriban D. Falleen

1053.

1054. At the time of the Battle of Coruscant, how old was the Jedi Temple?

A. 5,000 years C. 1,000 years
B. 2,000 years D. 4,000 years

1055. What do Utapauns use as structural material?

A. Stone C. Vines
B. Timber D. Bone

1056. What does the bas-relief hanging in the anteroom of Palpatine's office depict?

A. A battle between the Wookiees and the Trandoshans
C. A moving scene from one of Palpatine's favorite Alderaanian ballets, *The Divine Gothos*

B. A battle between the Jedi and the Sith during the Great Hyperspace Wars
D. An abstractionist's depiction of the formation of the Republic

1057. Which planet do gelagrubs call home?

A. Mygeeto C. Felucia
B. Muunilinst D. Cato Neimoidia

1058. What is Polis Massa?

A. A moon C. A planet
B. An asteroid belt D. A space station

1059. What covers the surface of Mygeeto?

A. Snow C. Crystallized ice
B. Rock D. Water

OBSESSED WITH *STAR WARS*

1053.

"I have brought peace, freedom, justice, and security to my new Empire," Anakin said to Obi-Wan as the two faced each other in their final confrontation on Mustafar.

"Your new Empire?" Obi-Wan said incredulously.

As the two continued their argument, Anakin said, "If you're not with me, then you're my enemy."

"Only a Sith deals in absolutes. I will do what I must," Obi-Wan said, removing his lightsaber.

"You will try," Anakin seethed, and the former partners began a legendary battle that would have reverberations for decades to come. Anakin fought with intense rage, keeping Obi-Wan on the defensive and driving him into the mining complex.

Their lightsabers flailed and struck equipment in the mining complex. Anakin and Obi-Wan had come to a stalemate—both were trying to use a Force push on each other. Finally, both went soaring across the room. Anakin leapt to his feet and jumped across a conference table. He struck out with his lightsaber at Obi-Wan but instead hit a control panel. What happened next?

A. The lights went out
B. The repulsor shields went down
C. The blast doors slammed shut
D. Armed droids entered the battle

1060. Why was Polis Massa a perfect location for Obi-Wan Kenobi and Yoda to select as a meeting place after they escaped the Empire?

A. The Polis Massans were known Jedi allies

B. The Polis Massans were Alderaanian allies

C. The Polis Massans operated discreetly to avoid excavation taxes

D. The Polis Massans operated discreetly to avoid space pirates who might steal their precious artifacts

1061. How hot is the lava on Mustafar?

A. 800 degrees Celsius

B. 700 degrees Celsius

C. 1,000 degrees Celsius

D. 900 degrees Celsius

1062. What is found at the very topmost level of the EmPal SuRecon?

A. A prison

B. A Sith holocron

C. Communications and intelligence equipment

D. Turbolasers

1063. What Separatist organization very jealously guarded the crystal treasures of Mygeeto?

A. The Trade Federation

B. The Commerce Guild

C. The Hyper-Communications Cartel

D. The IG Banking Clan

1064. On which planet did the Separatists build a secret bunker in which to hide should their plans go awry?

A. Mustafar

B. Jestefad

C. Utapau

D. Kamino

1065. Where did Darth Sidious tell General Grievous to send the Separatist leaders?

A. Utapau

B. Coruscant

C. Muunilinst

D. Mustafar

1066. Where was Darth Vader sent on his first mission?

A. Kuat

B. Mustafar

C. The Jedi Temple

D. Utapau

1067. Where did Obi-Wan Kenobi defeat the bounty hunter Durge?

A. Muunilinst

B. Saleucami

C. Yavin 4

D. Nelvaan

Revenge of the Sith **Era**

1068. What is in the center of the Chancellor's holding office?

A. A Sith Holocron

B. A HoloNet viewscreen

C. A resting area for visitors

D. The Chancellor's podium

1069. What broke as Mace Windu and Chancellor Palpatine were battling each other?

A. The statue of Braata

B. The desk

C. The window

D. The statue of Yanjon

1070. Who are depicted on the pylons at the entrance to the Jedi Temple?

A. The Founder Jedi

B. The Four Masters

C. The Mysterious Four

D. The Four Founders

1071. As of the fall of the Republic, how long had the Polis Massans been searching for Eellayin artifacts?

A. Five hundred years

B. Six hundred years

C. Four hundred years

D. Two hundred years

1072.

1073. What organization annexed Mustafar and turned it into a lava mining operation, extracting precious metals and ores?

A. The Commerce Guild

B. The IG Banking Clan

C. The Trade Federation

D. The Techno Union

1074. Where was the Sith ritual altar in the EmPal SuRecon originally located?

A. Onderon

B. Ziost

C. Yavin 4

D. Korriban

1075. What is in the top of the Temple Spire, the central spire of the Jedi Temple?

A. The Jedi High Council chamber

B. The Room of One Thousand Fountains

C. The Hall of Knighthood

D. The Pinnacle Room

1076. Where was the Chancellor's holding office located?

A. Directly below his main office

B. Directly below the Senate floor

C. Directly above his apartment

D. Directly above the Galactic Senate

1072.

The Wookiee planet Kashyyyk was pivotal in the struggle for victory in the battle-torn Republic. Its strategic location was so important to the Republic that although Jedi Master Luminara Unduli was already on Kashyyyk directing clone troops, Master Yoda left Coruscant to oversee what the Jedi Council knew would be a major battle.

Kashyyyk was important primarily because of its closeness to a major hyperspace trade route, and more urgently, an important navigation and communications relay station. The Claatuvac Guild, located in Kachirho, was an organization of Wookiee cartographers that maintained and updated hyperspace route surveys and kept the galaxy navigable.

It was also said that the Claatuvac Guild's ancient archives contained information so thorough that long-forgotten routes, gone from the Republic's hyperspace charts, were still maintained in their databases. If the Separatists were to get their hands on these ancient charts, giving them access to information that the Republic didn't know existed, their ability to overtake the galaxy would become that much easier.

What Wroshyr Tree in Kachirho contained all of the Claatuvac Guild's vital information?

A. Tree Kachirho

B. Tree Ylithcitchich

C. Tree Vikkilynn

D. Tree Wlatcherleroo

1077. To which planet did Obi-Wan Kenobi tell Anakin that General Vos had moved his troops?

A. Boz Pity
B. Mygeeto
C. Ord Mantell
D. Kessel

1078. What gas giant is located close to Mustafar and Jestefad?

A. Yavin
B. Enstrelle Pwistrax Prime
C. Pahl Tishi
D. Lefrani

1079. What is the Promenade of Seven Guilds in Pau City?

A. A dining court
B. The exhibition venue
C. The main thoroughfare
D. The varactyl holding area

1080. What is the source of Utapau's offworld trade, consisting mainly of minerals, salts, and chemicals?

A. The surface dunes
B. The world-ocean
C. The cavern walls
D. The bones of various beasts

1081. Where was Padmé while Anakin had been ordered by Mace Windu to remain in the Jedi Council chamber?

A. At the Senate
B. On Naboo
C. En route to her apartment
D. In her apartment

1082. On the fringe of which sector is Polis Massa located?

A. The Corporate sector
B. The Elrood sector
C. The Subterrel sector
D. The Cathol sector

1083. What was Polis Massa before it became an asteroid belt?

A. A planet
B. A moon
C. Twin moons
D. Twin planets

1084. What was the name of the ancient underground city the Polis Massans discovered and hence referred to as the Local Dig?

A. Klovaki
B. Wiyentaah
C. Frithis Ortal
D. Yan Yan Blistak

1085. What was the name of the lagoon city on Kashyyyk that Yoda was in charge of defending against the Separatist attack?

A. Kashiii
B. Katcholowach
C. Kachirho
D. Wottklootchoch

Revenge of the Sith Era

1086. In what Wroshyr tree was Yoda's command center on Kashyyyk?

A. Tree Vikkilynn

B. Tree Cholomotak

C. Tree Millickhtik

D. Tree Kachirho

1087. What is unique about Cato Neimoidian cities?

A. They are airborne

B. They are built on bridges above canyons

C. They are underground

D. They are underwater

1088. What covers the landscape of Felucia?

A. Multicolored fungi

B. Crystal canyons

C. Fluorescent plants

D. Oceans and swamps

1089.

1090. What did the citizens of Coruscant think the Emperor Palpatine Surgical Reconstruction Center was?

A. A high-rise apartment complex

B. A specialized hospital facility

C. A posh spa

D. A repository of Sith evil

1091. How many levels does Pau City boast?

A. Ten

B. Fourteen

C. Twelve

D. Eleven

1092. Which barren Outer Rim planet was a major battle site during the Outer Rim Sieges of the Clone Wars?

A. Tatooine

B. Saleucami

C. Boz Pity

D. Xantooine

1093. Why is Utapau's surface uninhabitable?

A. It is scorchingly hot

B. It is infested with carnivorous behemoths

C. It is frigidly cold

D. There is a constant gale-force wind

1094. How many different varieties of Wroshyr tree are there on Kashyyyk?

A. More than two hundred

B. More than five thousand

C. More than one thousand

D. More than two thousand

1089.

Pau City, the capital of Utapau, is built in one of the immense sinkholes that dot the planet. It was built primarily in existing natural caves, keeping the population safe from the brutal, scouring winds that sweep the surface of the planet.

The city contains several levels. The upper level of the city is the civil level, which contains all of Pau City's government offices. Also on this level are the Pahum Cultural Center, where most of the city's performances and exhibits are held, and the Grand Hall of the Trader's Guild. This building was taken over by the Techno Union when the Separatists invaded Utapau and transformed it into a factory.

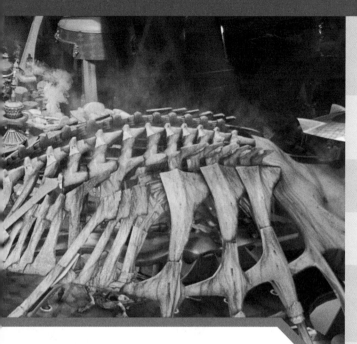

Below that is the wealth level, where the majority of Utapau's industries are housed, including mineral processing plants and pumping stations. Next comes the produce level, where all of Pau City's food supply is grown hydroponically in greenhouses. Animals are also raised for food on this level, and delivered daily to other levels of the city. This is the level where dactillions and varactyls are bred and trained. The second-to-lowest level is the mining level, where the raw material for the processing plants on the wealth level comes from.

What is at the very bottom of Pau City?

A. Gardens
B. A duracrete landing pad
C. Water
D. A dense rainforest

1095. Where did Emperor Palpatine find the massive Sith Holocron he had in his secret chamber atop EmPal SuRecon?
A. Ossus
B. Yavin 4
C. Onderon
D. Korriban

1096. What was stored throughout the walls of the gallery in the EmPal SuRecon?
A. Sith weapons
B. Sacred maps
C. Bodies
D. Bacta

1097. What does Saleucami translate into in Wroonian?
A. Desert
B. Rainforest
C. Oasis
D. Outpost

1098. What occurs in the lowest level of Pau City?
A. Farming
B. Mining
C. Cultural events
D. Government business

1099. What piece of Mustafarian equipment were Anakin and Obi-Wan fighting atop after it broke free from the control room and began to float down the molten river?
A. A loading turret
B. A propulsion turret
C. A loading arm
D. A collector arm

1100. Where did Obi-Wan go into hiding after receiving special instruction from Master Yoda?
A. Tatooine
B. Dantooine
C. Naboo
D. Polis Massa

1101. What droids drilled into the outer hull of Obi-Wan Kenobi's ship during the Battle of Coruscant?
A. Battle droids
B. Tri-fighters
C. Droidekas
D. Buzz droids

1102. What dangled in the middle of EmPal SuRecon's hospital tower reservoir?
A. Bacta reserves
B. Gigantic synthetic Sith crystals
C. Dark side amulets
D. Cryogenically frozen ancient Sith Lords

Revenge of the Sith **Era**

1103. Where did Yoda go into exile?

A. Xagobah

B. Dantooine

C. Dagobah

D. Polis Massa

1104. Where were the crystal caverns and temple that Luminara Unduli and Barriss Offee attempted to save from Separatist attack?

A. Hurikane

B. Ilum

C. Yavin 4

D. Dxun

1105. Where did Obi-Wan meet Bail Organa and Yoda after defeating Anakin Skywalker?

A. Polis Massa

B. Naboo

C. Tatooine

D. Dagobah

1106. What marked the surface of Saleucami?

A. Potholes

B. Stalagmites

C. Bulbous plantlife

D. Rivers

1107.

1108. What type of droid was destroyed when a Wookiee soldier swung onto it and slapped a detonator onto its outer shell?

A. Tank droid

B. Homing spider droid

C. Hailfire droid

D. Crab droid

1109. When Obi-Wan fell into the water on Utapau, what type of droid searched him out in the sinkhole basin?

A. Sith dark eye probe droid

B. Arakyd probe droid

C. Crab droid

D. Probot

1110. Which Separatist droid did clone troopers refer to as "the muckraker"?

A. Super battle droid

B. Dwarf-spider droid

C. Battle droid

D. Crab droid

1111. Why did C-3PO get gold plating?

A. The plating he received on Tatooine rusted off

B. His original plating was destroyed in a blaster fight

C. He had to look his best in the service of a Senator

D. His original plating was too small for his wiring

1107.

Anakin and Obi-Wan were recalled from the Outer Rim sieges after a catastrophe occurred—General Grievous had managed to evade the Jedi and kidnap Chancellor Palpatine. He was holding the Chancellor hostage in his flagship, the *Invisible Hand*, high above Coruscant, where a deadly battle was underway. Star Destroyers and Separatist ships clogged space above the city planet.

Obi-Wan and Anakin swooped their Jedi interceptors into the fray, with a clear mission: to save the Chancellor from the clutches of the sinister Count Dooku and his henchman, General Grievous.

1112. What droids were swarming General Grievous's flagship, *Invisible Hand*, when Anakin and Obi-Wan were flying toward it?
- **A.** Vulture droids
- **B.** Battle droids
- **C.** Droidekas
- **D.** Buzz droids

1113. What company manufactured MagnaGuards?
- **A.** Industrial Automaton
- **B.** Holowan Mechanicals
- **C.** Cybot Galactica
- **D.** Commerce Guild

1114. What type of droid was FX-9?
- **A.** Lava collector
- **B.** Astromech
- **C.** Battle droid
- **D.** Surgical assistant

1115. What was the Ubrikkian Model DD-13 droid's nickname?
- **A.** "Butch"
- **B.** "The Crusher"
- **C.** "Galactic Chopper"
- **D.** "Knuckles"

1116. What astromech droid piloted Obi-Wan's starfighter off Utapau as a diversion?
- **A.** R4-G9
- **B.** R2-D2
- **C.** R4-P17
- **D.** R5-D4

1117. What were IG-101 and IG-102?
- **A.** Battle droid captains
- **B.** MagnaGuards
- **C.** Protocol droids
- **D.** Medical droids

1118. What company manufactured Ordnance Lifters, which were designed for lifting cargo skids and missiles?
- **A.** Kuat Drive Yards
- **B.** Baktoid Armor Workshops
- **C.** Cybot Galactica
- **D.** Seinar Systems

1119. Which droid was modeled after eight-eyed vine stalkers found on Skako?
- **A.** Crab droid
- **B.** Octuparra droid
- **C.** Vulture droid
- **D.** Droideka

1120. What droid referred to R2-D2 as a "stupid little astro-droid"?
- **A.** A super battle droid
- **B.** A battle droid
- **C.** A droideka
- **D.** C-3PO

As the two Jedi soared ever nearer to their target, Anakin noticed that General Grievous's ship was heavily protected by vulture droids. Sensing attack, the droids launched themselves toward the Jedi. Obi-Wan called in Squad Seven to help fight off the vulture droids.

When the droids attacked a member of Squad Seven, Anakin told Obi-Wan that he was going to go help the clone trooper. What did Obi-Wan say to Anakin?

- **A.** "Yes, and do it quickly!"
- **B.** "Don't bother. They're only clones."
- **C.** "I'll help you."
- **D.** "No. They're doing their job, and we can do ours."

Revenge of the Sith Era

1121. Who told Obi-Wan, Bail Organa, and Yoda that Padmé was carrying twins?
- **A.** Maneeli Tuun
- **B.** GH-7
- **C.** Midwife droid
- **D.** Dznori Xam

1122. What was stored in the Octuparra droid's hollow, ball-shaped cognitive unit?
- **A.** Gaseous viruses
- **B.** Technical readouts
- **C.** Battle configurations
- **D.** Energy reserves

1123. Which droids were common at the Jedi Temple embarkation area, helping with cargo loading or traffic control?
- **A.** Ordnance lifters
- **B.** Hover loaders
- **C.** Pincer loaders
- **D.** Astromech droids

1124. How many MagnaGuards did General Grievous hand-pick to help kidnap Chancellor Palpatine during the Battle of Coruscant?
- **A.** Eleven
- **B.** Ten
- **C.** Fourteen
- **D.** Twelve

1125. What was on the top of GH-7's head?
- **A.** A probe arm
- **B.** A bacta reservoir
- **C.** An equipment tray
- **D.** A sterilization chamber

1126. Who was responsible for unleashing the Tri-Fighter droid on the Republic?
- **A.** Industrial Automaton
- **B.** Commerce Guild
- **C.** Colicoid Creation Nest
- **D.** Arakyd

1127. What was the Chroon-Tan B-Machine more commonly known as?
- **A.** Midwife droid
- **B.** "Galactic Chopper"
- **C.** Medical assistant
- **D.** Medical droid

1128.

1129. What were MagnaGuards' heads designed to look like?
- **A.** Ancient Sith droids
- **B.** Ancient Krath droids
- **C.** The species that designed them
- **D.** General Grievous

1128.

Anakin Skywalker had blasted the shield generator on General Grievous's ship, the *Invisible Hand*, so that he and Obi-Wan Kenobi could land on the ship and save Chancellor Palpatine from the Separatists. As the two leapt from their Jedi interceptors, they were attacked by battle droids, which they quickly destroyed.

Obi-Wan Kenobi told R2-D2 to locate the Chancellor. R2 plugged in to the ship's network and projected a holographic image of the Chancellor's location—the top spire of the ship. Sensing danger, Obi-Wan wryly suggested that the two Jedi "spring the trap." Obi-Wan tossed R2 a communicator and told him to wait for orders.

R2-D2 waited in the main hangar bay as the Jedi sprinted toward the Chancellor's projected location. Anakin and Obi-Wan were in a stalled elevator, attempting to give R2 instructions to reactivate it, when two super battle droids walked into the main hangar bay. Overhearing Obi-Wan talking to R2 through the communicator, the super battle droids looked around but found nothing. When R2 went over to activate the elevator, the super battle droids caught him in the act, and one of them picked him up. How did R2-D2 escape this droid's clutches?

- **A.** He shocked it
- **B.** He sprayed oil on it
- **C.** He cut it with a saw blade
- **D.** He deactivated it

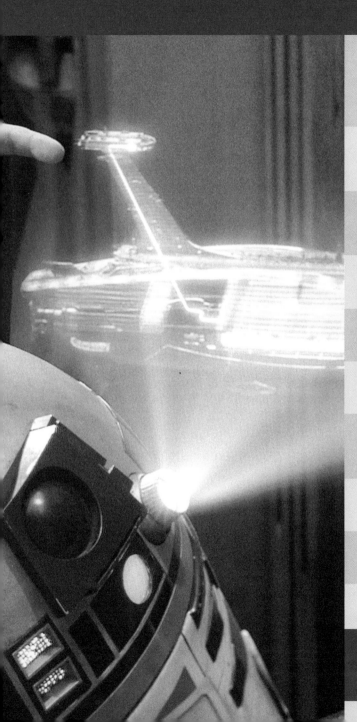

1130. What was the "Galactic Chopper" designed to oversee?
- **A.** Hardware installation
- **B.** Droid troop deployment
- **C.** The installation of cybernetic implants, prosthetic limbs, and synthetic organs
- **D.** Droid troop cleanup

1131. When the buzz droids attacked Obi-Wan's ship, which astromech droid was destroyed?
- **A.** R5-D9
- **B.** R4-F9
- **C.** R4-G9
- **D.** R4-P17

1132. Who yelled, "I'd like to have a serious talk with your programmer!" when he saw a droid army marching the streets of Coruscant?
- **A.** C-3PO
- **B.** Obi-Wan Kenobi
- **C.** Mace Windu
- **D.** Anakin Skywalker

1133. Who used Zenoti Arms HB-9 rifles?
- **A.** Mustafarians
- **B.** Battle droids
- **C.** Utapauns
- **D.** Clone troopers

1134. What color was Darth Sidious' lightsaber blade?
- **A.** Yellow
- **B.** Red
- **C.** Blue
- **D.** Green

1135. What were the MagnaGuards' electrostaffs constructed with?
- **A.** Mustafarian alloy
- **B.** Mygeetan alloy
- **C.** Sith alloy
- **D.** Phrik alloy

1136. How many lightsabers did General Grievous use in his battle with Obi-Wan Kenobi on Utapau?
- **A.** Six
- **B.** Four
- **C.** Three
- **D.** Two

1137. What was the name of the clone troopers' standard-issue rifle?
- **A.** DC-15A
- **B.** DC-207A
- **C.** DC-14SQ
- **D.** DC-15SQ

1138. Which is a traditional Wookiee weapon?
- **A.** Force pike
- **B.** Lightsaber
- **C.** Electrostaff
- **D.** Bowcaster

Revenge of the Sith **Era**

1139. What was special about Bail Organa's target blaster?

A. It could only be used on stun setting

B. It was hand-crafted for him by appreciative Gungans

C. It was hand-crafted for him by appreciative Alderaanians

D. It was for ceremonial purposes only and did not function

1140. What color was Aayla Secura's lightsaber blade?

A. Green

B. Blue

C. Purple

D. Red

1141. What blaster did General Grievous carry?

A. BlasTech Custom DT-47 "Annihilator"

B. BlasTech Custom DT-47 "Destroyer"

C. BlasTech Custom DT-57 "Destroyer"

D. BlasTech Custom DT-57 "Annihilator"

1142.

1143. What color was Zett Jukasa's lightsaber blade?

A. Blue

B. Purple

C. Green

D. Red

1144. How many lightsabers did Anakin use to kill Count Dooku?

A. Three

B. Two

C. One

D. None

1145. What did Pau'an warriors carry as weapons?

A. Energy staffs

B. Tridents

C. Bidents

D. Electrostaffs

1146. What is carried in a Wookiee ammo halter?

A. Pellets

B. Throwing knives

C. Poisonous spikes

D. Blaster gas cartidges

1147. What class of Star Destroyer was employed by the Republic at the time of the Battle of Coruscant?

A. *Nebula*

B. *Venator*

C. *Imperial*

D. *Victory*

1142.

A tragedy had occurred. The Jedi Temple was in flames—Padmé could see the smoke spiraling up from its majestic towers. She was beside herself with worry. C-3PO told Padmé that he had received word regarding Anakin Skywalker's location. "Don't worry—I'm sure he'll be all right." C-3PO turned and walked away and Padmé burst into tears.

Later, Anakin arrived at Padmé's apartment. She rushed to his arms. "Are you all right? I heard there was an attack on the Jedi Temple. You could see the smoke from here!" Padmé cried as Anakin consoled her. The fallen Jedi then told Padmé that the Jedi had tried to overthrow the Republic. He had uncovered their plot himself. He would maintain his current allegiances, however, and was now following orders from the Chancellor. He told Padmé that he had a very important mission to complete and that he would come back to her when it was over. "Have faith, my love. Everything will soon be set right," Anakin said. He told her where he was going, boarded his starship, and took off for his final mission.

After Anakin and R2-D2 left, C-3PO asked Padmé if there was anything he could do. "No, thank you, 3PO," Padmé whispered. What did C-3PO say to himself afterward?

A. "Some job this is."

B. "My lady, I'm under far too much stress."

C. "Oh, I feel so helpless."

D. "I'll be inside if you need me."

1148. When an ARC-170's S-foils are set to attack position, how many wings does it have?
- **A.** Four
- **B.** Eight
- **C.** Six
- **D.** Two

1149. Who manufactured the *Theta*-class T-2c shuttle?
- **A.** Cygnus Spaceworks
- **B.** Kuat Drive Yards
- **C.** Hoersch-Kessel Drive Inc.
- **D.** Gwori Revolutionary Industries

1150. What type of craft did Obi-Wan Kenobi fly on his journey to Utapau?
- **A.** ARC-170
- **B.** X-wing starfighter
- **C.** V-wing starfighter
- **D.** Jedi interceptor

1151. How many double laser cannons did the Tsmeu-6 have?
- **A.** Six
- **B.** Three
- **C.** One
- **D.** Two

1152. What are the hulls of Oevvaor catamarans made from?
- **A.** Oevvaor skeletons
- **B.** Phrik alloy
- **C.** Mustafarian alloy
- **D.** Wroshyr timber

1153. What craft did His Grace the Duke Gadal-Herm's Safety Inspectorate manufacture?
- **A.** Yoda's Kashyyyk escape pod
- **B.** Yoda's Dagobah landing pod
- **C.** General Grievous' escape pod
- **D.** The Techno Union starfighter

1154. Which Separatist group traveled in *Munificent*-class star frigates?
- **A.** The Commerce Guild
- **B.** The Hyper-Communications Cartel
- **C.** The IG Banking Clan
- **D.** The Corporate Alliance

1155. What were the clone troopers using to search for Yoda on Kashyyyk?
- **A.** AE-APs
- **B.** AT-RTs
- **C.** AE-OTs
- **D.** AT-PTs

1156. What was Stass Allie flying on Saleucami?
- **A.** BARC speeder
- **B.** Swoop skimmer
- **C.** Aratech 74-Z speeder
- **D.** ISP speeder

1157. How many nozzles does a firespeeder have?
- **A.** One
- **B.** Six
- **C.** Fifteen
- **D.** Four

Revenge of the Sith **Era**

1158. How did General Grievous remain seated in his wheel bike during fast, bumpy travel?

A. A containment field
B. Magnetic panels in the seat
C. He fit into custom-cut grooves
D. A holding strap

1159. How many deactivated battle droids can be stored on a Commerce Guild Support Destroyer?

A. Up to 130,000
B. Up to 80,000
C. Up to 40,000
D. Up to 100,000

1160. What is at the very topmost part of the HAVw A6 Juggernaut?

A. A domed turret
B. A remote activation antenna
C. A rapid-repeating heavy laser cannon
D. An observation post

1161. How did Obi-Wan Kenobi jump into hyperspace when on board his Jedi Interceptor?

A. He docked with a hyperdrive booster ring
B. His ship was equipped with a hyperdrive
C. He remained on a Star Destroyer until it jumped out of hyperspace
D. He didn't need to jump into hyperspace

1162.

1163. How many DBY-827 heavy turbolaser turrets does a *Venator*-class Star Destroyer have?

A. Two
B. Nine
C. Seven
D. Eight

1164. What type of craft did Obi-Wan Kenobi use to steal away from the clones on Utapau after they attacked him?

A. Jedi Interceptor
B. ARC-170
C. Belbullab-22 fighter
D. Porax-38 starfighter

1165. What did Anakin destroy in order to land on the *Invisible Hand*?

A. The blast door
B. The communications tower
C. The bridge
D. The atmosphere containment shield

1162.

Obi-Wan Kenobi and Yoda, hoping to change the false code broadcasting orders to all Jedi, managed to get past the clone troopers into the Jedi Temple, where they discovered a grisly scene. Younglings, Padawans, and Jedi lay dead throughout the Temple. Making matters more tragic, Yoda saw that some of the Jedi had not been killed by blasters, as originally suspected, but by a lightsaber. "Who? Who could have done this?" Obi-Wan Kenobi asked Master Yoda.

When Obi-Wan discovered that Anakin was responsible, he knew what he must do, even though he wasn't sure that he could. "Send me to kill the Emperor," Obi-Wan pleaded with Master Yoda. Yoda, however, was adamant. Obi-Wan had to fight his former apprentice.

Obi-Wan went to Padmé in order to discover Anakin's location. He told Padmé of Anakin's fall, but she refused to believe him even after he told her of the evidence, and would not tell Obi-Wan where Anakin had gone. Obi-Wan, however, kept watch over Padmé and stowed aboard her ship as she rushed to find Anakin. Where did he hide?

A. In a reserve fuel tank
B. In a storage locker
C. In the droid hold
D. In lounge

1166. How many proton torpedoes does an ARC-170 starfighter carry?
- **A.** Six
- **B.** Twenty
- **C.** Fourteen
- **D.** Two

1167. What was the HAVw A6 Juggernaut's maximum land speed?
- **A.** 90 kph
- **B.** 160 kph
- **C.** 190 kph
- **D.** 50 kph

1168. What does AT-PT stand for?
- **A.** All Terrain Private Transportation
- **B.** All Terrain Paramilitary Tank
- **C.** All Terrain Personal Transport
- **D.** All Terrain Patrol Transport

1169. What make is the *Invisible Hand*?
- **A.** Modified *Providence*-class carrier/destroyer
- **B.** *Defiance*-class carrier/destroyer
- **C.** Modified *Lancer*-class carrier/destroyer
- **D.** *Tormentor*-class carrier/destroyer

1170. What company manufactured the ARC-170 fighter?
- **A.** Kuat Drive Yards
- **B.** Kuat Systems Engineering
- **C.** Hoersch-Kessel Drive Inc.
- **D.** Incom/Subpro

1171. How many twin turbolaser cannons were in place on the Banking Clan's *Munificent*-class frigates?
- **A.** Thirty-six
- **B.** Ten
- **C.** Twenty-six
- **D.** Forty

1172. What Separatist organization produced the Mankvim-814 interceptor during the occupation of Utapau?
- **A.** Trade Federation
- **B.** Techno Union
- **C.** IG Banking Clan
- **D.** Commerce Guild

1173. What type of ship did Padmé take to Mustafar?
- **A.** Naboo star skiff
- **B.** Naboo cruiser
- **C.** Naboo royal starship
- **D.** Naboo yacht

Revenge of the Sith **Era**

1174. What ship did Bail Organa take to find Master Yoda?

A. *Alderaan Queen II*
B. *Radiant VII*
C. *Tantive IV*
D. *Alderaan Star II*

1175. Who said, "Another happy landing" after the *Invisible Hand*'s remnants landed safely on Coruscant?

A. Anakin Skywalker
B. Chancellor Palpatine
C. General Grievous
D. Obi-Wan Kenobi

1176. According to Master Yoda, where was General Grievous hiding?

A. In the Outer Rim
B. Beyond the Outer Rim
C. In the Rishi Maze
D. In the Galactic Core

1177. Which Jedi Master said he didn't trust Anakin Skywalker?

A. Ki-Adi-Mundi
B. Obi-Wan Kenobi
C. Mace Windu
D. Yoda

1178. What did Anakin tell Padmé she sounded like when she questioned the state of the Republic?

A. A Sith Lord
B. A Separatist
C. A mercenary
D. A Loyalist

1179. Who told Jar Jar to "watch it" as they were escorting Chancellor Palpatine from the landing platform?

A. Terr Taneel
B. Giddean Danu
C. Chi Eekway
D. Orn Free Taa

1180. Who discovered General Grievous' location?

A. Clone intelligence units
B. The Jedi
C. The Chancellor
D. Boba Fett

1181.

1182. What did Padmé tell Anakin the war represented?

A. A failure to act
B. A need for dialogue
C. A crumbling Republic
D. A failure to listen

1181.

After Obi-Wan Kenobi defeated General Grievous on Utapau, he found Commander Cody and gave him new orders, then mounted the varactyl Boga and sped away up the sinkhole wall. At that moment, the Emperor contacted Commander Cody and gave the signal for Order 66 to be executed. "Yes, my Lord," Cody responded. As clone troopers opened fire on them, Obi-Wan and Boga toppled from the sinkhole wall into the waters below. Obi-Wan used his A99 aquata breather to swim underwater away from the search area, while Boga climbed up the sinkhole to safety.

Obi-Wan escaped Utapau and joined Senator Organa, who had gone in search of any Jedi he could find. Obi-Wan talked with Yoda and Organa about the grave situation they were facing. Yoda told Obi-Wan that a coded retreat message was being broadcast from the Jedi Temple. Organa then told Obi-Wan what the message said. What did he say?

A. "It requests all Jedi to go directly to Mustafar for an emergency meeting."
B. "It requests all Jedi stay far away from Coruscant."
C. "It requests all Jedi to return to the Temple. It says the war is over."
D. "It requests that all Jedi arrest their clone troopers. It says they are dangerous."

1183. What was a pathway to many abilities some consider to be unnatural?

A. The Force

B. The dark side of the Force

C. The Separatist movement

D. The Jedi Order

1184. What did the Jedi Council ask Anakin to do after he was made a member?

A. Report on the Chancellor's actions

B. Lead the battle on Kashyyyk

C. Lead the battle on Utapau

D. Take on a Padawan

1185. What hallway were the Jedi in when the battle droid told General Grievous that they had been found?

A. Hallway 21

B. Hallway 832

C. Hallway 99

D. Hallway 328

1186. What did Obi-Wan Kenobi tell Tion Medon after Medon revealed that General Grievous was on Utapau?

A. "Tell your people to leave the city at once—they are in great danger."

B. "Tell your people to take shelter. If you have warriors, now is the time."

C. "Tell your people that all will be well—the Jedi are here now."

D. "Tell your people to get to their ships at once."

1187. What did Anakin tell the Jedi Council in regards to Chancellor Palpatine's news that General Grievous was in hiding on Utapau?

A. They had discovered scrambled transmissions from Grievous to Nute Gunray

B. They had placed a tracker on General Grievous' ship before he departed Coruscant

C. A partial message was intercepted in a diplomatic packet from the chairman of Utapau

D. The Utapauns had directly contacted the Chancellor and relayed the General's location to him

1188. What nightmare did Anakin Skywalker have?

A. He dreamed that Shmi Skywalker died

B. He dreamed that the Republic fell to the Separatists

C. He dreamed that he turned to the dark side

D. He dreamed that Padmé died giving birth

Revenge of the Sith Era

1189. What did Obi-Wan Kenobi use to chase General Grievous after Grievous escaped in his wheel bike?

A. A BARC speeder

B. An AT-RT

C. An AT-PT

D. Boga

1190. What did Palpatine tell Darth Vader the galaxy would have under Sith rule?

A. Organization

B. Peace

C. Security

D. Military rule

1191. What elevator were Anakin and Obi-Wan traveling on in their mission to save the Chancellor?

A. Elevator 6-5000

B. Elevator 1138

C. Elevator 911

D. Elevator 31174

1192. What sinister order did Emperor Palpatine give Commander Cody?

A. Order 29

B. Order 62

C. Order 66

D. Order 11

1193. What report did Mace Windu ask Anakin to deliver to Chancellor Palpatine?

A. Yoda had landed on Kashyyyk

B. Master Vos had won the Battle of Saleucami

C. Master Kenobi was on his way to Utapau

D. Master Kenobi had made contact with General Grievous

1194. What did Obi-Wan say his journey to Utapau might turn out to be?

A. A wild bantha chase

B. A wild eopie chase

C. A wild kowakian monkey-lizard chase

D. A wild nos monster chase

1195. Who said of the Chancellor, "If he does not give up his emergency powers after the destruction of Grievous, then he should be removed from office"?

A. Mace Windu

B. Aayla Secura

C. Yoda

D. Ki-Adi-Mundi

OBSESSED WITH *STAR WARS*

1200.

Commander Cody had just reported in to the Jedi Council that Obi-Wan Kenobi was actively pursuing Grievous on Utapau.

At the same time, Anakin was making a grim discovery: Chancellor Palpatine was the Sith Lord that the Jedi had been searching for since the demise of his first mentor, Qui-Gon Jinn. When Anakin reported his findings to Mace Windu, Mace told Anakin that he was going to the Chancellor's office to deliver the news that General Grievous had fallen and that the war was over.

"Master Windu!" the Chancellor burbled when the Jedi entered his office. "I take it General Grievous has been destroyed then." They ignited their lightsabers as Mace Windu told the Chancellor that he was under arrest and that the Senate would decide his fate. "I *am* the Senate," the Chancellor growled.

"Not yet," Mace replied. What did the Chancellor say in return?

A. "You Jedi are too smug for your own good."
B. "I will do as you say."
C. "It's treason then."
D. "You will not stop me, Jedi."

1196. What reason did the clone trooper give Senator Organa for the troopers' presence at the Jedi Temple?
A. There had been an attack on the Temple
B. There had been a rebellion
C. There had been a fire
D. There had been an invasion

1197. What did Chancellor Palpatine tell Anakin Skywalker that the Jedi Council wanted when the two were talking at the Galaxies Opera House?
A. An end to the war
B. General Grievous's capture
C. The Chancellor's re-election
D. Control of the Republic

1198. What did Obi-Wan tell R2-D2 to hit in order to destroy the buzz droid that was attacking Anakin's Jedi Interceptor?
A. The center eye
B. The drill head
C. The communications antenna
D. The outer hull

1199. Who said, "Army or not, you must realize you are doomed"?
A. Count Dooku
B. Chancellor Palpatine
C. General Grievous
D. Darth Sidious

1200.

1201. How many clone troopers tried to kill Master Yoda after they were given Order 66?
A. Two
B. Five
C. Eleven
D. One

1202. After Obi-Wan departed for Utapau, how did Anakin tell Padmé that he felt?
A. Angry
B. Depressed
C. Hopeless
D. Lost

1203. Who said, "The Chancellor's office indicated that Master Anakin returned to the Jedi Temple"?
A. Captain Typho
B. C-3PO
C. Obi-Wan Kenobi
D. Senator Organa

Revenge of the Sith **Era**

1204. How many super battle droids accompanied Count Dooku when he confronted Anakin Skywalker and Obi-Wan Kenobi?

A. Four   C. Three

B. Six   D. Two

1205. Who made sure that Yoda got to his escape pod on Kashyyyk?

A. Tarfful and Chewbacca   C. Chewbacca and Guanta

B. Tarfful and Guanta   D. Tarfful and Lachichuk

1206. What did Anakin Skywalker say he would "certainly like to" do after he discovered that Chancellor Palpatine was a Sith Lord?

A. Report his findings to the Jedi Council   C. Kill the Chancellor

B. Join the Sith   D. Learn how to save Padmé

1207. What emergency code did Obi-Wan begin transmitting after he escaped Utapau?

A. Emergency code 9-13   C. Emergency code 4-09

B. Emergency code 911   D. Emergency code 1

1208. How did Obi-Wan Kenobi defeat General Grievous?

A. In hand-to-hand combat   C. With a blaster

B. With a lightsaber   D. With an electrostaff

1209.

1210. Who, according to Chancellor Palpatine, was searching for a life of significance, of conscience?

A. Anakin Skywalker   C. Mace Windu

B. Yoda   D. Aayla Secura

1211. Who said, "The dark side of the Force surrounds the Chancellor"?

A. Yoda   C. Aayla Secura

B. Mace Windu   D. Ki-Adi-Mundi

1212. What did Padmé promise Anakin?

A. She was going to have their baby on Naboo   C. She would talk to the Chancellor and sort things out

B. She would stay by his side no matter what   D. She was not going to die in childbirth

1209.

"Hello there!" Obi-Wan Kenobi said after jumping into a massive group of battle droids, super battle droids, Magna-Guards, and, most importantly, General Grievous. Obi-Wan had been hiding above the General, listening to him give the Separatist leaders instructions. When the time was right, he made his move.

"General Kenobi! You are a bold one," General Grievous cackled. "Kill him," he ordered the MagnaGuards. Obi-Wan used the Force to trap the MagnaGuards, and as the battle droids made a move to attack Obi-Wan, General Grievous commanded them to stand back. He would deal with the Jedi himself.

"Your move," Obi-Wan said. With that, Grievous removed his cape and unhinged his arms, igniting several light-sabers. The two battled over the scaffolding of Pau City as Grievous's legions of droids watched in interest. Grievous battled ferociously, but his metal body was no match for Obi-Wan's abilities with the Force.

The clone troopers landed, distracting Grievous momentarily. Obi-Wan used a Force push that sent Grievous flying. Grievous then leapt to his feet and boarded a vehicle. What was it?

A. An AT-ST

B. A BARC speeder

C. An AT-PT

D. A wheel bike

1213. Which Jedi did Chancellor Palpatine kill first?
- **A.** Agen Kolar
- **B.** Kit Fisto
- **C.** Saesee Tiin
- **D.** Mace Windu

1214. Who said, "You have hate, you have anger, but you don't use them!"?
- **A.** Chancellor Palpatine
- **B.** Master Yoda
- **C.** Count Dooku
- **D.** Darth Sidious

1215. How did Darth Plagueis die?
- **A.** The Jedi hunted him down
- **B.** His apprentice killed him
- **C.** He died of old age
- **D.** His Master killed him

1216. Where did Mace Windu tell Anakin Skywalker to wait while the Jedi went to arrest the Chancellor?
- **A.** In the Room of One Thousand Fountains
- **B.** In the Jedi Temple's hangar
- **C.** In the Chancellor's outer office
- **D.** In the Jedi Council chamber

1217. What did Anakin's anger do, according to Chancellor Palpatine?
- **A.** It made him upset
- **B.** It made him confused
- **C.** It gave him focus and made him stronger
- **D.** It made him violent and unorganized

1218. What made Nute Gunray feel that General Grievous would be unable to keep the Separatist leaders safe?
- **A.** The Jedi were still on the loose
- **B.** Chancellor Palpatine managed to escape his grip
- **C.** General Grievous was just a droid
- **D.** General Grievous had failed before

1219. How many, according to the Emperor, had achieved the power to cheat death?
- **A.** One
- **B.** Three
- **C.** None
- **D.** Two

Revenge of the Sith **Era**

1220. How many of General Grievous's hands did Obi-Wan cut off during their lightsaber battle on Utapau?

A. One   **C.** Three

B. Four   **D.** Two

1221. What did Yoda tell Anakin was the "shadow of greed"?

A. Hatred   **C.** Jealousy

B. Longing   **D.** Anger

1222. After Anakin returned from his dark mission at the Jedi Temple, what did he tell Padmé was happening?

A. The Jedi had tried to overthrow the Republic   **C.** Obi-Wan Kenobi had been successful on Utapau and the war was over

B. The Chancellor had revealed himself as a Sith Lord   **D.** The Chancellor had given up his emergency powers

1223. What elevator did Anakin ask R2-D2 to activate after he had rescued the Chancellor?

A. Elevator 747   **C.** Elevator 99

B. Elevator 42   **D.** Elevator 3224

1224. Where did Anakin tell Padmé that he was going in order to end the war?

A. Mygeeto   **C.** Saleucami

B. Mustafar   **D.** Felucia

1225. What reason did Anakin have to tell Mace Windu not to kill Chancellor Palpatine?

A. Palpatine alone could help him save Padmé   **C.** Palpatine had to stand trial

B. Palpatine wasn't a Sith Lord after all   **D.** Palpatine was his friend

1226. What did Yoda tell Obi-Wan to use in order to find out where Darth Vader had gone?

A. A tracking device   **C.** Navigation maps

B. His feelings   **D.** His instinct

1231.

Darth Vader, once known as Anakin Skywalker, had been defeated by his former Master Obi-Wan Kenobi, who had severed both his legs and his left arm in a grim ending to their epic battle on Mustafar. Sensing that his new apprentice was in danger, the Emperor commanded a shuttle to take him to Mustafar immediately. The Emperor found Darth Vader lying on the molten edge of a lava river, barely conscious.

The ruler of the galaxy sped to Coruscant and escorted his apprentice into the secret surgery suite at the very top spire of a major medical facility. As droids worked tirelessly on Darth Vader's burned body, replacing flesh with machine, Vader cried out in pain. Finally, after the droids had finished operating, Darth Vader was encased in the helmet

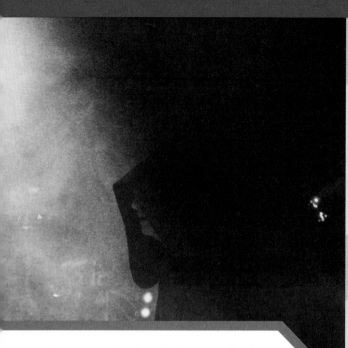

1227. Who did General Grievous contact upon landing on Utapau?
- **A.** Count Dooku
- **B.** Darth Tyranus
- **C.** Tion Medon
- **D.** Darth Sidious

1228. What was Emperor Palpatine's final order for Darth Vader before Padmé arrived on Mustafar?
- **A.** "Send a message to the ships of the Trade Federation. All droid units are needed on Coruscant."
- **B.** "Send a message to the ships of the Confederacy of Independent Systems. All droid units must shut down immediately."
- **C.** "Send a message to the ships of the Techno Union. All droid units must return to Metalorn."
- **D.** "Send a message to the ships of the Trade Federation. All droid units must shut down immediately."

1229. Who contacted Senator Organa regarding a special session of Congress?
- **A.** Sei Taria
- **B.** Mas Amedda
- **C.** Sly Moore
- **D.** Chancellor Palpatine

1230. Who said, "If one is to understand the great mystery, one must study all its aspects"?
- **A.** Chancellor Palpatine
- **B.** General Grievous
- **C.** Anakin Skywalker
- **D.** Count Dooku

1231.

1232. Who said, "Welcome Lord Vader. We've been expecting you"?
- **A.** Wat Tambor
- **B.** Shu Mai
- **C.** Nute Gunray
- **D.** Rune Haako

1233. Whose presence did Chancellor Palpatine announce when Obi-Wan Kenobi and Anakin Skywalker arrived to rescue him aboard the *Invisible Hand*?
- **A.** General Grievous
- **B.** Count Dooku
- **C.** Darth Sidious
- **D.** Darth Maul

that would spread fear throughout the galaxy. The Emperor leaned in close to his apprentice. "Lord Vader, can you hear me?" he asked.

"Yes, Master," Darth Vader breathed. "Where is Padmé? Is she safe? Is she all right?" he asked. What did the Emperor tell him?

- **A.** "She is well, Lord Vader. Do not worry."
- **B.** "Her whereabouts are still unknown, Lord Vader."
- **C.** "The Jedi assassinated her."
- **D.** "It seems in your anger, you killed her."

Revenge of the Sith Era

1234. Into what did Emperor Palpatine reorganize the Republic?
- **A.** The first Galactic Empire
- **B.** The Second Galactic Empire
- **C.** The Third Galactic Empire
- **D.** The New Republic

1235. What actor portrayed Senator Orn Free Taa in *Revenge of the Sith*?
- **A.** Ahmed Best
- **B.** Oliver Ford Davies
- **C.** Kee Chan
- **D.** Matt Rowan

1236. Aayla Secura was a Twi'lek Jedi. What actress portrayed her in *Revenge of the Sith*?
- **A.** Bonnie Piesse
- **B.** Michonne Bourriague
- **C.** Amy Allen
- **D.** Genevieve O'Reilly

1237. Who was the director of concept design for *Revenge of the Sith*?
- **A.** Peter Russell
- **B.** David Lee
- **C.** Phil Harvey
- **D.** Ian Gracie

1238. Which *Revenge of the Sith* scene used shots of Tunisia as the background?
- **A.** The Mustafar battle
- **B.** The Lars homestead
- **C.** The Mygeeto clone trooper attack
- **D.** The Theed funeral procession

1239. Who was the second assistant director?
- **A.** Stephen Jones
- **B.** Paul Sullivan
- **C.** Colin Fletcher
- **D.** Deborah Antoniou

1240. Which *Revenge of the Sith* scene was partially filmed in Phuket, Thailand?
- **A.** The Naboo Funeral Procession
- **B.** Yoda's landing on Dagobah
- **C.** The Battle of Kashyyyk
- **D.** The Battle of Felucia

1241. What actor reprised his role as Chewbacca in *Revenge of the Sith*?
- **A.** Michael Kingma
- **B.** Peter Mayhew
- **C.** Axel Dench
- **D.** James Rowland

1242. What character did Wayne Pygram play in *Revenge of the Sith*?
- **A.** Governor Tarkin
- **B.** Plo Koon
- **C.** Captain Typho
- **D.** Giddean Danu

OBSESSED WITH *STAR WARS*

1243. Who played Agen Kolar in *Revenge of the Sith*?
- **A.** Matt Sloan
- **B.** Kenji Oates
- **C.** David Bowers
- **D.** Tux Akindoyeni

1244. Who supplied the voice for General Grievous in *Revenge of the Sith*?
- **A.** Frank Oz
- **B.** Michael Kingma
- **C.** Matthew Wood
- **D.** Warren Owens

1245. Who played Commander Cody in *Revenge of the Sith*?
- **A.** Jay Laga'aia
- **B.** Temuera Morrison
- **C.** Ahmed Best
- **D.** Joel Edgerton

1246. What actor played Tion Medon in *Revenge of the Sith*?
- **A.** Bruce Spence
- **B.** David Bowers
- **C.** Silas Carson
- **D.** Jay Laga'aia

1247. What character did Sandi Finlay portray in *Revenge of the Sith*?
- **A.** Chi Eekway
- **B.** Sly Moore
- **C.** Mon Mothma
- **D.** Pooja Naberrie

1248. What was Marco Nero's role in production for *Revenge of the Sith*?
- **A.** Props runner
- **B.** Sculptor
- **C.** Model maker
- **D.** Concept designer

1249. What character did Joel Edgerton play in *Revenge of the Sith*?
- **A.** Ruwee Naberrie
- **B.** Owen Lars
- **C.** Captain Colton
- **D.** Captain Antilles

1250.

1250.

This actress became the youngest ever to be nominated for a Best Actress in a Leading Role Oscar, for her first starring film role in 2002's *Whale Rider*. Since that time, she has been nominated for, and has won, several awards, including the Broadcast Film Critics Association Award for Best Young Actor/Actress for the same film. When she was nominated for an Oscar, she said, "I keep having to pinch myself to make sure I'm actually awake."

She is part Maori and moved to New Zealand from Australia when she was four years old. She has been studying Maori dance since she was six. Since her role in *Whale Rider*, she has been seen in *The Nativity Story*, in which she played Mary.

In *Revenge of the Sith*, she played the new Queen of Naboo, Queen Apailana, and she can be seen following Padmé's funeral capsule through the streets of Theed. Who is she?

- **A.** Pernilla August
- **B.** Keira Knightley
- **C.** Keisha Castle-Hughes
- **D.** Amy Allen

1251. Baron Papanoida was a Wroonian, and some said a double agent. Who portrayed him in *Revenge of the Sith*?
- **A.** Rick McCallum
- **B.** George Lucas
- **C.** Anthony Daniels
- **D.** John Knoll

1252. Who portrayed Mas Amedda in *Revenge of the Sith*?
- **A.** Jerome Blake
- **B.** David Bowers
- **C.** Oliver Ford Davies
- **D.** Ahmed Best

Revenge of the Sith Era

STAR WARS

™

EPISODE IV

A NEW HOPE

1253. Who was jokingly called "Wormie" as a youngster?
- A. Luke Skywalker
- B. Han Solo
- C. Princess Leia
- D. Owen Lars

1254. How tall was Han Solo?
- A. 2.5 meters
- B. 1.5 meters
- C. 1.8 meters
- D. 2.3 meters

1255. What was Luke planning to pick up at Tosche Station?
- A. Energy converters
- B. Battery packs
- C. Power converters
- D. Power packs

1256. Who taught Han Solo how to understand Shyriiwook?
- A. Chewbacca
- B. Tarfful
- C. Dewlanna
- D. Mallatobuck

1257. To which planet did Bail Organa take Leia in order for her to witness the Great Meet herd ceremony?
- A. Naboo
- B. Aqualish
- C. Ithor
- D. Dantooine

1258. Princess Leia traveled to Kattada for talks regarding giving aid to Ralltiir. With whom did she speak?
- A. Captain Antilles
- B. Mia Ikova
- C. Lord Tion
- D. Commander Karg

1259. Whom did Darth Vader battle on Maryx Minor?
A. Boba Fett
C. Aurra Sing
B. The Dark Woman
D. Prince Xizor

1260. With whom did Obi-Wan Kenobi study during his exile on Tatooine?
A. Yoda
C. Ki-Adi-Mundi
B. Qui-Gon Jinn
D. Luke Skywalker

1261.

1262. What had Obi-Wan Kenobi come to be known as on Tatooine?
A. Ken
C. Obi
B. Ben
D. Wan

1263. Which galaxy-renowned professor taught history to Princess Leia Organa?
A. Giles Durane
C. Milis O'ball
B. Teek Plok
D. Arn Horada

1264. Where did Luke Skywalker race his skyhopper?
A. Waldo Flats
C. Beggar's Canyon
B. The Dune Sea
D. The Desert Plain

1265. Who was referred to as a "crazy old hermit" by the locals on Tatooine?
A. Owen Lars
C. Obi-Wan Kenobi
B. Huff Darklighter
D. Sharad Hett

1266. On which planet did Darth Vader's evil scientists accidentally release a lethal bioagent?
A. Muunilinst
C. Falleen
B. Xagobah
D. Ylesia

1261.

Princess Leia was being pursued by an Imperial Star Destroyer as she sped toward Tatooine in an attempt to fulfill her secret mission as an important member of the Rebel Alliance. As the Star Destroyer ensnared the *Tantive IV*, Leia raced to salvage her mission. Sequestered in a side corridor, Leia worked with a loyal droid to ensure the future of the Rebel Alliance and watched pensively as the droid fled the scene to carry out her instructions. Leia was discovered by Imperial stormtroopers, who captured her after a brief battle. "She'll be all right. Inform Lord Vader we have a prisoner," one stormtrooper said.

When Leia was taken before Darth Vader, she started to assert her rights as a diplomat, but she was cut off by the Dark Lord. "Don't act so surprised, Your Highness. You weren't on any mercy mission this time. Several transmissions were beamed to this ship by Rebel spies. I want to know what happened to the plans they sent you."

Leia scoffed. "I don't know what you're talking about." What did she tell him she was doing?

A. She was on a rescue mission
B. She was on a political mission
C. She was on a diplomatic mission
D. She was on a peacekeeping mission

1267. Who said, "One thing's for sure—we're all gonna be a lot thinner"?
- **A.** Princess Leia
- **B.** Han Solo
- **C.** C-3PO
- **D.** Luke Skywalker

1268. What did Luke Skywalker tell Han Solo about Princess Leia that made him change his mind about rescuing her?
- **A.** That she was a leader in the Rebellion
- **B.** That she could get him a good job
- **C.** That she was rich
- **D.** That she was famous

1269. How tall was Luke Skywalker?
- **A.** 1.48 meters
- **B.** 2.20 meters
- **C.** 1.72 meters
- **D.** 1.91 meters

1270. Who took Han Solo in as a small child?
- **A.** Talon Karrde
- **B.** Garris Shrike
- **C.** Jabba the Hutt
- **D.** Dexter Jettster

1271. Who was Princess Leia's best friend as a child?
- **A.** Winter
- **B.** Fall
- **C.** Summer
- **D.** Spring

1272. According to Obi-Wan Kenobi, for how long had the Jedi been the guardians of peace and justice in the galaxy?
- **A.** More than a hundred generations
- **B.** More than a thousand generations
- **C.** More than two millennia
- **D.** More than two thousand years

1273. On which planet did Darth Vader have a private retreat?
- **A.** Kamino
- **B.** Tatooine
- **C.** Vjun
- **D.** Onderon

1274. Who said to Princess Leia, "I care"?
- **A.** Obi-Wan Kenobi
- **B.** Luke Skywalker
- **C.** Han Solo
- **D.** C-3PO

A New Hope Era

1275. What criminal who had proclaimed himself "King of Corellia" did a young Han Solo discover he was related to through the genealogy charts he found?

A. Lana the Blue
B. Dalla the Red
C. Dalla the Black
D. Lana the Black

1276.

1277. What did Princess Leia discover from a wounded Rebel while on a diplomatic mission to Ralltiir?

A. That she was adopted
B. That the Emperor was going to dissolve the Senate
C. That the Empire was constructing the Death Star
D. That Darth Vader was tracking her

1278. What did Han Solo do after he arrived on Coruscant?

A. Joined the Rebel Alliance
B. Joined the Imperial Navy
C. Won the *Millennium Falcon* from Lando Calrissian
D. Enlisted with the Hutts as a spice smuggler

1279. What was Han Solo's homeworld?

A. Dantooine
B. Corellia
C. Coruscant
D. Alderaan

1280. How tall was Princess Leia?

A. 1.5 meters
B. 1.1 meters
C. 1.9 meters
D. 2.1 meters

1281. What infamous galactic denizen witnessed a seventeen-year-old Han Solo win the All-Human Free-For-All on Jubilar?

A. Aurra Sing
B. Jabba the Hutt
C. Boba Fett
D. Gardulla the Hutt

1282. Who trained Princess Leia in self-defense?

A. Bail Organa
B. Breha Organa
C. Jan Dodonna
D. Giles Durane

1276.

Obi-Wan Kenobi, Luke Skywalker, C-3PO, and R2-D2 had found what they thought was safe passage off Tatooine in the *Millennium Falcon*, a ship owned and piloted by Han Solo. Solo, eager to pay off debts, had been more than happy to accept the tidy sum Obi-Wan Kenobi had promised him once they reached their destination. He soon found out that he had gotten more than he bargained for: stormtroopers flooded the docking bay where the *Millennium Falcon* was housed and opened fire, attempting to stop Solo from taking off.

Solo was too quick for the troopers, however, and managed to fire a few shots before blasting out of Mos Eisley. Once out of the planet's atmosphere, Solo lamented his decision. "Our passengers must be hotter than I thought," Solo said, noting that Star Destroyers were now in pursuit of his ship.

Solo began making the calculations for the jump to lightspeed, but as he did so, he told Chewbacca to do something to hold off their attackers. What did he tell Chewbacca to do?

A. Activate the cloaking device
B. Open fire
C. Jettison the spare parts
D. Angle the deflector shield

1283. With whom did a young Han Solo fall in love on Ylesia?
- **A.** Renna Shi
- **B.** Bria Tharen
- **C.** Shira Brie
- **D.** Amaiza Foxtrain

1284. What was Darth Vader's homeworld?
- **A.** Dantooine
- **B.** Yavin 4
- **C.** Tatooine
- **D.** Coruscant

1285. What freighter did Han Solo spend most of his childhood on?
- **A.** The *Spicer's Hideaway*
- **B.** The *Miner's Penchant*
- **C.** The *Trader's Luck*
- **D.** The *Open Door*

1286. Who said, "I recognized your foul stench when I was brought on board"?
- **A.** Darth Vader
- **B.** Grand Moff Tarkin
- **C.** Princess Leia
- **D.** Obi-Wan Kenobi

1287. Who was one of the last Jedi to be struck down by Darth Vader before the Battle of Yavin?
- **A.** Yaddle
- **B.** The Dark Woman
- **C.** Bant
- **D.** Yoda

1288. Who exclaimed, "HE's the brains, sweetheart!"?
- **A.** Luke Skywalker
- **B.** Han Solo
- **C.** Princess Leia
- **D.** Obi-Wan Kenobi

1289. How tall was Darth Vader?
- **A.** 2.20 meters
- **B.** 1.81 meters
- **C.** 2.02 meters
- **D.** 2.50 meters

1290. Who lived beyond the Dune Sea?
- **A.** Biggs Darklighter
- **B.** Obi-Wan Kenobi
- **C.** Tank
- **D.** Toby

A New Hope Era

1291. What was the name of Darth Vader's castle?

A. Castle Vader

B. Castle Dark Side

C. Bast Castle

D. Lurdo Castle

1292. How many Falleen natives did Darth Vader order "sterilized" by orbital bombardment after an experiment conducted by his scientists went awry, releasing a tissue-destroying bacterium?

A. 100,000

B. 300,000

C. 200,000

D. 150,000

1293.

1294. Who referred to Obi-Wan Kenobi as a "crazy old man"?

A. Han Solo

B. Beru Lars

C. Owen Lars

D. Darth Vader

1295. What was Grand Moff Tarkin's first name?

A. Maurice

B. Wilhelm

C. Wilhuff

D. Moriz

1296. Who was lurking outside the *Millennium Falcon* when Han Solo arrived to prepare it for immediate departure?

A. Gardulla the Hutt

B. Jabba the Hutt

C. Aurra Sing

D. Greedo

1297. Who said, "If he gets a translator, be sure it speaks Bocce"?

A. Owen Lars

B. Luke Skywalker

C. Beru Lars

D. Han Solo

1298. What earned Tarkin his promotion from Governor to Moff?

A. The Raaltiir Massacre

B. The Alderaan Massacre

C. The Ghorman Massacre

D. The Naboo Massacre

1293.

Princess Leia had been captured and escorted to the Empire's secret weapon, the Death Star. There, she endured many tortures at the ruthless hands of Darth Vader, including exposure to the horrifying mind probe. Although she resisted the probe's influence, a testament to her strength and conviction, she would soon face an even greater peril.

As Darth Vader relayed to Grand Moff Tarkin Princess Leia's refusal to reveal the location of the Rebel base, Tarkin decided on an action that he thought would surely get the information from her, and he instructed Admiral Motti to set the station's course for Leia's home planet. As the station loomed over Leia's home planet, Tarkin summoned her to the Death Star's control room. "Governor Tarkin, I should have expected to find you holding Vader's leash," she sneered at the Governor.

He responded by saying that he had found a particular task difficult. What was it?

A. Ordering the capture of the *Tantive IV*

B. Choosing a planet to use as a demonstration of the Death Star's power

C. Signing the order to terminate her life

D. Coming to terms with the fact that she was a Rebel spy

1299. To whom did Han Solo say, "You're a wonderful human being"?
- **A.** Obi-Wan Kenobi
- **B.** Jabba the Hutt
- **C.** Luke Skywalker
- **D.** Darth Vader

1300. Who was Chewbacca's wife?
- **A.** Wishilirikk
- **B.** Vanessa
- **C.** Mallatobuck
- **D.** Lumpawarrump

1301. Over what was Tarkin given almost unlimited jurisdiction when Emperor Palpatine made him Grand Moff?
- **A.** Oversector Outer
- **B.** The Corporate Sector
- **C.** The Perlemian Trade Route
- **D.** The Core Worlds

1302. What was Jabba the Hutt's homeworld?
- **A.** Da Soocha V
- **B.** Tatooine
- **C.** Nal Hutta
- **D.** Nar Shaddaa

1303. After Luke Skywalker and his friend Windy were rescued from an attack by a vicious desert creature and taken back to the Lars homestead by Obi-Wan Kenobi, how did Owen Lars react?
- **A.** He was overjoyed that they were safe
- **B.** He yelled at Obi-Wan to get off his property and never come back
- **C.** He thanked Obi-Wan profusely
- **D.** He took away Luke's skyhopper privileges

1304. What was Beru Lars' homeworld?
- **A.** Ator
- **B.** Coruscant
- **C.** Tatooine
- **D.** Dantooine

1305. How tall was Chewbacca?
- **A.** 2.41 meters
- **B.** 2.28 meters
- **C.** 2.36 meters
- **D.** 2.52 meters

1306. What was Grand Moff Tarkin's impression of Princess Leia aboard the Death Star?
- **A.** "Impertinent to the last"
- **B.** "Charming to the last"
- **C.** "Pompous to the last"
- **D.** "Arrogant to the last"

A New Hope Era

1307. On which planet did Han Solo accept Chewbacca as his partner?

A. Tatooine
B. Devaron
C. Kashyyyk
D. Nar Shaddaa

1308. Who said, "You can waste time with your friends when your chores are done"?

A. Beru Lars
B. Tank
C. Biggs Darklighter
D. Owen Lars

1309. What was Grand Moff Tarkin's homeworld?

A. Coruscant
B. Dantooine
C. Eriadu
D. Alderaan

1310.

1311. What cargo was Jabba upset that Han Solo had jettisoned?

A. Slyth
B. Death sticks
C. Glitterstim
D. Dianoga spleens

1312. What organization did Grand Moff Tarkin join after graduating from the Academy?

A. The Republic Outland Regions Security Force
B. The Republic Outlands Task Force
C. The Imperial Reserve
D. The Imperial Outland Regions Security Reserve

1313. What was Jabba's full Huttese name?

A. Jabba Diamanda Tremaine
B. Jabba Quatrain Fromugguh
C. Jabba Desilijic Tiure
D. Jabba Quarrelle Prommudduh

1314. What was Owen Lars' job?

A. Eopie farmer
B. Dwarf nuna farmer
C. Moisture farmer
D. Dewback farmer

1310.

Luke was cleaning the protocol and astromech droids that he and his uncle had just purchased from the Jawas when he accidentally activated a holographic message in the R2 unit. Stuck on a loop, the image did not say anything except, "Help me, Obi-Wan Kenobi. You're my only hope." Luke wanted to see the entire message, but R2-D2 said that the restraining bolt had short-circuited his recording systems and suggested that Luke remove it. When Luke removed the bolt, however, the message stopped and R2-D2 clammed up. At that moment, Luke was called in to dinner.

Luke discussed what he had found with his aunt and uncle, who were disturbed by what they heard. "In the morning I

1315. What did Princess Leia call Chewbacca?

A. A fuzzball
B. A furry oaf
C. A walking carpet
D. A rug

1316. How tall was Grand Moff Tarkin?

A. 1.2 meters
B. 1.8 meters
C. 1.6 meters
D. 2.0 meters

1317. Over which penal colony planet did Grand Moff Tarkin supervise the construction of the Death Star?

A. Akrit'tar
B. Mytus VII
C. Despayre
D. Dorvalla

1318. Of whom was Grand Moff Tarkin speaking when he said, "Surely he must be dead by now"?

A. Qui-Gon Jinn
B. Yoda
C. Obi-Wan Kenobi
D. Quinlan Vos

1319. When young Luke Skywalker demonstrated his latent Force abilities by finding a missing tool without even searching for it, what did Owen Lars do?

A. He congratulated him on using the Force
B. He told him of his heritage
C. He scolded him
D. He acted as if nothing had happened

1320. How many seasons more did Owen Lars say he needed Luke to stay on at the farm?

A. Four
B. Two
C. One
D. Three

1321. Who said, "Evacuate? In our moment of triumph?"

A. Admiral Motti
B. Captain Yorr
C. Darth Vader
D. Grand Moff Tarkin

1322. What was the name of Grand Moff Tarkin's protégé and mistress, a woman he met on Carida?

A. Maala
B. Tasha
C. Daala
D. Yaala

want you to take those droids into Anchorhead and have their memories erased," Uncle Owen said. Luke then brought up wanting to transmit his application to the Academy and leave the farm, but Uncle Owen said he needed Luke. After Luke left to finish his chores, Beru Lars said something to Owen. What was it?

A. "If he's anything like his father, you should never let him leave."
B. "Don't try to keep Luke from growing up, Owen."
C. "Keep him here as long as you can."
D. "Owen, he can't stay here forever. Most of his friends have gone."

A New Hope Era

1323. What, according to Grand Moff Tarkin, would keep the local systems in line?

A. Fear

B. The Senate

C. Taxes

D. Allegiance

1324. What did Han Solo ask Chewbacca to do as they were approaching the Death Star?

A. Get the smuggling compartments ready

B. Turn the ship around

C. Lock in the auxiliary power

D. Fire at will

1325. Who introduced Obi-Wan Kenobi and Luke Skywalker to Han Solo?

A. Boshek

B. Chewbacca

C. Danz Borin

D. Dannik Jerriko

1326.

1327. How old was Chewbacca at the Battle of Yavin?

A. Approximately three hundred years old

B. Approximately four hundred years old

C. Approximately two hundred years old

D. Approximately six hundred years old

1328. How much extra did Jabba say he needed Han to pay him back?

A. 10 percent

B. 20 percent

C. 25 percent

D. 15 percent

1329. Who said, "He's got too much of his father in him"?

A. Owen Lars

B. Biggs Darklighter

C. Obi-Wan Kenobi

D. Beru Lars

1330. What was the name of Chewbacca's son?

A. Chumpawarrup

B. Tumpawarrump

C. Lumpawarrump

D. Dunpawarrup

1326.

While the *Millennium Falcon* was soaring through hyperspace toward its destination, Luke Skywalker was practicing his lightsaber skills with a remote. The tiny ball zoomed through the air randomly, emitting short, sharp shocks that Luke tried to evade or strike with his lightsaber.

While Luke was training, Obi-Wan felt a disturbance in the Force, as if millions of voices had suddenly cried out in terror and then were suddenly silenced. He felt that something terrible had happened. Not wanting to scare Luke, he told the boy to get on with his training. Han Solo then walked in and announced that he had outrun the Imperials, but Luke was too busy concentrating on the remote and Obi-Wan was too worried to acknowledge Han's news.

OBSESSED WITH *STAR WARS*

Chewbacca, R2-D2 and C-3PO were also too engaged to notice Han's entrance. R2-D2 and Chewie were playing a heated game of Dejarik, a holographic game in which monsters from around the galaxy battle each other. R2-D2 made a move that upset Chewbacca, who started growling in protest. "He made a fair move. Screaming about it won't help you," C-3PO incautiously scolded the Wookiee. What did Han Solo tell C-3PO the repercussions of upsetting a Wookiee were?

A. Getting your legs ripped off

B. Getting your arms pulled out of their sockets

C. Getting your kneecaps broken

D. Getting beaten up

1331. What did Jabba tell Han Solo would happen if he didn't pay him back?

A. He'd hunt him down and kill him

B. He would make it so Han Solo would never work again

C. He would detonate the bomb he had planted in the *Millennium Falcon*

D. He'd put a price on his head so big he wouldn't be able to go near a civilized system

1332. What rank did Wilhuff Tarkin reach in the Republic Outland Regions Security Force before retiring?

A. Captain

B. Commander

C. Lieutenant

D. Admiral

1333. What Commander in the Rebel Alliance assisted General Dodonna in devising the plan to destroy the Death Star?

A. Commander Nernon Flobonka

B. Commander Evram Lajaie

C. Commander Ellstris Gorlan

D. Commander Ed'iee Bealle

1334. To whom did Red Leader exclaim, "Cut the chatter"?

A. Red Five

B. Red Four

C. Red Two

D. Red Six

1335. Who said, "Until this battlestation is fully operational, we are vulnerable"?

A. General Venel

B. Admiral Sicirch

C. General Tagge

D. Admiral Motti

1336. What Rebel Commander was formerly the Sulorine Sector commander?

A. Commander Skywalker

B. Commander Trixe

C. Commander Willard

D. Commander Worlon

1337. What cantina patron in Mos Eisley piloted the *Scarlet Vertha*?

A. Nabrun Leids

B. Ponda Baba

C. Dr. Evazan

D. Greedo

1338. Who was tending the bar when Obi-Wan Kenobi and Luke Skywalker entered the cantina?

A. Wuher

B. Ackmena

C. Chalmun

D. Ponda Baba

A New Hope Era

1339. Who was Red Three?
- **A.** Biggs Darklighter
- **B.** Wedge Antilles
- **C.** Luke Skywalker
- **D.** Jek Porkins

1340. Whose ship was known as the *Herd Mother*?
- **A.** Momaw Nadon
- **B.** Ketwol
- **C.** Hem Dazon
- **D.** Ellorrs Madak

1341.

1342. Who was a colonel in the Imperial Security Bureau assigned to work with Grand Moff Tarkin?
- **A.** Cassio Tagge
- **B.** Jan Dodonna
- **C.** Wullf Yularen
- **D.** Maximillian Veers

1343. What Rebel Y-wing pilot found an Imperial tracking device that forced the evacuation of the Rebel base on Dantooine?
- **A.** Cera Sisirch
- **B.** Davish Krail
- **C.** Tiree
- **D.** Ryle Torsyn

1344. Who led the cantina band?
- **A.** Ickabel G'ont
- **B.** Doikk Na'ts
- **C.** Figrin D'an
- **D.** Lirin Car'n

1345. What was Jek Porkins' homeworld?
- **A.** Dantooine
- **B.** Bestine
- **C.** Corellia
- **D.** Tatooine

1346. What Shistavanen Wolfman fell in love with Dice Igebon while in Mos Eisley?
- **A.** Kal Karvis
- **B.** Lak Sivrak
- **C.** Paploo
- **D.** Yorga the Hutt

1341.

Luke Skywalker and Obi-Wan sped into Mos Eisley, C-3PO and R2-D2 on the back of their speeder. Stormtroopers stopped them at a checkpoint and asked about their droids and to see Luke's identification. "You don't need to see his identification," Obi-Wan said, waving his hand.

"We don't need to see his identification," the stormtrooper said back.

"These aren't the droids you're looking for," said Obi-Wan. The stormtrooper, momentarily under Obi-Wan's influence, allowed Luke to go by.

"I don't understand how we got past those troops! I thought we were done for," Luke said.

"The Force can have a strong influence on the weak-minded," Obi-Wan instructed him as they approached a cantina, where they hoped to find a pilot who would take them off Tatooine so they could complete their mission.

Luke entered the cantina and went up to the bar to order a drink. When he did, someone pushed him, grunting disapproval. "He doesn't like you," an unattractive bar patron told Luke. Who didn't like him?

- **A.** Greeata
- **B.** Greedo
- **C.** Figrin D'an
- **D.** Ponda Baba

1347. What Rodian accompanied Jabba the Hutt to confront Han Solo in Mos Eisley?
A. Greedo
B. Greeata
C. Thuku
D. Thulu

1348. What happened to Biggs Darklighter after his last flight through Beggar's Canyon with Luke Skywalker?
A. He was almost trapped by the Sarlacc
B. He was attacked by a Tusken Raider with a poison-tipped gaderffii
C. He haggled with Jawas to purchase an astromech droid
D. He and Luke went to Mos Eisley

1349. Who was Grand Moff Tarkin's chief personal aide aboard the Death Star?
A. Colonel Yularen
B. Chief Bast
C. Sergeant Torent
D. Admiral Motti

1350. Who was the night bartender at the Mos Eisley cantina?
A. Wuher
B. Chalmun
C. Ackmena
D. Lana

1351. Who ordered the scanning crew to search every part of the *Millennium Falcon* when it was captured on the Death Star?
A. Colonel Yularen
B. Captain Yorr
C. Captain Khurgee
D. Chief Bast

1352. Who was Red Seven during the Battle of Yavin?
A. Wedge Antilles
B. Elyhek Rue
C. Jek Porkins
D. Biggs Darklighter

1353. What bounty hunter accosted Han Solo in the Mos Eisley cantina?
A. Djas Puhr
B. Greeata
C. Greedo
D. Aurra Sing

1354. From whom did Chalmun purchase his cantina in Mos Eisley?
A. Wuher
B. Ackmena
C. The Vriichon brothers
D. Kitik Keed'kak

A New Hope Era

1355. Who fired an unsuccessful shot at the Death Star's thermal exhaust port during the Battle of Yavin?
- **A.** Wedge Antilles
- **B.** Garven Dreis
- **C.** Luke Skywalker
- **D.** Biggs Darklighter

1356. What was Theron Nett before he joined the Rebel Alliance?
- **A.** A smuggler
- **B.** A bounty hunter
- **C.** An Imperial officer
- **D.** A moisture farmer

1357.

1358. Who was Luke's best friend on Tatooine?
- **A.** Biggs Darklighter
- **B.** Tank
- **C.** Wedge Antilles
- **D.** Fixer

1359. What Rebel pilot learned his piloting skills by hunting sink-crabs in his T-16 Skyhopper?
- **A.** Wedge Antilles
- **B.** Biggs Darklighter
- **C.** Jek Porkins
- **D.** Luke Skywalker

1360. What were Shada D'ukal and Karoly D'ulin?
- **A.** Emperor's Hands
- **B.** Mistryl Shadow Guards
- **C.** Bounty hunters
- **D.** Dathomir Witches

1361. What short-tempered mantid cantina patron had a particularly strong love of eggs?
- **A.** Ponda Baba
- **B.** Kitik Keed'kak
- **C.** Greedo
- **D.** Ee'dit Massy

1362. Who played Ommni Box in the Modal Nodes?
- **A.** Tedn Dahai
- **B.** Tech M'or
- **C.** Figrin D'an
- **D.** Sy Snootles

1357.

This scruffy, angry-looking being had spent his entire life on the desert planet Tatooine. His parents deserted him on the desolate planet, which could have explained his angry demeanor. He graduated from a bartending correspondence school and was hired to work in one of the seedier, yet immensely popular, cantinas on Tatooine, which attracted galactic denizens of all species and sizes.

His mixing prowess was unmatched. Even without the use of the cantina's computer, he could whip up cocktails specific to any alien being's physiology, pleasing

customer after customer, all the while scowling and disapproving of them.

His main dream in life was to create a signature drink that would make him famous, and he decided that in order to gain that fame, he would have to make a beverage that would please none other than Jabba the Hutt. He eventually did make this cocktail (with a little help from his least favorite thing—a droid), and earned himself the respect he had so long desired. Who was he?

A. Chalmun
B. C2-R4
C. Wuher
D. Greedo

1363. Whose parents, Jagged and Zena, were killed by space pirates?
A. Wedge Antilles
B. Jek Porkins
C. Tott Doneeta
D. Biggs Darklighter

1364. Who played the Fanfar in the Modal Nodes?
A. Tech M'or
B. Tedn Dahai
C. Doikk Na'ts
D. Nalan Cheel

1365. Who said, "Where are you taking this thing?" to Han Solo and Luke Skywalker?
A. Captain Needa
B. Lieutenant Childsen
C. Captain Khurgee
D. Chief Bast

1366. What bounty hunter was just about to try to capture Han Solo when Greedo got to him first?
A. Boba Fett
B. Danz Borin
C. Aurra Sing
D. Bossk

1367. What Imperial informant told the stormtroopers in Mos Eisley which docking bay Luke Skywalker and Obi-Wan Kenobi were going to?
A. Greedo
B. Boba Fett
C. Garindan
D. Thuku

1368. Who could calculate hyperspace coordinates in his head?
A. Chewbacca
B. Myo
C. Brainiac
D. Teak Sidbam

1369. Whose father was a food magnate on Tatooine?
A. Biggs Darklighter
B. Wedge Antilles
C. Han Solo
D. Luke Skywalker

1370. What Imperial bureaucrat resigned from the Empire after the occupation of Ralltiir and spent his time as a fugitive in Mos Eisley?
A. Tagg Tanna
B. Yerka Mig
C. Yalla Tadra
D. Yorka Mag

1363A 1364B 1365B 1366B 1367C 1368C 1369A 1370B

1371. Who was Red Eight during the Battle of Yavin?

A. Elyhek Rue   C. Bren Quersey

B. Jek Porkins   D. Davish Krail

1372. What Stennes Shifter made his living turning criminals over to Imperial authorities in Mos Eisley?

A. Tech M'or   C. Merc Sunlet

B. Trinto Duaba   D. Labria

1373. Who had the death sentence on twelve systems?

A. Jabba the Hutt   C. Dr. Evazan

B. Han Solo   D. Ponda Baba

1374. Who said, "Don't try to frighten us with your sorcerer's ways, Lord Vader"?

A. General Tagge   C. Grand Moff Tarkin

B. Admiral Ozzel   D. Admiral Motti

1375. How old was Dannik Jerriko when Luke Skywalker happened into the Mos Eisley cantina?

A. One thousand four hundred thirty-three   C. One thousand ten

B. Two thousand thirteen   D. Seven hundred ninety

1376. Who served as a test pilot on various TIE prototype ships?

A. Captain Khurgee   C. Colonel Yularen

B. Captain Yorr   D. Colonel Kilb

1377.

1378. What smuggler despised his own species?

A. Han Solo   C. Theron Nett

B. Bom Vimdim   D. Arleil Schous

1377.

This Tatooine native was one of Luke Skywalker's oldest friends. The two grew up together and spent their spare time racing through Beggar's Canyon in their skyhoppers. They loved racing so much that they referred to each other as "shooting stars."

The time came, however, when Luke's friend left him behind and went off in search of his future. He landed at the Academy, while Luke remained on Owen Lars' moisture farm, dreaming of a time when he could join his friend.

1379. Who honed his piloting skills by poaching Bothan sky dragons?

A. Black One

B. Red Six

C. Black Two

D. Red Five

1380. What Sakiyan bounty hunter was working in the cantina when Luke Skywalker and Obi-Wan Kenobi arrived?

A. Aurra Sing

B. Greedo

C. Djas Puhr

D. Boba Fett

1381. Who served in the Tierfon Yellow Squadron at Tierfon Rebel Outpost?

A. Jek Porkins

B. Biggs Darklighter

C. Luke Skywalker

D. Wedge Antilles

1382. What Vuvrian bought Luke's landspeeder from him before he left Tatooine?

A. Wandett

B. Baykuh

C. Wioslea

D. Mollii

1383. What Talz pickpocket lived in abandoned tunnels under Mos Eisley?

A. Mollock

B. Muftak

C. Loriaz

D. Mornna

1384. What Rebel leader had previously led a squadron at Renforra base?

A. Troylus Naeruda

B. Dutch Vander

C. Jarin Fed

D. Inostor Yzus

1385. Who was infamous for rearranging body parts on living creatures?

A. Chewbacca

B. Dr. Evazan

C. Djas Phur

D. Teak Sidbam

1386. Which pilot in the Battle of Yavin had previously led the relief effort of Clak'dor VII in the Mayagil sector?

A. Red Five

B. Red Three

C. Red Nine

D. Red Leader

This person's eyes were opened to the true nature of the Empire at the Academy, and he quickly made friends with young Rebels. They convinced him to turn his back on the Empire and his dream and instead join the fight for the galaxy. His friends arranged a meeting for him with a Rebel agent on the planet Bestine, and he joined the Rebel Alliance.

He returned to Tatooine one last time and confided in Luke his true feelings for the Empire, before having to regroup with the Alliance. Luke would meet him again, however. Who was he?

A. Laze Loneozner

B. Biggs Darklighter

C. Janek Sunber

D. Derek Klivian

A New Hope Era

1387. Whom were Shada D'ukal and Karoly D'ulin impersonating while in the cantina?

A. The Toggle brothers   C. The Tonnika sisters

B. The Tonelle twins   D. The Tonunduh twins

1388. What Mos Eisley resident had a secret safehouse for Rebel agents under a vesuvague hanging tree in his home?

A. Wuher   C. Bom Vimdim

B. Ponda Baba   D. Moma Nadon

1389. What instrument did Lirin Car'n play?

A. Ommni Box   C. Bandfill

B. Kloo Horn   D. Fizzz

1390. Who was Mauler Mithel?

A. Black Two   C. Gold Seven

B. Gold Three   D. Red Nine

1391. Who was the Ranat thief lurking in the Mos Eisley cantina when Luke arrived?

A. Reegesk   C. Toval

B. Grixland   D. Yashma

1392.

1393. What was Figrin D'an's species?

A. Duros   C. Neimoidian

B. Bith   D. Saurin

1394. Which of the following species helped create the hyperspace routes for trade throughout the galaxy?

A. Dugs   C. Pacithhips

B. Duros   D. Swokes Swokes

1392.

This Corellian native was brought up in outer Gus Treta, a spaceport owned by his parents. When much of the spaceport was destroyed by a craft piloted by suspected criminals who were attempting to escape and had forgotten to release their mooring clamps, this Corellian was left an orphan. He collected enough insurance credits from the accident, however, to allow him to purchase his first ship.

He used his first vessel, a stock light freighter, in his attempts to become a smuggler or gunrunner. Fortunately, he was not successful at either endeavor, and he turned his piloting skills into a career with the Rebel Alliance.

He fought valiantly in the Battle of Yavin up until the final moments, at which point he conceded to Luke Skywalker that he could no longer fight because his ship was not functioning properly. "I'm hit! I can't stay with you," the pilot called to Luke.

"Get clear," Luke responded. The pilot apologized and maneuvered his damaged ship away from the battle. He was one of the few Rebel heroes to survive the Battle of Yavin and fight the Empire to the end. Who was he?

A. Wedge Antilles

B. Jek Porkins

C. Biggs Darklighter

D. Garven Dreis

1395. How long do Talz larvae remain in chrysalis form?

- **A.** Two months
- **B.** Two years
- **C.** One month
- **D.** One year

1396. What species possesses long, thin fingers with suction cups at the tips?

- **A.** Rodians
- **B.** Duros
- **C.** Abyssins
- **D.** Jawas

1397. Which species is rumored to have descended from the ancient Kumungah?

- **A.** Hutts
- **B.** Jawas
- **C.** Chadra-Fans
- **D.** Ithorians

1398. What species has based its religion, language, and culture on mathematics?

- **A.** Sakiyan
- **B.** Pacithhip
- **C.** Givin
- **D.** Bith

1399. How many nostrils do Chadra-Fan have?

- **A.** Two
- **B.** Four
- **C.** One
- **D.** Six

1400. What language do Pacithhips speak?

- **A.** Pacithhip
- **B.** Paccy
- **C.** Lanaese
- **D.** Shimiese

1401. What was Nabrun Leids' species?

- **A.** Saurin
- **B.** Morseerian
- **C.** Toydarian
- **D.** Umbaran

1402. Which species lacks a sense of individuality and when speaking uses the pronoun "we"?

- **A.** Devaronians
- **B.** Aqualish
- **C.** Rodians
- **D.** Arcona

A New Hope Era

1403. Which species has hidden prehensile proboscises with which they suck out others' life essences through their nostrils?

A. Morseerians

B. Rodians

C. Anzati

D. Ranats

1404. How many livers do Devaronians have?

A. Three

B. Two

C. One

D. None

1405. Which species eschews sleep, instead meditating for short periods of time to restore themselves?

A. Bothans

B. Jawas

C. Bith

D. Rodians

1406. How many toes do Kubaz have on each foot?

A. Three

B. Two

C. Six

D. Four

1407.

1408. Which alien species was involved in a bloody civil war on its homeworld approximately three hundred years before the Battle of Yavin that decimated its population and forced survivors to live in hermetically sealed environments to survive?

A. Rodian

B. Bith

C. Hutt

D. Saurin

1409. What was Elis Helrot's species?

A. Gand

B. Givin

C. Gamorrean

D. Gotal

1410. In order to make a living, which species scours the desert for junk they hope to repair and sell?

A. Tusken Raiders

B. Hutts

C. Jawas

D. Humans

1407.

Some scientists believe that this diminutive, humanoid species, which evolved from rodents, eventually became bipedal from reaching for the lichens and fungi that grow on cave walls. These beings emit a foul, rancid odor that is difficult for other beings to stand, but they don't seem to mind it at all. To protect themselves, they cover themselves head to toe in homemade cloaks with hoods.

These beings live in tight clans. Each one of their vessels, in which they live, travel, and work, can hold up to three hundred members of a single clan. The clans come together annually to share stories, swap goods, and even trade sons and daughters, referring to their children as "marriage merchandise." They have come to believe that trading children for marriage with other clans will keep their bloodlines diverse. Although they trade their children, they place great importance on family. They revere their heritage and ancestry so much that their language includes forty-three different terms to describe relationship, lineage, and bloodline.

The most important member of each clan is referred to as the shaman, a female who is said to be able to see the future. Some tests done on these shamans have shown that they may possess something similar to Force abilities, and each shaman takes on an apprentice in order to keep their traditions alive. Which species is this?

A. Tusken Raider

B. Jawa

C. Pacithhip

D. Swokes Swokes

1411. Which species is a distant relative of the Verpine?
- A. Chadra-Fan
- B. Duros
- C. Quor'sav
- D. Yam'rii

1412. Which species is native to Antar 4?
- A. Anzati
- B. Gotal
- C. Balosar
- D. Amanaman

1413. What was M'iiyoom Onith's species?
- A. Kubaz
- B. Quor'sav
- C. H'memthe
- D. Saurin

1414. How many lungs do Bith have?
- A. Three
- B. Seven
- C. Two
- D. One

1415. Which species' prime source of food comes in the form of the hubba gourd?
- A. Tusken Raiders
- B. Rodians
- C. Givins
- D. Jawas

1416. How many arms do Morseerians have?
- A. Six
- B. Four
- C. Eight
- D. Two

1417. If left alone, which species will die of loneliness within a matter of weeks?
- A. Swokes Swokes
- B. Chadra-Fan
- C. Jawas
- D. Vurks

1418. Where are Biths' olfactory senses located?
- A. In their noses
- B. In the folds of their cheeks
- C. In their fingers
- D. In the palms of their hands

A New Hope Era

1419. What was Feltipern Trevagg's species?
A. Saurin
C. Gotal
B. Givin
D. Pacithhip

1420. Which species' devastating near-extinction was reversed when they channeled their need for violence into theater?
A. Dugs
C. Chadra-Fans
B. Rodians
D. Talz

1421. What was Ellors Madak's species?
A. Hutt
C. Kubaz
B. Duros
D. Yam'rii

1422.

1423. Which species magnifies its eyes by using polished orange gemstones called "durindfire"?
A. Duros
C. Jawas
B. Tusken Raiders
D. Kubaz

1424. Which species attacked Luke Skywalker as he was retrieving R2-D2?
A. Jawas
C. Nikto
B. Tusken Raiders
D. Klatooinians

1425. Which species' outer frame is actually an exoskeleton?
A. Aqualish
C. Devaronian
B. Duros
D. Givin

1426. Which species contains two rows of teeth and odor-detecting glands within their long snouts?
A. Trandoshans
C. Kubaz
B. Rodians
D. Anzati

1422.

This species hails from the Tyrius system in the galaxy's Mid Rim, and are known for their prowess as hunters. To their advantage in that field, they have multifaceted eyes that can see heat emanating from their prey even in darkness. They also have long, tapered snouts that serve as filters for their incredibly developed sense of smell. Their coloring allows them to blend in with vegetation.

This species emits an odor that most other species find revolting. This scent is actually a pheromonal excretion that attracts others of the species and also indicates the individual's family heritage to others in the species. This odor is particularly important to members of this species because their society is built around clans. Family units

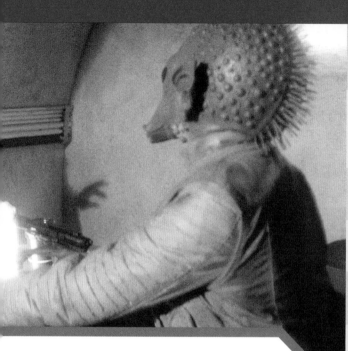

have been important to this species since their ancestors first built primitive tools to protect themselves. Since that time, this species has developed a love of hunting so strong that they never acquired any agricultural tendencies. They have hunted all of the natural prey on their planet to extinction, so they have to import most of their food from offworld.

Their love of hunting has grown so powerful that they are obsessed with violence, even romanticizing it in their arts. Their dramatic pieces are highly regarded around the galaxy.

What is this violent species?

A. Dug
B. Trandoshan
C. Rodian
D. Hutt

1427. What was Iasa's species?
- **A.** Aqualish
- **B.** Jawa
- **C.** Saurin
- **D.** Skakoan

1428. When do Anzati youth reach puberty?
- **A.** At around three hundred years of age
- **B.** At around one hundred years of age
- **C.** At around two hundred years of age
- **D.** At around fifty years of age

1429. What was Leesub Sirin's species?
- **A.** Quarren
- **B.** Qiraash
- **C.** Nikto
- **D.** Human

1430. What color is Devaronians' blood?
- **A.** Red
- **B.** Blue
- **C.** Black
- **D.** Green

1431. Into which category do Rodians fall?
- **A.** Mammalian
- **B.** Reptilian
- **C.** Amphibian
- **D.** Avian

1432. Which species' huge craniums house immensely oversized brains, the development of which was due to years of calculated breeding practices?
- **A.** Humans
- **B.** Duros
- **C.** Bith
- **D.** Wookiees

1433. What creatures do Tusken Raiders ride?
- **A.** Eopies
- **B.** Banthas
- **C.** Dewbacks
- **D.** Rontos

1434. What beautiful and invaluable item is found in krayt dragons' gizzards?
- **A.** Krayt diamonds
- **B.** Dragon opals
- **C.** Krayt crystals
- **D.** Dragon pearls

A New Hope Era

1435. How long do dianogas grow on average?
- **A.** 8 meters
- **B.** 6 meters
- **C.** 10 meters
- **D.** 4 meters

1436. What creatures did Luke Skywalker hunt in Beggar's Canyon?
- **A.** Rontos
- **B.** Womp rats
- **C.** Dwarf nunas
- **D.** Skettos

1437.

1438. What creatures live mainly in the mountains surrounding the Jundland Wastes on Tatooine?
- **A.** Greater Krayt Dragons
- **B.** Canyon Krayt Dragons
- **C.** Krell Dragons
- **D.** Dewbacks

1439. Which creature's long neck allows it to stretch for desert lichens and mosses that grow on high canyon walls?
- **A.** Eopie
- **B.** Ronto
- **C.** Galoomp
- **D.** Anooba

1440. How many segments of a bantha's horn grow each year?
- **A.** Two
- **B.** Five
- **C.** Three
- **D.** One

1441. What creature is used in some space stations and on some planets as an easy means of waste disposal?
- **A.** Womp rat
- **B.** Ronto
- **C.** Sketto
- **D.** Dianoga

1442. What is a bantha's average lifespan?
- **A.** Forty to sixty years
- **B.** Twenty to forty years
- **C.** Eighty to one hundred years
- **D.** Ten to twenty years

1437.

One of these creatures is ceremonially presented to every Tusken Raider child at the age of seven, and becomes the Tusken Raider's life partner. The young Tusken Raider learns to raise, care for, and ride this important companion, and develops an intense bond with it that will last a lifetime. When the creature reaches maturity, the Tusken Raider saddles it and rides it into the desert, where the two perform ceremonial tasks and initiation rituals. Upon completion, the Tusken Raider is considered an adult.

When Tusken Raiders marry, their respective creatures also mate, bringing the two species closer together in their bond. Even more curious, when a Tusken Raider couple has a son or daughter, these mated creatures often produce equivalent male or female offspring.

What Tatooine creature forms this unique bond with the Tusken Raiders?

- **A.** Dewbacks
- **B.** Banthas
- **C.** Rontos
- **D.** Eopies

1443. How many banthas did Luke Skywalker spot after R2-D2 had alerted him to the fact that several creatures were approaching from the southeast?
- **A.** One
- **B.** Three
- **C.** Two
- **D.** Five

1444. How many legs do greater krayt dragons have?
- **A.** Four
- **B.** Ten
- **C.** Eight
- **D.** Six

1445. What creature evolved on the swamp world of Vodran and then escaped the planet in the hold of a space freighter, spreading across the galaxy?
- **A.** Dewback
- **B.** Krayt dragon
- **C.** Womp rat
- **D.** Dianoga

1446. How many legs do dewbacks have?
- **A.** Eight
- **B.** Six
- **C.** Four
- **D.** Two

1447. Where are dianogas' mouths located?
- **A.** On their ocular stems
- **B.** On the bottom of their bodies
- **C.** On their chests
- **D.** On the ends of their tentacles

1448. From what creature did Obi-Wan Kenobi once save Luke Skywalker and Windy?
- **A.** Ronto
- **B.** Krayt dragon
- **C.** Dewback
- **D.** Sarlacc

1449. What bipedal reptavian survives on dewback eggs and carrion?
- **A.** Sketto
- **B.** Woodoo
- **C.** Sarlacc
- **D.** Urusai

1450. What nocturnal creature survives by eating insects and sucking the blood out of sleeping animals?
- **A.** Grekko
- **B.** Sketto
- **C.** Urusai
- **D.** Paladia

A New Hope Era

1451. What is the maximum number of womp rats usually sighted in a pack?
- **A.** Ten
- **B.** Thirty
- **C.** Twenty
- **D.** Fifty

1452. Which species participates in "neck fights" for dominance?
- **A.** Krayt dragon
- **B.** Bantha
- **C.** Eopie
- **D.** Ronto

1453. How many legs do canyon krayt dragons have?
- **A.** Ten
- **B.** Four
- **C.** Six
- **D.** Eight

1454. What species contains olfactory glands in its tongue?
- **A.** Ronto
- **B.** Eopie
- **C.** Dewback
- **D.** Bantha

1455. What species' orange eyes refract sunlight?
- **A.** Womp rat
- **B.** Sketto
- **C.** Urusai
- **D.** Eopie

1456.

1457. What attacked Luke Skywalker and eventually pulled him underwater on the Death Star?
- **A.** Took
- **B.** Dianoga
- **C.** Nos monster
- **D.** Krayt dragon

1458. What creature has a larger mutant relative found in the Jundland Wastes that has wing-like ears?
- **A.** Worrt
- **B.** Womp rat
- **C.** Woodoo
- **D.** Dewback

1456.

An Imperial officer aboard the *Tantive IV* had news for Darth Vader. "An escape pod was jettisoned during the fighting, but no life forms were aboard." Darth Vader told the officer that the Princess must have hidden the plans they were searching for in the escape pod.

"Send a detachment down to retrieve them. See to it personally, commander. There'll be no one to stop us this time!" the Dark Lord said.

Down on the surface, two weary droids were trundling through the desert sands, away from the escape pod. R2-D2 wanted to go in one direction, but C-3PO wanted to go in another one. "Go that way. You'll be

malfunctioning within a day, you near-sighted scrap pile!" C-3PO snapped, heading off in the direction he thought seemed more easily maneuverable.

The two droids were long gone from the escape pod's crash-landing site when Imperial stormtroopers arrived on the scene to investigate. "Someone was in the pod. The footsteps go off in this direction," a stormtrooper announced. In the background, stormtroopers could be seen mounted on native Tatooine beasts.

What creatures were the stormtroopers riding near the escape pod's landing site?

A. Dewbacks
B. Rontos
C. Banthas
D. Eopies

1459. What bipedal rodent travels in packs of up to thirty?
A. Womp rat   **C.** Scurrier
B. Sketto   **D.** Jackrab

1460. Which creature is hermaphroditic?
A. Ronto   **C.** Dewback
B. Womp rat   **D.** Dianoga

1461. Which creature is easily domesticated when raised from the egg?
A. Ronto   **C.** Bantha
B. Dewback   **D.** Eopie

1462. Which creature buries itself in the sand during the daytime?
A. Dewback   **C.** Eopie
B. Greater krayt dragon   **D.** Bantha

1463. What are banthas known to do after the death of their Tusken Raider riders?
A. Find a new rider   **C.** Commit suicide
B. Become hermits   **D.** Become ill

1464. How many tentacles do dianogas have?
A. Six   **C.** Seven
B. Nine   **D.** Eight

1465. Which species is the favored pack animal of the Jawas?
A. Ronto   **C.** Eopie
B. Dewback   **D.** Bantha

1466. How many wings do male urusais have?
A. Five   **C.** Six
B. Four   **D.** Three

A New Hope Era

1467. What species travels single file at a very leisurely pace?

A. Ronto　　　　　　　C. Canyon krayt dragon

B. Dewback　　　　　　D. Bantha

1468. How many horns do krayt dragons have?

A. Six　　　　　　　　C. Four

B. Two　　　　　　　　D. One

1469. What species travels in bands mostly comprising females that form protective rings around their young?

A. Dewback　　　　　　C. Scurrier

B. Ronto　　　　　　　D. Bantha

1470.

1471. How many wings do skettos have?

A. Two　　　　　　　　C. Six

B. Four　　　　　　　　D. None

1472. Which creature's venom can be used as poison?

A. Bantha　　　　　　　C. Krayt dragon

B. Dewback　　　　　　D. Sketto

1473. Where did Princess Leia tell Grand Moff Tarkin the Rebel base was?

A. Tatooine　　　　　　C. Dantooine

B. Yavin 4　　　　　　　D. Alderaan

1474. What, according to Obi-Wan Kenobi, was a "wretched hive of scum and villainy"?

A. Mos Olaf　　　　　　C. Mos Espa

B. Mos Eisley　　　　　D. Mos Entha

OBSESSED WITH *STAR WARS*

1470.

These creatures' bodies, aside from their extremities, are one giant stomach sac and digestive system. They can unhinge their jaws to swallow things that are much larger than their body size and their bodies stretch to accommodate these larger food items. Their digestive system contains powerful acids that break down things that most other creatures would find indigestible. Depending on the situation, this feature can make these creatures either very handy to have around or the cause of nightmares.

These creatures are not sentient but have been shown through research to display traits that show some form of intelligence. They have the ability to discern between food items and to migrate from one home to another. They also can tell the difference between living and dead creatures. Dead creatures are their preferred form of food, but that does not mean they won't consume a living being if no dead animals are available.

These creatures are self-fertilizing. When they lay eggs, their larvae are microscopic and form colonies. As the creatures grow and their number becomes too great for their current location, some of the offspring will attempt to migrate to a new, less populated area where they can flourish. Most of them are generally passive unless attacked or startled. What are they?

A. Dewbacks

B. Krayt dragons

C. Dianogas

D. Skettos

1475. What Death Star bay needed to be cleared in order to open the magnetic field so the *Millennium Falcon* could be brought in for inspection?

A. Bay 38   **C.** Bay 29

B. Bay 626   **D.** Bay 327

1476. Where, in fact, was the Rebel base?

A. Yavin   **C.** Tatooine

B. Yavin 4   **D.** Dantooine

1477. Where did Luke Skywalker tell C-3PO that Obi-Wan Kenobi lived?

A. Out beyond the Jundland Wastes   **C.** Out beyond Beggar's Canyon

B. Out beyond the Dune Sea   **D.** Out beyond Ben's Mesa

1478. What cell was Princess Leia being held in?

A. 197   **C.** 288

B. 2187   **D.** 2298

1479. What docking bay in Mos Eisley housed the *Millennium Falcon*?

A. Docking bay 84   **C.** Docking bay 94

B. Docking bay 9   **D.** Docking bay 8

1480. What had the Mos Eisley cantina's previous owners, the Vriichon brothers, buried in the basement?

A. Glitterstim spice   **C.** A vast store of credits

B. Bodies   **D.** Illegal weapons

1481. Where did Luke Skywalker try to convince Biggs Darklighter that he had witnessed a space battle?

A. Anchorhead   **C.** Mos Eisley

B. Tosche Station   **D.** The Lars homestead

1482. In what salt flat community was the Lars homestead located?

A. Greater Jundland   **C.** Greater Mesa

B. Great Mesa   **D.** Great Chott

A New Hope Era

1483. Where on Tatooine did the droids' escape pod land?
- **A.** The Eastern Dune Sea
- **B.** The Western Dune Sea
- **C.** Great Mesa
- **D.** Beggar's Canyon

1484. What did Obi-Wan Kenobi tell Luke Skywalker was not to be traveled lightly?
- **A.** Beggar's Canyon
- **B.** The Jundland Wastes
- **C.** The Dune Sea
- **D.** Mos Eisley

1485. What does the sign above the entrance to Chalmun's cantina say in Basic?
- **A.** "NO DROIDS"
- **B.** "Watch Your Step"
- **C.** "Watch Your Head(s)"
- **D.** "CASH ONLY"

1486. What ancient ship's crash-landed hull remains in the center of Mos Eisley as a testament to its occupants, the first colonists to travel to Tatooine?
- **A.** The *Dromogon King*
- **B.** The *Dowager Queen*
- **C.** The *Dowager King*
- **D.** The *Dragon Queen*

1487. According to Princess Leia, to which planet was she headed when Darth Vader intercepted her ship?
- **A.** Dantooine
- **B.** Onderon
- **C.** Alderaan
- **D.** Tatooine

1488. In which Tatooine settlement was the Sandcrawler formerly carrying C-3PO and R2-D2 intercepted by stormtroopers?
- **A.** Mos Entha
- **B.** Anchorhead
- **C.** Mos Olaf
- **D.** Bestine

1489. In what detention block was Princess Leia being held?
- **A.** AC-24
- **B.** AC-13
- **C.** AA-23
- **D.** AA-14

1490.

1490.

Planned since before the advent of the Clone Wars, the Death Star was considered the Empire's ultimate weapon. The Emperor wanted to use this doomsday device to impose his version of order throughout the galaxy. Surely, he thought, no one would defy him after witnessing the unlimited destructive power he held within his grasp.

The project had been funded largely by the agents of the Confederacy of Independent Systems—in particular, the Trade Federation, the InterGalactic Banking Clan, and the Techno Union. Unbeknownst to most, the Republic itself had also funded the project, although unwillingly. The Death Star was

constructed in secret in the Outer Rim of the galaxy, utilizing engineers and scientists from all over the galaxy, including beings from Geonosis, Ryloth, Eriadu, and Fondor.

The Emperor would only get to boast over his ultimate weapon for a short time, however. The Rebels stole the plans and found a weakness, attacking and ultimately destroying the battle station. He did manage to show its full power, though. How many planets did the Death Star destroy before it met a similar fate?

A. One
B. Two
C. Three
D. Six

1491. How far apart are Pretormin's Environmental GX-8 Water Vaporators supposed to be positioned from one another in order to collect the maximum amount of condensation from the Tatooine atmosphere?

A. 200 meters   C. 250 meters
B. 150 meters   D. 300 meters

1492. In which trash compactor were the Rebel heroes trapped after attempting to rescue Princess Leia?

A. 42-6   C. 32-4
B. 32-6-3827   D. 42-9-3830

1493. What civilization built the Temple in which the Rebel base was housed on Yavin 4?

A. The Sith   C. The Massassi
B. The Devaronians   D. The Lepi

1494. What game did Luke and his friends play while at Tosche Station?

A. Skyhopper   C. Dejarik
B. Sabacc   D. Billiards

1495. After whom was the arena in Mos Eisley named?

A. Aurra Sing   C. Boba Fett
B. Jango Fett   D. Jabba the Hutt

1496. What was the Death Star's diameter?

A. 200 kilometers   C. 120 kilometers
B. 140 kilometers   D. 160 kilometers

1497. What was the domed entry to the Lars homestead constructed of?

A. Duracrete   C. Pourstone
B. Sandstone   D. Tatooine clay

1498. While en route to Mos Eisley from Obi-Wan Kenobi's home, where did Luke, Obi-Wan, and the droids stop for the night?

A. Pika Oasis   C. Arnthout
B. Mos Taike   D. Bestine

A New Hope Era

1499. Under whose evil reign had the Massassi been ordered to build the giant temples found on Yavin 4?

A. Naga Sadow   **C.** Exar Kun

B. Ulic Qel-Droma   **D.** Ludo Kressh

1500. What was the cantina's original purpose when its basic structure was constructed by early settlers?

A. Protection against sandstorms   **C.** A trading post

B. A mess hall   **D.** A fortification against Tusken Raiders

1501. From what cellblock was Chewbacca supposedly being transferred as part of Luke Skywalker's plan to rescue Princess Leia?

A. Cellblock 2-87   **C.** Cellblock 1-49

B. Cellblock 8012   **D.** Cellblock 1138

1502. Across what did Princess Leia and Luke Skywalker swing while evading stormtroopers?

A. The equatorial trench   **C.** A sub-core shaft

B. A repulsorlift tube   **D.** A maintenance gantry

1503. What was at the apex of the Great Temple on Yavin 4?

A. The briefing room   **C.** The mess hall

B. The audience chamber   **D.** The barracks

1504. What was Jabba the Hutt's Mos Eisley townhouse known as?

A. Hutt Hideaway   **C.** The Hutt Haven

B. The Tiure Complex   **D.** The Desilijic Complex

1505. What was housed in the uppermost spire of the Great Temple in which the Rebels set up their hidden base?

A. The audience chamber   **C.** The command center

B. The observation and communication room   **D.** The auxiliary power generator

1506. On what level of the Death Star was Princess Leia being held prisoner?

A. Level five   **C.** Level three

B. Level four   **D.** Level six

OBSESSED WITH *STAR WARS*

1514.

The Rebel heroes had, as they thought, evaded the Imperials and escaped the Death Star. As they landed on Yavin 4, they immediately took R2-D2 away in order to analyze the information he had so bravely carried throughout their adventures. General Dodonna then used R2-D2's information to brief the Rebel forces on their plan of attack. As Dodonna revealed the only way to destroy the station, many Rebels shifted nervously. Luke, however, remained positive. "It's not impossible," he said smugly, adding that he had bull's-eyed similarly sized targets on his homeworld.

As the pilots were preparing for battle, Luke climbed up to the cockpit of his X-wing fighter. The chief, who was placing R2-D2 into the astromech hold, said to Luke, "This R2 unit of yours seems a bit beat up. Do you want a new one?"

"Not on your life," Luke replied. "That little droid and I have been through a lot together!"

Luke relied on R2-D2 to help him maintain control of his fighter as the Rebels battled the Imperials above the surface of the Death Star. When Luke began his final attack run on the Death Star, Darth Vader was close behind and fired at Luke's X-wing. What did Luke report to the Rebel base?

A. "I'm hit, but not bad."
B. "I've lost R2!"
C. "I'm all right."
D. "Everything's under control."

1507. How many sides did the Great Temple on Yavin 4 have?
A. Six
B. Four
C. Eight
D. Ten

1508. Where did Luke Skywalker bull's-eye womp rats?
A. Beggar's Canyon
B. Ben's Mesa
C. Mushroom Flats
D. Hutt Flats

1509. What did some archeologists propose that the temples on Yavin 4 had originally been used for?
A. Sith Lord burial chambers
B. Communication devices to contact Sith Lords across the galaxy
C. Sith army training camps
D. Sith meditation and training retreat centers

1510. What were the Rebels targeting in their attack on the Death Star?
A. An emergency air dump
B. The equatorial trench
C. An antigravity chamber
D. A thermal exhaust port

1511. Whose spirit was trapped in the Great Temple on Yavin 4?
A. Ludo Kressh's
B. Darth Bane's
C. Exar Kun's
D. Naga Sadow's

1512. Approximately how long before the Battle of Yavin were the temples of Yavin 4 built?
A. Three thousand years
B. Eight thousand years
C. Four thousand years
D. Five thousand years

1513. Which was Jek Porkins's astromech droid?
A. R5-D8
B. R9-D9
C. R3-D2
D. R2-D5

1514.

A New Hope Era

1515. What protocol droid accompanied R2-D2 and C-3PO as they walked the hall of the consular ship before it was boarded by Imperial troops?

A. N-3PO
B. U-3PO
C. R-3PO
D. K-3PO

1516. What astromech droid did Owen Lars purchase before begrudgingly picking R2-D2?

A. R5-D3
B. R5-D4
C. R5-E9
D. R5-D6

1517. What did Luke Skywalker notice about R2-D2 as he was cleaning him on the Lars homestead?

A. He was dirty
B. He had worn treads
C. He had a lot of carbon scoring
D. His servomotor was faulty

1518. Why did C-3PO exclaim, "Curse my metal body"?

A. He thought he had given Obi-Wan Kenobi faulty directions
B. He and R2-D2 were captured by stormtroopers
C. He thought that he hadn't been quick enough in getting R2 to shut down the trash compactor
D. He thought he wasn't going to be able to make it to the *Millennium Falcon* in time for takeoff

1519. Which astromech droid series was referred to as "a meter-tall stack of the worst business decisions you could possibly want" by *Mechtech Illustrated*?

A. The R5 series
B. The R6 series
C. The R2 series
D. The R1 series

1520. Which droid was entrusted with the secret plans to the Death Star?

A. R2-D2
B. C-3PO
C. R5-D4
D. R1-G4

1521. Which manufacturer produced the CZ series?

A. Arakyd
B. Cybot Galactica
C. Serv-O-Droid
D. Industrial Automaton

1522. What was wrong with R5-D4?

A. It had a bad motivator
B. It had a bad servomotor
C. It had a bad communicator
D. It had a bad power coupling

1529.

Luke Skywalker, Obi-Wan Kenobi, R2-D2, and C-3PO had managed to evade the stormtroopers, much to Luke's surprise. They parked Luke's landspeeder and planned to search for a pilot who would be able to take them to the Alderaan system. As C-3PO was climbing off the back, a nosy Jawa ran up to Luke's landspeeder and began fussing over it. "I can't abide those Jawas. Disgusting creatures," C-3PO said boldly, still feeling a bit queasy from his experience aboard the sandcrawler.

"Go on," Luke said, brushing the Jawa away from his speeder. "Do you really think we'll find a pilot here who can take us to Alderaan?" he asked Obi-Wan. Obi-Wan told him that most of the best starpilots could be found in the cantina, but to

watch his step; it could be a little rough. "I'm ready for anything," Luke said smugly.

Luke and Obi-Wan entered the dank, smoky cantina and headed toward the bar. Luke took in the sights—he had never seen so many different alien beings in one place.

C-3PO and R2-D2 followed Obi-Wan and Luke into the bar, but the bartender, seeing the droids, yelled at Luke. What did he say?

A. "Droids have to pay a cover charge!"

B. "Your astromech droid was reported stolen!"

C. "We don't serve their kind here!"

D. "Droids can't drink, but they sure can dance!"

1523. What company produced astromech droids?
- **A.** Cybot Galactica
- **B.** Go-Corp/Utilitech
- **C.** Industrial Automaton
- **D.** Arakyd

1524. Which astromech unit was among the droids taken by Imperial stormtroopers after they searched the sandcrawler that R2-D2 and C-3PO had been on?
- **A.** R2-G2
- **B.** R1-G4
- **C.** R4-G3
- **D.** R6-G6

1525. How many arms does an MSE-6 droid have?
- **A.** Two
- **B.** One
- **C.** None
- **D.** Three

1526. Which was Theron Nett's astromech droid?
- **A.** R2-X0
- **B.** R2-X1
- **C.** R2-X5
- **D.** R2-X2

1527. Which of the Lars' droids preferred working for Beru because she gave it simple, repetitious jobs?
- **A.** WED-02-13
- **B.** WED-15-77
- **C.** WED-11-62
- **D.** WED-02-66

1528. Which type of droid did Chewbacca frighten by roaring at it on the Death Star?
- **A.** An MSE-6 droid
- **B.** A CZ droid
- **C.** An R2 unit
- **D.** An R5 unit

1529.

1530. Which was an Imperial maintenance droid?
- **A.** R1-G4
- **B.** R5-D8
- **C.** R4-I9
- **D.** R2-X2

A New Hope Era

1531. For whose staff did 5D6-RA7 work?
- **A.** Captain Khurgee
- **B.** Admiral Motti
- **C.** Captain Yorr
- **D.** Grand Moff Tarkin

1532. Which droid's job was adding comm repeaters to the Mos Eisley communications network?
- **A.** ASP-704
- **B.** R4-D9
- **C.** ASP-702
- **D.** R4-D3

1533. Which language do some GNK droids speak?
- **A.** Huttese
- **B.** Servo
- **C.** Dillific
- **D.** Gonkian

1534. Which type of droid helped stormtroopers search the streets of Mos Eisley for R2-D2 and C-3PO?
- **A.** Mark V patrol droid
- **B.** Mark IV patrol droid
- **C.** An R4 unit
- **D.** An R5 unit

1535. What did C-3PO "thank the maker" for?
- **A.** A tuneup
- **B.** A polish
- **C.** An oil bath
- **D.** A rewiring

1536. What did C-3PO think his first job had been when talking to Owen Lars?
- **A.** Programming moisture vaporators
- **B.** Tending to the Senator from Naboo
- **C.** Programming binary loadlifters
- **D.** Assisting Owen's stepmother

1537. Which droid, illegal during the Republic, was employed to get secrets out of Princess Leia?
- **A.** Death Star Droid
- **B.** Interrogator Droid
- **C.** Probot
- **D.** IG assassin droid

1538. Which manufacturer produced the RA-7 series, casually known as "Death Star Droids"?
- **A.** Serv-O-Droid
- **B.** Arakyd
- **C.** TaggeCo
- **D.** SoroSuub

OBSESSED WITH *STAR WARS*

1539. Where did C-3PO tell stormtroopers who entered the control room on the Death Star he had to take his counterpart?

A. To the repair shop
C. To maintenance
B. To the hangar bay
D. To the turbolift

1540. What was the CZ droid's primary function?

A. Secretarial
C. Mechanic
B. Sabotage
D. Heavy lifting

1541. Which manufacturer produced the IT-O interrogation droid?

A. Arakyd
C. Phlut Design Systems
B. Imperial Department of Military Research
D. MedTech Industries

1542. Which was Red Five's astromech droid?

A. R4-I9
C. R2-D2
B. R2-D5
D. R4-G7

1543. Which droid was able to see through radiation, fog, sand, and groundfill, and was refurbished by Jawas on Tatooine?

A. LIN-V7H
C. LIN-V8K
B. LiN-88B-2
D. LiN-87B-2

1544. To whom did the lightsaber Luke Skywalker received from Obi-Wan Kenobi belong originally?

A. Anakin Skywalker
C. Qui-Gon Jinn
B. Yoda
D. Obi-Wan Kenobi

1545.

1546. When the stormtroopers attacked the sandcrawler that had held R2-D2 and C-3PO, what kind of weapons did they have?

A. EE-3 rifles
C. E-11B blaster pistols
B. E-11 blaster rifles
D. E-11A1 blasters

1545.

Being a smuggler afforded Han Solo very little safety—he never knew when he was going to have to protect himself from any number of galactic thugs. He had always managed to stay on many an important crime lord's good side, but recent bad luck had brought with it a bounty that had the galaxy's most famous and most dangerous assassins and bounty hunters tracking the pilot. Solo, intent on staying alive, remained armed at all times, always ready to defend himself in a fight.

After discussing business with Obi-Wan Kenobi and feeling that his problems could potentially be over in the near future, Solo ran into one such galactic thug who was bent on making sure he would be able to capture Solo and collect big. Cornering him in a busy cantina, the bounty hunter threatened to turn over the wanted man, dead if possible. Solo pulled out his weapon and, after dodging a blast, shot the bounty hunter. After apologizing to the bartender for making a mess, Solo then left the cantina to meet his new clients.

What type of weapon did Han Solo use?

A. DH-17 blaster pistol
B. Ionization blaster
C. DL-44 pistol
D. Merr-Sonn Power 5 blaster pistol

A New Hope Era

1547. What color was Darth Vader's lightsaber blade?
- **A.** Blue
- **B.** Green
- **C.** Yellow
- **D.** Red

1548. Who used a Drearian Defense Conglomerate Defender sporting blaster?
- **A.** Princess Leia
- **B.** Luke Skywalker
- **C.** Han Solo
- **D.** Chewbacca

1549. What color was Obi-Wan Kenobi's lightsaber blade?
- **A.** Red
- **B.** Green
- **C.** Blue
- **D.** Purple

1550. Which manufacturer produced the E-11 blaster rifle?
- **A.** BlasTech
- **B.** Merr-Sonn Munitions, Inc.
- **C.** Golan Arms
- **D.** Imperial Department of Military Research

1551. Which weapon short-circuited droid electrical systems?
- **A.** Bowcaster
- **B.** Ionization blaster
- **C.** Lightsaber
- **D.** Blaster rifle

1552. Who used a DT-12 blaster pistol in Mos Eisley?
- **A.** Greedo
- **B.** Ponda Baba
- **C.** Han Solo
- **D.** Chewbacca

1553. How many laser cannons does the TIE Advanced x1 have?
- **A.** One
- **B.** Three
- **C.** Four
- **D.** Two

1554.

1555. Which Star Destroyer pursued Princess Leia's ship over Tatooine?
- **A.** Star Destroyer *Detritus*
- **B.** Star Destroyer *Devastator*
- **C.** Star Destroyer *Avenger*
- **D.** Star Destroyer *Destructor*

1556. How many small escape pods was the *Tantive IV* equipped with?
- **A.** Eight
- **B.** Nine
- **C.** Six
- **D.** Ten

1554.

"Chewbacca here is first mate in a ship that might suit us," Obi-Wan Kenobi said as he helped Luke up from a misunderstanding the farmboy'd just had with a grumpy Aqualish. Chewbacca led the Jedi Master and the boy over to a table where the ship's captain, Han Solo, was sitting.

"Chewie here tells me you're looking for passage to the Alderaan system," Han said to Obi-Wan Kenobi.

"Yes, indeed. If it's a fast ship," Kenobi replied. The two haggled over terms and then came to an agreement. Solo told Kenobi that they'd leave as soon as the passengers were ready, and told them which docking bay to go to.

Luke sold his speeder, saying, "I'm never coming back to this planet again," and they regrouped with R2-D2 and C-3PO, who had been evading stormtroopers throughout Mos Eisley.

As they entered the docking bay, Luke was incredulous. "What a piece of junk!" he said. Solo, getting a little defensive, told Luke that the ship could go past light speed, and then noted that he had made a few special modifications himself. How fast past light speed did Solo say the *Millennium Falcon* could go?

- **A.** 0.6
- **B.** 0.5
- **C.** 0.4
- **D.** 0.3

1557. What ship was the *Millennium Falcon* a modified version of?
- **A.** YT-2300
- **B.** YT-1400
- **C.** YT-1300
- **D.** YT-2400

1558. How many TIE fighters make up a typical attack squadron?
- **A.** Twelve
- **B.** Twenty
- **C.** Fourteen
- **D.** Ten

1559. How long are Y-wing fighters?
- **A.** 10 meters
- **B.** 14 meters
- **C.** 15 meters
- **D.** 16 meters

1560. What skyhopper model did Luke use to bull's-eye womp rats?
- **A.** T-16
- **B.** T-14
- **C.** T-19
- **D.** T-13

1561. Which ship was intentionally built without life-support systems?
- **A.** Y-wing
- **B.** TIE fighter
- **C.** X-wing
- **D.** YT-1300

1562. What was the original manufacturer of the sandcrawler?
- **A.** SoroSuub
- **B.** Kuat Systems Engineering
- **C.** Corellia Mining
- **D.** Gallofree Yards, Inc.

1563. What did the TIE Advanced x1 have that regular TIE fighters lacked?
- **A.** Solar panels
- **B.** A targeting computer
- **C.** A hyperdrive
- **D.** A life support system

1564. How many wings does a T-16 skyhopper have?
- **A.** Four
- **B.** Two
- **C.** Six
- **D.** Three

1565. Who owned a SoroSuub V-35 landspeeder?
- **A.** Obi-Wan Kenobi
- **B.** Fixer
- **C.** Biggs Darklighter
- **D.** Owen Lars

1566. What are the panels on the exterior of TIE fighters' wings?
- **A.** Heat-exchange matrices
- **B.** Solar panels
- **C.** Shield generators
- **D.** Cloaking panels

A New Hope **Era**

1567. Which manufacturer created Y-wing fighters?
- **A.** Kuat Drive Yards
- **B.** SoroSuub
- **C.** Koensayr
- **D.** Sienar Fleet Systems

1568. How did the droids stay on the back of Luke Skywalker's landspeeder during travel?
- **A.** Magnetic clamps
- **B.** They were tethered to the speeder
- **C.** They balanced
- **D.** The Force

1569. How many quad laser cannons did the *Millennium Falcon* have?
- **A.** Two
- **B.** Three
- **C.** Four
- **D.** One

1570. How long are *Imperial*-class Star Destroyers?
- **A.** 1,500 meters
- **B.** 1,700 meters
- **C.** 1,600 meters
- **D.** 1,800 meters

1571. How fast did the *Millennium Falcon* make the Kessel Run?
- **A.** In less than eleven parsecs
- **B.** In less than twelve parsecs
- **C.** In less than ten parsecs
- **D.** In less than fourteen parsecs

1572. Which model of landspeeder made it difficult for Luke Skywalker to get a good price when he sold his landspeeder in Mos Eisley?
- **A.** XP-29
- **B.** XP-38
- **C.** XP-39
- **D.** CP-28

1573.

1574. How many Y-wings deployed in the Battle of Yavin survived the fighting?
- **A.** One
- **B.** Three
- **C.** Six
- **D.** None

1575. What does TIE stand for?
- **A.** Turbo Infused Engine
- **B.** Translon Engine
- **C.** Transfer Interior Engine
- **D.** Twin Ion Engine

1573.

When the Empire took control of the company that manufactured this ship, technicians and suppliers under the company's employ defected to the Rebellion, taking their ships' prototypes with them. The Rebellion began manufacturing these ships in small numbers, and the ships became integral to the Alliance's fleet. These ships became known for their speed and agility, as well as their ability to absorb substantial damage.

Each of the ships' wings contains a Taim & Bak KX9 laser cannon, which can be fired individually, simultaneously, in pairs, or other combinations. The ships also carry proton

OBSESSED WITH *STAR WARS*

1576. How many large escape pods was the *Tantive IV* equipped with?
A. Two
C. Four
B. Six
D. None

1577. How many proton torpedoes does an X-wing fighter carry?
A. Nine
C. Three
B. Two
D. Six

1578. How many TIE ships are housed in *Imperial*-class Star Destroyers?
A. Seventy-two
C. Sixty-two
B. Eighty-two
D. Ninety-two

1579. What model was Luke Skywalker's landspeeder?
A. X-32
C. X-34
B. XP-38
D. X-30

1580. How many wings does an X-wing have?
A. Four
C. Six
B. Two
D. Eight

1581. Which manufacturer created the *Tantive IV*?
A. SoroSuub
C. Kuat Drive Yards
B. Corellian Engineering Corporation
D. Incom

1582. Which ship lacks landing gear?
A. Y-wing
C. X-wing
B. YT-1300
D. TIE fighter

1583. What was the droid holding chamber on the Jawas' sandcrawler originally used for?
A. Water storage
C. Troop barracks
B. Ore hold
D. Mess hall

1584. How many Arakyd Flex Tube proton-torpedo launchers does a Y-wing fighter have?
A. One
C. Four
B. Six
D. Two

torpedoes, which are ejected from Krupx MG7 launchers located near the ships' bottoms.

These ships contain life-support systems that can last up to a week in non-combat situations, and GBK-585 motivator hyperspace control units. There is a motivator on each of the ships' engines. In the event of emergencies, the ships also have ejection seats to throw pilots clear of the fighters.

These ships received their name from their unique wing configuration. Which are they?

A. Y-wing starfighters
B. T-wing starfighters
C. X-wing starfighters
D. E-wing starfighters

A New Hope Era

1585. How many turbolaser cannons did the *Tantive IV* have?
- **A.** Six
- **B.** Nine
- **C.** Four
- **D.** Twelve

1586. What else did the TIE Advanced x1 have that regular TIE fighters lacked?
- **A.** Landing gear
- **B.** Binocular sensor array
- **C.** A shield generator
- **D.** Ion cannons

1587. How many stormtroopers are carried on *Imperial*-class Star Destroyers?
- **A.** 10,700
- **B.** 9,700
- **C.** 5,700
- **D.** 8,700

1588. How many ion cannons does a Y-wing fighter have?
- **A.** One
- **B.** Two
- **C.** Three
- **D.** None

1589. What class was the escape pod used by C-3PO and R2-D2?
- **A.** Class-6
- **B.** Class-2
- **C.** Class-4
- **D.** Class-9

1590.

1591. How long are sandcrawlers?
- **A.** 62.1 meters
- **B.** 36.8 meters
- **C.** 24.2 meters
- **D.** 49.8 meters

1592. How many giant turret gun stations does an *Imperial*-class Star Destroyer have?
- **A.** Six
- **B.** Eight
- **C.** Ten
- **D.** Four

1593. Which stormtrooper wasn't at his post and was surprised by Han Solo?
- **A.** TK-421
- **B.** CK-421
- **C.** TK-429
- **D.** CK-423

1594. Who placed the secret plans into R2-D2's memory banks?
- **A.** Princess Leia
- **B.** C-3PO
- **C.** Jan Dodonna
- **D.** Captain Antilles

1590.

A harried Imperial officer rushed toward Darth Vader inside the Death Star, orbiting the planet Yavin above the Rebel Base, alerting the Dark Lord to the small Rebel ships attacking the Death Star. According to the officer, the ships' size made them difficult to attack with turbolasers.

"We'll have to destroy them ship to ship," Darth Vader instructed. "Get the crews to their fighters." TIE fighters soon besieged the Rebel pilots, decimating their forces.

Now the Death Star was almost in range of the Rebel base, spelling almost certain doom for the Rebellion. Darth Vader had joined the fight and was targeting Luke Skywalker's X-wing starfighter as Luke careened through the Death Star's trench. "The Force is strong with this one," the Dark Lord said as Luke continued to evade his targeting computer. Darth Vader finally had Luke in his scope. "I have you now," he said, pressing the trigger. His attack was foiled, however, when a blast destroyed his right wingman. In the confusion, his left wingman lost control, spinning into his ship. The impact sent him out of control and away from the trench. Who fired on his right wingman?

- **A.** Han Solo
- **B.** Wedge Antilles
- **C.** Biggs Darklighter
- **D.** Garven Dreis

1595. How much did Obi-Wan Kenobi promise Han Solo as payment for passage to Alderaan?
A. 16,000
B. 17,000
C. 18,000
D. 11,000

1596. What did Owen Lars tell Luke Skywalker his father had been?
A. A Jedi Knight
B. A Sith Lord
C. A navigator on a spice freighter
D. A fighter pilot

1597. When did Han Solo expect to arrive at Alderaan?
A. 0500 hours
B. 0300 hours
C. 0400 hours
D. 0200 hours

1598. What did C-3PO say they had done to the *Tantive IV*?
A. Shut down the main reactor
B. Disarmed it
C. Boarded it
D. Shut down the life-support systems

1599. What did Princess Leia say when Luke Skywalker came to rescue her?
A. "Thank goodness!"
B. "Aren't you a little short for a stormtrooper?"
C. "Aren't you a little young for a Jedi?"
D. "I'm so glad you've arrived!"

1600. How long did Luke Skywalker tell the stormtrooper patrol in Mos Eisley he had owned R2-D2 and C-3PO?
A. About two or three seasons
B. About six or seven seasons
C. About one or two seasons
D. About three or four seasons

1601. How did Darth Vader know that Obi-Wan Kenobi was on the Death Star?
A. He saw him
B. He felt a tremor in the Force
C. The Emperor told him
D. He found a piece of his robe on the *Millennium Falcon*

1602. Who rescued Luke Skywalker from the Tusken Raiders?
A. Obi-Wan Kenobi
B. Han Solo
C. Biggs Darklighter
D. Owen Lars

A New Hope Era

1603. According to Princess Leia, why was their escape from the Death Star so easy?

A. They were smarter than the Imperials

B. Things always went her way

C. They were just lucky

D. The Imperials were tracking them

1604. How did Luke Skywalker and Princess Leia get across the unextended bridge on the Death Star after Luke blasted the controls?

A. With a grappling hook

B. They used the Force

C. They jumped

D. They didn't—they went back the way they came

1605. What did Obi-Wan Kenobi say would happen if Darth Vader struck him down?

A. He would be dead

B. He would become one with the Force

C. He would become more powerful than Darth Vader could possibly imagine

D. He would come back again

1606.

1607. What did Han Solo say was wrong in the detention center when he was contacted?

A. Damaged wiring

B. A weapons malfunction

C. A dianoga attack

D. A prisoner uprising

1608. What did C-3PO call R2-D2 as they were bickering over the escape pod?

A. A mechanical poltroon

B. A walking garbage can

C. An overweight glob of grease

D. An ignominious mechanical troll

1609. What did Han Solo tell Luke to do after Obi-Wan Kenobi had been killed?

A. Run

B. Shoot Darth Vader

C. Avenge Obi-Wan's death

D. Blast the door

1610. Who said, "That's no moon—it's a space station"?

A. Luke Skywalker

B. C-3PO

C. Han Solo

D. Obi-Wan Kenobi

OBSESSED WITH *STAR WARS*

1606.

After R2-D2 had led Luke Skywalker and C-3PO to Obi-Wan Kenobi, Obi-Wan took them to his home. He told Luke about his father's demise and gave Luke his father's lightsaber. Then R2-D2 played a message for Obi-Wan from Princess Leia asking him to transport R2-D2 to Bail Organa on Alderaan. R2-D2 was carrying information vital to the Rebellion, and Leia's ship had been attacked by the Empire, so she couldn't complete the mission. Leia begged Obi-Wan to take over. "This is our most desperate hour," she said via hologram. "Help me, Obi-Wan Kenobi. You're my only hope." With that, the message faded.

Luke said he would take Obi-Wan to Anchorhead, but then he had to get home. On the way, they happened upon the sandcrawler from which Owen had purchased R2-D2 and C-3PO. The Jawas had all been killed, and the sandcrawler ransacked. It looked as if Tusken Raiders had done it, but Obi-Wan knew better. "These blast points, too accurate for Sand People. Only Imperial stormtroopers are so precise." Luke realized that the stormtroopers were searching for his droids and raced back to the Lars homestead—which lay in ruins. What did he discover there?

A. Owen and Beru were nowhere to be found

B. Stormtroopers had the homestead surrounded

C. Owen and Beru had been killed

D. Owen and Beru were being led off by Imperial troops

1611. How many Rebel ships, so small that they were evading the Death Star's turbolasers, did the Imperial officer tell Darth Vader that they had counted?

A. Twenty   **C.** Twenty-five

B. Thirty   **D.** Thirty-five

1612. How many stormtroopers did Princess Leia kill before she was stunned on *Tantive IV*?

A. Three   **C.** Nine

B. One   **D.** Two

1613. Who said, "You're all clear, kid! Now let's blow this thing and go home!"?

A. Biggs Darklighter   **C.** Luke Skywalker

B. Wedge Antilles   **D.** Han Solo

1614. For which planet did Grand Moff Tarkin tell Admiral Motti to set the Death Star's course?

A. Alderaan   **C.** Dantooine

B. Tatooine   **D.** Onderon

1615. Who said, "Sir, Luke is the best bush pilot in the Outer Rim territories"?

A. Han Solo   **C.** Tank

B. Biggs Darklighter   **D.** Wedge Antilles

1616. How wide was the target area the Rebel pilots had to fire at when attacking the Death Star?

A. 1 meter   **C.** 2 meters

B. 3 meters   **D.** 4 meters

1617. Who boarded the *Tantive IV* after it was intercepted by an Imperial Star Destroyer?

A. The Emperor   **C.** Darth Vader

B. Grand Moff Tarkin   **D.** Admiral Motti

1618. What did Luke Skywalker do toward the end of the Battle of Yavin that distressed the Rebels?

A. He turned off his targeting computer   **C.** He turned his ship around

B. He ejected his astromech droid   **D.** He fired and missed

A New Hope Era

1619. Who said, "There'll be no escape for the princess this time"?

A. C-3PO　　　　　　　C. Darth Vader

B. Obi-Wan Kenobi　　D. Luke Skywalker

1620. Who attacked R2-D2 and disabled him as he was traversing the rocky canyons of Tatooine?

A. Tusken Raiders　　C. Smugglers

B. Pirates　　　　　　D. Jawas

1621. Who said, "Help me, Obi-Wan Kenobi. You're my only hope"?

A. R2-D2　　　　　　　C. Luke Skywalker

B. Princess Leia　　　D. Captain Antilles

1622. What had brought the two droids into Luke Skywalker's service, according to C-3PO?

A. An escape pod　　　C. Jawa traders

B. The Rebellion against　D. Bad luck
　　the Empire

1623. What were Obi-Wan's last words to Luke Skywalker after the Battle of Yavin?

A. "Good work, Luke."　　C. "The Force will be with
　　　　　　　　　　　　　　you, always."

B. "May the Force be with you."　D. "Use the Force as your guide."

1624. According to Luke Skywalker, if there was a bright center to the universe, what was Tatooine?

A. A bustling megalopolis　　C. The planet that was farthest
　　　　　　　　　　　　　　　　from it

B. A desert ditch　　　　　D. A distant nightmare

1625. What did Princess Leia announce the *Millennium Falcon* had lost when they were under attack by TIE fighters after escaping the Death Star?

A. The horizontal controls　　C. The shield generator

B. The hyperdrive motivator　　D. The lateral controls

1626.

1627. Who said, "I find your lack of faith disturbing"?

A. Darth Vader　　　　C. Grand Moff Tarkin

B. Obi-Wan Kenobi　　D. The Emperor

OBSESSED WITH *STAR WARS*

1626.

"What an incredible smell you've discovered!" Han Solo snapped after landing in the trash compactor on the Death Star. Luke, Han, and Chewbacca had attempted to rescue the Princess from her cell, only to find that the only way out of the cellblock was blocked by stormtroopers. Princess Leia had come up with the bright idea of blasting through a vent and jumping into the garbage chute, but the door to the chute was magnetically sealed.

"It could be worse," Princess Leia replied, but she spoke too soon—the walls of the compactor came smashing in toward each other. As they scrambled to come up with a way to escape the mess, C-3PO finally remembered to turn his comlink back on and contacted Luke, who screamed at him to shut down all garbage smashers on the detention level. C-3PO managed to get R2-D2 to shut down the trash compactor and open the door.

Out in the hallway, Han was snippy. "If we can just avoid any more female advice, we ought to be able to get out of here," he said. After some bickering, Princess Leia responded, "Listen. I don't know who you are, or where you came from, but from now on, you do as I tell you. Okay?" What did Han Solo call her in response?

A. Lady

B. Your Worshipfulness

C. Your Highness

D. Sister

1628. Where did the exhaust port the Rebel pilots had to target lead directly to?
- **A.** The reactor system
- **B.** The ventilation system
- **C.** The fuel system
- **D.** The molten core

1629. Who did Darth Vader think was missing from a consular ship?
- **A.** The counselor
- **B.** The viceroy
- **C.** The senator
- **D.** The ambassador

1630. What were Han Solo's last words to Luke Skywalker before the Battle of Yavin?
- **A.** "We could use you."
- **B.** "It's more like suicide."
- **C.** "May the Force be with you."
- **D.** "What good's a reward if you ain't around to use it?"

1631. What did Owen Lars tell C-3PO to do?
- **A.** Get moving
- **B.** Shut up
- **C.** Get to work
- **D.** Pipe down

1632. What did the Imperial officer think was wrong with TK-421 when he saw the stromtrooper pointing to his helmet?
- **A.** Bad receiver
- **B.** Bad visualizer
- **C.** Bad communicator
- **D.** Bad transmitter

1633. Who asked, "Who's the more foolish—the fool, or the fool who follows him?"
- **A.** Obi-Wan Kenobi
- **B.** Grand Moff Tarkin
- **C.** Han Solo
- **D.** Luke Skywalker

1634. Where did C-3PO think he and R2-D2 were going to end up?
- **A.** The droid foundry of Geonosis
- **B.** The spice mines of Kessel
- **C.** The spice mines of Nal Hutta
- **D.** The wheel

1635. What did Han Solo call Obi-Wan Kenobi?
- **A.** An old idiot
- **B.** An old fossil
- **C.** A geriatric fossil
- **D.** An old geezer

1636. Where did Owen Lars tell Luke Skywalker he wanted R2-D2 and C-3PO to be working on the condensors in the morning?
- **A.** The north ridge
- **B.** The west ridge
- **C.** The south ridge
- **D.** The east ridge

A New Hope Era

1637. Why was C-3PO reluctant to go in the direction R2-D2 was suggesting after their escape pod landed on Tatooine?
- **A.** It was much too rocky
- **B.** There was too much moisture
- **C.** It was too mountainous
- **D.** It was too treacherous to maneuver in his fragile state

1638. Who exclaimed, "Into the garbage chute, fly boy!"?
- **A.** Han Solo
- **B.** C-3PO
- **C.** Luke Skywalker
- **D.** Princess Leia

1639. Who said, "Your sad devotion to that ancient religion has not given you clairvoyance enough to conjure up the stolen datatapes," to Darth Vader?
- **A.** Grand Moff Tarkin
- **B.** Captain Yorr
- **C.** Chief Bast
- **D.** Admiral Motti

1640. According to C-3PO, in how many locations was the tractor beam coupled to the main reactor on the Death Star?
- **A.** Six
- **B.** Seven
- **C.** Nine
- **D.** Eight

1641.

1642. What word did Grand Moff Tarkin receive about the Imperial Senate?
- **A.** The Emperor had dissolved it
- **B.** They were voting the Emperor emergency powers
- **C.** They were holding new elections
- **D.** They had approved the use of the Death Star against the Rebellion

1643. Who destroyed the Death Star?
- **A.** Biggs Darklighter
- **B.** Han Solo
- **C.** Obi-Wan Kenobi
- **D.** Luke Skywalker

1644. Where did C-3PO tell the stormtroopers the "madmen" were headed?
- **A.** To the hangar bay
- **B.** To the prison level
- **C.** To the tractor beam
- **D.** To maintenance

1645. What did C-3PO think he had found when he spotted the sandcrawler from afar?
- **A.** A settlement
- **B.** An oasis
- **C.** A transport
- **D.** A village

OBSESSED WITH *STAR WARS*

1641.

Darth Vader realized that Obi-Wan Kenobi was on the Death Star. He had felt his former Master's presence as soon as the Death Star's tractor beam caught the *Millennium Falcon*. When news came to him and to Grand Moff Tarkin that Princess Leia had escaped her cell, he said, "Obi-Wan is here. The Force is with him." Tarkin told him that Kenobi must not be allowed to escape. "Escape is not his plan. I must face him alone," the Dark Lord said.

The two met in an empty hallway, Darth Vader's lightsaber blazing red. "The circle is now complete," Darth Vader said as Kenobi ignited his lightsaber. "When I left you, I was but the learner. Now I am the master."

The two swung lightsabers, and as Kenobi blocked an attack, he said, "You can't win, Darth." No matter the physical outcome of the battle, Kenobi knew that the Force was with him.

The battle raged, and Kenobi saw Luke running into the hangar bay toward the *Millennium Falcon*. With a serene smile, Kenobi raised his lightsaber, closed his eyes, and allowed Darth Vader to strike him down. What puzzled Darth Vader after he had killed Kenobi?

- **A.** Obi-Wan's body had disappeared
- **B.** The cut wasn't cauterized by the lightsaber
- **C.** Obi-Wan's spirit remained
- **D.** Vader lost his ability to feel the Force

1646. Who said, "Good against remotes is one thing. Good against the living—that's something else"?

A. Han Solo

B. Luke Skywalker

C. Obi-Wan Kenobi

D. Princess Leia

1647. What was Luke Skywalker referring to when he said, "What a piece of junk!"?

A. His landspeeder

B. The *Millennium Falcon*

C. The Death Star

D. His X-wing

1648. What did Luke Skywalker say Han Solo was best at when Han refused to help battle the Death Star?

A. Being a loser

B. Running away from problems

C. Being selfish

D. Taking care of himself

1649. Whom did R2-D2 tell Luke Skywalker he belonged to?

A. Princess Leia

B. Owen Lars

C. Obi-Wan Kenobi

D. Padmé Amidala

1650. Why couldn't Luke, Han, Leia, and Chewbacca blast their way out of the trash compactor?

A. It was magnetically sealed

B. Their blasters fizzled out in the water

C. There was no door

D. The door was locked from the outside

1651. What mission did Princess Leia give Obi-Wan Kenobi?

A. To destroy the Death Star

B. To train Luke Skywalker as a Jedi

C. To take R2-D2 to Alderaan

D. To defeat Darth Vader

1652. What did the *Millennium Falcon*'s log read when the Imperials checked it on the Death Star?

A. The crew abandoned ship right after takeoff

B. The crew abandoned ship right after jumping out of hyperspace

C. The crew abandoned ship before entering hyperspace

D. The crew was taken prisoner by pirates

1653. Which character did Phil Brown play in *A New Hope*?

A. Admiral Motti

B. Jek Porkins

C. Biggs Darklighter

D. Owen Lars

A New Hope Era

1654. Who was the special photographic effects supervisor for *A New Hope*?
- **A.** John Stears
- **B.** John Dykstra
- **C.** Norman Reynolds
- **D.** Leslie Dilley

1655. Who played Chewbacca in *A New Hope*?
- **A.** Jack Purvis
- **B.** David Prowse
- **C.** Anthony Daniels
- **D.** Peter Mayhew

1656. Which actor portrayed General Dodonna in *A New Hope*?
- **A.** Alex McCrindle
- **B.** Phil Brown
- **C.** Don Henderson
- **D.** Graham Ashley

1657.

1658. Which character did Shelagh Fraser play in *A New Hope*?
- **A.** Leesub Sirin
- **B.** Brindy Truchong
- **C.** Beru Lars
- **D.** Swilla Corey

1659. Who supplied the voice for Darth Vader in *A New Hope*?
- **A.** James Earl Jones
- **B.** Richard LeParmentier
- **C.** David Prowse
- **D.** Garrick Hagon

1660. Which actor played Wedge Antilles in *A New Hope*?
- **A.** Denis Lawson
- **B.** Jack Purvis
- **C.** Garrick Hagon
- **D.** Phil Brown

1661. Who was the costume designer for *A New Hope*?
- **A.** John Stears
- **B.** John Mollo
- **C.** John Dykstra
- **D.** John Barry

1657.

This actor was born in 1913 in England. He was inspired to be an actor by his favorite aunt, who was an actress on the stage. He went to school to pursue a career in acting, but he also studied drawing, which turned out to be useful in his first job as a government surveyor's assistant. While doing this job, he also performed in local amateur theater. Deciding that acting was his life's pursuit, he moved to London and attended the Guildhall School of Music and Drama. He performed in repertory theater, and then decided to take a risk and relocated to Hollywood. His first film role was in *The Man in the Iron Mask* in 1939.

After a few more films in Hollywood, he returned to England, where he contributed to the war effort during World War II by joining the Entertainment National Services Association. Throughout the 1950s, he worked in British television.

At the end of the 1950s, he began a long association with Hammer Productions. He became synonymous with British horror, starring in such films as *The Curse of Frankenstein*, *The Satanic Rites of Dracula*, *Dr. Phibes Rises Again*, *Frankenstein Must Be Destroyed*, and *The Blood Beast Terror*.

Appropriately, he was cast as the sinister Grand Moff Tarkin in *A New Hope*. Who was he?

- **A.** Sir Alec Guinness
- **B.** David Prowse
- **C.** Peter Cushing
- **D.** Phil Brown

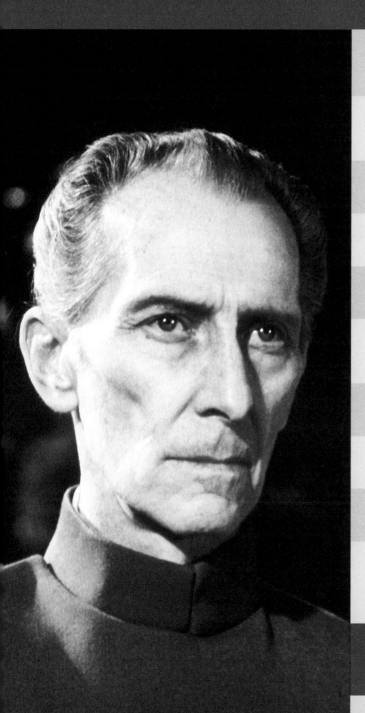

1662. Which actor portrayed Admiral Motti in *A New Hope*?
- **A.** Jack Klaff
- **B.** William Hootkins
- **C.** Don Henderson
- **D.** Richard Le Parmentier

1663. Who was in charge of special dialogue and sound effects for *A New Hope*?
- **A.** Ray West
- **B.** Ben Burtt
- **C.** Lester Fresholtz
- **D.** Stephen Katz

1664. Which actor was inside R2-D2 in *A New Hope*?
- **A.** Jack Purvis
- **B.** Kenny Baker
- **C.** Anthony Daniels
- **D.** Peter Mayhew

1665. Which actor portrayed the chief Jawa in *A New Hope*?
- **A.** Kenny Baker
- **B.** Jack Purvis
- **C.** Jeremy Sinden
- **D.** Drewe Hemley

1666. Who was the production designer for *A New Hope*?
- **A.** John Barry
- **B.** John Mollo
- **C.** John Stears
- **D.** John Dykstra

1667. Who was the special production and mechanical effects supervisor for *A New Hope*?
- **A.** Ray West
- **B.** Paul Hirsch
- **C.** John Dykstra
- **D.** John Stears

1668. Who played Biggs Darklighter in *A New Hope*?
- **A.** Jeremy Sinden
- **B.** Richard LeParmentier
- **C.** Garrick Hagon
- **D.** Denis Lawson

1669. Who produced the special edition of *A New Hope*?
- **A.** George Lucas
- **B.** Rick McCallum
- **C.** Gary Kurtz
- **D.** Howard Kazanjian

1670. Where were the Yavin 4 scenes shot for *A New Hope*?
- **A.** Guatemala
- **B.** Brazil
- **C.** Venezuela
- **D.** Peru

A New Hope Era

1671. Who was Echo Seven?

A. Luke Skywalker
B. Carlist Rieekan
C. Han Solo
D. Princess Leia

1672. What game did Luke want to play on Vorzyd 5?

A. Sabacc
B. Dejarik
C. Billiards
D. Cosmic Chance

1673. To which planet were Luke Skywalker and Princess Leia headed for a diplomatic meeting with resistance groups and government leaders when they crash-landed on Mimban?

A. Mimban
B. Circarpous IV
C. Corellia
D. Ralltiir

1674. Who rescued Han Solo from the clutches of Boba Fett on Nar Shaddaa?

A. Lando Calrissian
B. Chewbacca
C. Princess Leia
D. Luke Skywalker

1675. Who oversaw the development of a mind-altering aerosol weapon called Pacifog on a laboratory orbiting the planet Kadril?

A. Darth Vader
B. Emperor Palpatine
C. Blackhole
D. Grand Admiral Thrawn

1676. What did Luke Skywalker and Princess Leia search for on Mimban?

A. The Ilum crystal
B. The Chronelle crystal
C. The Kaiburr crystal
D. The Sadgie crystal

1671C 1672D 1673B 1674A 1675A 1676C

1677. Who said, "He is as clumsy as he is stupid"?
A. The Emperor
B. Darth Vader
C. Captain Needa
D. Admiral Ozzel

1678. Who was Rogue Leader in the Battle of Hoth?
A. Han Solo
B. Wedge Antilles
C. Cal Alder
D. Luke Skywalker

1679. Who taught Lando Calrissian how to fly a spaceship?
A. Han Solo
B. Amaiza Foxtrain
C. Jodelle Foxtrain
D. Lobot

1680. Who, disguised as a serving girl, snuck into Lady Tarkin's estate on Phelarion?
A. Princess Leia
B. Han Solo
C. Luke Skywalker
D. Lando Calrissian

1681. Who discovered a hidden civilization in the Rafa system?
A. Han Solo
B. Luke Skywalker
C. Lando Calrissian
D. Yoda

1682.

1683. Who referred to Princess Leia as a "steel kitten" on Mimban?
A. Lando Calrissian
B. Prince Xizor
C. Han Solo
D. Darth Vader

1684. Who was in charge of Echo Base on Hoth?
A. General Rieekan
B. General Veers
C. General Dodonna
D. General Mills

1682.

Luke Skywalker was faced with a difficult situation. His snowspeeder had been hit and his gunner had been either knocked unconscious or killed in the blast. The smoking speeder slid to the ground in the direct path of one of the Empire's gargantuan, deadly transports.

On the ground, Luke scrambled to drag the gunner from his seat in the downed speeder. Luke knew that it was only a matter of moments before his ship would be smashed to bits under the walker's large foot. He ran out of time, and jumped out of the speeder barely seconds before it was smashed under the mammoth machine. Thinking fast, Luke Skywalker ran away from the crushed remains of his

downed speeder and after the walker as it lumbered toward Echo Base. He shot a grappling cable up underneath the transport's hull, pulling himself up close to the main body of the mechanical leviathan. What did he do next?

A. He fired on the pilots

B. He cut a hole in the hull with his light-saber and threw in a detonation device

C. He cut a hole in the hull, entered the walker, and fought the crew

D. He used his lightsaber to cut the cockpit off of the walker

1685. What did Luke Skywalker use to heal Princess Leia after she had been mortally wounded on Mimban?

A. The Coachelle crystal   **C.** The Chronelle crystal

B. The Kaiburr crystal   **D.** The Force

1686. What was Luke Skywalker's rank in the Rebel Alliance at the Battle of Hoth?

A. General   **C.** Captain

B. Admiral   **D.** Commander

1687. Who was Echo Three?

A. Wedge Antilles   **C.** Luke Skywalker

B. Han Solo   **D.** Princess Leia

1688. Who did the bounty hunter Skorr find on Ord Mantell?

A. Lando Calrissian   **C.** Boba Fett

B. Han Solo   **D.** Luke Skywalker

1689. Who, according to legend, was recruited to fight a marauder named Sergi-X Arragontus?

A. Han Solo   **C.** Luke Skywalker

B. Lando Calrissian   **D.** R2-D2

1690. Who said, "You truly belong with us here among the clouds"?

A. Han Solo   **C.** Lobot

B. Lando Calrissian   **D.** C-3PO

1691. Whom did Boba Fett attempt to take prisoner after witnessing an X-wing crash on Ota?

A. Luke Skywalker   **C.** Han Solo

B. Wedge Antilles   **D.** Princess Leia

1692. Who helped Luke Skywalker defeat Darth Vader on Mimban?

A. Yoda   **C.** Obi-Wan Kenobi

B. Qui-Gon Jinn   **D.** Halla

The Empire Strikes Back Era

1693. Who helped Keyan Farlander with the rollout of the new B-wing starfighter?

A. Luke Skywalker

B. Princess Leia

C. Han Solo

D. Wedge Antilles

1694. What did Senator Simon Greyshade want in return for keeping silent regarding the Empire's plot to blame the Rebel Alliance for a theft aboard the gambling station The Wheel?

A. 500,000 credits

B. Princess Leia

C. An audience with the Emperor

D. An audience with Darth Vader

1695. How did Darth Vader accept Captain Needa's apology?

A. He increased his rank

B. He decreased his rank

C. He shook his hand

D. He choked him

1696. Who said, "I am not a committee!"?

A. C-3PO

B. Princess Leia

C. Luke Skywalker

D. Han Solo

1697. What appendage of Darth Vader's did Luke Skywalker cut off in their lightsaber duel on Mimban?

A. His left leg

B. His left arm

C. His right leg

D. His right arm

1698. To whom was Princess Leia referring when she said, "Laser brain"?

A. Han Solo

B. Chewbacca

C. Luke Skywalker

D. Lando Calrissian

1699. Who earned a death sentence by stealing treasure from the Glottalphib crime lord Nandreeson?

A. Han Solo

B. Lando Calrissian

C. Dengar

D. Boba Fett

1700. Who said, "Then I'll see you in Hell!" after receiving a stern warning from a concerned Rebel officer?

A. Luke Skywalker

B. Han Solo

C. Obi-Wan Kenobi

D. Princess Leia

OBSESSED WITH *STAR WARS*

1704.

Han Solo, Princess Leia, Chewbacca, and C-3PO were seeking a safe haven in which they could hide from Darth Vader, who was bent on capturing the *Millennium Falcon*. So obsessed had the Dark Lord become by the idea of capturing the Rebels that he had sent his fleet into harm's way by following the elusive ship into a deadly asteroid field.

The Rebels had managed to hide from the Imperial fleet, but someone had followed them after the fleet broke up and relayed their whereabouts to the Empire. Unaware of all this, Han raced toward what he thought would be a safe haven in the clouds—but Han, Leia, and Chewbacca were betrayed and handed over to the Empire.

Darth Vader had Han Solo strapped to a device that sent electric shocks throughout his body. As the Dark Lord watched, presumably enjoying the proceedings, Han Solo screamed in agony.

Han was then dragged to a holding cell where he joined Princess Leia and Chewbacca. What did he tell Princess Leia about his ordeal?

A. "They wanted to know about Luke Skywalker."

B. "Darth Vader doesn't want us at all."

C. "I wouldn't talk, no matter how hard they tried to get me to."

D. "They never even asked me any questions."

1701. Who fought and defeated Rokur Gepta, the last of the Sorcerers of Tund?
- **A.** Yoda
- **B.** Princess Leia
- **C.** Lando Calrissian
- **D.** Han Solo

1702. Who was attacked by a squill and caught Bledsoe's disease on Tatooine?
- **A.** Chewbacca
- **B.** Han Solo
- **C.** Luke Skywalker
- **D.** Wedge Antilles

1703. Who helped the Oswaft of the planet ThonBoka win their freedom from an Imperial blockade that was causing them to starve?
- **A.** Luke Skywalker
- **B.** Han Solo
- **C.** Yoda
- **D.** Lando Calrissian

1704.

1705. Who said, "You are beaten!"?
- **A.** Darth Vader
- **B.** Yoda
- **C.** Luke Skywalker
- **D.** The Emperor

1706. Against which organization on Corellia did Darth Vader enlist Grand Admiral Thrawn's aid?
- **A.** Black Moon
- **B.** Black Sun
- **C.** Black Hole
- **D.** Black Star

1707. What did Princess Leia use to fight Darth Vader on Mimban?
- **A.** A blaster
- **B.** A whip
- **C.** A staff
- **D.** A lightsaber

1708. Who called Han Solo a "nerf herder"?
- **A.** Princess Leia
- **B.** Lando Calrissian
- **C.** C-3PO
- **D.** Luke Skywalker

The Empire Strikes Back **Era**

1709. What was Han Solo's rank in the Rebel Alliance at the Battle of Hoth?
- **A.** Lieutenant
- **B.** General
- **C.** Admiral
- **D.** Captain

1710. Who owned the droid Vuffi Raa?
- **A.** Lando Calrissian
- **B.** Darth Vader
- **C.** Luke Skywalker
- **D.** Han Solo

1711. For what celebration did Chewbacca return to Kashyyyk to be with Mallatobuck and Lumpawarump?
- **A.** Kashyyyk Day
- **B.** Wroshyr Day
- **C.** Tarfful Day
- **D.** Life Day

1712. Who instructed Luke Skywalker to go to the Dagobah system?
- **A.** Han Solo
- **B.** Qui-Gon Jinn
- **C.** Obi-Wan Kenobi
- **D.** Yoda

1713. Who was the first to track Han Solo to Cloud City?
- **A.** Dengar
- **B.** Boba Fett
- **C.** Darth Vader
- **D.** Captain Valance

1714. What strange creature did Luke Skywalker encounter on Dagobah?
- **A.** Yoda
- **B.** Oppo Rancisis
- **C.** An Aqualish
- **D.** Chewbacca

1715. Who, due to his superior's incompetence, was promoted from Captain to Admiral during the Battle of Hoth?
- **A.** Captain Needa
- **B.** Captain Piett
- **C.** Captain Charge
- **D.** Captain Solo

1716. With whom did Darth Vader need to make contact when he asked Admiral Piett to move the Super Star Destroyer *Executor* so they could send a clear transmission?
- **A.** Mara Jade
- **B.** Blackhole
- **C.** Emperor Palpatine
- **D.** Shire Brie

OBSESSED WITH *STAR WARS*

1720.

Although the Empire had been successful at the Battle of Hoth, all of the Rebel transports had been able to make safe getaways. The Rebels' base on the planet had been ransacked and destroyed, but their casualties were minimal. Darth Vader's Super Star Destroyer, as well as a large fleet of Star Destroyers and fighters, continued to pursue a ship full of Rebels whom Darth Vader considered to be first on his list of enemies.

When the Rebels fled into an asteroid field, Vader's ships were pummeled by asteroids, but his order remained clear: "I want that ship, not excuses." As his fleet continued their search, Admiral Piett rushed to him and told him that the Emperor commanded him to make contact.

Darth Vader knelt as the huge, holographic image of Emperor Palpatine flickered before him. "What is thy bidding, my Master?" Vader asked the Dark Lord of the Sith.

"There is a great disturbance in the Force," the Emperor said. "We have a new enemy." Who was this enemy?

A. The young Rebel who knew Obi-Wan Kenobi

B. The young Rebel who had destroyed the probe droid on Hoth

C. The young Rebel who had destroyed the Death Star

D. The young Rebel en route to train with Master Yoda

1717. Whom did Darth Vader hire an actor to impersonate, setting a trap for Luke Skywalker on the planet Aridus?
- **A.** Owen Lars
- **B.** Beru Lars
- **C.** Biggs Darklighter
- **D.** Obi-Wan Kenobi

1718. Who co-founded Rogue Squadron with Luke Skywalker?
- **A.** Han Solo
- **B.** Carlist Rieekan
- **C.** Cal Alder
- **D.** Wedge Antilles

1719. What did Yoda say was always in motion when Luke asked him about a vision?
- **A.** The future
- **B.** The Force
- **C.** The galaxy
- **D.** The mind

1720.

1721. C-3PO assured R2-D2 that one person could fix the hyperdrive on the *Millennium Falcon*—who was it?
- **A.** Han Solo
- **B.** Chewbacca
- **C.** R2-D2
- **D.** Lando Calrissian

1722. Dr. Evazan, the Mos Eisley cantina patron who said, "He doesn't like you," to Luke Skywalker, was experimenting in the reanimation of dead bodies on the planet Necropolis when he was killed by which notorious bounty hunter?
- **A.** Boba Fett
- **B.** Aurra Sing
- **C.** Dengar
- **D.** 4-LOM

1723. Who told Han Solo that he was a good fighter in Echo Station on Hoth?
- **A.** Princess Leia
- **B.** Carlist Rieekan
- **C.** Lobot
- **D.** Lando Calrissian

1724. What type of stew was Yoda preparing when Luke Skywalker was visiting his hut?
- **A.** Grimeworm
- **B.** Skimmerleaf
- **C.** Pillbug
- **D.** Rootleaf

The Empire Strikes Back **Era**

1725. To what did General Rieekan order all power in Echo Base rerouted?

A. The ion cannon

B. The energy shield

C. The medical facility

D. The hangar bay

1726. While the Rebel Alliance's secret base was on the planet Thila, which Rebel pilot flew into battle in his T-47 without realizing that Chewbacca was dangling from his fuselage?

A. Luke Skywalker

B. Han Solo

C. Wedge Antilles

D. Zev Senesca

1727. What did Yoda tell Luke Skywalker about his father?

A. He was a great friend

B. He was a Sith Lord

C. He was the best star pilot in the galaxy

D. He was a powerful Jedi

1728. Whom did General Moch hire to kill Rebel Agent Kyle Katarn?

A. Bossk

B. 4-LOM

C. Skorr

D. Boba Fett

1729.

1730. Due to his flawless reputation and massive record of "arrests and suppressions" in the Outer Rim, who was promoted to the Imperial Death Squadron, the most visible fleet in the Empire?

A. Captain Needa

B. Admiral Ozzel

C. Captain Piett

D. General Veers

1731. Who came across Tash and Zak Arranda on Dagobah and tried to capture them, but instead ran into a band of cannibals?

A. Yoda

B. Dengar

C. Boba Fett

D. Luke Skywalker

1732. How old was General Carlist Rieekan when he began his military career?

A. Seventeen

B. Twenty

C. Forty-two

D. Thirty-one

1729.

Princess Leia, Chewbacca, Lando Calrissian, C-3PO, and R2-D2 were making a hasty retreat from Cloud City, which had been overtaken by Imperial troops. As they struggled to reach the *Millennium Falcon* on the landing platform, they battled Imperial stormtroopers at every turn. Finally arriving at the platform, they managed to break through the code (which the Empire had changed), battle off more stormtroopers, and rush to their ship. They blasted out of the doomed mining facility and toward freedom.

Their escape would be temporary, however. As they were fleeing the Empire, Leia got a feeling and commanded

1733. What did Yoda levitate out of the water?
- **A.** His landing pod
- **B.** A dragonsnake
- **C.** Luke's X-wing
- **D.** R2-D2

1734. To whom did C-3PO say, "You have a responsibility to me, so don't do anything foolish"?
- **A.** Lando Calrissian
- **B.** R2-D2
- **C.** Han Solo
- **D.** Chewbacca

1735. Who uttered the words "Luke, don't give in to hate" to Luke Skywalker?
- **A.** Obi-Wan Kenobi
- **B.** Yoda
- **C.** Han Solo
- **D.** Princess Leia

1736. Who said, "He's no good to me dead"?
- **A.** Darth Vader
- **B.** Boba Fett
- **C.** Lando Calrissian
- **D.** Dengar

1737. What did Luke Skywalker promise Yoda as he was leaving?
- **A.** To return and finish what he had begun
- **B.** To mind the Force
- **C.** To fight the dark side
- **D.** To practice levitation

1738. Whom did Han Solo tell Chewbacca he had to take care of?
- **A.** Lando Calrissian
- **B.** Boba Fett
- **C.** Luke Skywalker
- **D.** Princess Leia

1739. Who tried to capture Luke Skywalker in the Panna system?
- **A.** Darth Vader
- **B.** IG-88
- **C.** Boba Fett
- **D.** Aurra Sing

1740. What, according to Yoda, was "quicker, easier, more seductive"?
- **A.** The dark side
- **B.** Training as a Jedi in the old Republic
- **C.** The light side
- **D.** Urban living

Chewbacca to turn the ship around. "I know where Luke is," she told Chewbacca, who immediately did as Leia commanded. When Lando protested, Chewbacca roared in anger.

They rushed back to Cloud City and saw a form Leia knew to be Luke Skywalker. What did Leia tell Lando Calrissian to do as they approached Luke?

- **A.** "Open the top hatch."
- **B.** "Go to the back and stay there."
- **C.** "Open fire."
- **D.** "Remain calm."

The Empire Strikes Back Era

1741. Who did the Emperor have no doubt their new enemy was?

A. The offspring of Mon Mothma

B. The offspring of Obi-Wan Kenobi

C. The offspring of Anakin Skywalker

D. The offspring of Bail Organa

1742. What was Yoda balancing on before Luke's X-wing sank?

A. Luke's left hand

B. Luke's right leg

C. Luke's left leg

D. Luke's right hand

1743. What did Darth Vader tell Admiral Piett did not concern him?

A. Uncharted settlements

B. Admiral Ozzel

C. A clear transmission

D. Asteroids

1744. What Alderaan native was offworld inspecting a satellite transmission system around the planet Delaya when Alderaan was destroyed by the Death Star?

A. Carlist Rieekan

B. Dack Ralter

C. Simon Greyshade

D. Bren Derlin

1745. What reason did Yoda give Obi-Wan for not being able to train Luke Skywalker?

A. He didn't like Luke's bangs

B. Luke was too old

C. Luke hadn't brought proper clothing

D. Luke didn't have a high enough midi-chlorian count

1746. Who told Luke he couldn't control the Force after Luke said, "I feel the Force"?

A. Yoda

B. Darth Vader

C. Obi-Wan Kenobi

D. Princess Leia

1747.

1748. To whom did Darth Vader make a point of stressing, "No disintegrations"?

A. Boba Fett

B. IG-88

C. Dengar

D. Bossk

1747.

Yoda knew from the start that he had a difficult student in the reckless, headstrong Luke Skywalker. Luke had been sent to Yoda to complete the training that Obi-Wan was unable to finish before he sacrificed himself aboard the Death Star, and although Luke desperately wanted to become a Jedi like his father, he kept allowing his emotions to get the upper hand. Luke's ultimate failure came when his X-wing starfighter sank into the swamp. He tried to levitate the ship out of the murky water. Stirring, the X-wing began to lift as Luke became visibly shaken. "I can't . . . it's too big," Luke said, collapsing.

OBSESSED WITH *STAR WARS*

1749. What did Obi-Wan think Luke Skywalker was?
- **A.** "The future of the Jedi"
- **B.** "Our last hope"
- **C.** "The galaxy's last chance"
- **D.** "The key to freedom"

1750. What did Yoda have to say to Luke Skywalker about size?
- **A.** "Size is important."
- **B.** "Size matters not."
- **C.** "In your mind size is."
- **D.** "Overcome your obsession with size you must."

1751. Who was Luke Skywalker's tailgunner in the Battle of Hoth?
- **A.** Wedge Antilles
- **B.** Dack Ralter
- **C.** Derek Klivian
- **D.** Wes Janson

1752. Who kidnapped Princess Leia and Luke Skywalker in an attempt to capture Han Solo?
- **A.** Bossk
- **B.** Cradossk
- **C.** Skorr
- **D.** Aurra Sing

1753. Who was Rogue Four?
- **A.** Cal Alder
- **B.** Tarrin Datch
- **C.** Dack Ralter
- **D.** Derek Klivian

1754. Which Imperial appeared to agents and to Darth Vader only through a distorter and sent troops to Vorzyd 5 to capture Princess Leia and Luke Skywalker?
- **A.** Mara Jade
- **B.** Blackhole
- **C.** Prince Xizor
- **D.** General Veers

1755. Which bounty hunter was obsessed with catching and skinning Chewbacca?
- **A.** Aurra Sing
- **B.** Boba Fett
- **C.** Bossk
- **D.** Dengar

1756. Who was Rogue Seven?
- **A.** Kasan Moor
- **B.** Nala Hetsime
- **C.** Tenk Lesko
- **D.** Coleytho Mason

"Judge me by my size, do you?" Yoda asked.

Luke stomped off into the swamp in a huff, but Yoda closed his eyes and concentrated. R2-D2's beeps got Luke Skywalker's attention, and he went to Yoda's side. Luke ran to his resurrected X-wing and touched it to make sure it was real.

"I don't believe it," Luke stammered. What did Yoda say in return?

- **A.** "The Force is strong in me, yes."
- **B.** "Size matters not at all, as I said."
- **C.** "That is why you fail."
- **D.** "In time, you will."

The Empire Strikes Back Era

1757. Who reported in to Echo Base that he had found Commander Skywalker and Captain Solo on Hoth?
- **A.** Rogue Four
- **B.** Rogue Six
- **C.** Rogue Ten
- **D.** Rogue Two

1758. What was Captain Needa's first name?
- **A.** Lorth
- **B.** Tygo
- **C.** Lurdo
- **D.** Buvil

1759. Which Rebel soldier was a child of prisoners in a Kalist VI labor colony?
- **A.** Cal Alder
- **B.** Wedge Antilles
- **C.** Dack Ralter
- **D.** Zev Senesca

1760. What was Wes Janson's rank at the Battle of Hoth?
- **A.** Lieutenant
- **B.** Major
- **C.** Captain
- **D.** General

1761. What Force-sensitive being did Luke Skywalker and Princess Leia encounter on Mimban?
- **A.** Malla
- **B.** Dalla
- **C.** Halla
- **D.** Nalla

1762. Who had to inform Princess Leia that the shield doors to the Rebel Base on Hoth had to be closed for the night?
- **A.** Carlist Rieekan
- **B.** Cal Alder
- **C.** Bren Derlin
- **D.** Wedge Antilles

1763.

1764. Who was Cloud City's computer liaison officer?
- **A.** Vuffi Raa
- **B.** Lobot
- **C.** Ugloste
- **D.** King Ozz

1763.

This mercenary could be spotted among the bounty-hunter vermin on the deck of the Super Star Destroyer *Executor*, hired by Darth Vader to search the galaxy for the Rebel ship *Millennium Falcon* and its passengers.

When he was young, he spent his time repairing damaged swoops with his father. He raced them as well, until he was in a terrible accident. It just so happened that the person he believed had caused the accident was Han Solo. After this being sideswiped Solo's main repulsor-fin, he crashed. The crash ended his career in racing, and began his life-long hatred of Solo and his desperate need for revenge against the Corellian.

He began working as an assassin for the Empire, all the while fantasizing that each of his kills was Han Solo. Driven by revenge, he became a merciless killer. He actually captured Solo once in the Hoth system, after teaming up with other bounty hunters, but Solo escaped, further fueling this being's need for revenge. When the Empire called for bounty hunters to scour the galaxy for Solo, this being jumped at the chance. Who was he?

- **A.** Boba Fett
- **B.** Bossk
- **C.** Dengar
- **D.** Zuckuss

1765. Which bounty hunter acquired the title Monarch of the Qotile System?
- **A.** Bossk
- **B.** 4-LOM
- **C.** Dengar
- **D.** Boba Fett

1766. Which member of Rogue Squadron deserted the Imperial Academy with Biggs Darklighter?
- **A.** Dack Ralter
- **B.** Kasan Moor
- **C.** Samoc Farr
- **D.** Derek Klivian

1767. Which bounty hunter was native to Trandosha?
- **A.** Boba Fett
- **B.** Dengar
- **C.** Bossk
- **D.** Zuckuss

1768. When Princess Leia was explaining the evacuation plan to Rebel Pilots in Echo Base, who said, "Two fighters against a Star Destroyer?"?
- **A.** Rogue Four
- **B.** Rogue Two
- **C.** Rogue Eleven
- **D.** Rogue Three

1769. Before being hired by the Empire to search for the *Millennium Falcon* and its passengers, which bounty hunter had previously killed Hal Horn, the head of CorSec on Corellia?
- **A.** Zuckuss
- **B.** Bossk
- **C.** IG-88
- **D.** Boba Fett

1770. Whom did Cradossk accept as a member of the Bounty Hunters' Guild, an acceptance that Zuckuss saw as a bad omen?
- **A.** Dengar
- **B.** 4-LOM
- **C.** Boba Fett
- **D.** IG-88

1771. What was Derek Klivian's nickname?
- **A.** Lurdo
- **B.** Hobbie
- **C.** Pee-wee
- **D.** Turner

1772. Who was a findsman?
- **A.** Zuckuss
- **B.** Dengar
- **C.** Skorr
- **D.** La'Taun

The Empire Strikes Back Era

1773. Whose designation was Rogue Ten?

A. Dash Rendar   **C.** Tycho Celchu

B. Tarrin Datch   **D.** Tenk Lenso

1774. What was Zuckuss's homeworld?

A. Gand   **C.** Dantooine

B. Ord Mantell   **D.** Bith

1775.

1776. Who was promoted from Lieutenant to Major after saving his commanding officer, General Irrv, from a native insurrection on Culroon III?

A. Captain Needa   **C.** Admiral Ozzel

B. General Veers   **D.** Admiral Piett

1777. Who was the first Alliance gunner to harpoon an AT-AT during the Battle of Hoth?

A. Dack Ralter   **C.** Jehaw Graneet

B. Kesin Ommis   **D.** Wes Janson

1778. Whose father had been an Outer Rim slaver before being killed by pirates?

A. Dengar   **C.** Lobot

B. Bren Derlin   **D.** Tarrin Datch

1779. Who was originally from Kestic Station in the Bestine System?

A. Dash Rendar   **C.** Torl Ogo

B. Zev Senesca   **D.** Wes Janson

1780. What was Dengar's homeworld?

A. Coruscant   **C.** Corellia

B. Tatooine   **D.** Nar Shaddaa

1775.

This being's father had been a merciless slaver in the Outer Rim territories, terrifying and subjugating millions before being murdered by rival slavers during the Clone Wars. Orphaned and taken prisoner, this being longed to upstage his father and earn even greater notoriety through the Outer Rim. Eventually escaping his captors after being imprisoned for two years, he fled to Bespin and became a petty thief in order to get by.

Finally captured and taken before Baroness—Administrator Shallence, he was put to work in Cloud City. His head was shaved and holes were bored into his head, where a Biotech Aj^6 cyborg headband was attached.

With this attachment, this being had constant access to all information involving Cloud City and was gifted with boosted intelligence and increased strength. His emotions, memory, and linguistic skills eventually disappeared, leaving him with little or no remaining knowledge of his troubled past; he simply acted as a loyal worker in Cloud City. What was his name?

A. Lobot

B. Loman

C. RoMan

D. Mobot

1781. Who said, "They can't have disappeared. No ship that small has a cloaking device"?

A. General Veers C. Admiral Ozzel
B. Captain Piett D. Captain Needa

1782. Who won a spot on the Ferini racing team when he was young?

A. Han Solo C. Dengar
B. Zev Senesca D. Bossk

1783. Who came out of lightspeed too close to the Hoth system?

A. Admiral Ozzel C. Captain Needa
B. General Veers D. Captain Piett

1784. Who felt like he could take on the whole Empire himself?

A. Dash Rendar C. Dack Ralter
B. Wes Janson D. Zev Senesca

1785. What was Admiral Ozzel's first name?

A. Leroy C. Yen
B. Gerard D. Kendal

1786. What was Tenk Lenso's designation during the Battle of Hoth?

A. Rogue Three C. Rogue Nine
B. Rogue Eleven D. Rogue Eight

1787. Which Imperial officer had escaped from the Death Star in a shuttle and crash-landed on Yavin 4?

A. Captain Needa C. Admiral Piett
B. Admiral Ozzel D. General Veers

1788. Who was paired with 4-LOM on many missions?

A. Lobot C. Zuckuss
B. Aurra Sing D. Boba Fett

The Empire Strikes Back Era

1789. Who had a son named Zevulon?
- **A.** General Veers
- **B.** General Rieekan
- **C.** Admiral Ozzel
- **D.** Captain Valance

1790. Who had an elite force of stormtroopers under his command whose black armor had been modified with stygian-triprismatic polymer?
- **A.** Blackhole
- **B.** Darth Vader
- **C.** Emperor Palpatine
- **D.** General Veers

1791.

1792. With whom did bounty hunter Zuckuss pair up when attempting to capture the accountant Nil Posondum?
- **A.** Cradossk
- **B.** Skorr
- **C.** Boba Fett
- **D.** Bossk

1793. How long was Lobot's original term in his position on Cloud City?
- **A.** Five years
- **B.** Fifteen years
- **C.** Twelve years
- **D.** Twenty years

1794. What was Admiral Ozzel's homeworld?
- **A.** Coruscant
- **B.** Ord Mantell
- **C.** Carida
- **D.** Corellia

1795. How many bounties had Bossk collected for the Empire as of the Battle of Hoth?
- **A.** Sixteen
- **B.** Thirty
- **C.** Nine
- **D.** Twelve

1796. Whose hypothalamus had been replaced with circuitry, deadening almost all emotions?
- **A.** Darth Vader
- **B.** Boba Fett
- **C.** Dengar
- **D.** Zuckuss

1791.

The *Millennium Falcon* had evaded the Imperial fleet, and Darth Vader was losing patience. No longer relying on his own troops, Vader had brought in a group of mercenaries and offered a large sum to whoever could bring in Han Solo and his crew. As Vader was going over regulations with the bounty hunters, primarily his desire to have Solo's crew delivered to him alive, Admiral Piett piped up. "My Lord, we have them."

After taking refuge in what Han Solo had mistakenly thought to be a safe haven, the *Millennium Falcon* had blasted out of the asteroid field and now had the Star Destroyer *Avenger* on its tail. The smaller ship had suffered heavy damage and was unable to blast into hyperspace. Captain Solo, always resourceful, chose an alternate means of escape. "Turn the ship around," he commanded. "I said turn her around!" With that, Chewbacca aimed the *Falcon* directly at the Star Destroyer.

"They're moving into attack position," the baffled Captain Needa exclaimed as the smaller ship charged at the bridge of the menacing Star Destroyer. "Shields up," he ordered, right before the rebel ship flew past them. What was his next order?

- **A.** "Open fire!"
- **B.** "Track them. They may come round for another pass."
- **C.** "Initiate tractor beam!"
- **D.** "Damage their ship, but don't destroy it!"

1797. Which Imperial officer was in charge of the ground asault against the Rebels on Hoth?

A. General Veers
C. Admiral Ozzel
B. Captain Needa
D. Captain Piett

1798. Who was referred to as "The Uncanny One"?

A. Boba Fett
C. Bossk
B. 4-LOM
D. Zuckuss

1799. What did Halla do after her mission on Mimban was completed?

A. She retired
C. She joined the Rebellion
B. She ran for office
D. She opened a general store for the miners on Mimban

1800. Who worked from time to time as a gladiator in the pits of Loovria?

A. Boba Fett
C. Bossk
B. Dengar
D. Lobot

1801. Who, as a Captain, served as a Naval Academy instructor on Coruscant?

A. Admiral Ozzel
C. Captain Piett
B. Captain Needa
D. General Gith

1802. Who tried to capture a pack of Wookiees on Gandolo IV, only to be foiled by Han Solo?

A. Darth Vader
C. Dengar
B. IG-88
D. Bossk

1803. How many years had Halla been searching for the elusive Kaiburr Crystal?

A. Seven
C. Six
B. Two
D. Three

1804. Whose skull was speared by a crystal shard when he crashed during an illegal race through the Agrilat swamps on Corellia?

A. Lobot
C. Bossk
B. Dengar
D. Cal Alder

The Empire Strikes Back Era

1805. For how many centuries had Zuckuss' family followed the findsmen tradition?

- **A.** Three
- **B.** Two
- **C.** Six
- **D.** One

1806. What did Bossk do to gain control of the Bounty Hunters' Guild?

- **A.** He ran a keen election campaign
- **B.** He dug up dirt on his competition
- **C.** He framed his main competitor for murder
- **D.** He killed and ate his own father

1807. How old was Lobot when he was orphaned?

- **A.** Ten
- **B.** Twelve
- **C.** Fifteen
- **D.** Four

1808.

1809. What was General Veers' first name?

- **A.** Handel
- **B.** Lennox
- **C.** Aloysius
- **D.** Maximilian

1810. Who was Rogue Two?

- **A.** Sadgie Yarl
- **B.** Zev Senesca
- **C.** Morl Aglat
- **D.** Kasan Moor

1811. Which alien species has a rare subspecies referred to as "the breathers"?

- **A.** Lepus Carnivorus
- **B.** Trandoshan
- **C.** Wookiee
- **D.** Gand

1812. During Han Solo's legendary trip to Aduba-3, he encountered a giant green alien. What did this alien look like?

- **A.** A rabbit
- **B.** A newt
- **C.** A velociraptor
- **D.** A cat

1808.

Admiral Ozzel took the Imperial fleet out of lightspeed close to the Hoth system, believing that an element of surprise would hinder the Rebels' chances of escape. They found, however, a shield protecting the ice planet, which made an attack from space impossible. Not to be deterred, Darth Vader ordered General Veers to ready his troops for a surface attack, before taking Admiral Ozzel to task for the final time in the Admiral's shaky career.

On the surface, General Veers was commanding one of the large transports lumbering toward the Rebel base. His main goal was to target and destroy the generator creating the protective shield. As he neared the base, the Rebels countered with an attack, but he persevered. Just as he had the shield generator in his scope, he received holographic contact from Darth Vader. What did he tell the Dark Lord?

- **A.** "Yes, Lord Vader. The shield will be down in moments. You may start your landing."
- **B.** "We need more time, my Lord."
- **C.** "We will need more transports."
- **D.** "They've downed several transports, my Lord. I will contact you once I reach the generator."

1813. Which species has come to be known as "Greenies"?
- **A.** Trandoshans
- **B.** Rodians
- **C.** Mimbanites
- **D.** Lepi

1814. Which of the following species is known for its tireless work ethic?
- **A.** Greenies
- **B.** S'kytri
- **C.** Trandoshans
- **D.** Ugnaughts

1815. Which species lives underground on Mimban?
- **A.** Coway
- **B.** Mimbanites
- **C.** Thrella
- **D.** Hrakians

1816. Ufflor are elected officials within the tribes for which species?
- **A.** Mimbanites
- **B.** Wookiees
- **C.** Coway
- **D.** Ugnaughts

1817. How many claws do Trandoshans have on each appendage?
- **A.** Four
- **B.** Five
- **C.** Three
- **D.** Six

1818. How many times a year do the reptilian Trandoshans shed their skin?
- **A.** Two times
- **B.** One time
- **C.** Three times
- **D.** Four times

1819. Which species is native to the planet Gentes?
- **A.** Trandoshans
- **B.** Lepi
- **C.** Gands
- **D.** Ugnaughts

1820. According to legend, Han Solo hired Hedji on Aduba-3 to protect the farmers. What was Hedji's species?
- **A.** Spiner
- **B.** Quiller
- **C.** Needler
- **D.** Prickler

The Empire Strikes Back **Era**

1821. Which species had one of its largest galactic populations in Cloud City?
A. Gands
C. Lannik
B. Trandoshans
D. Ugnaughts

1822. Which species is native to the Coachelle system in the Mid Rim?
A. Trandoshan
C. Gand
B. Spiner
D. Lepi

1823. What is the name of the female deity the Trandoshans worship?
A. The Trapper-Keeper
C. The Score-Keeper
B. The Karcc'lamp
D. Trandosha

1824. Which species refers to themselves as T'doshok?
A. Trandoshans
C. Gands
B. S'kytri
D. Wookiees

1825.

1826. How many fingers do Gands have on each hand?
A. Two
C. Three
B. Four
D. Six

1827. Which species was enslaved by the Empire on a planet the Empire called Marat V?
A. The S'kytri
C. The Hrakians
B. The Hoojibs
D. The Kivviks

1828. Lord Figg rounded up three tribes of which species by force?
A. Trandoshans
C. Wookiees
B. Ugnaughts
D. Lepi

1825.

Certain members of this alien species have a very rare gift and are revered by other members of their species and denizens of the galaxy for their skills. These beings perform divine rituals and interpret omens that have been sent to them in order to track prey. They are hired throughout the galaxy based on these mystical powers and have been used as bounty hunters, assassins, advisors, and bodyguards. Although some think the powers of this species are overrated, their track record speaks for itself.

Some sects in this religious order maintain the need for chemical baths or genetic tampering in order to be true hunters. The genetic tampering causes knob-like growths to protrude from the beings' chitinous exoskeletons, which the beings use as weapons.

These beings can be identified by their weapon of choice, which is a staff that ends in a V-shaped pair of electrically charged prods. Most members of this species require little or no sleep, which means that these mystical hunters can spend that much more time reading omens and tracking their prey. Which species is this?

A. Trandoshan
B. Gand
C. Ssi-ruuk
D. Rodian

1829. What is special about Coways' eyesight?

- **A.** They see in the ultraviolet spectrum
- **B.** They are colorblind
- **C.** They have infrared vision
- **D.** They are blind

1830. Which species has a durable exoskeleton?

- **A.** Trandoshans
- **B.** Lepi
- **C.** Wookiees
- **D.** Gands

1831. What was Yoda's species?

- **A.** Unknown
- **B.** Trilith
- **C.** Yolor
- **D.** Yangral

1832. For which species is Terend the name of the ruling council within each individual tribe?

- **A.** Hrakian
- **B.** Trandoshan
- **C.** Wookiee
- **D.** Ugnaught

1833. Which species only allows outsiders onto its homeworld in designated areas called "Alien Quarters"?

- **A.** Gands
- **B.** Trandoshans
- **C.** Hrakians
- **D.** Ugnaughts

1834. Canu is worshipped by which of the following species?

- **A.** Ugnaughts
- **B.** Wookiees
- **C.** Coway
- **D.** S'kytri

1835. What near-human species with feathers crowning their bald skulls and eye ridges did R2-D2 and C-3PO encounter on Vorzyd 5, when they escorted a drunk member of the species back to his ship in order to find Luke Skywalker and Princess Leia?

- **A.** Balosars
- **B.** Hrakians
- **C.** Fosh
- **D.** H'nemthe

1836. What does Coway skin look like?

- **A.** It is covered in green scales
- **B.** It is covered in gray scales
- **C.** It is covered in spines
- **D.** It is covered in gray down

The Empire Strikes Back Era

1837. Which species holds an annual ritual in which the males come together to meet females who are considered eligible for marriage?

A. Gands
B. Ugnaughts
C. Trandoshans
D. Wookiees

1838. Which species' culture is based solely on hunting and tracking beings they consider weaker than themselves?

A. Wookiees
B. Gands
C. Coway
D. Trandoshans

1839. Which species do the Trandoshans consider to be archenemies?

A. Wookiees
B. Humans
C. Aqualish
D. Gands

1840. Which species remains largely a scientific mystery because they refuse to allow themselves to be studied?

A. Trandoshans
B. Lepi
C. Gands
D. Ugnaughts

1841. Which species fought with Chewbacca on Cloud City?

A. Trandoshans
B. Lepi
C. Jawas
D. Ugnaughts

1842. What language do the Lepi speak?

A. Lepan
B. Lepese
C. Lepanese
D. Lepala

1843.

1844. What color are Trandoshans' eyes?

A. Blue
B. Green
C. Orange
D. Black

1843.

These beings hatch from eggs and are raised in clutches. When they emerge, they already have the ability to walk and exhibit the basic instinct that is the most important aspect of their culture. When they are two years old, their parents take them out into the world and teach them the skills they will need in order to survive in their society. By the age of ten, most members of this species are already highly skilled.

Male members of this species perform basically one task: they hunt. They are awarded points for every successful hunting mission. These points, referred to as "jagannath points" in their society, are very important—the more points a member of this species accumulates, the higher the esteem he has in society.

The males with the most jagannath points are considered to be viable mates. When they return from their hunts, they mate with females, or clutch mothers, who then lay eggs and watch over them until they hatch. When the children are old enough, the males set out to accumulate their own jagannath points. Which species is this?

A. Gand
B. Trandoshan
C. Rodian
D. Ugnaught

1845. Which species is genetic cousin to the Coway?
- **A.** Trandoshans
- **B.** Mimbanites
- **C.** Ugnaughts
- **D.** Spiners

1846. Which species' digestive system utilizes very strong amino acids to digest lichens, fungi, and uncooked meats?
- **A.** Coway
- **B.** Greenies
- **C.** Trandoshans
- **D.** Gands

1847. Which species has what they call "blood professions," or professions passed down from one generation to the next?
- **A.** Wookiees
- **B.** Ugnaughts
- **C.** Lepi
- **D.** Spiners

1848. How many eggs do female Trandoshans lay at one time?
- **A.** Six
- **B.** Four
- **C.** One
- **D.** Twenty

1849. What substance do the rare subspecies of Gands called "Breathers" inhale?
- **A.** Water
- **B.** Tibanna
- **C.** Oxygen
- **D.** Ammonia

1850. What was Jaxxon's homeworld?
- **A.** Ord Mantell
- **B.** Nar Shaddaa
- **C.** Dantooine
- **D.** Coachelle Prime

1851. What species is also referred to as a "snow lizard"?
- **A.** Yamak
- **B.** Tauntaun
- **C.** Wampa
- **D.** Mynock

1852. Which creatures prefer to walk on four legs except when attacking?
- **A.** Wampas
- **B.** Tauntauns
- **C.** Hoth hogs
- **D.** Glidditches

The Empire Strikes Back Era

1853. What creature anchors itself deep into caverns with tendrils and digests the rock and stone surrounding it?

A. A mynock

B. A dragonsnake

C. A duracrete slug

D. A giant space slug

1854. How many varieties of tauntaun have so far been identified?

A. Two

B. Fifteen

C. Twenty

D. Nine

1855. How long can space slugs grow?

A. Up to 900 meters

B. Up to 500 meters

C. Up to 50 meters

D. Up to 100 meters

1856. What do wampas use to stick their prey to the ceilings of their dwellings?

A. Water

B. Blood

C. Mud

D. Saliva

1857. What is the knobby white spider?

A. The young form of the greater white spider

B. The larval form of the knobby white bat

C. The spore form of the gnarltree

D. The young form of the white climbing snill

1858.

1859. What creature, which is the only remaining species indigenous to Alderaan, can be found in Bespin's atmosphere?

A. The aiwha

B. The beldon

C. The velker

D. The thranta

1860. How many arms do dragonsnakes have?

A. Two

B. Six

C. Four

D. Three

1858.

Luke Skywalker and Han Solo were out patrolling the perimeter of Echo Base when Luke spotted what he assumed was a meteor landing nearby. Han contacted him and told him that he was returning to base, and Luke responded that he was going to check out the meteor crash site. After signing off, he noticed that his tauntaun was acting strangely. Before he knew it, his tauntaun had been mauled by a wampa and he was knocked unconscious.

He awoke to find himself hanging from the ceiling of the wampa's cave, his lightsaber lying in the snow. Gathering his strength, Luke used the Force to bring his lightsaber to him, and just in time—the wampa, done snacking on the tauntaun, was moving in to devour Luke. Igniting his lightsaber, Luke attacked the wampa, rendering it harmless, before he rushed out into the snowstorm and collapsed.

Back at Echo Base, a worried Han Solo went out into the storm on tauntaun in search of Luke, who he found babbling and nearly unconscious. As he tried to snap Luke out of it, Han's tauntaun collapsed. To keep Luke from freezing to death, Han took Luke's lightsaber and slit the dead tauntaun's belly open, shoving Luke inside. What did Han say?

A. "You'll be warm in here, kid."

B. "I thought they smelled bad on the outside!"

C. "I'm sorry to have to do this to you."

D. "Watch out for those intestines, kid!"

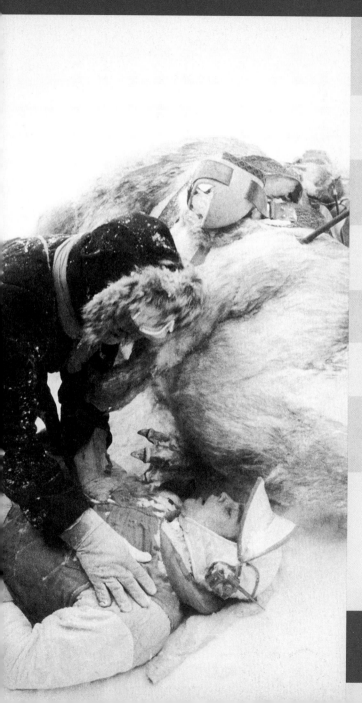

1861. What have aggravated tauntauns been known to do, causing distress to their handlers?

A. Kick

B. Butt

C. Spit

D. Bite

1862. To what was C-3PO referring when he screamed, "Oh, go away! Beastly thing! Shoo! Shoo!"?

A. A tauntaun

B. A mynock

C. A wampa

D. A space slug

1863. What is the blanket term for the thousands of small, usually winged creatures that inhabit Bespin's atmosphere?

A. Leapers

B. Jumpers

C. Wingers

D. Floaters

1864. How soon after birth can baby tauntauns begin to feed themselves without assistance from their mothers?

A. Three weeks

B. Two weeks

C. Immediately

D. One month

1865. What silicon-based lifeform can exist in no atmosphere?

A. Tauntauns

B. Wampas

C. Duracrete slugs

D. Giant space slugs

1866. What unique effect does wampa saliva have on its victims?

A. It acts as an anesthetic

B. It stuns them

C. It poisons them

D. It instantly kills them

1867. Which creature swallowed R2-D2, thinking he would make a good snack, then reacted by spitting R2-D2 out when it found out that droids were not to its liking?

A. A giant space slug

B. A dragonsnake

C. A dianoga

D. A gorg

1868. What is the tauntaun's primary source of food?

A. Fungus that grows beneath the frost layer

B. Hoth hogs

C. Ion eels

D. Snow mice

The Empire Strikes Back Era

1869. What enormous Tibanna gas-filled creatures float through the slushy gas-liquid-solid interface of Bespin's lower atmosphere?

A. Thrantas

B. Beldons

C. Velkers

D. Aiwhas

1870. What hermaphroditic Dagobah creature sucks up and consumes any organic material it comes across?

A. The dragonsnake

B. The butcherbug

C. The Dagobah python

D. The giant swamp slug

1871. Which variety of tauntaun is known for its high-pitched and comical screech?

A. The common tauntaun

B. The glacier tauntaun

C. The climbing tauntaun

D. The scaly tauntaun

1872. Up to how many times its body weight can a Dagobah python swallow?

A. Seven times

B. Fifteen times

C. Ten times

D. Five times

1873.

1874. Which furry Dagobah mammal has phosphorescent patches on its chest that cause the lahdia plant, its main diet, to open, revealing edible berries and flowers?

A. The scrange

B. The timid worrat

C. The spade-headed smooka

D. The spot-light sloth

1875. How large are tauntaun herds?

A. Twenty to thirty individuals

B. Forty to fifty individuals

C. Sixty to eighty individuals

D. Ten to twenty individuals

1876. Which reptavian flies through the lower levels of the Dagobah rainforest?

A. The greater bogwing

B. The accipitero

C. The lesser bogwing

D. The spade-headed smooka

OBSESSED WITH STAR WARS

1873.

Han Solo had defied logic and stormed headlong into an asteroid field in order to evade the pursuing Imperial fleet. After several near-misses and shouts of protest from his passengers, Han had decided to go in closer to one of the larger asteroids in hopes of finding a safe place to land so he could make much-needed repairs to the *Millennium Falcon*. He spotted one that he thought would make a safe haven, and glided over its surface into a large cave.

The crew had been working throughout the ship for quite some time when Leia decided to take a break. Resting in the cockpit, she thought she noticed something flying outside. Looking closer, she screamed when a hideous creature clamped itself onto the cockpit and made a shrieking noise. "There's something out there," she yelled as she ran to find Han.

Out in the cave, Leia, Han, and Chewbacca were investigating when Han saw something and shot at it. As it fell to the ground, Solo said. "That's what I thought—mynock. Chewie, check the rest of the ship and make sure there are no more attached."

What did Han Solo say the creature was chewing on?

A. The hull

B. The piping

C. Transparisteel

D. Power cables

1877. How many hearts do giant space slugs have?
- **A.** Eight
- **B.** Two
- **C.** Six
- **D.** One

1878. What quality did all tauntauns trained and used by the Rebel Alliance on Hoth have in common?
- **A.** They were all cyborgs
- **B.** They were all male
- **C.** They were all female
- **D.** They were all declawed

1879. Which creatures capture energy particles emitted by stars as they fly through space?
- **A.** Space slugs
- **B.** Mynocks
- **C.** Bogwings
- **D.** Spade-headed smookas

1880. Which airborne creatures form large packs to attack beldons by tearing holes in the beldons' skin?
- **A.** Aiwhas
- **B.** Thrantas
- **C.** Rawwks
- **D.** Velkers

1881. How many nostrils do tauntauns have?
- **A.** Two
- **B.** Four
- **C.** Six
- **D.** Eight

1882. Although their homeworld is unknown, which planet is popularly called the "birthplace of the Mynock"?
- **A.** Ord Mantell
- **B.** Mynock IV
- **C.** Ord Mynock
- **D.** Mynock Prime

1883. Which creatures are allergic to helium, which causes them to bloat and, more often than not, explode?
- **A.** Wampas
- **B.** Mynocks
- **C.** Knobby white spiders
- **D.** Thrantas

1884. Up to how many cubs do wampa females give birth to in each pregnancy?
- **A.** Six
- **B.** Four
- **C.** Three
- **D.** One

The Empire Strikes Back Era

1885. What surprising sound attracts wampas?
A. Tauntaun cries
B. Human voices
C. Snowspeeders
D. Astromech beeps

1886. What is the highest speed at which the common tauntaun can run?
A. 90 kph
B. 60 kph
C. 80 kph
D. 50 kph

1887. Which wormlike beast on Mimban moves by using suction organs located on its underside?
A. The poordra
B. The frelloma
C. The wandrella
D. The kiskin

1888. What do spaceports sometimes try to keep in the vicinity to cut down on mynock populations?
A. Helium pellets
B. Space slugs
C. Ion blasters
D. Ion nets

1889.

1890. What is the smallest known variety of tauntaun?
A. The climbing tauntaun
B. The scaly tauntaun
C. The tinytaun
D. The glacier tauntaun

1891. Where did Princess Leia send all troops in sector twelve during the Imperial invasion of Echo Base?
A. The top of the mountain
B. The lowest level of the base
C. The south slope
D. Bespin

1892. What did Han Solo do in order to evade the Imperial ships that were pursuing him after he blasted off from Hoth?
A. He went into hyperspace
B. He entered an asteroid field
C. He activated a cloaking device
D. Nothing—they were captured

1889.

While investigating the creatures that were flocking around the *Millennium Falcon* in the asteroid cave where Han Solo had hidden it, Leia noticed that the interior of the cave was a little odd. "This ground sure feels strange," she said. "It doesn't feel like rock!"

"There's an awful lot of moisture in here," Han added. As Han Solo fired on one of the creatures and watched it fall to the ground, a flock of them flew over Leia's head. Chewbacca was battling a swarm when his bowcaster misfired and hit the cave's floor, setting off a shockwave. When it calmed down, Solo, suspicious, shot the floor

OBSESSED WITH *STAR WARS*

1893. Where did Luke Skywalker crash on Dagobah?

A. Gnarlroot Bog   C. Blackvine Bog

B. Dragonsnake Bog   D. Gnarltree Bog

1894. What is Hoth covered with?

A. Lava and rocks   C. Snow and ice

B. Grassy plains   D. A vast ocean

1895. What forms natural bridges throughout the expansive Dagobah jungle?

A. Blackvines   C. Galla

B. Gnarltrees   D. Sohli

1896. Above which planet does Cloud City hover?

A. Coruscant   C. Hoth

B. Dagobah   D. Bespin

1897. How many moons does Hoth have?

A. Six   C. Nine

B. Three   D. None

1898. What, according to C-3PO, were the odds of successfully navigating an asteroid field?

A. 4,890 to 1   C. 3,720 to 1

B. 8,900 to 1   D. 725 to 1

1899. Where were the Rebel ground troops under Trey Callum's command located in the Battle of Hoth?

A. The Alpha Outpost   C. The Omega Outpost

B. The Delta Outpost   D. The Beta Outpost

1900. How many beings call Cloud City home?

A. Seven million   C. Twelve million

B. Five million   D. Eight hundred thousand

again, setting off another tremor. Realizing what was happening and that they had few options, Solo ordered everyone back onto the *Millennium Falcon*, and snapped at the arguing Princess Leia, "Sit down, sweetheart, we're taking off!"

As they frantically sped out of their hiding place, Leia saw the entrance growing smaller and shouted, "The cave is collapsing!"

"This is no cave," Han responded. What was it?

A. A mutant mynock

B. A giant space slug

C. A nos monster

D. A Hoth trenchslug

The Empire Strikes Back Era

1901. What did the deck officer tell Han Solo would happen before he reached the first marker?

- **A.** He would experience frostbite
- **B.** He would lose sight of Echo Base
- **C.** His tauntaun would freeze
- **D.** He would find Commander Skywalker

1902. What is the breathable, upper atmosphere of Bespin called?

- **A.** The Air Zone
- **B.** The Life Arena
- **C.** The Air Arena
- **D.** The Life Zone

1903. Where was Echo Base located on Hoth?

- **A.** Mount Ison
- **B.** Clabburn Range
- **C.** Lanteel Glacier
- **D.** Kerane Valley

1904. How wide is Cloud City?

- **A.** 16 kilometers
- **B.** 20 kilometers
- **C.** 80 kilometers
- **D.** 9 kilometers

1905. Into what was Han Solo placed in Cloud City?

- **A.** A Cellomite freezing chamber
- **B.** A Tibanna freezing chamber
- **C.** A thoralite freezing chamber
- **D.** A carbonite freezing chamber

1906.

1907. How far above Bespin's core does Cloud City hover?

- **A.** 200,000 kilometers
- **B.** 39,000 kilometers
- **C.** 59,000 kilometers
- **D.** 82,000 kilometers

1908. What occurrence in Sector Four did the Controller in Echo Base alert General Rieekan to?

- **A.** Echo Three had reported a meteorite
- **B.** Echo Three had not reported in
- **C.** A fleet of Star Destroyers had come out of hyperspace
- **D.** Imperial walkers had landed on Hoth

1906.

Luke Skywalker had been training very intensely with Jedi Master Yoda. "Tell me why . . ." Luke started to ask Yoda after Yoda had lectured him about the dark side of the Force.

"No, no. There is no why," Yoda responded. "Nothing more will I teach you today. Clear your mind of questions."

"There's something not right here," Luke said, looking at the entrance to a cave. "I feel cold."

"That place is strong with the dark side of the Force. A domain of evil it is. In you must go," Master Yoda instructed,

telling Luke that there was nothing inside except what Luke took with him.

Luke brought his lightsaber with him and entered the cave. Going deeper and deeper into the gnarled, dank cavern, he was terrified to see Darth Vader coming toward him. Luke ignited his lightsaber, and the two began to duel. Luke struck a deadly blow to the Sith Lord, decapitating him. As Darth Vader's head rolled to Luke's feet, sparks flew, and the mask split, revealing the face inside. Whose face was it?

A. Anakin Skywalker
B. Obi-Wan Kenobi
C. Princess Leia
D. Luke Skywalker

1909. What information did Luke Skywalker obtain about Dagobah before he landed?
A. Technology   **C.** No lifeforms
B. Cities   **D.** Massive lifeforms

1910. Where was the ice cave in which the wampa intended to consume Luke Skywalker located?
A. Cirque Glacier   **C.** Mount Ison
B. Lanteel Glacier   **D.** Moorsh Moraine

1911. What was Cloud City's original name?
A. Great Floating Cloud   **C.** Sky City
B. Floating Home Mining Colony **D.** Great Floating Miners' Colony

1912. What did Echo Station Three-T-Eight report that they had spotted?
A. Imperial walkers   **C.** A probe droid
B. A meteorite   **D.** A wampa

1913. What, according to R2-D2, were the chances of surviving the harsh night weather of Hoth?
A. 893 to 1   **C.** 725 to 1
B. 1,298 to 1   **D.** 3,720 to 1

1914. Which position does Hoth occupy in the Hoth system?
A. The sixth planet   **C.** The third planet
B. The ninth planet   **D.** The eighth planet

1915. Into what did Luke Skywalker allow himself to fall on Cloud City?
A. A Tibanna duct   **C.** A sewage tunnel
B. A ventilation trench   **D.** A reactor shaft

1916. What did Han Solo say he was going to do after he entered the asteroid field above Hoth?
A. Leave the asteroid field as soon as possible   **C.** Hide himself in a flurry of small asteroids
B. Go in closer to one of the big asteroids   **D.** Lure as many Imperial ships in after him as possible

The Empire Strikes Back Era

1917. Where was the carbon-freeze chamber located in Cloud City?

A. A processing vane
C. The Tibanna warehouse
B. The carbon wing
D. A transport docking bay

1918. What was Luke clinging to before he allowed himself to plummet to the bottom of Cloud City?

A. A weathervane
C. An antenna
B. An atmosphere sensor
D. A repulsorlift

1919. Where on Hoth did the Imperial ground assault forces land?

A. Lanteel Glacier
C. Moorsh Moraine
B. Nev Ice Flow
D. Kerane Valley

1920. What did Luke see in his vision of the future?

A. A city in the clouds
C. A battle with Darth Vader
B. A palace in the desert
D. The death of Yoda

1921. Where was the rendezvous point at which Luke Skywalker told Lando Calrissian he would meet him?

A. Dantooine
C. Dagobah
B. Tatooine
D. Hoth

1922.

1923. What was Luke Skywalker dangling from beneath Cloud City when he summoned Leia?

A. A satellite dish
C. A weathervane
B. An antenna
D. A sensor array

1924. Where was the Echo Base evacuation fleet located?

A. The western ridge
C. The eastern ridge
B. The north ridge
D. The south ridge

1922.

Luke Skywalker had seen a vision of Obi-Wan Kenobi while in a state of shock on the ice planet Hoth. Kenobi had instructed his former apprentice to venture to Dagobah, where he would receive further training as a Jedi Knight from Yoda, the Jedi Master who had instructed Kenobi. Although he was unsure that he had actually seen the vision, Luke headed toward Dagobah.

Careening through mists, unable to see what was in front of him, a frantic Skywalker tried to comfort R2-D2 and began the landing cycle on his X-wing starfighter. They splashed down, and realized that the ship was partially submerged in the waters of a swamp. After struggling to shore, they began to set up camp.

The two were questioning their reasons for being there when Luke saw a strange green creature watching them. The inquisitive being began rifling through Luke's belongings and tasting his food. Finally, the little menace grabbed Luke's lamp. "Hey, give me that!" Luke ordered.

"Mine! Or I will help you not," the creature responded.

"I don't want your help. I want my lamp back!" Luke demanded, adding that he was going to need it in a place like this. What did he call Dagobah?

A. A slimy mudhole
B. A filthy sinkhole
C. A swampy mudpit
D. A watery deathpit

1925. Onto what did Darth Vader force Luke Skywalker toward the bitter end of their fateful lightsaber duel in Cloud City?

A. A sensor balcony   C. A moving walkway

B. A Tibanna block warehouse   D. An airlock

1926. Where did Lando tell Lobot to hold the Imperial forces?

A. In the prison level   C. In the carbon-freezing chamber

B. In the mining level   D. In the security tower

1927. What lies under the ice in Hoth's southern hemisphere?

A. A vast system of caves   C. A vast, churning ocean

B. A subterranean city   D. More ice

1928. Where was *Slave I* docked at Cloud City?

A. The north platform   C. The south platform

B. The east platform   D. The west platform

1929. What does Cloud City extract from the lower atmosphere of its host planet?

A. Tibanna gas   C. Turducken gas

B. Noralla gas   D. Mlivilick gas

1930. Along which galactic trade route would one come across Hoth?

A. Hydian Way   C. Rimma Trade Route

B. Perlemian Trade Route   D. Corellian Trade Spine

1931. To what phrase did C-3PO reply, "How rude!"?

A. "Tee chuta hhat yudd!"   C. "Lana!"

B. "E chu ta!"   D. "Paploo!"

1932. Which manufacturer was responsible for the LOM series protocol droid?

A. Arakyd   C. Industrial Automaton

B. Commerce Guild   D. TaggeCo

The Empire Strikes Back Era

1933. Which famed jewel did 4-LOM steal during his first job, successfully overriding his programming and beginning an existence of crime and danger?

A. The Coruscant Fire
B. The Adrinna Connix sapphire
C. The Lana Visillix diamond
D. The Ankarres sapphire

1934. What was in zone twelve, moving east on the ice planet Hoth, and emitting a transmission that, according to C-3PO, was not used by the Alliance?

A. The wampa
B. The probe droid
C. AT-ATs
D. Echo Three and Echo Seven

1935. Which manufacturer unleashed IG-88 on the galaxy?

A. Industrial Automaton
B. Techno Union
C. Holowan Laboratories
D. Serv-O-Droid

1936. What was 4-LOM's first job?

A. He worked on the *Kuari Princess*
B. He was a translator in the Senate
C. He was Ackmena's bar assistant in Mos Eisley
D. He was a valet on The Wheel

1937. Who fixed the hyperdrive on the *Millennium Falcon*?

A. C-3PO
B. R2-D2
C. Chewbacca
D. Lando Calrissian

1938. What was the name given to the Imperial program that attempted to build droid warriors to crush the Rebellion, but resulted in IG-88?

A. Project Starscream
B. Gurdun's Folly
C. Project Phlutdroid
D. Loruss' Folly

1939.

1940. What did R2-D2 turn on in Princess Leia's chamber in Echo Base?

A. The environmental control
B. The atmospheric correction unit
C. The "Fresh-Aire" cylinder
D. The thermal heater

1939.

Han Solo had been frozen in carbonite and Lando Calrissian was trying to make things right. As stormtroopers were escorting Princess Leia and Chewbacca to Darth Vader's shuttle, Lando programmed Lobot to arrive on the scene with Bespin security, who removed the stormtroopers' weapons and took them to a security tower. As soon as Lando removed Chewbacca's binders, the angry Wookiee began to choke him. "Ha . . . ha . . ." was all Lando was able to get out.

"What?" Princess Leia said mockingly.

"It sounds like 'Han'!" C-3PO interjected.

"Han! There's still a chance to save Han!" Lando wheezed before Chewbacca released his grip.

They all rushed off to stop Boba Fett from leaving Cloud City, but they were too late: His ship was blasting off just as they got to the landing platform doors. R2-D2 plugged into the computer terminal to override the code so they could get through the doors. As the doors opened, stormtroopers poured onto the scene. What did R2-D2 do to slow them down and allow his friends time to get to the *Millennium Falcon*?

A. He sprayed grease on the floor
B. He shocked them
C. He closed the blast doors
D. He sprayed his fire extinguisher, creating a thick cloud

1941. Whose head was put on backward when he was being reassembled?

A. R2-D2's

B. C-3PO's

C. FX-7's

D. 4-LOM's

1942. Who updated 4-LOM's programming, initiating the droid's career as a bounty hunter?

A. Jabba the Hutt

B. Aurra Sing

C. Gardulla the Hutt

D. Zuckuss

1943. What was C-3PO's first exclamation after he was turned back on?

A. "Who was that rude protocol droid?"

B. "Stormtroopers? Here? I've got to warn the others! Oh no, I've been shot!"

C. "Where is R2 when I need him? I'll never find the Princess at this rate!"

D. "With all we've been through, I don't know how we've stayed in one piece!"

1944. What did Cloud City's central computer tell R2-D2?

A. The Lando Calrissian was a fink

B. That C-3PO had been disassembled

C. That the Empire was taking over Cloud City

D. That the hyperdrive on the *Millennium Falcon* had been deactivated

1945. How many IG-series prototypes were created?

A. Six

B. Seventeen

C. Five

D. Eleven

1946. Who was 4-LOM's partner in many bounty hunting jobs?

A. Aurra Sing

B. Zuckuss

C. Boba Fett

D. IG-88

1947. Who revived Luke Skywalker on Hoth?

A. 3-1A

B. 4-19

C. 8-5A

D. 2-1B

1948. Which white protocol droid worked with the Rebel Alliance in Echo Base?

A. C-3PX

B. R-3PO

C. K-3PO

D. N-3PO

The Empire Strikes Back Era

1949. Who was 2-1B's assistant in Echo Base?
- **A.** FX-12
- **B.** FY-9
- **C.** FX-7
- **D.** FY-12

1950. Who tended to Luke Skywalker's wounds on the medical frigate?
- **A.** FX-7
- **B.** 2-1B
- **C.** R2-D2
- **D.** Dr. Evazan

1951. What company manufactured FX-7?
- **A.** Arakyd Industries
- **B.** Serv-O-Droid
- **C.** Genetech
- **D.** MedTech Industries

1952. Who manufactured 2-1B?
- **A.** Geentech
- **B.** Geentech/ Industrial Automaton
- **C.** Industrial Automaton
- **D.** Genetech/ Arakyd

1953. Which droid served as Droid Coordinator in Echo Base?
- **A.** C-3PO
- **B.** R2-D2
- **C.** K-3PO
- **D.** FX-7

1954.

1955. How many articulated tentacles did Vuffi Raa have?
- **A.** Five
- **B.** Seven
- **C.** Three
- **D.** Eight

1956. How many arms does a Viper probot have?
- **A.** Seven
- **B.** Two
- **C.** Three
- **D.** Six

1954.

C-3PO had stumbled across something he wasn't supposed to see, and he had ended up blasted into many parts. Chewbacca had scoured Cloud City to find him, and wrestled several Ugnaughts to get the droid's parts back.

After the Empire had made its presence in Cloud City known and Chewbacca had been imprisoned, he sat down to piece the prissy protocol droid back together, starting by placing C3PO's head back on his body. As he activated the droid, C-3PO began to whine incessantly, so the Wookiee shut C-3PO back down. Chewbacca never got a chance to put the droid back together completely. The Rebels had been summoned to the carbon freeze chamber to witness Darth Vader's test run.

C-3PO, reactivated, was slung on Chewbacca's back in a net. As Chewbacca followed Boba Fett, Han Solo, and Princess Leia up the platform to the carbon freeze, C-3PO was whining the entire way. What did he say?

- **A.** "You woolly oaf! If you'd put me back together, I could get there by myself!"
- **B.** "If only you had reattached my legs, I wouldn't be in this ridiculous position!"
- **C.** "Pay attention to me so I can see what's going on!"
- **D.** "I demand that you put me together at once!"

OBSESSED WITH *STAR WARS*

1957. Which droid downloaded sentience programming during a routine test and assassinated its creators?

A. IG-88   C. FX-7

B. 4-LOM   D. C-3PX

1958. Which company produced the Viper probe droid?

A. Industrial Automaton   C. Arakyd

B. TaggeCo   D. Malkite Poisoners

1959. How was the probe droid destroyed on Hoth?

A. A wampa attacked it   C. Chewbacca fired on it

B. It self-destructed   D. Han Solo fired on it

1960. Which IG-88 disguised itself as a bounty hunter and attempted to trace the *Millennium Falcon* for the Empire?

A. IG-88D   C. IG-88C

B. IG-88A   D. IG-88B

1961. Who manufactured the KDY v-150 Planet Defender?

A. Golan Arms   C. Kuat Drive Yards

B. SoroSuub   D. Industrial Automaton

1962. Which weapon did snowtroopers take time to set up in an attempt to stop the *Millennium Falcon* from blasting out of Echo Base?

A. A Merr-Sonn Munitions PLX-2M   C. A Tenloss DXR-6 Disruptor

B. A BlasTech E-Web heavy repeating blaster   D. A Merr-Sonn CR-24 Flame Rifle

1963. Who used a Merr-Sonn Munitions GRS-1 snare rifle?

A. Zuckuss   C. Dengar

B. 4-LOM   D. IG-88

1964. Which bounty hunter used a stun-gas blower?

A. Boba Fett   C. Skorr

B. Dengar   D. 4-LOM

The Empire Strikes Back Era

1965. What did the Rebel Alliance use on Hoth to allow its transports to get past the Imperial blockade?

A. Cloaking devices

B. A plasma cannon

C. An ion cannon

D. A planetary turbolaser

1966. Who carries Relby-K23 blaster pistols?

A. Rebel soldiers

B. Bespin security guards

C. Snowtroopers

D. Imperial officers

1967. Who used an EE-3 blaster rifle?

A. Boba Fett

B. 4-LOM

C. Zuckuss

D. Bossk

1968. What did Yoda tell Luke Skywalker about his weapons when Luke was going into the cave?

A. "Your weapons—with you, take them."

B. "Take only what you need."

C. "No good will your weapons serve."

D. "Your weapons—you will not need them."

1969. What anti-infantry device did the Rebels use in the ground battle on Hoth?

A. Atgar 1.4 FD P-Tower Laser Cannon

B. KDY w-165 Planetary Turbolaser

C. Golan Arms DF.9

D. Borstel NK-7 Ion Cannon

1970. Who used the Monnotor DAS-430 electromagnetic projectile launcher, among many, many other weapons?

A. Dengar

B. IG-88

C. Boba Fett

D. Bossk

1971.

1972. What was the name of the AT-AT assault group on Hoth?

A. Blizzard Force

B. Tundra Force

C. Snowstorm Armada

D. Snowblast Assault Force

1971.

Princess Leia sensed that Luke Skywalker was in danger, and she told Chewbacca to turn the *Millennium Falcon* around after they had made their initial escape from Cloud City. "I know where Luke is," Leia told Chewbacca. After they found Luke and brought him on board, they had another problem: an Imperial blockade around Cloud City. "Star Destroyer," Princess Leia said to Lando and Chewbacca as they evaded Imperial ships.

Darth Vader had left Cloud City and was now monitoring the *Millennium Falcon*'s flight from the bridge of the Super Star Destroyer *Executor*. "Did your men deactivate the hyperdrive on the *Millennium Falcon*?" Darth Vader asked Admiral Piett, who told him that they had. "Good. Prepare the boarding party, and set your weapons for stun."

The Empire wouldn't get the chance to board the *Millennium Falcon*, however. As Darth Vader and Admiral Piett watched, the ship unexpectedly blasted off into hyperspace and parts unknown. Darth Vader, in an uncharacteristically passive move, simply turned and walked away.

Back with the Rebel fleet, Luke Skywalker was getting his hand tended to by 2-1B as he talked to Lando about their plans to rescue Han Solo. What ship was Luke recovering on?

A. The *Millennium Falcon*

B. A Gallofree Yards GR-75 transport

C. A Mon Cal cruiser

D. A Nebulon-B Frigate

1973. Which Star Destroyer is seen launching a slew of probe droids to search the galaxy for hints of the Rebel Base's location?

A. The *Executor*　　**C.** The *Stalker*
B. The *Avenger*　　**D.** The *Impaler*

1974. What does AT-AT stand for?

A. All Terrain Armored Transport　　**C.** All Terrain Assault Tank
B. All Terrain Assault Titan　　**D.** All Terrain Armored Tyrant

1975. Which Star Destroyer pursued the *Millennium Falcon* into the asteroid field above Hoth?

A. The *Tormentor*　　**C.** The *Adjudicator*
B. The *Crippler*　　**D.** The *Avenger*

1976. Who piloted the *Punishing One*?

A. Lando Calrissian　　**C.** Dengar
B. IG-88　　**D.** Boba Fett

1977. What was Darth Vader's flagship?

A. Super Star Destroyer *Eclipse*　　**C.** Super Star Destroyer *Allegiance*
B. Super Star Destroyer *Executor*　　**D.** Super Star Destroyer *Intimidator*

1978. Which type of ship did the Rebels use as evacuation transports from Echo Base on Hoth?

A. Gallofree YKL-37r Nova couriers　　**C.** Gallofree Yards GT-45 transports
B. Gallofree HTT-26 transports　　**D.** Gallofree Yards GR-75 transports

1979. What bounty hunter flew the *Hound's Tooth*?

A. Skorr　　**C.** Bossk
B. Zuckuss　　**D.** Boba Fett

1980. What was the last transport to escape the Imperial blockade of Hoth?

A. The *Bright Hope*　　**C.** *Thon's Orchard*
B. The *Dutyfree*　　**D.** *Lana's Lament*

The Empire Strikes Back Era

1981. Which ship was actually a modified T-47 airspeeder?
- **A.** The cloud car
- **B.** The snowspeeder
- **C.** The TIE bomber
- **D.** The TIE interceptor

1982. How many Class II heavy laser cannons is an AT-AT equipped with?
- **A.** Four
- **B.** Six
- **C.** Eight
- **D.** Two

1983. Why couldn't Han Solo take a snowspeeder out when he needed to search Hoth for Luke?
- **A.** They were all getting serviced
- **B.** They were all damaged in transport
- **C.** They were having difficulty adapting the speeders to the cold
- **D.** Han didn't know how to fly a snowspeeder

1984. Which bounty hunter haunted the galaxy in the *Mist Hunter*?
- **A.** Dengar
- **B.** Boba Fett
- **C.** Skorr
- **D.** Zuckuss

1985. What is the snowspeeder's maximum speed?
- **A.** 1000 kph
- **B.** 700 kph
- **C.** 500 kph
- **D.** 300 kph

1986. How many blaster cannons do cloud cars come equipped with?
- **A.** Four
- **B.** Six
- **C.** Two
- **D.** Eight

1987.

1988. How many stormtroopers can an AT-AT transport, excluding those in the cockpit?
- **A.** Thirty-two
- **B.** Twenty
- **C.** Forty
- **D.** Sixty

1987.

Han Solo was unable to get the *Millennium Falcon* to blast into hyperspace although it was surrounded by the Imperial fleet that had been sweeping the asteroid field to find his ship. "Sir, we just lost the main rear deflector shield," C-3PO warned. "One more direct hit on the back quarter and we're done for!" Solo ordered Chewbacca to turn the ship around, unexpectedly moving into attack position.

As the *Falcon* roared past the *Avenger*, Captain Needa ordered his officers to track the ship. "Captain Needa, the ship no longer appears on our scopes!" an officer alerted him.

"They can't have disappeared!" Captain Needa said nervously, not wanting to relate the bad news to Darth Vader.

"Well, there's no trace of them, sir," the officer responded. Where was the *Millennium Falcon*?

- **A.** It had blasted into hyperspace
- **B.** It was on the Star Destroyer *Avenger*'s conning tower
- **C.** It was well behind Star Destroyer *Avenger*, headed in the opposite direction
- **D.** It was in the Star Destroyer *Avenger*'s rear hangar

1989. What was the name of IG-88's ship?
- **A.** The *IG Annihilator*
- **B.** The *IG 8000*
- **C.** The *IG Assassin*
- **D.** The *IG 2000*

1990. How tall are AT-ATs?
- **A.** 10.5 meters
- **B.** 15.5 meters
- **C.** 20.5 meters
- **D.** 30.5 meters

1991. What does AT-ST stand for?
- **A.** All Terrain Scout Transport
- **B.** All Terrain Single Transport
- **C.** Assault Trooper Security Transport
- **D.** All Terrain Security Tank

1992. How many medium blaster cannons is an AT-AT fitted with?
- **A.** Two
- **B.** Four
- **C.** Eight
- **D.** Six

1993. What feature did Sienar Fleet Systems include in TIE bombers that was not seen in earlier TIE ships?
- **A.** Twin ion engines
- **B.** Solar arrays
- **C.** Cloaking devices
- **D.** A life-support system

1994. How many engine thrusters does a Super Star Destroyer have?
- **A.** Nine
- **B.** Seven
- **C.** Thirteen
- **D.** Nineteen

1995. How many cloud cars escorted the *Millennium Falcon* into Cloud City?
- **A.** Three
- **B.** Two
- **C.** Six
- **D.** One

1996. Where in *Slave I* did Boba Fett direct Cloud City security personnel to place his prize?
- **A.** The sleeping quarters
- **B.** One of the prisoner cages
- **C.** The cockpit
- **D.** The cargo hold

The Empire Strikes Back Era

1997. Who was the other bounty hunter who scoured the galaxy in the *Mist Hunter*?

- **A.** Aurra Sing
- **B.** Dengar
- **C.** 4-LOM
- **D.** IG-88

1998. How many passengers can an AT-ST accommodate?

- **A.** Two
- **B.** Six
- **C.** Three
- **D.** Four

1999. What is a cloud car's maximum speed?

- **A.** 2,300 kph
- **B.** 950 kph
- **C.** 1,500 kph
- **D.** 450 kph

2000. How many pilots does an AT-AT require?

- **A.** One
- **B.** Three
- **C.** Two
- **D.** Five

2001. Which AT-AT did Luke Skywalker destroy?

- **A.** Blizzard One
- **B.** Blizzard Three
- **C.** Blizzard Four
- **D.** Blizzard Two

2002. What did C-3PO giddily announce that he had isolated on the *Millennium Falcon*?

- **A.** The hyperdrive motivator
- **B.** The reverse powerflux coupling
- **C.** The fuel drive pressure stabilizer
- **D.** The warp vortex stabilizer

2003. How many AT-ATs is a Y-86 Titan capable of housing?

- **A.** Six
- **B.** Four
- **C.** Nine
- **D.** Ten

2004. What type of ship was the *Hound's Tooth*?

- **A.** YT-1300
- **B.** YV-545
- **C.** YT-2400
- **D.** YV-666

OBSESSED WITH *STAR WARS*

2010.

Admiral Ozzel was in serious trouble with Darth Vader. The Admiral had taken his fleet out of lightspeed too close to the Hoth system, and the Rebel Alliance had been alerted to their presence. He ordered General Veers to prepare his troops for a surface attack against the Rebel base, with the goal of destroying the power generator that produced the energy shield surrounding the planet.

The Rebel Alliance knew that their shield wouldn't stop the Empire, so they prepared for ground assault. As the soldiers lined up in trenches, they spotted Imperial walkers marching toward the shield generator.

Luke Skywalker commanded a group of snowspeeders that were tasked with defeating the walkers before they could reach the base. As the speeders engaged the walkers, it became very clear that their weapons were going to be absolutely useless against the superior armor from which the walkers were constructed.

"That armor's too strong for blasters," Luke Skywalker said to his pilots. What did he tell them to use instead?

A. Proton torpedoes
B. Concussion missiles
C. Harpoons and tow cables
D. Ion cannons

2005. Which AT-AT did Wedge and Janson topple?
A. Blizzard Two   **C.** Blizzard Four
B. Blizzard One   **D.** Blizzard Five

2006. In addition to AT-ATs, how many AT-STs is a Y-86 Titan capable of transporting?
A. Ten   **C.** Sixteen
B. Four   **D.** Twenty

2007. What type of ship was the *Punishing One*?
A. A Nubian LuderVat Steamer   **C.** A Corellian Jumpmaster 5000
B. A TIE Advanced X-1   **D.** A B-wing fighter

2008. Where is an AT-AT's vulnerable point?
A. Its sensor array   **C.** Its drive motor
B. Its neck   **D.** One of its escape hatches

2009. Which manufacturer was responsible for unleashing the horror of the *Executor* on the galaxy?
A. Subpro Corporation   **C.** FreiTek, Inc.
B. Kuat Systems Engineering   **D.** Kuat Drive Yards

2010.

2011. Where did Obi-Wan Kenobi tell Luke Skywalker to go?
A. Back to Echo Base   **C.** To Coruscant
B. To Dagobah   **D.** To Tatooine

2012. Who was suffering from delusions of grandeur, according to C-3PO?
A. Han Solo   **C.** R2-D2
B. Chewbacca   **D.** Princess Leia

The Empire Strikes Back Era

2013. What wasn't quite enough to get Princess Leia excited?
- **A.** Escaping the Empire
- **B.** Being held by Han Solo
- **C.** Racing through the asteroid field
- **D.** Flying to Bespin

2014. What did Yoda tell Obi-Wan Kenobi he felt in Luke Skywalker?
- **A.** Much fear
- **B.** No commitment
- **C.** Much anger
- **D.** Daydreaming

2015. What, according to Luke, was perfectly safe for droids?
- **A.** Dagobah
- **B.** Swimming
- **C.** Swamps
- **D.** Space flight

2016. How did Han Solo discover that the *Millennium Falcon* wasn't in a cave?
- **A.** He stepped on a vein
- **B.** He shot the ground while fighting off mynocks
- **C.** He smelled stomach acid
- **D.** He stabbed the ground while fighting off mynocks

2017.

2018. Who did C-3PO call a noisy brute aboard the *Millennium Falcon*?
- **A.** Lando Calrissian
- **B.** Chewbacca
- **C.** Han Solo
- **D.** Luke Skywalker

2019. After a jolt, what did C-3PO tell Han Solo was quite possible about the asteroid in which they had landed the *Millennium Falcon*?
- **A.** It was too porous to be safe
- **B.** It was not entirely stable
- **C.** The Empire would find them quickly
- **D.** It was going to collide with another asteroid and destroy them

2020. What were anger, fear, and aggression, according to Yoda?
- **A.** Fun
- **B.** The Jedi way
- **C.** The dark side
- **D.** Luke's next lesson

OBSESSED WITH *STAR WARS*

2017.

When Luke Skywalker didn't return from patrolling the perimeter of Echo Base, Princess Leia grew increasingly worried about him. She sent C-3PO to ask Han if he had seen Luke. Han hadn't seen him either and, realizing that Luke would be done for if he was injured in the freezing cold, went out to look for him, ignoring protests that it was too cold to continue the search.

Han went out into the blinding snow, hoping he would be able to find his friend before it was too late. He did find Luke, but Luke was injured and apparently delusional. Han was forced to set up a temporary shelter for the two of them, but they managed to make it through the night.

When they were discovered the next day, Luke was rushed to the medical center and placed in bacta. How strong did Han say Luke looked after his stay in the bacta tank?

- **A.** "Strong enough to rip the arms off a rancor"
- **B.** "Strong enough to pull the ears off a gundark"
- **C.** "Strong enough to beat up a Wookiee"
- **D.** "Strong enough to defeat an acklay"

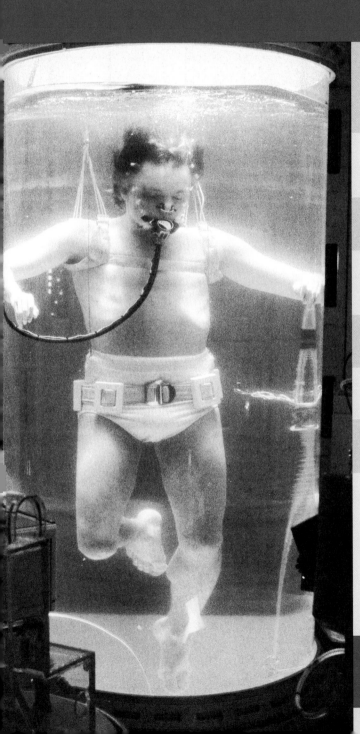

2021. What did Luke feel after he set up camp on Dagobah?

A. The Force

B. The presence of a great Jedi Master

C. Like he and R2-D2 were being watched

D. The dark side

2022. What was standard Imperial procedure when going to lightspeed?

A. Alerting all ships of intended course

B. Routine check of all devices

C. Dumping garbage

D. A test flight

2023. What did Luke Skywalker lose in his battle with Darth Vader?

A. His left hand

B. His left foot

C. His right hand

D. His right leg

2024. What did Luke Skywalker tell Han Solo he was going to investigate on Hoth?

A. A wampa

B. A meteorite

C. A probe droid

D. An uncharted settlement

2025. Where did Chewbacca find a troubled C-3PO in Cloud City?

A. Platform 3-2-7

B. In the droid cleansing center

C. In a junk pile

D. On a mining belt

2026. What did Han Solo say to Princess Leia after she said, "I love you"?

A. "I love you, too."

B. "I know."

C. "Finally she admits it."

D. "Will you marry me?"

2027. What does a Jedi use for knowledge and defense, never for attack?

A. His lightsaber

B. The Force

C. Levitation

D. Mind tricks

2028. What guild did Princess Leia ask Lando whether Cloud City was a part of?

A. The Tibanna Guild

B. The Mining Guild

C. The Gas Workers Guild

D. The Ugnaught Guild

The Empire Strikes Back Era

2029. How many forms of communication did C-3PO pompously announce he was fluent in when General Rieekan picked up a strange code emanating outside of Echo Base?

A. Fifteen million
B. Twelve million
C. Nine million
D. Six million

2030. What system was the *Millennium Falcon* in when the Imperial fleet broke up?

A. Hutt Space
B. The Anoat system
C. The Hoth system
D. The Dagobah system

2031. What did Han Solo need C-3PO to do when they were hiding from the Empire?

A. Clean the smuggling compartments
B. Bring him the hydrospanner
C. Talk to the *Millennium Falcon* to find out what was wrong with the hyperdrive
D. Stay out of the way

2032. Why did Darth Vader place Han Solo in the carbon freeze?

A. He hated him
B. For Boba Fett
C. To test it on a living being before using it on Luke Skywalker
D. He wanted to make an example of Han Solo for other members of the Rebel Alliance

2033.

2034. What did Darth Vader tell Lando Calrissian about Princess Leia and Chewbacca after he tortured Han Solo?

A. That they were going to be placed in the carbon freeze
B. That they must never again leave Cloud City
C. That they were now official property of the Empire
D. That they were going to die

2035. What would forever dominate Luke's destiny once he started down its path, according to Yoda?

A. The Force
B. The dark side
C. His Jedi training
D. His relationship with Darth Vader

OBSESSED WITH *STAR WARS*

2033.

The bounty hunter Boba Fett figured that Han Solo would pull something devious when charging the Star Destroyer *Avenger*, and he remained behind after the Imperial fleet blasted into hyperspace. As he suspected, Boba Fett saw the *Millennium Falcon* zooming off in the opposite direction toward Cloud City.

Solo hoped that his old friend Lando Calrissian would help him in a time of desperate need. Lando played a bit of a practical joke upon their arrival at Cloud City, making it appear that he was holding a grudge against Solo. His façade faded quickly, though, and he let Solo know that he and his friends were more than welcome. Everything seemed to be going well, but Calrissian was giving the Rebels a tour that ended in a meeting with Darth Vader and Boba Fett. Solo was tortured, and then used as a test subject to make sure that living beings would be able to survive the process of being placed in carbon freeze.

As Solo was being lowered into the carbon freeze, Boba Fett said something to Darth Vader. What was it?

A. "He's no good to me dead."
B. "There can be no mistakes."
C. "Make sure he doesn't die—he's worthless to me that way."
D. "What if he doesn't survive? He's worth a lot to me."

2036. Who said, "The Force is with you, young Skywalker, but you are not a Jedi yet"?

A. Yoda

B. Darth Vader

C. Obi-Wan Kenobi

D. The Emperor

2037. How many AT-ATs were spotted on Hoth?

A. Six

B. Five

C. Nine

D. Four

2038. When escaping Cloud City, Lando Calrissian made an announcement to the entire facility. What was it?

A. "I am no longer administrator of this facility."

B. "The Empire has taken control of the city. I advise everyone to leave before more troops arrive."

C. "Be on the lookout for stormtroopers—the Empire has taken over Cloud City."

D. "Darth Vader never keeps a promise, and now I'm leaving."

2039. Who said "We would be honored if you would join us" to Han Solo, Princess Leia, and Chewbacca in Cloud City?

A. Boba Fett

B. Darth Vader

C. Lando Calrissian

D. Lobot

2040. What limb did R2-D2 still have to attach to C-3PO when he stopped working on him to fix the hyperdrive on the *Millennium Falcon*?

A. His left leg

B. His left arm

C. His right leg

D. His right arm

2041. What did Princess Leia say she would just as soon kiss when Han Solo asked her whether she was afraid he would leave without giving her a goodbye kiss?

A. A gundark

B. A Wookiee

C. A tauntaun

D. A wampa

2042. What did Luke Skywalker ask Yoda about his vision of the future?

A. "What are they wearing?"

B. "Will they die?"

C. "Can I help them?"

D. "How far into the future is it?"

The Empire Strikes Back **Era**

2043. What did Han Solo ask Chewbacca to bring him when he was trying to repair the hyperdrive motivator?

A. A coupling
C. A negative ionizer
B. A hydrospanner
D. A dampening axis

2044.

2045. What did the Emperor tell Darth Vader about the son of Skywalker?

A. He was too weak in the Force to be a threat
C. He would reveal himself to them soon
B. He must not become a Jedi
D. He was on Dagobah

2046. Who said, "Hurry up, goldenrod, or you're gonna be a permanent resident!"?

A. Princess Leia
C. Lando Calrissian
B. Luke Skywalker
D. Han Solo

2047. What order did Darth Vader give Admiral Piett after Captain Needa reported that he had lost the *Millennium Falcon*?

A. "Find them, Admiral, or join Captain Needa."
C. "Calculate every possible destination along their last known trajectory."
B. "Tell the bounty hunters they are now in our employ."
D. "Set a new course for Coruscant."

2048. What did Admiral Piett call the bounty hunters assembled on the bridge of the *Executor*?

A. Trash
C. Junk
B. Scum
D. Pigs

2049. What attacked Luke Skywalker on Hoth?

A. A tauntaun
C. A wampa
B. A Hoth hog
D. An ice bat

2044.

Luke Skywalker was training with Master Yoda, who gave him a new lesson in seeing visions through the Force. Luke mastered this quickly. "Han! Leia!" he cried, tumbling to the ground. "I saw a city in the clouds . . ." Luke told Yoda that his friends were in pain, and he asked Yoda if they would die.

"Difficult to see," Yoda told him, stressing that the future was not fixed. When Luke seemed determined to go to their rescue, Yoda rebuked him. "If you leave now, help them you could, but you would destroy all for which they have fought and suffered."

Later, as Luke was packing his X-wing starfighter to depart, Obi-Wan Kenobi appeared to help Master Yoda convince Luke that he was making a mistake in abandoning his training at this stage. "It is you and your abilities the Emperor wants; that is why your friends are made to suffer," Obi-Wan told Luke. "Patience!"

"And sacrifice Han and Leia?" Luke asked. What did Yoda say in reply?

A. "Follow their destinies they must."
B. "If you honor what they fight for—yes."
C. "In motion, the future is. Their fates you know not."
D. "Consume you, the dark side will, if you take this easy path."

2050. What did Yoda say to Luke Skywalker, cutting him off, when Luke asked, "But tell me why . . ."?

A. "You will learn, my young apprentice."

B. "Figure it out yourself, you must."

C. "There is no why."

D. "How embarrassing your questions are."

2051. What did Princess Leia say to Han Solo when the *Millennium Falcon* wouldn't start in hangar seven?

A. "Would it help if I got out and pushed?"

B. "This ship's a disaster."

C. "Trade this hunk of junk in already!"

D. "Any day now."

2052. What was Yoda's reply when Obi-Wan Kenobi said, "That boy is our last hope"?

A. "Return for more training, he must."

B. "Too quick to anger he is."

C. "No, there is another."

D. "Return he will not."

2053. What attack pattern did Luke Skywalker order at the beginning of the Hoth ground battle?

A. Attack pattern alpha

B. Attack pattern delta

C. Attack pattern omega

D. Attack pattern epsilon

2054. Darth Vader told Luke Skywalker there was only one thing Luke could use to destroy Vader. What was it?

A. The Force

B. Sith lightning

C. Luke's anger

D. A lightsaber

2055. Who arrived just before Han Solo at Cloud City, leaving Lando Calrissian no choice but to betray his old friend?

A. Luke Skywalker

B. Miners

C. The Empire

D. Yoda

2056. How many Star Destroyers did Han Solo see coming right at the *Millennium Falcon* after it blasted out of Echo Base?

A. Three

B. One

C. Two

D. Four

The Empire Strikes Back **Era**

2057. Who went to look for C-3PO in Cloud City after he went missing?

A. Princess Leia

B. Han Solo

C. Chewbacca

D. Lobot

2058. What had Han Solo heard that made him remain in Echo Base after he was supposed to leave?

A. That the ion cannon was temporarily offline

B. That no ships were allowed to take off

C. That Luke's snowspeeder had been hit

D. That the command center had been hit

2059. What did Princess Leia tell Luke Skywalker when he saw her being escorted by stormtroopers in Cloud City?

A. "Go back, Luke!"

B. "Watch out for Darth Vader!"

C. "It's a trap!"

D. "They got Han!"

2060. What did Yoda tell Luke Skywalker he would be?

A. Tired

B. Powerful

C. Strong

D. Afraid

2061.

2062. How did Darth Vader alter his deal with Lando Calrissian after freezing Han Solo in carbonite?

A. He had Lando placed in prison

B. He ordered Chewbacca and Princess Leia to be taken to his ship

C. He took control of Cloud City

D. He left a garrison

2063. Of whom was Darth Vader speaking when he said, "He will join us or die"?

A. Yoda

B. Han Solo

C. Luke Skywalker

D. Chewbacca

2064. What did the Emperor want, according to Obi-Wan Kenobi?

A. The *Millennium Falcon*

B. Luke Skywalker and his abilities

C. The end of the Rebellion

D. Total domination

2061.

Everything had proceeded exactly as Darth Vader had planned. Luke Skywalker had rushed to the aid of his friends in Cloud City, walking directly into Vader's trap. As an overconfident Skywalker ignited his lightsaber, Darth Vader followed suit.

The two engaged in a brutal lightsaber battle over the carbon freeze chamber, and Darth Vader believed he had pushed his young opponent down into it. "All too easy," he said. Then he noticed that Skywalker was dangling from some tubes above the chamber. Flipping down from the tubes, Luke kicked Vader off the carbon freeze platform. The fight moved into the control room of a processing vane, where Darth Vader used the Force to hurl objects at the inexperienced Jedi.

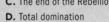

OBSESSED WITH *STAR WARS*

2065. What did Yoda tell Luke Skywalker would happen if he were to leave Dagobah to help Han and Leia in Cloud City?

A. He would be a valuable help to them

B. He would need his lightsaber

C. He would destroy all for which they had fought and suffered

D. He should steer clear of carbon-freezing chambers

2066. How did the Imperial probe droid know that Han Solo and Chewbacca had discovered it?

A. Chewbacca roared

B. Han Solo yelled at it

C. Chewbacca slipped on the ice

D. Han Solo fired at it

2067. Who was a "slimy, double-crossing, no-good swindler"?

A. Luke Skywalker

B. Han Solo

C. Darth Vader

D. Boba Fett

2068. What reason did Luke Skywalker give Yoda for wanting to become a Jedi?

A. Because of Obi-Wan Kenobi

B. Because of his father

C. Because of his lightsaber

D. Because of his uncle

2069. When did Princess Leia say that she "occasionally, maybe" liked Han Solo?

A. When he was acting like a scoundrel

B. When he wasn't acting like a scoundrel

C. When he wasn't acting stuck-up

D. When he wasn't scruffy-looking

2070. How would Luke Skywalker know the good side from the bad, according to Yoda?

A. Through years of training

B. He would need to ask Yoda

C. When he was calm, at peace

D. By studying his holonotes

Luke crashed through a window and clung to the railing of a sensor balcony. Vader cornered Skywalker on the balcony, and Luke managed to land a blow on the Dark Lord before Vader disabled Skywalker completely. Backing up onto an atmosphere sensor, Luke tried not to listen as Vader tempted him to the dark side. "Obi-Wan never told you what happened to your father," Darth Vader said finally.

"He told me enough," Luke yelled. "He told me *you* killed him." What did Darth Vader say in response?

A. "No, Obi-Wan killed your father."

B. "No, *I* am your father."

C. "No, you have no father."

D. "No, Obi-Wan is your father."

The Empire Strikes Back Era

2071. Who wrote the screenplay for *The Empire Strikes Back*?

A. George Lucas and Leigh Brackett

B. Leigh Brackett and Lawrence Kasdan

C. Lawrence Kasdan and George Lucas

D. Lawrence Kasdan

2072. Which actor portrayed Lobot in *The Empire Strikes Back*?

A. Julian Glover

B. Michael Sheard

C. John Hollis

D. Milton Johns

2073. Who played Boba Fett in *The Empire Strikes Back*?

A. Temuera Morrison

B. Daniel Logan

C. Jeremy Bulloch

D. David Prowse

2074. Captain Piett was promoted to Admiral in *The Empire Strikes Back*. Who played him?

A. John Dicks

B. Michael Culver

C. Kenneth Colley

D. Clive Revill

2075. Who portrayed the Emperor in the 2004 version of *The Empire Strikes Back*?

A. Clive Revill

B. Ian McDiarmid

C. Bruce Boa

D. Christopher Malcolm

2076. Who was the conceptual artist for *The Empire Strikes Back*?

A. Leslie Dilley

B. Alan Tomkins

C. Harry Lange

D. Ralph McQuarrie

2077. Where were the Hoth sequences filmed for *The Empire Strikes Back*?

A. Norway

B. Denmark

C. Iceland

D. Greenland

2078. Who was the chief model maker for *The Empire Strikes Back*?
- **A.** Steve Gawley
- **B.** Lorne Peterson
- **C.** Paul Huston
- **D.** Tom Rudduck

2079. Who portrayed General Rieekan in *The Empire Strikes Back*?
- **A.** Oliver Maguire
- **B.** Kenneth Colley
- **C.** Mark Jones
- **D.** Bruce Boa

2080. Who played Rogue Four in *The Empire Strikes Back*?
- **A.** Christopher Malcolm
- **B.** Richard Oldfield
- **C.** John Ratzenberger
- **D.** Denis Lawson

2081.

This actor was born in 1946 in Aberdeen, Scotland, and has had a long career in film, theater and television. He originated the character of Brad Majors in the first production of the cult hit musical *The Rocky Horror Show* in a small, upstairs theater in London called the Royal Court Theatre in 1973.

He continued working with *Rocky Horror* and was the artistic director for the Rocky Horror Company from 1989 to 2004, responsible for all licensing and stage productions of the show.

In addition to other roles, he also had a recurring part on the cult hit television program *Absolutely Fabulous* as Justin, one of fashion victim Edina Monsoon's ex-husbands, and father to Saffron Monsoon.

He has also been seen in *Superman III*, *Reds*, *Labyrinth*, and *Shock Treatment*, the little-known sequel to *The Rocky Horror Picture Show*.

In *The Empire Strikes Back*, he played Rogue Two, the snow-speeder pilot who found Luke Skywalker and Han Solo after their icy night in the wilds of Hoth. Who is he?

- **A.** Denis Lawson
- **B.** Christopher Malcolm
- **C.** Julian Glover
- **D.** Michael Sheard

2082. Who was the effects director of photography for *The Empire Strikes Back*?
- **A.** Ken Ralston
- **B.** Dennis Muren
- **C.** Jim Veilleux
- **D.** Selwyn Eddy

2083. Who was in charge of set decoration for *The Empire Strikes Back*?
- **A.** John Mollo
- **B.** Leslie Dilley
- **C.** Michael Ford
- **D.** Barbara Ritchie

2084. Who played the clumsy and stupid Admiral Ozzel in *The Empire Strikes Back*?
- **A.** Julian Glover
- **B.** Milton Johns
- **C.** Michael Sheard
- **D.** Oliver Maguire

2085. Who was the costume designer for *The Empire Strikes Back*?
- **A.** John Mollo
- **B.** Harry Lange
- **C.** Alan Tomkins
- **D.** Stuart Freeborn

The Empire Strikes Back **Era**

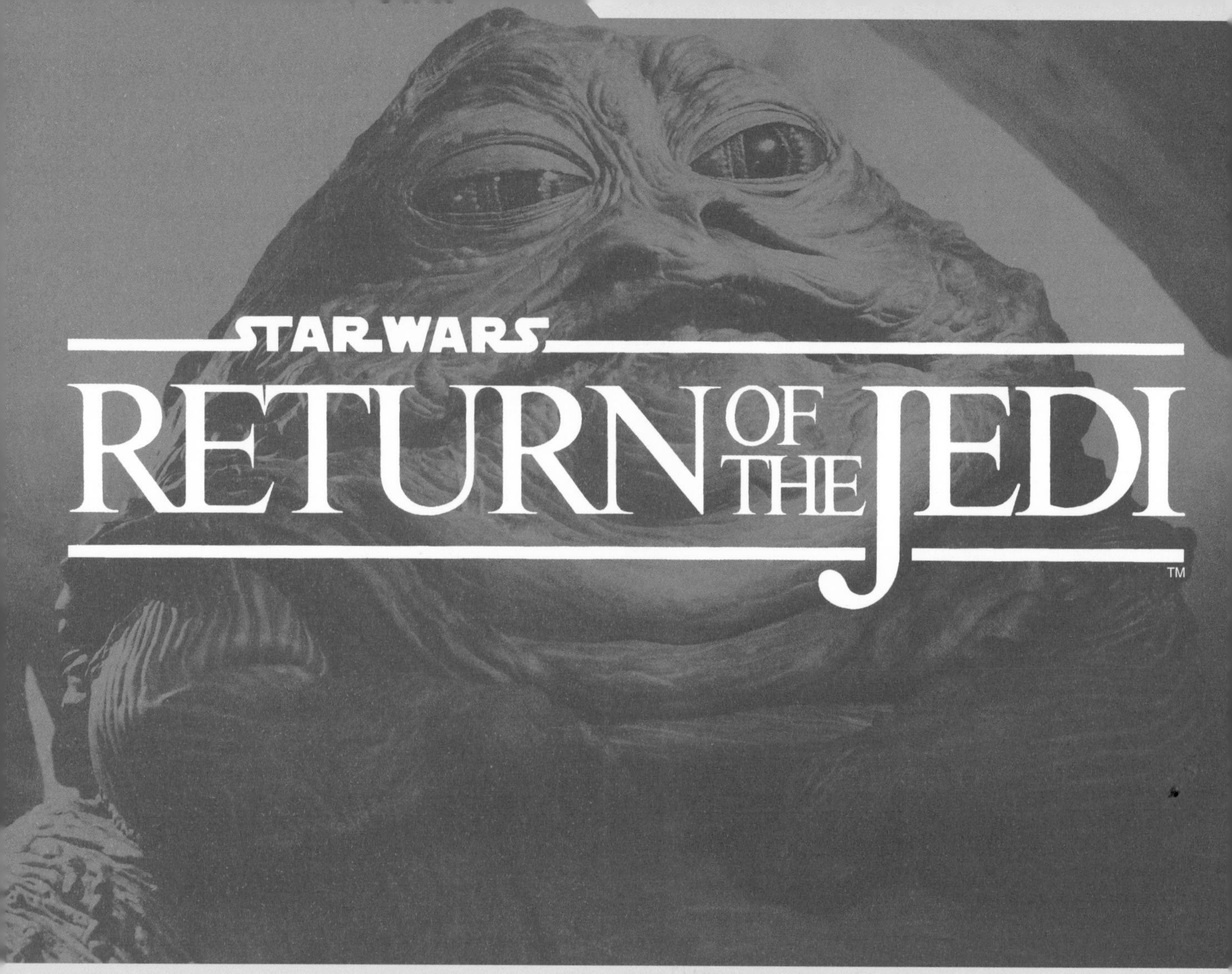
STAR WARS
RETURN OF THE JEDI
TM

2086. Who claimed that a maneuver at the Battle of Tanaab was what promoted him to General?

A. Luke Skywalker
B. Han Solo
C. Wedge Antilles
D. Lando Calrissian

2087. Where was Princess Leia shot when Han Solo was attempting to hotwire the entrance to the shield generator bunker on Endor?

A. Her right shoulder
B. Her left leg
C. Her left shoulder
D. Her right leg

2088. What was Luke Skywalker's weakness, according to the Emperor?

A. His faith in the light side of the Force
B. His faith in his friends
C. His lack of vision
D. His resistance to the dark side of the Force

2089. Who was rescued from Prince Xizor's castle on Coruscant by Luke Skywalker and Lando Calrissian?

A. Han Solo
B. Princess Leia
C. Chewbacca
D. C-3PO and R2-D2

2090. Where did Luke Skywalker go to study the Force before his mission to rescue Han Solo?

A. Dagobah
B. Tatooine
C. Dantooine
D. Coruscant

2091. Who was Gold Leader in the Battle of Endor?

A. Lando Calrissian
B. Luke Skywalker
C. Han Solo
D. Wedge Antilles

2086D 2087C 2088B 2089B 2090B 2091A

2092. Whom did Prince Xizor attempt to assassinate, hoping it would impress the Emperor and cause Darth Vader's downfall?

A. Han Solo

B. Luke Skywalker

C. Princess Leia

D. Mon Mothma

2093. Regarding whom did Princess Leia only retain images and feelings?

A. Her real mother

B. Her real father

C. Her adoptive mother

D. Her adoptive father

2094. What was Darth Vader's reason for arriving unexpectedly at the second Death Star, much to Moff Jerjerrod's chagrin?

A. He had an important meeting

B. He was there to put the Death Star's construction back on schedule

C. He was there to relieve Moff Jerjerrod of his duties

D. He was there to inspect the forest moon of Endor

2095. Whom did Jabba's swoop gang attempt to assassinate on Tatooine, believing Darth Vader had ordered the assassination?

A. Princess Leia

B. Luke Skywalker

C. Han Solo

D. Boba Fett

2096.

2097. What did hibernation sickness do to Han Solo?

A. He couldn't see

B. He was emaciated

C. He couldn't walk

D. He was dehydrated

2098. Who, according to Darth Vader, once thought as Luke did?

A. Yoda

B. Mace Windu

C. Obi-Wan Kenobi

D. The Emperor

2099. Who personally oversaw the final stages of construction on the second Death Star?

A. Darth Vader

B. Admiral Piett

C. Emperor Palpatine

D. Moff Jerjerrod

OBSESSED WITH *STAR WARS*

2096.

Scout troopers had discovered the Rebel presence on the Endor moon and were headed back to alert the Empire. Ever resourceful, Princess Leia impulsively grabbed a nearby speeder bike and prepared to race after them. Luke Skywalker jumped onto the speeder bike with her before she took off, and the two raced through the trees, trying to catch up to the troopers. As they got alongside one, Luke jumped from Leia's speeder and shoved the trooper off, commandeering the speeder for himself.

Eventually, the two got separated, and one of the troopers forced Leia off her speeder; she blacked out just after seeing the trooper smash into a tree stump and explode. She regained consciousness after being prodded by a crude, primitive spear. "Hey, cut it out!" she yelled, looking at the miniscule creature who was threatening her. Disregarding the being's somewhat aggressive attitude, Leia got up and dusted herself off.

Realizing that she was lost, she knew that the creature was probably her best chance to get out of the forest and back to her friends. He was cautious, however, and wouldn't back down from his defensive stance. What did Leia do to make him more comfortable?

A. She gave him her pistol

B. She offered him some food

C. She patted his head

D. She raised her hands in surrender

2100. What happened to Lando Calrissian when he returned to Cloud City, which had been occupied by the Empire?

- **A.** A malfunctioning Lobot attacked him
- **B.** He was arrested by stormtroopers
- **C.** Ugnaughts attacked him for back pay
- **D.** He fell in love

2101. What was Bib Fortuna's response when Luke Skywalker said to him, "You will take me to Jabba now"?

- **A.** "Whatever the Jedi desires."
- **B.** "You should be running for your life."
- **C.** "Jabba will see no one."
- **D.** "I will take you to Jabba now."

2102. Who said, "Hey. It's me!"?

- **A.** Luke Skywalker
- **B.** Princess Leia
- **C.** Han Solo
- **D.** Admiral Ackbar

2103. Where did Darth Vader report that the Rebel fleet was massing?

- **A.** Near Coruscant
- **B.** Near Naboo
- **C.** Near Sullust
- **D.** Near Aduba-3

2104. What did Han Solo call Jabba the Hutt as they were about to be hurled into the sarlacc?

- **A.** A fat, drooling slug
- **B.** A pernicious, offal-ridden goiter
- **C.** A wonderful person
- **D.** A slimy piece of worm-ridden filth

2105. How did Lando Calrissian destroy Prince Xizor's castle on Coruscant?

- **A.** He discovered a secret self-destruct button that Xizor had installed in case of invasion
- **B.** He set exotic drapes from the Moons of Ohontris on fire
- **C.** He fired on it from the *Millennium Falcon*
- **D.** He threw a thermal detonator down the garbage chute

2106. Who freed Han Solo from the carbonite?

- **A.** Luke Skywalker
- **B.** Dash Rendar
- **C.** Princess Leia
- **D.** Chewbacca

2107. What, according to Luke Skywalker, was the Emperor's weakness?

- **A.** His bad dentition
- **B.** His overconfidence
- **C.** His reliance on the dark side of the Force
- **D.** His faith in his apprentice

Return of the Jedi **Era**

2108. With whom did Lando Calrissian have a nasty run-in on the third moon of Blimph?

A. Gardulla the Hutt
B. Nardraa the Hutt
C. Jabba the Hutt
D. Quaffug the Hutt

2109. What did the Emperor tell Luke Skywalker he was looking forward to?

A. Reuniting Luke with his father
B. Completing Luke's training
C. Unveiling a well-kept secret
D. Destroying the Rebellion

2110. Who did Han Solo rescue from the grip of the sarlacc?

A. Chewbacca
B. Lando Calrissian
C. Boba Fett
D. Luke Skywalker

2111. Where did Luke Skywalker go after rescuing Han Solo from Jabba the Hutt?

A. Sullust
B. Dagobah
C. Endor
D. Boz Pity

2112.

2113. Who volunteered to lead the attack against the Death Star?

A. Han Solo
B. Luke Skywalker
C. Lando Calrissian
D. Nien Nunb

2114. How much did Han Solo offer to pay Jabba the Hutt as he was being dragged away to a prison cell?

A. Double
B. Quadruple
C. Triple
D. In full

2115. Who did Emperor's Hand Mara Jade attempt to assassinate in Jabba's palace?

A. Princess Leia
B. Han Solo
C. Luke Skywalker
D. Jabba the Hutt

2112.

Princess Leia had been unsuccessful in her attempt to rescue Han Solo from Jabba the Hutt, and now she, Chewbacca, C-3PO, and R2-D2 were at the mercy of the vile gangster. "We have powerful friends," she told the crime lord. "You're going to regret this."

One of her powerful friends showed up soon. Luke Skywalker arrived at Jabba's palace and gained entrance, only to be approached by two Gamorrean guards. Using the Force, he caused the two to withdraw their advances and, then came face-to-face with Bib Fortuna. Skywalker manipulated his thoughts and commanded Fortuna to take him to Jabba. Upon entering Jabba's chamber, Skywalker demanded, "You will bring Captain Solo and the Wookiee to me." The Hutt laughed maniacally, letting Luke know he was immune to Jedi mind tricks. "Nevertheless, I'm taking Captain Solo and his friends," Luke said smugly. "You can either profit from this or be destroyed. It's your choice, but I warn you not to underestimate my powers."

"There will be no bargain, young Jedi. I shall enjoy watching you die," Jabba responded. What did Luke Skywalker do next?

A. He lunged at Jabba with his lightsaber
B. He asked Jabba to reconsider accepting money for Solo
C. He used the Force to grab a guard's pistol
D. He Force-choked the Hutt

2116. Who went undercover and adopted the name Tamtel Skreej after joining the Hutt Guardsman's Guild?
- **A.** Princess Leia
- **B.** Lando Calrissian
- **C.** Chewbacca
- **D.** Luke Skywalker

2117. How did Han Solo tell Chewbacca to fly as they were approaching the second Death Star in a stolen shuttle?
- **A.** Rigidly
- **B.** Imperial
- **C.** Casual
- **D.** Recklessly

2118. What did Luke Skywalker ask Yoda when he returned to Dagobah?
- **A.** "Am I a Jedi Knight?"
- **B.** "Is the dark side stronger?"
- **C.** "Are you going to die?"
- **D.** "Is Darth Vader my father?"

2119. What did Princess Leia say to Han Solo when he told her he loved her?
- **A.** "I love you, too."
- **B.** "Too late, mister."
- **C.** "I know."
- **D.** "Let's get married."

2120. Who allowed the Rebellion to know the location of the shield generator?
- **A.** Darth Vader
- **B.** Mon Mothma
- **C.** Emperor Palpatine
- **D.** Moff Jerjerrod

2121. What did Emperor Palpatine tell Darth Vader would be Luke Skywalker's undoing?
- **A.** His faith in the Rebellion
- **B.** His trust in the Force
- **C.** His compassion for Darth Vader
- **D.** His trust in Obi-Wan Kenobi's teachings

2122. What did Luke Skywalker tell Princess Leia about his mother?
- **A.** She was lovely
- **B.** He never knew her
- **C.** She died when he was very young
- **D.** He thought he might have been adopted

2123. Who went undercover as a bounty hunter named Boussh in an attempt to rescue Han Solo?
- **A.** Luke Skywalker
- **B.** Chewbacca
- **C.** Princess Leia
- **D.** Lando Calrissian

Return of the Jedi Era

2124. Who said, "You are unwise to lower your defenses"?

A. Luke Skywalker C. Emperor Palpatine

B. Darth Vader D. Boba Fett

2125. What did Darth Vader tell Luke Skywalker about the name Anakin Skywalker?

A. It no longer had any meaning for him C. He had never liked that name

B. He hadn't used it for a long time D. He didn't know who his father was

2126. Who commanded *Home One* in the Battle of Endor?

A. Lando Calrissian C. Mon Mothma

B. Admiral Ackbar D. Wedge Antilles

2127. How old was Yoda when Luke Skywalker returned to Dagobah to complete his training?

A. Eight hundred years old C. Nine hundred years old

B. One thousand years old D. Seven hundred years old

2128. Who discovered an unconscious Leia Organa on the forest moon of Endor?

A. Logray C. Lana

B. Wicket D. Paploo

2129. What did Luke Skywalker need to do in order to complete his training and become a Jedi Knight, according to Master Yoda?

A. Levitate an X-wing out of the swamp C. Destroy the Emperor

B. Confront Darth Vader again D. Study the Holocrons in Yoda's hut

2130. Who disguised himself as the bounty hunter Snoova in order to infiltrate Black Sun?

A. Lando Calrissian C. Chewbacca

B. Luke Skywalker D. Dash Rendar

2131. What, according to Obi-Wan Kenobi, was true, from a certain point of view?

A. That Luke Skywalker had completed his training C. That Darth Vader had betrayed and murdered Luke's father

B. That Yoda was still with Luke even though he had died D. That Luke needed to confront Darth Vader

OBSESSED WITH *STAR WARS*

2139.

Boussh snaked stealthily through Jabba's throne room, trying very hard not to make a sound. The crime lord and his toadies were passed out all over, presumably after having had their fill of debauchery. Accidentally bumping a wind chime, the bounty hunter steadied it before heading across the main floor toward the space where Captain Solo's frozen frame hung from the wall.

Sneaking up alongside the block of carbonite, the masked hunter fiddled with the controls on the side panel, causing the block to lower to the floor with a thud. Boussh deactivated the carbon freeze, and Solo began to thaw out, his frozen, pained expression giving way to live flesh. Completely free of the carbonite, Solo slid to the floor in a quivering heap. Trembling, the Rebel hero asked, "Where am I?"

Boussh replied, "Jabba's palace." Boussh went on to tell Solo what the effects of being frozen in carbonite were and that he would be back to normal soon.

"Who are you?" Solo asked, feeling the strange mask on the bounty hunter's face. As the bounty hunter removed the mask, a laugh came booming through the throne room. Who was laughing?

A. Bib Fortuna
B. Jabba the Hutt
C. Salacious Crumb
D. Boba Fett

2132. How much did Jabba offer Boussh when the bounty hunter presented the crime lord with a shackled Chewbacca?
A. Thirty thousand
B. Twenty-five thousand
C. Fifty thousand
D. Ninety thousand

2133. Who had been kidnapped from his homeworld and offered to Grand Moff Tarkin as a slave?
A. Chewbacca
B. Admiral Ackbar
C. Nien Nunb
D. Doda Bodonawieedo

2134. Where did Wicket spend his childhood?
A. Lazy Days Village
B. Moon Lake Village
C. Tree Sun Village
D. Bright Tree Village

2135. What did Jabba the Hutt receive as a birthday gift from Bib Fortuna?
A. His sail barge
B. Salacious Crumb
C. Oola
D. His rancor

2136. Who was rescued by Han Solo and Princess Leia after crash-landing in a lifepod on the planet Daluuj?
A. Dash Rendar
B. Mon Mothma
C. Admiral Ackbar
D. Wedge Antilles

2137. What price did Jabba actually settle on as bounty for Chewbacca from the bounty hunter Boussh?
A. Fifty thousand
B. Thirty-five thousand
C. Forty thousand
D. Ten thousand

2138. Which Rebel officer detailed the need to deactivate the shield generator on Endor in order to attack the Death Star?
A. General Madine
B. Mon Mothma
C. Admiral Ackbar
D. General Dodonna

2139.

Return of the Jedi Era

2140. What was the name of Admiral Ackbar's home city?
- **A.** Phantom Key
- **B.** Whispering Conch
- **C.** Shellview Pines
- **D.** Coral City

2141. Who told Luke that there was another Skywalker?
- **A.** Obi-Wan Kenobi
- **B.** Yoda
- **C.** The Emperor
- **D.** Darth Vader

2142. Who had a sister named Winda?
- **A.** Wicket
- **B.** Chewbacca
- **C.** Admiral Ackbar
- **D.** Jabba the Hutt

2143. Who gave the order, "Move the fleet away from the Death Star!" toward the end of the Battle of Endor?
- **A.** Lando Calrissian
- **B.** Admiral Ackbar
- **C.** Mon Mothma
- **D.** General Madine

2144. Whose parents were named Deej and Shodu?
- **A.** Wicket
- **B.** Lana
- **C.** Admiral Ackbar
- **D.** Jabba the Hutt

2145. Who asked, "Look I so old to young eyes?"
- **A.** Yoda
- **B.** Obi-Wan Kenobi
- **C.** The Emperor
- **D.** Jabba the Hutt

2146.

2147. Who helped Mace and Cindel Towani reunite with their parents on Endor?
- **A.** Wicket
- **B.** Gorax
- **C.** King Terak
- **D.** Chewbacca

2146.

The Ewoks accepted the Rebels and committed to help them defeat the Empire on Endor. They led the Rebel ground troops to a secret back entrance to the bunker from which the shield protecting the second Death Star was emanating. As Han Solo, Princess Leia, C-3PO, and R2-D2 were contemplating how they were going to get past the guards protecting the entrance, an Ewok rashly created a diversion that led most of the troopers away from the bunker. Free to proceed, the Rebel troops snuck down to the side and Solo tapped a soldier on the shoulder, leading him over to the Rebel troops, who captured him.

Once inside, Solo and his troops worked fast to set up charges that would destroy the shield and allow access to the Death Star. "Han, hurry! The fleet will be here any moment," Leia said urgently, looking at a monitor.

Outside, C-3PO, R2-D2, and Wicket were watching from a distance, where they couldn't be seen. They watched as an entire fleet of troopers arrived. "Oh no, they'll be captured!" C-3PO said to his companions. What did Wicket do?

- **A.** He rushed down to defend the Rebels
- **B.** He ran off into the forest, chattering
- **C.** He told C-3PO to remain calm
- **D.** He hid behind R2-D2

OBSESSED WITH *STAR WARS*

2148. Who was the first to volunteer for Han Solo's command crew on their mission to Endor?

A. Luke Skywalker

B. Chewbacca

C. Princess Leia

D. Lando Calrissian

2149. Who did Jabba the Hutt order into the sarlacc pit first?

A. Han Solo

B. Chewbacca

C. Luke Skywalker

D. Lando Calrissian

2150. Who did Princess Leia call a "jittery little thing"?

A. Logray

B. Wicket

C. Chief Chirpa

D. Teebo

2151. Who said, "Twilight is upon me, and soon night must fall"?

A. Obi-Wan Kenobi

B. Darth Vader

C. Yoda

D. Anakin Skywalker

2152. Who killed Jabba the Hutt?

A. Han Solo

B. C-3PO

C. Luke Skywalker

D. Princess Leia

2153. What did Wicket do that got him banished from all Ewok rituals?

A. He set fire to a sacred amulet

B. He spoke out against Logray, who was practicing Dark Rituals

C. He endangered the Ewok Temple by letting blurggs stampede through it

D. He accidentally turned Chief Chirpa's hair pink while trying to perform a rain ritual

2154. Who called Han Solo "bantha fodder"?

A. Bib Fortuna

B. Jabba the Hutt

C. Princess Leia

D. Lando Calrissian

2155. Who set off a trap, allowing the Rebels to be captured by the Ewoks?

A. R2-D2

B. Chewbacca

C. C-3PO

D. Han Solo

Return of the Jedi Era

2156. How many meals a day did Jabba the Hutt eat?
- **A.** Six
- **B.** One
- **C.** Nine
- **D.** Twenty-three

2157. Who did Luke Skywalker see upon exiting Yoda's hut on Dagobah?
- **A.** Qui-Gon Jinn
- **B.** Darth Vader
- **C.** Obi-Wan Kenobi
- **D.** The Emperor

2158. Whose father was named Zorba?
- **A.** Wicket
- **B.** Admiral Ackbar
- **C.** Jabba the Hutt
- **D.** Bib Fortuna

2159. Who shared a cell with Han Solo in Jabba's palace?
- **A.** Chewbacca
- **B.** Luke Skywalker
- **C.** Princess Leia
- **D.** Hermi Odle

2160. Approximately how old was Jabba the Hutt at the time of his demise?
- **A.** Nine hundred
- **B.** Two hundred
- **C.** Six hundred
- **D.** One hundred

2161. What did Wicket witness that helped the Ewoks in the Battle of Endor?
- **A.** The location of the Imperial troops
- **B.** The access code to the shield generator bunker
- **C.** Darth Vader landing on Endor
- **D.** An AT-ST stumbling off the Yawari cliffs

2162. Who referred to Darth Vader as "twisted and evil"?
- **A.** Obi-Wan Kenobi
- **B.** Princess Leia
- **C.** Yoda
- **D.** Mon Mothma

2163. Who said, "Concentrate all fire on that Super Star Destroyer"?
- **A.** Mon Mothma
- **B.** General Madine
- **C.** Admiral Ackbar
- **D.** Lando Calrissian

2169.

This being defiantly battled Luke Skywalker, Han Solo, Chewbacca, and Lando Calrissian, launching himself from Jabba's sail barge onto the skiff with the prisoners. He tried to fire on Luke Skywalker, but Luke sliced the being's blaster in two with his lightsaber. The being then bound Skywalker with rope that he shot from one of his various tools, but Luke managed to free himself from that as well. He met his match when his arch-nemesis, Han Solo, still disabled from the carbonite freeze, accidentally hit him in the back and sent him flying into the sarlacc's waiting beak.

Inside the sarlacc, fibrous suckers attached themselves to his body and kept him alive, maintaining his consciousness

2164. Who commandeered an AT-ST during the Battle of Endor?
- **A.** Han Solo
- **B.** Wicket
- **C.** Princess Leia
- **D.** Chewbacca

2165. What was Wicket's last name?
- **A.** Waldo
- **B.** Warrick
- **C.** Woldorst
- **D.** Wellits

2166. Who played a Red Ball Jett keyboard?
- **A.** Sy Snootles
- **B.** Greeata
- **C.** Doda Bodonawieedo
- **D.** Max Rebo

2167. How was Barquin D'an related to Figrin D'an?
- **A.** He was Figrin's younger brother
- **B.** He was Figrin's father
- **C.** He was Figrin's older brother
- **D.** He was Figrin's uncle

2168. Which member of Max Rebo's band was raised by adoptive Ortolan parents?
- **A.** Barquin D'an
- **B.** Max Rebo
- **C.** Rystáll Sant
- **D.** Sy Snootles

2169.

2170. When he was asked why the Star Destroyer fleet surrounding the Death Star wasn't battling the Rebel fleet, who said, "I have my orders from the Emperor himself. He has something special planned for them. We only need to keep them from escaping"?
- **A.** Admiral Ozzel
- **B.** Lieutenant Venka
- **C.** Admiral Piett
- **D.** Captain Kallic

2171. Who was Supreme Commander of the Rebel Alliance?
- **A.** Princess Leia
- **B.** Mon Mothma
- **C.** Crix Madine
- **D.** Carlist Rieekan

while extracting moisture. He struggled to maintain his identity as his body was filled with the toxins that the sarlacc used to keep its prey alive yet dependent. Finally managing the strength to escape, he proved that his reputation was warranted by managing to get back to the surface of the dune sea, where he passed out, bloody and barely alive.

The vicious bounty hunter Dengar found him, and, seeing an opportunity, nursed him back to health. Who was this being?

- **A.** Bossk
- **B.** Boba Fett
- **C.** Bib Fortuna
- **D.** Boussh

Return of the Jedi Era

2172. Who was Logray's first shaman apprentice, an Ewok who was banished from Bright Tree Village for turning to the dark arts of magic?
- **A.** Korva
- **B.** Nirrik
- **C.** Zarrak
- **D.** Yoo Yoo Killis

2173. To which Ewok was C-3PO referring when he said, "I'm afraid our furry companion has gone and done something rather rash"?
- **A.** Wicket
- **B.** Paploo
- **C.** Logray
- **D.** Chief Chirpa

2174. Who sang the hit song, "Lapti Nek"?
- **A.** Greeata
- **B.** Sy Snootles
- **C.** Joh Yowza
- **D.** Lyn Me

2175. Who wrote the "Declaration of Rebellion," personally addressing Emperor Palpatine and his crimes against the galaxy?
- **A.** Princess Leia
- **B.** Luke Skywalker
- **C.** Bail Organa
- **D.** Mon Mothma

2176. Who helped Paploo remove a curse that had been placed on Bright Tree Village?
- **A.** R2-D2
- **B.** C-3PO
- **C.** The ghost of Yoda
- **D.** Luke Skywalker

2177. Which Rebel pilot had been inspired by bootleg copies of "A Call to Reason" and "Declaration of Rebellion" to join the Rebel Alliance?
- **A.** Grizz Frix
- **B.** Airen Cracken
- **C.** Wedge Antilles
- **D.** Dorovio Bold

2178. Who played slitherhorn in the Max Rebo Band?
- **A.** Greeata
- **B.** Doda Bodonawieedo
- **C.** Max Rebo
- **D.** Barquin D'an

2179. Whose estate on Tinnel IV was burglarized by the infamous jewel thief known only as Tombat?
- **A.** Admiral Piett
- **B.** Moff Jerjerrod
- **C.** Emperor Palpatine
- **D.** Darth Vader

OBSESSED WITH *STAR WARS*

2185.

Imperial records state that this officer had recently been promoted to Director of Imperial Energy Systems, although this was merely a front. Allegedly, he was responsible for overseeing a new sub-department of the Ministry of Energy, which would develop large-scale portable power plants for disaster relief. In reality, he had been charged with the top-secret construction of a second Death Star, superior to the battle station destroyed during the Battle of Yavin.

Although this being didn't know it, the Emperor's sole reason for constructing this second Death Star was to lure the Rebellion to its doom. The Emperor knew that when the Rebellion heard of this second superweapon, they would stop at nothing to make sure it wasn't completed. In fact, the Emperor was so smug that he had taken it upon himself to be there when the battle began, so he could watch the Rebellion's destruction firsthand.

The Rebels had fallen for the Emperor's trap, and young Skywalker was on board the new Death Star. In a final show of arrogance, the Emperor gave the order to demonstrate the firepower of his new superweapon. "Fire at will," he told this Director of Imperial Energy Systems. What was the Director's name?

A. Admiral Piett
B. Moff Jerjerrod
C. Admiral Griff
D. Lieutenant Venka

2180. Who, after his stint in the underworld with Jabba, retired to his homeworld of Vinsoth and founded a sect that worshipped the Force?
A. Bib Fortuna   **C.** Tessek
B. Ephant Mon   **D.** Bossk

2181. Which member of the Max Rebo Band was actually a double agent, spying on Jabba for many of his enemies?
A. Greeata   **C.** Sy Snootles
B. Barquin D'an   **D.** Max Rebo

2182. Who was in charge of the Rebel troops who captured the Imperial Shuttle *Tydirium*?
A. General Solo   **C.** General Madine
B. General Calrissian   **D.** Admiral Ackbar

2183. How was Paploo related to Chief Chirpa?
A. He was Chief Chirpa's son   **C.** He was Chief Chirpa's nephew
B. He was Chief Chirpa's cousin   **D.** He was Chief Chirpa's brother

2184. Who greeted Luke Skywalker at the entrance of Jabba's palace?
A. Oola   **C.** Boba Fett
B. Sy Snootles   **D.** Bib Fortuna

2185.

2186. Who was Governor of the Quanta sector prior to his role in the Battle of Endor?
A. General Madine   **C.** Moff Jerjerrod
B. Admiral Piett   **D.** Grand Admiral Thrawn

2187. Which member of the Max Rebo Band was, at one time, enslaved by a Vigo, a high-ranking member of the Black Sun criminal syndicate?
A. Greeata   **C.** Lyn Me
B. Rystáll Sant   **D.** Doda Bodonawieedo

Return of the Jedi Era

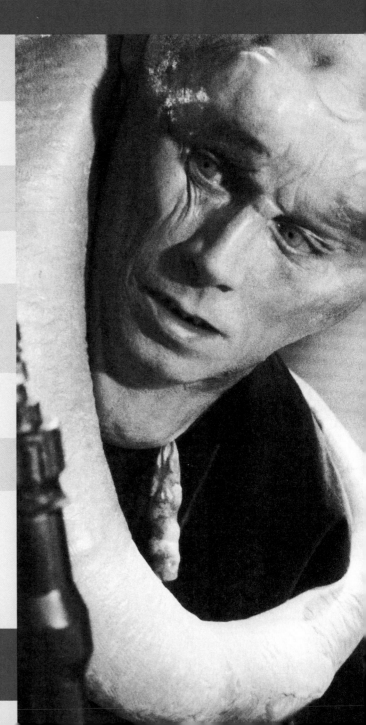

2188. Who was Number One on the Empire's Most Wanted list?
- **A.** Luke Skywalker
- **B.** Mon Mothma
- **C.** Leia Organa
- **D.** Borsk Fey'lya

2189. Who stole a number of priceless sculptures from Jabba's palace after hearing of the events that had taken place over the Pit of Carkoon?
- **A.** Yarna d'al Gargan
- **B.** Malakili
- **C.** Doda Bodonawieedo
- **D.** Tessek

2190. Who was saved from slavery as a child when Boba Fett was hired to kill all of the slavers who were attempting to kidnap the children of the village?
- **A.** Greeata
- **B.** Snoova
- **C.** Lyn Me
- **D.** Malakili

2191. Over how many seasons had Chief Chirpa ruled Bright Tree Village?
- **A.** Thirty-five
- **B.** Forty-two
- **C.** Nine
- **D.** Twenty-three

2192. Which Quarren escaped from Jabba's sail barge on a speeder bike moments before the craft exploded, returned to Jabba's palace, and tried to take over Jabba's business, only to fall prey to the B'omarr monks that roamed the palace's halls?
- **A.** Bib Fortuna
- **B.** Bossk
- **C.** Tessek
- **D.** Sy Snootles

2193. Who did Han Solo accidentally hit with a vibro-ax and send careening into the open beak of the sarlacc?
- **A.** Bossk
- **B.** Aurra Sing
- **C.** Boba Fett
- **D.** Bib Fortuna

2194. Who did Lando Calrissian free after winning her in a sabacc game?
- **A.** Greeata
- **B.** Lyn Me
- **C.** Rystáll Sant
- **D.** Yarna d'al Gargan

2195. Who was Lando Calrissian's co-pilot aboard the *Millennium Falcon* during the Battle of Endor?
- **A.** Airen Cracken
- **B.** Nien Nunb
- **C.** Grizz Frix
- **D.** Dorovio Bold

OBSESSED WITH *STAR WARS*

2203.

This close advisor to Jabba the Hutt had been employed by him for nearly forty years at the time that Luke Skywalker and the Rebel Alliance leaders toppled Jabba's crime empire. Although he worked tirelessly for Jabba, he also despised him and wished for nothing more than Jabba's death.

He had been born in the Una clan on his homeworld. A very industrious youth, he amassed considerable wealth by trafficking ryll spice offworld. Dabbling in contraband trading had its price, however, and his actions brought slavers to his home planet. Other beings on his planet were disgusted by his actions, and he was sentenced to death. He managed to escape his execution, but he left with a tarnished reputation and none of his assets.

At the time of his expulsion from his homeworld, he gained employment in Jabba's massive organization. He had many shifty side projects that, if Jabba knew about them, would have led either to his firing or, more likely, his execution. He managed to maintain a loyal façade, however, and worked his way up through Jabba's syndicate until he achieved the high position he occupied on the fateful day that Jabba sentenced Luke Skywalker and his friends to death. Who was he?

A. Ephant Mon
B. J'Quille
C. Max Rebo
D. Bib Fortuna

2196. Which member of Max Rebo's band was horrified by Oola's fate and quit the band immediately?
A. Barquin D'an
B. Max Rebo
C. Greeata
D. Doda Bodonawieedo

2197. Who in Jabba's entourage had the unfortunate nickname "The Ugly One"?
A. Sy Snootles
B. Yarna d'al Gargan
C. Bib Fortuna
D. C-3PO

2198. Whose first manager was named Evar Orbus?
A. Droopy McCool
B. Rystall Sant
C. Greeata
D. Max Rebo

2199. Which Ewok kept an iguana as his pet and advisor?
A. Logray
B. Chief Chirpa
C. Wicket
D. Lana

2200. Whom did Jabba secretly appoint as his internal security officer?
A. Tessek
B. Bossk
C. Ephant Mon
D. Malakili

2201. Which seemingly trusted member of Jabba's entourage was, in fact, funneling some of the gangster's profits into a secret account?
A. Oola
B. Yarna d'al Gargan
C. Tessek
D. Bib Fortuna

2202. What did Max Rebo's contract with Jabba the Hutt specify his band would receive as payment?
A. Credits
B. Food
C. Bantha pelts
D. Sabacc lessons

2203.

Return of the Jedi Era

2204. What did Droopy McCool's former boss, Evar Orbus, call him?
- **A.** Ticky
- **B.** J'May
- **C.** Snit
- **D.** Pickles

2205. Which Ewok leader wore a gurrek skull headdress and had a striped pelt?
- **A.** Logray
- **B.** Lana
- **C.** Teebo
- **D.** Wicket

2206. Who was Red Leader during the Battle of Endor?
- **A.** Lando Calrissian
- **B.** Luke Skywalker
- **C.** Wedge Antilles
- **D.** Han Solo

2207. Which former leader of the Storm Commandos, an elite Imperial army unit, deserted the Empire and joined the Rebel Alliance?
- **A.** Mon Mothma
- **B.** Admiral Ackbar
- **C.** Keir Santage
- **D.** Crix Madine

2208. Who spent most of his life on Tatooine after his ship was shot out of orbit by an Imperial patrol?
- **A.** Pote Snitkin
- **B.** J'Quille
- **C.** Hermi Odle
- **D.** Nizzles

2209. Who was the keeper of Jabba the Hutt's rancor?
- **A.** Hermi Odle
- **B.** Malakili
- **C.** Droopy McCool
- **D.** J'Quille

2210. Who was a spy sent into Jabba's Palace by one of his rivals, Lady Valarian?
- **A.** Droopy McCool
- **B.** Ak-rev
- **C.** J'Quille
- **D.** Hermi Odle

2211. Who was fed to Jabba the Hutt's rancor after she refused Jabba's advances?
- **A.** Sy Snootles
- **B.** Oola
- **C.** Lyn Me
- **D.** Rystáll Sant

OBSESSED WITH *STAR WARS*

2212. Who left the rubble of Jabba's empire to search the Tatooine wastes for his cousins and was never heard from again?
- **A.** Max Rebo
- **B.** Bib Fortuna
- **C.** Droopy McCool
- **D.** Ephant Mon

2213. Who spent time in a monastery devoted to the Weequay god of thunder, Am-Shak, before taking up percussion in the Max Rebo band?
- **A.** Barquin D'an
- **B.** Ak-rev
- **C.** Malakili
- **D.** Snoova

2214. Who was an accountant in Jabba the Hutt's crime organization?
- **A.** Guri
- **B.** Tessek
- **C.** Hermi Odle
- **D.** J'Quille

2215. Who was the medicine man in Bright Tree Village?
- **A.** Sadgie
- **B.** Coley
- **C.** Logray
- **D.** Lana

2216. After finishing school, whose first job was playing the kloo horn aboard the *Kuari Princess* luxury ship?
- **A.** Barquin D'an
- **B.** Lyn Me
- **C.** Sy Snootles
- **D.** Greeata

2217. How many pairs of breathing tubes lined Pote Snitkin's face?
- **A.** Four
- **B.** Two
- **C.** Eight
- **D.** Ten

2218.

2219. Who played the chidinkalu horn in Max Rebo's band?
- **A.** Max Rebo
- **B.** Droopy McCool
- **C.** Rappertunie
- **D.** Doda Bodonawieedo

2218.

This talented being had developed an infatuation with Boba Fett at a very young age; she kept track of his career and refused to believe the shocking stories about him. As luck would have it, her skill as a dancer ultimately got her a job in Max Rebo's Band in Jabba's palace, where she would finally be able to meet the object of her affection. She managed to speak with him briefly, but stayed in the palace when duty called Boba Fett to Jabba's sail barge.

A famous prisoner, Luke Skywalker, had defied Jabba one too many times. Jabba vowed that Luke and his friends would pay with their lives, decreeing that they were to be fed to a deadly creature in the desert expanse of Tatooine. Boba Fett accompanied the Hutt crime lord to witness the executions, and, when Luke Skywalker managed to free himself and the other prisoners, launched himself from Jabba's ship to keep the rebel heroes from escaping.

Which member of Max Rebo's band was enraged when Boba Fett was presumed dead in the battle aboard Jabba's sail barge and vowed revenge on Luke Skywalker, Han Solo, and Princess Leia?

- **A.** Rystáll Sant
- **B.** Lyn Me
- **C.** Sy Snootles
- **D.** Greeata

Return of the Jedi **Era**

2220. Who replaced Logray as the medicine man of Bright Tree Village after Chief Chirpa removed Logray from his position?
A. Paploo
C. Wicket
B. Jonka
D. La'Taun

2221.

2222. Before joining the Rebel Alliance, who had been a cargo runner for the SoroSuub Corporation, piloting a ship called the *Sublight Queen*?
A. Airen Cracken
C. Nien Nunb
B. Grizz Frix
D. Crix Madine

2223. Which member of Max Rebo's band was a Shawda Ubb from the planet Manpha?
A. Greeata
C. Droopy McCool
B. Rappertunie
D. Sy Snootles

2224. Whose fugitive parents were killed by Rodian bounty hunters when he was ten years old?
A. Greedo
C. Doda Bodonawieedo
B. Bossk
D. Max Rebo

2225. Which Dressellian joined the Rebel Alliance and was on active duty during the Battle of Endor?
A. Amanaman
C. Lana
B. Snoova
D. Orrimaarko

2226. Hermi Odle was a tuberous, greasy being with droopy eyes and drooling lips. What was his species?
A. Baragwin
C. Bothan
B. Besalisk
D. Bith

2227. Into which category does the species Pa'lowick fall?
A. Reptilian
C. Mammalian
B. Avian
D. Amphibian

2221.

Once a loyal Senator, this being had grown discouraged after watching Chancellor Palpatine's ever-growing power, through the Clone Wars to the time of his ascension to the position of Emperor. Not wanting to be branded a traitor, she maintained the outward appearance of a loyalist, even though the Senate was merely a formality after the Emperor seized control of the galaxy. Underneath the mask of a loyal politician, she was a staunch believer in the need to overthrow the Emperor and regain freedom in the galaxy, and this being worked most fervently to this end up to and beyond the Battle of Endor.

This being managed to balance a love of freedom and a family life with a daughter named Lieda. Leading a double

2228. Which species are sentient planarian hunter-gatherers?
A. Shawda Ubb
C. Falleen
B. Klatooinians
D. Amanin

2229. Which species are often referred to as "prune faces" due to their wrinkled skin?
A. Twi'leks
C. Ewoks
B. Dressellians
D. Askajians

2230. Which beings have pig-like snouts?
A. Rodians
C. Gamorreans
B. Yuzzum
D. Mon Calamari

2231. In which species do some youth have a second mouth, located under their characteristic long trunk, which disappears into their facial skin once they reach adulthood?
A. Pa'lowick
C. Whiphid
B. Ortolan
D. Shawda Ubb

2232. Which species plants a tree every time a baby is born, referring to it as that being's "life tree"?
A. Wookiees
C. Eloms
B. Ewoks
D. Sullustans

2233. What portly species has adapted to the arid climate of its homeworld by hoarding water in epidermal sacs that help them to survive long periods without water?
A. Hutts
C. Baragwin
B. Askajians
D. Gamorreans

2234. Which species planned to eat Luke Skywalker?
A. Twi'leks
C. Sullustans
B. Ewoks
D. Bith

2235. How many fingers do the Yarkora have on each hand?
A. Six
C. Three
B. Five
D. Four

life was difficult, and ultimately she received aid from Malan Tugrina, an Alderaanian who worked devotedly.

She managed to gather key political and military figures from the Republic to join the struggle and ultimately helped unite the three largest existing resistance groups into the Rebel Alliance. Unfortunately, her activities came to Emperor Palpatine's attention. Forced into hiding, this being continued to work selflessly for the furtherance of peace and freedom, culminating in an announcement that the Emperor had made a critical error and that the time for the Rebellion to strike was at hand. Who was this key figure in the Rebel Alliance?

A. Padmé Amidala
B. Chi Eekway
C. Mon Mothma
D. Bana Breemu

Return of the Jedi Era

2236. Up to how many children can Askajian females give birth to at a time?

A. Four

B. Three

C. Six

D. Two

2237. Which species has a matriarchal culture, with each clan led by a Council of Matrons?

A. Ortolans

B. Ewoks

C. Gamorreans

D. Yarkora

2238. Which species has the ability to spit a poison that will immobilize its recipient for up to fifteen minutes?

A. Quarren

B. Chevin

C. Weequay

D. Shawda Ubb

2239.

2240. Which species' skin is so thick and strong that it can withstand blaster fire?

A. Rodians

B. Shawda Ubb

C. Weequays

D. Dressellians

2241. Which canine-based species has been in the service of the Hutts for almost twenty-five thousand standard years?

A. Wookiees

B. Ewoks

C. Klatooinians

D. Weequays

2242. Which species served as guards in Jabba's palace?

A. Amanin

B. Trandoshans

C. Gamorreans

D. Bothans

2243. Many members of this species died to get the Rebel Alliance information regarding the second Death Star. Which is it?

A. Ewoks

B. Sullustans

C. Bothans

D. Gamorreans

2239.

These amphibious beings have long, slender legs and arms that attach to plump, squat bodies. Their skin is patterned in yellows, browns, and greens, allowing them to blend in with the rainforest environment on their home planet. Their oddest feature is their lips, which are almost human.

Their bodies are perfectly adapted for the marshes and rainforests of their planet. Their long legs make wading through water in search of food very easy for these beings, and the formation of their mouths allows them to snack on marlello duck eggs with ease, puncturing the shells with their tongues and sucking the yolks through their mouths. In order to evade predators, these beings can almost entirely submerge themselves while being able to keep their eyes, on bulbs atop their heads, above the water so they know when it's safe to resurface. They reproduce by laying eggs that the females will guard in their homes until the eggs hatch. Children are raised in agrarian, feudal-style communities.

These beings are somewhat primitive, and singing is a religious ritual to them. The few who go offworld tend to make their way in show business, as seen in Jabba's palace. Which species is this?

A. Twi'lek

B. Pa'lowick

C. Yuzzum

D. Bith

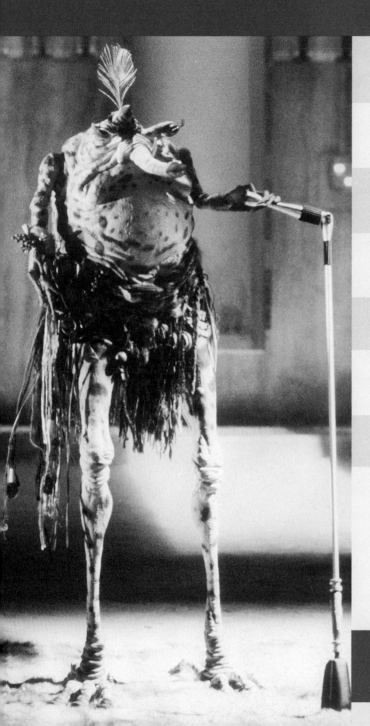

2244. Which species communicates through singing?
- **A.** Pa'lowick
- **B.** Yuzzum
- **C.** Twi'leks
- **D.** Rodians

2245. The members of this species tend to carry staffs from which they dangle the skulls of their vanquished enemies. Which is it?
- **A.** Ewoks
- **B.** Amanin
- **C.** Klatooinians
- **D.** Gamorreans

2246. Which subterranean species works for SoroSuub almost exclusively, which is located on its home planet?
- **A.** Polis Massans
- **B.** Sullustans
- **C.** Klatooinians
- **D.** Weequays

2247. Which species developed from feline ancestors and has retractable claws on its five-fingered hands?
- **A.** Askajians
- **B.** Wookiees
- **C.** Bothans
- **D.** Yarkora

2248. How many stomachs do the Yarkora, a sentient ungulate species, have?
- **A.** One
- **B.** Three
- **C.** Four
- **D.** Two

2249. What Trandoshan was lurking about in Jabba's Palace and on Jabba's sail barge when the Rebel heroes were fighting to rescue Han Solo?
- **A.** Bossk
- **B.** Zanolf
- **C.** Cradossk
- **D.** Pekt

2250. Which species' fingers contain suction cups on the tips?
- **A.** Whiphids
- **B.** Ortolans
- **C.** Yarkora
- **D.** Yuzzum

2251. What do young Ortolans do for fun?
- **A.** Dye their fur with food coloring
- **B.** Get tattoos
- **C.** Pierce their trunks
- **D.** Join gangs

Return of the Jedi Era

2252. Which species' primary deity is the Moon Lady?
- **A.** Askajians
- **B.** Ewoks
- **C.** Falleen
- **D.** Bothans

2253. Which species has a sixth sense that has been compared to Jedi Force traits?
- **A.** Dressellians
- **B.** Wookiees
- **C.** Ewoks
- **D.** Bothans

2254. Which species' written language was primarily in picture format until they formed diplomatic ties with the Bothans and adopted the Bothan alphabet?
- **A.** Dressellians
- **B.** Baragwins
- **C.** Chevins
- **D.** Jawas

2255. From which world do the musically inclined Yuzzum hail?
- **A.** Kashyyyk
- **B.** Endor
- **C.** Ragna III
- **D.** Tatooine

2256. What is Ephant Mon's species?
- **A.** Baragwin
- **B.** Chevin
- **C.** Pa'lowick
- **D.** Ortolan

2257. How many fingers do Baragwin have on each hand?
- **A.** Six
- **B.** Two
- **C.** Eight
- **D.** Three

2258. Which species is born as tadpoles?
- **A.** Mon Calamari
- **B.** Klatooinians
- **C.** Ortolans
- **D.** Whiphids

2259. Which species develops two tusks after the age of two that protrude from their lower jaw?
- **A.** Quarren
- **B.** Whiphids
- **C.** Askajians
- **D.** Falleen

2264.

A mystery throughout the galaxy, these beings are highly intelligent, but their logic is almost completely incomprehensible to the galaxy at large. Would-be philosophers amuse themselves by trying to decipher this species' great works, generally with little success. This species's language makes it even more difficult to understand: it is a strange manipulation of phonemic pulses of energy, into which they insert syntactic contours. Some members of this species have learned to communicate directly with the neurons of other beings, but that generally necessitates direct contact.

These beings reproduce asexually by vomiting out their stomach linings, creating pupal beings that in turn grow into full-sized individuals. They can also reproduce by means of mutual tongue grooming, which creates new individuals exhibiting traits of both parent beings. Mostly stomach, these beings eat constantly, extracting nutrients from almost anything they touch. They contain two brains— one specifically designed to aid with digestion, and one for reasoning purposes.

Distinguishable by their long tongues, these beings affix themselves to surfaces and eat. One was seen near the ceiling in Jabba's palace. Which species is this?

A. Kowakian monkey-lizard
B. Elom
C. Yarkora
D. Wol Cabasshite

2260. What is the most important thing to Ortolans?
- **A.** Family
- **B.** Money
- **C.** Employment
- **D.** Food

2261. Which species' language is primarily made up of subsonic to ultrasonic waves produced through their trunks?
- **A.** Ortolans
- **B.** Pa'lowicks
- **C.** Twi'leks
- **D.** Yarkora

2262. To which species does Max Rebo belong?
- **A.** Chevin
- **B.** Ortolan
- **C.** Elom
- **D.** Yuzzum

2263. How many fingers do Whiphids have on each hand?
- **A.** Five
- **B.** Three
- **C.** Six
- **D.** Four

2264.

2265. What species developed from giant mammals that roamed the plains of Vinsoth?
- **A.** Chevin
- **B.** Wookiees
- **C.** Elom
- **D.** Elomin

2266. Which Endor species does the deadly condor dragon find unpalatable?
- **A.** Ewok ponies
- **B.** Blurggs
- **C.** Bordoks
- **D.** Ruggers

2267. Which species was Jabba the Hutt's pet, whom he named Attark?
- **A.** Rancor
- **B.** Sarlacc
- **C.** Hoover
- **D.** Kowakian monkey-lizard

Return of the Jedi Era

2268. How many eggs do blurggs lay at one time?

    A. Five to six   **C.** Ten to twenty

    B. Twelve to fourteen   **D.** Twenty to twenty-five

2269. Which huge and deadly creature reproduces through spores that travel through space until they find a suitable planet to grow on?

    A. Kowakian monkey-lizards   **C.** Banthas

    B. Blurggs   **D.** Sarlaccs

2270. What was Salacious Crumb?

    A. A blurgg   **C.** A rock wart

    B. A worrt   **D.** A Kowakian monkey-lizard

2271. What is unique about the sarlacc's tongue?

    A. It is sentient   **C.** It is a separate creature

    B. It has arms   **D.** It is beaked

2272.

2273. Which species digests its meals with a distinctive burp?

    A. Dewback   **C.** Gorg

    B. Worrt   **D.** Bantha

2274. How tall are full-grown rancors?

    A. Over 5 meters   **C.** Under 5 meters

    B. Over 10 meters   **D.** Approximately 1 meter

2275. Which creature buries most of itself underground, spreading out to 100 meters or more?

    A. Worrt   **C.** Rancor

    B. Sarlacc   **D.** Gorax

2272.

Luke Skywalker had entered Jabba's palace and attempted to get to the Hutt crime lord through Jedi mind control. Laughing at his attempt, Jabba made it quite clear that Jedi tricks would not be effective on him. He sprang open the trap door in the floor in front of his dais, and Luke went tumbling to the pit below, along with an unfortunate guard who had been standing in the wrong place at the wrong time.

Squealing and terrified, the guard was an easy catch for the rancor, who grabbed the guard and shoved him into its mouth. As the rancor chewed on the last visible piece of the guard, he turned his gaze to his other victim, who was trying very hard to remain calm.

Running first to what looked like an exit, Luke discovered bars blocking the doorway. He turned and ran across the pit and dove into a very small space beneath the rock, which was littered with bones from previous victims and other debris. The rancor reached for him, and Luke fended it off by grabbing something and hitting one of the rancor's deadly claws with it. What did he use to defend himself against the beast?

    A. A skull

    B. A rock

    C. A blaster

    D. His lightsaber

2276. Which creature on Endor keeps boar-wolves as "pets"?
- **A.** Ewok
- **B.** Gorax
- **C.** Dulok
- **D.** Temptor

2277. Which species has been domesticated by the Witches of Dathomir?
- **A.** Rancor
- **B.** Gorax
- **C.** Temptor
- **D.** Boar-wolf

2278. Which creature on Endor uses its furry, lure-like tongue to trap unsuspecting animals and eat them?
- **A.** Blurgg
- **B.** Geejaw
- **C.** Temptor
- **D.** Boar-wolf

2279. How old is a young rancor when it leaves its mother's care?
- **A.** Three years old
- **B.** Six months old
- **C.** Eight years old
- **D.** Ten months old

2280. How many boar-wolves generally make up a hunting party on Endor?
- **A.** Three
- **B.** Six
- **C.** Two
- **D.** Four

2281. For how long does a sarlacc digest the creatures it swallows?
- **A.** A thousand years
- **B.** A few days
- **C.** A month
- **D.** One hundred years

2282. What species do the Marauders of Endor use as beasts of burden?
- **A.** Ewok ponies
- **B.** Boar-wolves
- **C.** Blurggs
- **D.** Bordoks

2283. Which creature in Jabba the Hutt's palace proved its intelligence by swallowing a detonation link needed to activate a bomb, therefore thwarting an attempt on its master's life?
- **A.** The rancor
- **B.** Salacious Crumb
- **C.** A worrt
- **D.** Buboicullaar

Return of the Jedi Era

2284. Which creature stowed aboard Jabba the Hutt's ship when the Hutt was visiting the Kwenn Space Station?

A. A rancor
C. A worrt
B. Attark
D. Salacious Crumb

2285. According to legend, what do sarlaccs sap from their victims?

A. Their personalities
C. Their intelligence
B. Their life force
D. Their languages

2286. What is the condor dragon's approximate wingspan?

A. 5 meters
C. 3 meters
B. 10 meters
D. 8 meters

2287. Which species annoys passersby by laughing incessantly and apparently making fun of them?

A. Rontos
C. Hoovers
B. Kowakian monkey-lizards
D. Boar-wolves

2288. Which amphibious Tatooine species only reproduces during Tatooine's infrequent humidity showers?

A. Ronto
C. Worrt
B. Kreetle
D. Rock wart

2289. How many clawed fingers does a rancor have on each deadly hand?

A. Five
C. Six
B. Three
D. Four

2290. What did Jabba the Hutt's seemingly harmless pet Attark do to sleeping victims?

A. Injected them with poison
C. Sucked their blood
B. Ate their toes
D. Extracted their brains through their ears

2291. Which Endor species has a brain the size of a jubba nut and uses its dense skull as a battering ram?

A. Blurggs
C. Boar-wolves
B. Ewoks
D. Duloks

OBSESSED WITH *STAR WARS*

2292. How do the rock warts of Tatooine kill prey?

A. Large claws

B. Razor-sharp teeth

C. Neurotoxic venom

D. Whip-like tails

2293. Jabba the Hutt was rumored to keep these creatures as pets in his palace, which would explain the large population of the species surrounding the palace grounds. Which species is it?

A. Ibians

B. Worrts

C. Dewbacks

D. Rontos

2294. What did the rancor in Jabba the Hutt's palace eat right before turning its attention toward a hapless Luke Skywalker?

A. A Twi'lek

B. A Gamorrean

C. A Jawa

C. A Trandoshan

2295.

Chaos had overtaken Jabba's sail barge. The party that had zoomed out to the dune sea to watch as Luke Skywalker and his friends were thrown into the sarlacc pit had gotten an unexpected surprise when Luke Skywalker retrieved his lightsaber, freed his companions, and began to fight the guards trying to throw him into the gaping beak of the creature below.

Inside Jabba's sail barge, Princess Leia had taken the opportunity to join the fight by smashing a control panel, throwing the deck into darkness. As Jabba's henchmen ran everywhere, Leia tried to free herself from Jabba's clutches with R2-D2's help.

All the while, C-3PO was under an attack of his own. One of Jabba's pets had trapped him flat on the floor and was picking at his eyes, and had already successfully dislodged one of the protocol droid's photoreceptors, which was dangling from wires out of the droid's head. C-3PO was flailing and screaming, "Not my eyes! R2! Help!" when R2-D2 went over and shocked the beast, sending it flying. Which creature had attacked C-3PO?

A. Salacious Crumb

B. Bubo

C. Attark

D. Penny

2296. What idiotic creature will attack anything that is near, living or otherwise, with its lightning-fast tongue?

A. Temptor

B. Rock wart

C. Worrt

D. Hoover

2297. Which Endor species has greenish-white fur?

A. Ruggers

B. Geejaws

C. Yuzzums

D. Temptors

2298. Which species has been found to be Force-sensitive?

A. Kowakian monkey-lizards

B. Blurggs

C. Goraxes

D. Ewok ponies

2299. What is a sarlacc's estimated lifespan?

A. Five to ten thousand years

B. Twenty to fifty thousand years

C. One to two hundred thousand years

D. One to five thousand years

Return of the Jedi Era

2300. Which species has one large, central, upper fang used for tearing into live prey?

A. Blurgg

B. Rancor

C. Temptor

D. Condor dragon

2301. What did Jabba the Hutt try to do the first time he encountered Salacious Crumb?

A. He tried to eat him

B. He tried to tame him

C. He sang to him

D. He laughed at him and decided to keep him

2302. Which creatures are objects of derision in Ewok culture and folklore?

A. Goraxes

B. Blurggs

C. Condor dragons

D. Boar-wolves

2303. In which species is the female a huge, dangerous predator, while the male is a small, useless parasite?

A. Sarlacc

B. Space slug

C. Rancor

D. Gorax

2304. How many eggs do the reptomammalian rancors lay at one time?

A. Six

B. Twelve

C. Eight

D. Two

2305. Which small quadruped is used as a beast of burden by the Ewoks?

A. Condor dragon

B. Bordok

C. Rancor

D. Phlog

2306. Which architect designed the dungeons in Jabba the Hutt's palace?

A. Enstrelle Pwistrax

B. Chrukkuh Cerruckuh

C. Bant Estelle

D. Derren Flet

2307. Where was Jabba the Hutt's palace located on Tatooine?

A. The Jundland Wastes

B. The Northern Dune Sea

C. Hutt Flats

D. Beggar's Canyon

OBSESSED WITH *STAR WARS*

2308. Over which lake's strait did the Ewoks lead the Rebel forces en route to the shield generator?

A. Lake Marudi

C. Lake Stapina

B. Lake Pinatubo

D. Lake Littlenut

2309.

2310. How long was the underground Imperial power generator and shield projector complex on Endor?

A. 50 kilometers

C. 70 kilometers

B. 10 kilometers

D. 200 kilometers

2311. What are the roofs of the Ewoks' huts in Bright Tree Village woven from?

A. Condor dragon leather

C. Mizzlegritch wheat

B. Savanna grass

D. Dried blurgg tendons

2312. Where is the Dragon's Pelt Savanna located?

A. Endor

C. Sullust

B. Tatooine

D. Bothawui

2313. Which Ewoks live below the lowest levels of Bright Tree Village?

A. Shamans

C. Sentries and unmarried males

B. Outcasts

D. Outcasts and the terminally ill

2314. What was directly in front of Jabba the Hutt's dais?

A. A trap door to the rancor pit

C. Han Solo's frozen figure

B. A Red Ball Jett keyboard

D. The stairway to the entrance

2315. How many kilometers in diameter was the second Death Star?

A. Over 2,000 kilometers

C. Over 500 kilometers

B. Over 900 kilometers

D. Over 1,500 kilometers

2309.

C-3PO had gone along with R2-D2 to deliver a message to the revolting gangster Jabba the Hutt, but he had never expected that the message would involve being a gift to the infamous crime lord. "R2, you're playing the wrong message!" he protested, which raised a guffaw from Salacious Crumb. The two droids were then escorted through the lower levels of Jabba's palace. Looking into a prison cell, C-3PO got the chills. "Oh . . . how horrid," he gasped, backing up. He was then grabbed by a tentacle slithering out from behind the bars of a cell.

Running to catch up with R2-D2, he entered a chamber of horrors: parts of dissected droids decorated the walls, and C-3PO noticed with chagrin that droids were actively being tortured. "You are a protocol droid, are you not?" the droid in charge said to C-3PO. C-3PO attempted to introduce himself, but the droid was not interested in pleasantries, only in how many languages C-3PO spoke. After C-3PO rather pompously announced the number of languages in which he was fluent, the droid told the attending guard to fit C-3PO with a restraining bolt. Where did the droid tell the guard to take C-3PO after that?

A. To his Excellency's main audience chamber

B. To the master's sail barge

C. To the boiler room

D. To the library

Return of the Jedi Era

2316. Why was the being who designed the dungeons in Jabba's palace executed?

A. Jabba deemed the cells to be too accommodating for his prisoners—he wanted them to suffer

B. Jabba didn't care for the color scheme the architect had chosen

C. He hadn't anticipated the number of prisoners Jabba would have, and he designed the dungeons too small

D. The cells were designed so that smaller beings could escape

2317. Where was the Emperor's isolation tower located on the second Death Star?

A. The western equator

B. The north pole

C. The south pole

D. The eastern equator

2318.

2319. What is the name of the hut in which healers use medicinal plants and magic to cure the ill in Bright Tree Village?

A. Hut of Health

B. Place of Sickness

C. Wellness Barn

D. Hut of Wellness

2320. Where was Luke Skywalker brought to face the Emperor aboard the second Death Star?

A. The receiving area

B. The tower pinnacle

C. The maintenance hatch

D. The Emperor's throne room

2321. How many moons orbit Endor, a gas giant?

A. Eighteen

B. Nine

C. Eleven

D. Twenty-three

2322. What did Lando Calrissian tell Wedge Antilles to target when they attacked the second Death Star?

A. The power regulator on the east equator

B. The power regulator on the north tower

C. The power regulator on the south pole

D. The power regulator on the west tower

2318.

Han Solo needed his mission on Endor to be a success. If he couldn't get to the shield bunker and deactivate it, then the entire Rebel fleet would be at risk. It took him some time to find Leia after she and Luke got separated chasing scout troopers on speeder bikes, and in the meantime he had gotten caught in a trap planted by the Ewoks. This had wasted a considerable amount of time, but he was relieved at last to find that Leia was alive and safe with the Ewoks. After a bit of a misunderstanding, the Ewoks released their Rebel prisoners and pledged their aid to the cause.

The Ewok scouts took Han, Leia, Chewbacca, and the droids to the location of the shield generator. At that point, Wicket and Paploo started talking to C-3PO, who announced to Han Solo that there was a secret entrance to the bunker on the other side of the ridge.

The Ewoks led Han and his command team to the secret entryway, and Paploo pointed it out. What did Han call it, telling Paploo that it had been a good idea to take them there?

A. A back door

B. A secret entrance

C. A hidden door

D. A trick entrance

2323. Where was the Pit of Carkoon located?
- **A.** The Western Dune Sea
- **B.** The Jundland Wastes
- **C.** Ben's Mesa
- **D.** The outskirts of Mos Olaf

2324. In which lake were the Ewok stilt villages located?
- **A.** Lake Lana
- **B.** Lake Tena
- **C.** Lake City
- **D.** Lake Sui

2325. What was the Pit of Carkoon famous for?
- **A.** Its sarlacc
- **B.** Its jubba juice
- **C.** The sand surfing
- **D.** Its moisture farms

2326. What is the uppermost spire of the tower at Jabba the Hutt's palace?
- **A.** A landing pad
- **B.** A communications dome
- **C.** A prison
- **D.** An observation deck

2327. On the second Death Star, what replaced the two-meter-wide thermal exhaust port that was the downfall of the first Death Star?
- **A.** Millions of millimeter-sized heat dispersion tubes
- **B.** Nothing—the Emperor demanded that they follow the original design exactly
- **C.** Meter-wide thermal exhaust ports
- **D.** Open trenches leading into space through which heat could dissipate on its own

2328. How high above the forest floor is Bright Tree Village situated?
- **A.** 90 meters
- **B.** 8 meters
- **C.** 15 meters
- **D.** 25 meters

2329. Who allegedly built Jabba the Hutt's palace long before any colonists ever landed on Tatooine?
- **A.** The B'omarr monks
- **B.** Tusken Raiders
- **C.** Jawas
- **D.** Hutts

2330. Where were the Rebels accepted as part of the Bright Tree Village tribe?
- **A.** In the village center
- **B.** In the totem tree
- **C.** In Chief Chirpa's hut
- **D.** In the shaman hut

Return of the Jedi Era

2331. How tall was the Emperor's isolation tower on the second Death Star?

- **A.** Two hundred stories
- **B.** One hundred stories
- **C.** Fifty stories
- **D.** Twenty stories

2332. Where were R2-D2 and C-3PO escorted after C-3PO relayed Luke Skywalker's message to Jabba the Hutt?

- **A.** A B'omarr room
- **B.** The boiler room
- **C.** The power facility
- **D.** The monastery complex

2333. What height can the most ancient life trees on the forest moon of Endor reach?

- **A.** 500 meters
- **B.** 200 meters
- **C.** 1,000 meters
- **D.** 50 meters

2334. What was in the Room of Arches in the lower levels of Jabba the Hutt's palace?

- **A.** Salacious Crumb's secret lair
- **B.** The rancor keeper's sleeping chamber
- **C.** A colony of outcast Jawas
- **D.** A prison cell

2335. How many stories tall is the tower in Jabba the Hutt's palace?

- **A.** Six
- **B.** Twelve
- **C.** Nine
- **D.** Eleven

2336. Where was Jabba the Hutt's throne room located in his palace?

- **A.** In the upper portion of the main building
- **B.** In the upper level of the tower
- **C.** Underground
- **D.** At ground level in the main building

2337. Where was Luke Skywalker hiding when Darth Vader, reading Luke's thoughts, realized that he also had a daughter?

- **A.** Under the fallen catwalk
- **B.** Beneath the Emperor's dais
- **C.** Behind the turbolift to the observation tower pinnacle
- **D.** In an unused Imperial guard duty post

2338. Which beings excavated a secret tunnel into Jabba's palace?

- **A.** Hutts
- **B.** Tusken Raiders
- **C.** Jawas
- **D.** Rodians

OBSESSED WITH *STAR WARS*

2344.

Luke Skywalker did as he knew he must and turned himself over to Imperial troops. His presence on Endor was endangering the Rebels' mission, and he knew that in order to complete his training, he had to face Darth Vader a final time. There was still good in his father—he had felt it. Luke faced his ultimate test aboard the Death Star, as both Darth Vader and the Emperor used every trick in their power to turn Luke to the dark side of the Force. Ultimately, Luke succeeded in his mission, although at a very great price.

Luke held Darth Vader as the fallen Jedi gasped for air. The Death Star was falling apart all around them, but Vader wanted to see Luke as Anakin Skywalker just once before he died. "Luke, help me take this mask off," Vader said.

"But you'll die," Luke responded.

"Nothing can stop that now. Just once, let me look on you with my own eyes." Luke then helped Vader remove his casing, and his transformation from Dark Lord to Jedi was complete. Where were they on the Death Star when Luke and Anakin Skywalker were reunited as father and son?

A. In the Emperor's throne room

B. In the main hangar bay

C. In the Emperor's receiving area

D. On the command bridge

2339. Where did Luke Skywalker turn himself in to Imperial troops on Endor?

A. The main entrance to the shield generator

B. The rear entrance to the shield generator

C. An Imperial landing platform

D. An Imperial turbolaser outpost

2340. How many Ewoks reside in Bright Tree Village?

A. Five thousand

B. Two hundred

C. Eighty

D. One million

2341. How long did the previous occupant of Jabba the Hutt's palace, a pirate named Alkhara, live there before Jabba forced him out?

A. Twelve years

B. Thirty-four years

C. Twenty-nine years

D. Eight years

2342. Where, when hearing the news of the Empire's fall, did citizens topple a statue of Emperor Palpatine?

A. Tatooine

B. Naboo

C. Coruscant

D. Cloud City

2343. What purpose did the rancor pit allegedly serve before Jabba the Hutt had it converted into its current, bloody state?

A. It was a dining hall

B. It was a sleeping area

C. It was a sacred B'omarr grotto

D. It was a storage facility

2344.

2345. In which sector of the galaxy is Endor located?

A. The Correllian sector

B. The Meridian sector

C. The Moddell sector

D. The Centrality

2346. What did C-3PO yell to distract stormtroopers outside the rear entrance to the shield bunker?

A. "Come and get us, Imperial scum!"

B. "You can't catch all of us!"

C. "I say! Over there! Were you looking for me?"

D. "You stormtroopers are a sorry bunch!"

Return of the Jedi Era

2347. What was R2-D2 doing on Jabba the Hutt's sail barge?

A. Asking beings to dance   **C.** Collecting trash

B. Serving drinks   **D.** Passing out gift bags

2348. Given the fact that Ewoks had never actually left the forest moon of Endor, what language was C-3PO speaking when he communicated with them?

A. Gorax   **C.** Yuzzum

B. Basic   **D.** Teek

2349. What was AV-6R7's duty on the second Death Star?

A. It was in charge of maintenance   **C.** It worked in the mess hall

B. It was in charge of regulating the trash compactors   **D.** It was in charge of the work droids building the Death Star

2350. What had happened to the last interpreter in Jabba the Hutt's palace when Jabba got angry with him?

A. He was cast into the Pit of Carkoon   **C.** He was melted

B. He was disintegrated   **D.** He was shredded for scrap

2351. What did Luke Skywalker give to Jabba the Hutt as a token of his goodwill?

A. 50,000 wupiupi   **C.** Han Solo's frozen figure

B. R2-D2 and C-3PO   **D.** A new landspeeder

2352. What did the Ewoks think C-3PO was?

A. A friend   **C.** A god

B. A devil   **D.** A ghost

2353. Which company manufactured the droid frames used by the disembodied B'omarr monks?

A. Serv-O-Droid   **C.** SoroSuub

B. Arakyd Industries   **D.** Colicoid Creation Nest

2354. What was R2-D2 hiding while working on Jabba the Hutt's sail barge?

A. A blaster   **C.** The keys to Leia's shackles

B. Luke's lightsaber   **D.** Poison capsules

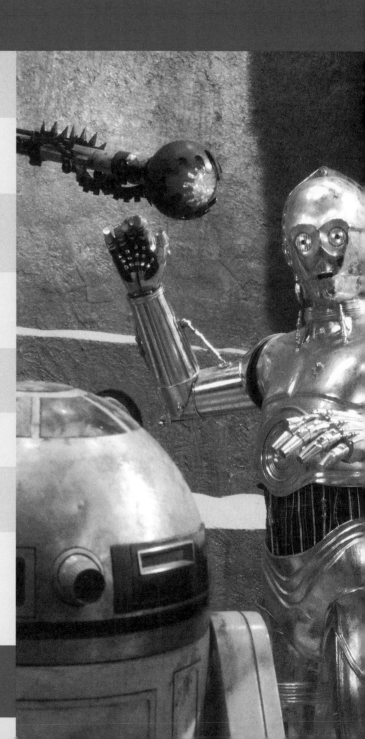

OBSESSED WITH *STAR WARS*

C-3PO and R2-D2, dispatched to Tatooine, were approaching Jabba's palace to deliver a message to Jabba from their master, Luke Skywalker. "R2, are you sure this is the right place?" C-3PO quavered, knowing that they were indeed where they were supposed to be. "I'd better knock, I suppose," he said, tapping gingerly against the gate. "There doesn't seem to be anyone there. Let's go back and tell Master Luke," he said hopefully.

Just then, a small, round hatch opened, and out popped an optical lens with optical shutters attached to a hydraulic lift. It began jabbering at C-3PO in Huttese. Taken aback, C-3PO exclaimed, "Goodness gracious me!" before launching into a Huttese explanation of their mission.

"Artoo detoowha bo Seethreepiowha eya toota odd mischka Jabba du Hutt," C-3PO said tentatively, only to be guffawed at before the eye retracted and the hatch snapped shut. "I don't think they're going to let us in, R2," C-3PO said, surprised. "We'd better go." As he spoke, however, the great gate opened with a churning screech.

What droid was C-3PO interacting with?

A. EV-9D9
B. TT-8L
C. 8D8
D. GNK

2355. What series was AV-6R7?
   A. V-series   **C.** B-series
   B. A-series   **D.** R-series

2356. Where did the stuck-up TT-8L droid work?
   A. The second Death Star   **C.** On the shuttle *Tydirum*
   B. Jabba the Hutt's palace   **D.** In the shield bunker

2357. Who exclaimed, "It's against my programming to impersonate a deity"?
   A. R2-D2   **C.** C-3PO
   B. EV-9D9   **D.** 8D8

2358.

2359. Which company was responsible for the TT-8L?
   A. SoroSuub   **C.** Arakyd Industries
   B. Serv-O-Droid   **D.** LeisureMech Enterprises

2360. What happened to allow 8D8 to spend its days torturing other droids in Jabba the Hutt's palace?
   A. It watched its series mates destroyed and wanted revenge   **C.** It had a mechanical flaw that allowed it to torture
   B. It had been lobotomized   **D.** It was mean

2361. Who destroyed a quarter of the droid population on Cloud City before hijacking a ship and landing on Tatooine?
   A. 8D8   **C.** EV-9D9
   B. AV-6R7   **D.** C-3PX

2362. How was AV-6R7 punished for failing to keep track of a faulty power droid?
   A. Its photoreceptors were removed   **C.** Its arms were removed
   B. Its vocoder was removed   **D.** Its legs were removed

2363. Whom did R2-D2 push overboard on Jabba the Hutt's sail barge?

A. Princess Leia

B. C-3PO

C. Lando Calrissian

D. Luke Skywalker

2364. Who supervised an incredibly overworked droid workforce in the now-defunct GoCorp repulsor plant long before going to Tatooine?

A. 8D8

B. EV-9D9

C. R2-D2

D. LIN-V8K

2365. Which droid was overwhelmingly voted "most annoying" in an annual poll of *Popular Automaton*'s readers?

A. GNK droid

B. TT-8L

C. 8D8

D. EV droid

2366. Which species designed the 8D8 droid?

A. Colicoids

B. Vurks

C. Muuns

D. Verpines

2367. Who broke Princess Leia free of her chains in Jabba the Hutt's palace?

A. C-3PO

B. Chewbacca

C. Luke Skywalker

D. R2-D2

2368. What did C-3PO do to win the Ewoks over to the Rebellion?

A. He told them he was a god and they must obey him

B. He gave them trinkets supplied by Princess Leia

C. He recounted the Rebellion's plight in their struggle against the Empire

D. He promised them a happy future if they did what he said

2369. Into what was the TT-8L/Y7 designed to be directly installed?

A. Ship computers

B. Kitchens

C. Doors

D. Ship cockpits

2370. Which type of droid was 8D8 torturing when C-3PO and R2-D2 were being given their assignments in Jabba the Hutt's palace?

A. An astromech droid

B. A droideka

C. A power droid

D. A protocol droid

OBSESSED WITH *STAR WARS*

2373.

The ground battle on the forest moon of Endor was going very poorly, and it appeared that the Rebels might be defeated. Han Solo and Princess Leia stood at the back door of the bunker, trying desperately to enter the code to get the door open so they could plant charges inside and destroy the shield generator. Han shielded Leia, who announced that the code had been changed. "We need R2," she exclaimed, before picking up her comlink. "R2, where are you? We need you at the terminal right away!" she yelled into the contraption.

R2-D2 and C-3PO had taken refuge in the forest as the battle raged around them, not sure what they should do. R2-D2 beeped to C-3PO, who said, "Going? What do you mean, you're going?" frantically adding, "This is no time for heroics! Come back!" before following the astromech droid out of their hiding place.

Han Solo and Princess Leia remained in their position at the bunker as the two droids raced to their side. "We're coming!" C-3PO shouted as they approached the locked bunker door. R2-D2 rushed to the computer terminal and plugged in, ready to access and override the security code, but as he was accessing the computer terminal, something stopped him. What was it?

A. A stormtrooper shot him

B. He was electrocuted

C. A stray arrow hit him

D. The blast door shut on him

2371. What did C-3PO tell the Ewoks he would do if they didn't release his friends?
- **A.** Set fire to Bright Tree Village
- **B.** Cast a spell that would dry up their wells
- **C.** Leave forever
- **D.** Become angry and use his magic

2372. Who carried a gaffi stick given to him by grateful Tusken Raiders after he killed a giant womp rat that had taken over their clan cave?
- **A.** Bib Fortuna
- **B.** Dossk
- **C.** Malakili
- **D.** Boba Fett

2373.

2374. Who carried heavy-duty axes?
- **A.** Jawas
- **B.** Bib Fortuna
- **C.** Gamorrean guards
- **D.** The Max Rebo band

2375. What weapon did Ak-rev carry?
- **A.** A purloined lightsaber
- **B.** A vibroblade
- **C.** A vibro-lance
- **D.** A blaster

2376. What did Boushh activate in Jabba's palace?
- **A.** A glop grenade
- **B.** A concussion grenade
- **C.** A thermal detonator
- **D.** A fragmentation grenade

2377. Who carried a dagger that he would poison with chall granules, krayt dragon venom, or rock wart sting juice?
- **A.** J'Quille
- **B.** Jabba the Hutt
- **C.** Bib Fortuna
- **D.** Snoova

2378. Which blaster rifles did the Rebel forces use in the Battle of Endor?
- **A.** DC-15
- **B.** BAW E-5
- **C.** A280
- **D.** E-11B

2379. What did Princess Leia use to defeat the scout trooper who was planning to take her into custody?
- **A.** A blaster
- **B.** A rifle
- **C.** A lightsaber
- **D.** A stick

2380. What color was the blade of Luke Skywalker's new lightsaber?
- **A.** Green
- **B.** Red
- **C.** Blue
- **D.** Purple

Return of the Jedi Era

2381. What did the Emperor use to fight Luke Skywalker?
A. A lightsaber
B. Martial arts
C. A blaster
D. Sith lightning

2382. Which Ewok weapon backfired when Wicket attempted to use it?
A. A club
B. A rock
C. Twine tied around a rock
D. A stone axe

2383. What did the Ewoks use in their initial attack on the Imperial forces outside the rear entrance to the shield generator bunker?
A. Rocks
B. Spears
C. Bows and arrows
D. Blowguns

2384. How did the Ewoks topple various AT-STs?
A. With rope
B. With blasters
C. With logs
D. With rocks

2385. Where did Luke Skywalker learn how to construct a lightsaber?
A. From Yoda
B. From the Force
C. From a book in Obi-Wan Kenobi's house
D. From the HoloNet

2386. How many TIE fighters escorted Darth Vader's shuttle as it approached the second Death Star?
A. Four
B. Six
C. Eight
D. Two

2387. Who designed the A-wing starfighter?
A. General Madine
B. General Rieekan
C. General Dodonna
D. General Solo

2388. Who owned the Ubrikkian luxury sail barge *Khetanna*?
A. Darth Vader
B. Emperor Palpatine
C. Bib Fortuna
D. Jabba the Hutt

2389.

2390. How many sand skiffs accompanied Jabba the Hutt's sail barge?
A. Three
B. Two
C. Nine
D. Four

2389.

The Rebel leaders outlined their plan of attack against the Emperor and his second dreaded Death Star. General Solo volunteered to lead a strike team on the forest moon of Endor, while his old friend General Calrissian chose to lead the strike against the Death Star itself. Solo told Calrissian that he could take the *Millennium Falcon*. "You need all the help you can get," Solo said. "She's the fastest ship in the fleet." As the two parted ways on their separate missions, Solo turned for one last look at his trusted ship.

During the battle, Calrissian and the rest of the rebel fleet fought gallantly against the attacking TIE fighters while they waited for the shield surrounding the Death Star to deactivate. Then Admiral Ackbar made the announcement: "The shield is down! Commence attack on the Death Star's main reactor!"

Zooming through the Death Star, Wedge Antilles announced to the group, "Stay alert. We could run out of room real fast." As if on cue, the *Millennium Falcon* struck a beam, losing an important piece of equipment. What did it lose?

A. The hyperspace integrator
B. The main sensor rectenna
C. The upper quad laser cannon
D. The warp vortex stabilizer

2391. How many Sienar Fleet Systems L-s9.3 laser cannons arm a TIE interceptor?

A. Six

B. Two

C. Eight

D. Four

2392. Which manufacturer produced the speeder bikes used by the Empire on the forest moon of Endor?

A. Gallofree Yards, Inc.

B. MandalMotors

C. Mobquet Swoops and Speeders

D. Aratech Repulsor Company

2393. How many sails did Jabba the Hutt's sail barge have?

A. Four

B. Two

C. Three

D. Five

2394. Which company manufactured the escort frigate used by the Rebellion?

A. Incom Corporation

B. Kuat Drive Yards

C. Hoersch-Kessel Drive, Inc.

D. Corellian Engineering Corporation

2395. Who designed the B-wing starfighter?

A. General Madine

B. Commander Ackbar

C. Mon Mothma

D. General Calrissian

2396. What was the name of Admiral Ackbar's command ship in the Battle of Endor?

A. *Mon Cal One*

B. *Home One*

C. *Rebels' Choice*

D. *Ackbar One*

2397. How many missiles can each missile launcher on an A-wing hold?

A. Six

B. Seven

C. Nine

D. Four

2398. How many turbolasers does a standard Mon Cal cruiser contain?

A. Thirty-two

B. Forty-eight

C. Ninety

D. Six

2399. Which company manufactured the B-wing starfighter?

A. Incom Corporation

B. Kuat Drive Yards

C. Slayn & Korpil

D. Sienar Fleet Systems

Return of the Jedi **Era**

2400. How many tractor beam projectors does a Nebulon-B frigate have?

A. One   C. Four

B. Two   D. None

2401. How many Karydee KD57 3-chamber repulsorlift engines kept Jabba the Hutt's sail barge afloat?

A. Three   C. Nine

B. Six   D. Twenty

2402. What is an Imperial speeder bike's maximum speed?

A. 300 kph   C. 500 kph

B. 200 kph   D. 100 kph

2403. How many Novaldex J-77 "Event Horizon" engines come standard in an A-wing starfighter?

A. One   C. Six

B. Two   D. Four

2404. Who pointed the blaster cannon at the deck of Jabba the Hutt's sail barge during the battle over the Pit of Carkoon?

A. Luke Skywalker   C. Han Solo

B. Princess Leia   D. Chewbacca

2405.

2406. Which type of ship did General Solo commandeer in order to infiltrate the shield surrounding the forest moon of Endor?

A. TIE fighter   C. TIE bomber

B. *Lambda*-class shuttle   D. Star Destroyer

2407. Which type of ship did Rebel pilot Ten Numb fly during the Battle of Endor?

A. Y-wing starfighter   C. X-wing starfighter

B. A-wing starfighter   D. B-wing starfighter

2408. Which type of ship smashed into the bridge of the Super Star Destroyer *Executor*, sending it plummeting into the second Death Star's surface?

A. Y-wing starfighter   C. B-wing starfighter

B. X-wing starfighter   D. A-wing starfighter

2405.

When the Mon Calamari officially joined the Rebel Alliance, they brought with them a fleet of large, sturdy ships that would become an integral part of the Alliance's fleet from that point on.

These starships were originally intended for colonization and civilian transport but were easily adapted to the Alliance's needs. When these ships were modified for use in battle, they were fitted with multiple ion cannons, turbolasers and tractor beam projectors. Each ship also featured a docking bay that could house a large number of Rebel starfighters. These ships boasted thick hull plating and

2409. Which type of vessel did Luke Skywalker use to escape the second Death Star?

A. TIE fighter
B. TIE interceptor
C. *Lambda*-class shuttle
D. TIE bomber

2410. How many Borstel RG9 laser cannons does an A-wing starfighter have?

A. Four
B. Six
C. Three
D. Two

2411. Which vehicle has a cockpit that can be jettisoned and flown at sublight speed for a short time in the event that the main ship is damaged?

A. A-wing
B. *Lambda*-class shuttle
C. TIE interceptor
D. B-wing

2412. How many troops can a *Lambda*-class shuttle carry?

A. Forty
B. Twenty
C. Ten
D. Fifty

2413. How many thrust nozzles does the B-wing's standard Quadex Kyromaster engine come equipped with?

A. Six
B. Two
C. Four
D. Eight

2414. Which craft's cockpit remains stable around a gyroscopically rotatable main body?

A. A-wing starfighter
B. B-wing starfighter
C. X-wing starfighter
D. Y-wing starfighter

2415. Who was the officer in command of the Super Star Destroyer *Executor* during the Battle of Endor?

A. Admiral Ozzel
B. Lieutenant Venka
C. Admiral Piett
D. Captain Kallic

2416. How many 3 ArMek SW-7a ion cannons does a B-wing starfighter come equipped with?

A. Five
B. Six
C. Two
D. Three

2417. Which type of ship did Rebel pilot Grizz Frix fly in the Battle of Endor?

A. Y-wing starfighter
B. X-wing starfighter
C. A-wing starfighter
D. B-wing starfighter

extremely powerful shields created by dozens of overlapping shield generators.

These ships were key to the success of the Battle of Endor, as noted by Mon Mothma in her memoirs: "Their cruisers protected our fleet at the Battle of Endor, allowing the starfighters to penetrate the second Death Star's core." One of these cruisers served as the Rebellion's flagship during the assault. What ships were they?

A. YT-1300s
B. MC80 Star Cruisers
C. Nebulon-B Frigates
D. Z-95 Headhunters

Return of the Jedi Era

2418. What was the maximum speed at which Jabba the Hutt's sail barge could travel?
- **A.** 50 kph
- **B.** 25 kph
- **C.** 100 kph
- **D.** 200 kph

2419. How many SFS-204 sublight ion engines does a *Lambda*-class shuttle contain?
- **A.** Four
- **B.** Two
- **C.** Six
- **D.** One

2420. Who said, "I don't think the Empire had Wookiees in mind when they designed her, Chewie"?
- **A.** Luke Skywalker
- **B.** Princess Leia
- **D.** C-3PO
- **D.** Han Solo

2421. How many days' worth of air and food can a TIE interceptor store?
- **A.** Two days' worth
- **B.** Six days' worth
- **C.** Nine days' worth
- **D.** None

2422.

2423. How many decks did Jabba the Hutt's sail barge have?
- **A.** Six
- **B.** Two
- **C.** Three
- **D.** Four

2424. Which type of ship did Wedge Antilles pilot in the Battle of Endor?
- **A.** Y-wing starfighter
- **B.** X-wing starfighter
- **C.** B-wing starfighter
- **D.** A-wing starfighter

2425. How long are Mon Cal cruisers?
- **A.** 1,500 meters
- **B.** 1,200 meters
- **C.** 2,000 meters
- **D.** 800 meters

2426. Who said, "Bo Shuda!"?
- **A.** Jabba the Hutt
- **B.** Bib Fortuna
- **C.** Lana
- **D.** Chief Chirpa

2427. What were Yoda's final words to Luke Skywalker?
- **A.** "Luke, mind the Force."
- **B.** "Face Vader, you must, if a Jedi you wish to become."
- **C.** "Luke, there is another Skywalker."
- **D.** "Obi-Wan and I always with you will be."

2422.

Han Solo had volunteered for the dangerous job of leading a strike team in a stolen Imperial shuttle. He had been tasked with flying the shuttle to the Death Star, using an Imperial code to get permission to go through the shield generated from the moon below the Death Star's orbit, and to deactivate the shield so the Rebel fleet could stage a last attack against the Galactic Empire. In a Rebel Alliance meeting, Han announced that he was still in need of a command crew. Chewbacca volunteered with a hearty roar. "General, count me in," Leia added, smiling.

"I'm with you, too!" said Luke Skywalker, and C-3PO and R2-D2 rounded out the team.

Things seemed to be going smoothly as the shuttle approached the Super Star Destroyer *Executor*. Han Solo had stated the Imperial shuttle's alleged purpose and transmitted the stolen code for clearance to lower the shield. There was a long pause as they waited for their code to clear. What reason did Luke Skywalker give for the Empire's hesitation?

- **A.** The code had been reported stolen
- **B.** Luke's own presence was endangering the mission
- **C.** The shuttle had been reported stolen
- **D.** The code was too outdated to be worth the price they paid

OBSESSED WITH *STAR WARS*

2428. What was ST-321?

   A. A code clearance   **C.** An officer's ranking

   B. Darth Vader's shuttle   **D.** A docking bay on the Death Star

2429. What did Admiral Ackbar say had to be deactivated if any attack was to be attempted against the second Death Star?

   A. The shield   **C.** The Death Star's defense fleet

   B. The Death Star's main power source   **D.** The *Executor*

2430. What did Han Solo say when asked what his cargo and destination was as the shuttle *Tydirium* awaited code clearance from the Empire?

   A. "Droid delivery for the Death Star."   **C.** "Parts and technical crew for the forest moon."

   B. "Troop reinforcements for the forest moon."   **D.** "Mechanic crew for the forest moon."

2431. How did the Emperor say that Luke Skywalker, who had grown strong, could be turned to the dark side of the Force?

   A. The Emperor could turn him to the dark side   **C.** He would be easily turned to the dark side

   B. Darth Vader could turn him to the dark side   **D.** Only the Emperor and Darth Vader together could turn him to the dark side

2432. Where did the Emperor tell Darth Vader to send the fleet?

   A. To Coruscant   **C.** To the far side of Endor

   B. To Bright Tree Village   **D.** To Sullust

2433. Who did Luke Skywalker say was on the ship requesting the shuttle *Tydirium*'s code clearance?

   A. The Emperor   **C.** Moff Jerjerrod

   B. Admiral Piett   **D.** Darth Vader

2434. What did Admiral Ackbar say the Rebel fleet's cruisers would do during the attack on the Death Star?

   A. Attack the Death Star   **C.** Create a perimeter

   B. Attack Star Destroyers   **D.** Remain at a safe distance

Return of the Jedi Era

2435. How were the scout troopers alerted to Han Solo's presence on Endor?

A. Chewbacca growled

B. He fired at them

C. He stepped on a stick

D. They spotted him behind a tree

2436. How much more training did Luke require, according to Yoda?

A. A few years' worth

B. Quite a bit

C. He was too reckless—he would never become a Jedi

D. He didn't require any more training

2437. Which switch did Luke tell Leia to hit in order to jam the scout troopers' comlinks?

A. The first switch

B. The center switch

C. The bottom switch

D. The left switch

2438.

2439. When Han Solo ordered a Rebel soldier to take the squad ahead, when did he say to meet at the shield generator?

A. 0200

B. 0400

C. 0300

D. 1100

2440. How did Jabba the Hutt describe Boussh?

A. "Bold and stupid"

B. "Fearless and inventive"

C. "Stupid and brave"

D. "Foolish and creative"

2441. Who said, "Why don't you use your divine influence and get us out of this?"

A. Luke Skywalker

B. Han Solo

C. R2-D2

D. Lando Calrissian

2442. What did Darth Vader tell Admiral Piett regarding the shuttle *Tydirium*?

A. "Hold them until I contact the Emperor."

B. "Leave them to me."

C. "Tell them to go on their way."

D. "Deny them entrance."

2443. Who did C-3PO say had never returned from Jabba the Hutt's palace as he and R2-D2 were approaching it?

A. Lando Calrissian and poor Chewbacca

B. Han Solo and poor Chewbacca

C. Princess Leia and poor Master Luke

D. Master Luke and poor Chewbacca

2438.

Luke's mission to Tatooine had been a success. Han Solo was free of the carbonite, Princess Leia was no longer Jabba's slave, and the droids had been rescued from their servitude. On top of that, Jabba's vile crime syndicate had been dissolved, making the galaxy a slightly safer place. Now Luke was on his way to make good on his promise—he was going back to Dagobah to finish his training with Jedi Master Yoda.

When he arrived at Yoda's hut, he found the Jedi Master in poor health, struggling to walk and having difficulty breathing. The ancient Jedi made light of the situation, joking even as he struggled to get into his bed. "Master Yoda, you can't die," Luke pleaded with his instructor.

"Strong am I with the Force," Yoda replied. "But not that strong. Twilight is upon me, and soon night must fall."

Luke told Yoda that he had returned to complete his training, but Yoda let Luke know that he already knew what he needed to succeed. "Then I am a Jedi," Luke said. Afterward, Yoda told him there was one final task Luke needed to complete in order to fulfill his destiny and become a Jedi. When Yoda informed Luke of his final assignment, Luke asked him a question. What was it?

A. "Am I the last of the Jedi?"

B. "Is Darth Vader my father?"

C. "Why did Obi-Wan lie to me?"

D. "How can I go on without you?"

2444. What did Darth Vader tell Luke Skywalker the Emperor was going to show him?

A. The dark side of the Force   **C.** The true nature of the Force

B. Force lightning   **D.** The ways of the Force

2445. What did Obi-Wan tell Luke could be made to serve the Emperor?

A. His powers   **C.** The Force

B. His sister   **D.** His feelings

2446. Who gave the command for the Rebel fleet to jump into hyperspace?

A. General Madine   **C.** General Dodonna

B. Lando Calrissian   **D.** Admiral Ackbar

2447. What did EV-9D9 call R2-D2?

A. "Feisty little one"   **C.** "Perky little thing"

B. "Nasty little ashcan"   **D.** "Ignorant little bucket"

2448. How many scout troopers were left after Paploo commandeered a speeder bike?

A. Three   **C.** Four

B. One   **D.** None

2449. How did Luke Skywalker destroy the scout trooper who was firing on him after he fell off his speeder?

A. With a blaster   **C.** With his lightsaber

B. With the Force   **D.** With a log

2450. What did Moff Jerjerrod tell Darth Vader he needed in order to complete the second Death Star on schedule?

A. More droids   **C.** More materials

B. More credits   **D.** More men

2451. What did Admiral Ackbar tell Green Group to stick to as the Rebel fleet attempted a retreat from the Death Star?

A. Holding Sector EKP   **C.** Holding Sector TK-421

B. Holding Sector MV-7   **D.** Holding Sector BFT

2452. What did Obi-Wan tell Luke that Anakin was?

A. "A fine Jedi"   **C.** "A good friend"

B. "A cocky kid"   **D.** "A dark lord"

Return of the Jedi **Era**

2453. How many additional scout troopers did Leia see after she rushed to stop the ones who had been alerted to the Rebels' presence and were going for help?

A. Two
B. Three
C. Six
D. Four

2454. What did Princess Leia tell Han Solo when he asked her who she was after she released him from the carbonite?

A. "Your hero."
B. "It's me, Leia."
C. "Someone who loves you."
D. "I am Boussh."

2455.

2456. What did General Madine say the stolen shuttle they were flying to Endor would be disguised as?

A. A troop transport
B. A mechanic vessel
C. A droid transport vessel
D. A cargo ship

2457. What news did Darth Vader have for the Emperor when he disobeyed orders and returned to the Death Star from the command ship?

A. That the Rebel fleet was massing near Sullust
B. That the Rebel fleet was planning an attack on the Death Star
C. That the Rebel fleet would soon be crushed
D. That Luke Skywalker was on Endor

2458. What code clearance did ST-321 have?

A. Code clearance blue
B. Code clearance green
C. Code clearance red
D. Code clearance orange

2459. What did Princess Leia have that scared Wicket?

A. A knife
B. A hat
C. A snake
D. A gun

2460. What did Admiral Ackbar say the fighters were going to do during the attack on the Death Star?

A. Fight off the Imperial fleet
B. Concentrate their fire on the Emperor's tower
C. Fly into the superstructure and attempt to knock out the main reactor
D. Attempt to fire into a thermal exhaust port

2455.

Luke watched as the small form of his Jedi Master passed from the physical realm and into the Force. As he left Yoda's hut, he walked over to his X-wing fighter, where R2-D2 was busy making small repairs. Luke leaned down next to R2 and said, "I can't do it, R2. I can't go on alone." As he spoke, a familiar voice responded to him. "Yoda will always be with you," said his first Master, Obi-Wan Kenobi.

Turning, Luke saw a vision of his old friend. "Obi-Wan, why didn't you tell me?" Luke asked. "You told me Vader betrayed and murdered my father."

"Your father was seduced by the dark side of the Force," Obi-Wan told Luke. "He ceased to be Anakin Skywalker and became Darth Vader. When that happened, the good man who was your father was destroyed. So, what I told you was true." Obi-Wan related to young Skywalker the tale of his former apprentice's fall, saying finally, "I thought that I could instruct him as well as Yoda. I was wrong."

"I can't do it, Ben," Luke insisted. "I can't kill my own father." Obi-Wan paused, and then said something. What was it?

A. "Then the Emperor has already won."
B. "You must face Darth Vader. The future of the galaxy depends on it."
C. "Then we will ask your sister to do it."
D. "Yoda has failed as an instructor just as I did."

OBSESSED WITH *STAR WARS*

2461. In which sector did the Mon Calamari soldier tell Admiral Ackbar there were enemy ships?
A. Sector 47
B. Sector 12
C. Sector 23
D. Sector 2187

2462. What did Bib Fortuna tell Jabba the Hutt about Luke Skywalker after R2-D2's message?
A. "Beware the Jedi."
B. "He's a boy."
C. "He's no match for you."
D. "He's no Jedi."

2463. Who snapped, "And you said it was pretty here"?
A. Luke Skywalker
B. Princess Leia
C. C-3PO
D. Han Solo

2464. What did Lando Calrissian order the Rebel fleet to do after they discovered that the Death Star was operational?
A. Fight to the death
B. Surrender to the Empire
C. Engage the Star Destroyers at point-blank range
D. Retreat

2465. What did R2-D2 run into, surprising him in the entrance of Jabba the Hutt's palace?
A. A B'omarr monk
B. A Gamorrean guard
C. Bib Fortuna
D. Salacious Crumb

2466. Who impersonated an AT-ST pilot, getting the Imperials to open the bunker door?
A. Luke Skywalker
B. Princess Leia
C. Han Solo
D. Wedge Antilles

2467. Who cried, "Why do you always have to be so brave!" after R2-D2 was shot attempting to open the bunker doors on Endor?
A. Princess Leia
B. Han Solo
C. C-3PO
D. Luke Skywalker

2468. What did Darth Vader tell Luke Skywalker that Obi-Wan had been wise to hide from Vader?
A. Luke Skywalker
B. Master Yoda
C. The dark side
D. Princess Leia

Return of the Jedi Era

2469. Who said, "You have paid the price for your lack of vision"?
- **A.** Emperor Palpatine
- **B.** Moff Jerjerrod
- **C.** Darth Vader
- **D.** Admiral Piett

2470. Who said, "I'm out of it for a little while, and everyone gets delusions of grandeur"?
- **A.** Han Solo
- **B.** Luke Skywalker
- **C.** C-3PO
- **D.** Princess Leia

2471. What did an officer report to Admiral Piett they had lost on the Super Star Destroyer *Executor*?
- **A.** All shields
- **B.** Turbolasers
- **C.** Bridge deflector shields
- **D.** Forward batteries

2472.

2473. Which groups did Lando Calrissian order to follow him in his attack on the Death Star once the shield was down?
- **A.** Red group
- **B.** Green group
- **C.** Green and Blue groups
- **D.** Red and Gold groups

2474. Where did Luke Skywalker get shot during the battle over the Pit of Carkoon?
- **A.** His left hand
- **B.** His right hand
- **C.** His left leg
- **D.** His right leg

2475. Who said, "Han, old buddy, don't let me down," during the Battle of Endor?
- **A.** Luke Skywalker
- **B.** Lando Calrissian
- **C.** Princess Leia
- **D.** C-3PO

2476. What did Luke Skywalker tell Jabba the Hutt before he was prodded to walk the plank?
- **A.** "Jabba, please don't kill us!"
- **B.** "Jabba, you're making a grave mistake."
- **C.** "Jabba, at least spare Leia."
- **D.** "Jabba, this is your last chance. Free us or die."

2472.

The Rebels had won the ground battle against Imperial forces on the forest moon of Endor, and deactivated the shield protecting the Death Star. Now they waited, hoping that their compatriots in space would be as successful. Suddenly, they saw a huge explosion in the sky, tails of light falling in all directions from a giant orange glow. The ground forces cheered—the Death Star was destroyed, and with it, decades of tyrannical rule. One celebrant seemed more pensive than ecstatic, and Han Solo noticed. "Hey, I'm sure Luke wasn't on that thing when it blew," he said, trying to comfort Leia.

"He wasn't," she responded. "I can feel it."

With that, Han got slightly upset. "You love him, don't you?"

"Yes," Leia replied.

Han, defeated, said, "All right. Fine. When he comes back, I won't get in the way." Leia smiled, finally ready to tell him what she hadn't been able to say before. What did she tell him?

- **A.** "Thank you for understanding."
- **B.** "You don't understand. I love him as a friend."
- **C.** "It's not like that at all. He's my brother."
- **D.** "It's not like that at all. I'm his sister."

2477. What did Anakin Skywalker ask Luke Skywalker to tell Leia?
- **A.** "You were right about me."
- **B.** "She would have made a great Sith Lord."
- **C.** "I wish I knew her."
- **D.** "I'm sorry."

2478. Who killed the Emperor?
- **A.** Luke Skywalker
- **B.** Darth Vader
- **C.** He died in the Death Star
- **D.** He didn't die

2479. How did Luke Skywalker address Jabba the Hutt in his holographic message?
- **A.** "Exalted one"
- **B.** "Honorable one"
- **C.** "Royal Highness"
- **D.** "Grand one"

2480. What did Darth Vader say when Luke Skywalker said, "I've got to save you"?
- **A.** "It's too late for me."
- **B.** "You already have."
- **C.** "Don't waste your time."
- **D.** "I cannot be saved."

2481. To what was the Emperor referring when he said, "You want this, don't you," to Luke Skywalker?
- **A.** Training as a Sith Lord
- **B.** To be with his father
- **C.** To watch the battle from his tower
- **D.** His lightsaber

2482. How many squads did the Imperial officer within the shield generator bunker order to be sent to help after receiving word that the Rebels were fleeing into the woods?
- **A.** Three squads
- **B.** Six squads
- **C.** Five squads
- **D.** Two squads

2483. How many Royal Guards escorted Emperor Palpatine from his shuttle?
- **A.** Six
- **B.** Four
- **C.** Two
- **D.** Eight

Return of the Jedi **Era**

2484. What did the celebrating Gungan in Theed yell after he learned that the Empire had been destroyed?
- **A.** "Wesa ganna have a party!"
- **C.** "Wesa free!"
- **B.** "Da Rebellion is bombad!"
- **D.** "Yousa guys bombad!"

2485. What did Luke Skywalker do with Darth Vader's armor?
- **A.** He burned it on a funeral pyre
- **C.** He shot it out of his shuttle in an escape pod
- **B.** He left it on the Death Star
- **D.** He threw it down the same shaft that the Emperor's body had been thrown into

2486. Who directed *Return of the Jedi*?
- **A.** George Lucas
- **C.** David Lynch
- **B.** Irvin Kirshner
- **D.** Richard Marquand

2487. Which actor portrayed the feisty Ewok Wicket W. Warrick?
- **A.** Kenny Baker
- **C.** Jack Purvis
- **B.** Warwick Davis
- **D.** Mike Edmonds

2488. Which character did Michael Carter portray in *Return of the Jedi*?
- **A.** Jabba the Hutt
- **C.** Malakili
- **B.** Boba Fett
- **D.** Bib Fortuna

2489.

2490. Who was the chief makeup artist in *Return of the Jedi*?
- **A.** Kay Freeborn
- **C.** Graham Dudman
- **B.** Nick Dudman
- **D.** Stuart Freeborn

2491. Which actor portrayed Anakin Skywalker in *Return of the Jedi*?
- **A.** Sebastian Shaw
- **C.** James Earl Jones
- **B.** Jake Lloyd
- **D.** David Prowse

2492. Who supplied the voice for Sy Snootles?
- **A.** Femi Taylor
- **C.** Jane Busby
- **B.** Claire Davenport
- **D.** Annie Arbogast

2489.

The original ending to *Return of the Jedi* featured a major celebration on the forest moon of Endor in which the Ewoks and the Rebel Alliance joined together in a massive party. Ewoks drummed on fallen stormtroopers' helmets and danced around bonfires as the Rebels congratulated each other and watched a massive fireworks display supplied by X-wing pilots.

For the special edition of the film, George Lucas wanted to expand on the celebratory nature of the ending by showing the reverberations of the Emperor's downfall across the galaxy. In doing so, he commissioned a new piece of music to replace the original closing song, and inserted new digital

OBSESSED WITH *STAR WARS*

paintings and blue-screen Ewok elements for the celebration on Endor. Additionally, he created scenes from several other important locations using digital matte paintings, digitally enhanced miniature photography and blue-screen footage, and 3-D computer graphics. Celebrations across the galaxy were now seen at the end of the film, giving a real sense of just how important the Alliance's victory over the Empire and its ruthless leader truly was.

Which of the following key galactic locations didn't make it into the updated celebration scene at the end of *Return of the Jedi* Special Edition?

A. Naboo
B. Dagobah
C. Cloud City
D. Tatooine

2493. Which character did Claire Davenport portray in *Return of the Jedi*?
A. Oola   **C.** Yarna d'al Gargan
B. Lyn Me   **D.** Malakali

2494. How many puppeteers did it take to operate Jabba the Hutt for *Return of the Jedi*?
A. Nine   **C.** Six
B. Three   **D.** Two

2495. Who played the hapless Twi'lek dancer Oola?
A. Annie Arbogast   **C.** Claire Davenport
B. Dawn Davenport   **D.** Femi Taylor

2496. What angst-ridden character did Ernie Fosselius play in *Return of the Jedi*?
A. Salacious Crumb   **C.** J'Quille
B. Bib Fortuna   **D.** Malakili

2497. Who did Timothy M. Rose portray in *Return of the Jedi*?
A. General Madine   **C.** Salacious Crumb
B. Admiral Ackbar   **D.** Logray

2498. Which *Return of the Jedi* scenes were shot in Redwood National Park?
A. Jabba the Hutt's palace   **C.** The Pit of Carkoon
B. Endor   **D.** Naboo

2499. Who did Dermot Crowley portray in *Return of the Jedi*?
A. Admiral Piett   **C.** Moff Jerjerrod
B. General Madine   **D.** Grizz Frix

2500. Which actor portrayed Chief Chirpa in *Return of the Jedi*?
A. Jack Purvis   **C.** Warwick Davis
B. Jane Busby   **D.** Malcolm Dixon

Return of the Jedi Era

ABOUT THE AUTHOR

Benjamin Harper has published more than 30 titles, including *DC Super Friends Going Bananas, Superman Returns Movie Storybook*; *Batman Begins Movie Storybook*; *Thank You, Superman*; *Marvel Heroes Swing Into Action*; three previous *Star Wars* trivia books; and many more. Born in St. Petersburg, Florida, he currently lives in Los Angeles with his traveling companion, Edith Bouvier Beale III. He currently works as an editor at Warner Bros. Global Publishing. He has worked in children's publishing for the past 17 years as an author, an editor at DC Comics, and at Lucas Licensing, and a manager at Scholastic, Inc. He has also worked as a maxillofacial surgery assistant and a garbageman.

ACKNOWLEDGMENTS

"A long time ago, in a galaxy far, far away . . ." Ever since I saw those fateful words on the screen for the first time on opening day in 1977, I have, truly, been obsessed with *Star Wars*. My family saw that movie together countless times—it became more than a movie for us. That Christmas, my mother and my Aunt Margaret sewed Jedi robes for both my cousin Justin and me, and found what were apparently the only two lightsaber toys in existence at that time (non-licensed, even). We were Jedi that Christmas, and the feeling has never left. With each film, my adoration grew, culminating in what I never even considered would happen—actually working at Skywalker Ranch with an amazing group of people. After leaving Lucasfilm, I stayed in touch, and jumped at the chance when Amy Gary asked me to work on this project.

I'd like to thank Kjersti Egerdahl for being a fabulous and patient editor, Frank Parisi, Amy Gary, Steve Korté, Lucy Autrey Wilson for introducing me to the world of Lucasfilm, Steve Sansweet and Sue Rostoni for being supportive in the face of adversity, Alice Alfonsi for starting it all, Sarah Hines Stephens and Jane Mason, Pablo Hidalgo, Leland Chee, all of the *Star Wars* authors whose work inspired these questions, George Lucas, and my parents—Frances and Jeff Harper, who have put up with and fostered many obsessions over the years.